OXFORD ENGLISH MONOGRAPHS

General Editors

CHRISTOPHER BUTLER   KATHERINE DUNCAN-JONES
MALCOLM GODDEN   HERMIONE LEE
A. D. NUTTALL   FIONA STAFFORD
PAUL STROHM

The Holy Land in English Culture 1799–1917

Palestine and the Question of Orientalism

EITAN BAR-YOSEF

CLARENDON PRESS · OXFORD

OXFORD
UNIVERSITY PRESS

Great Clarendon Street, Oxford OX2 6DP

Oxford University Press is a department of the University of Oxford.
It furthers the University's objective of excellence in research, scholarship,
and education by publishing worldwide in

Oxford New York

Auckland Cape Town Dar es Salaam Hong Kong Karachi
Kuala Lumpur Madrid Melbourne MexicoCity Nairobi
New Delhi Shanghai Taipei Toronto

With offices in

Argentina Austria Brazil Chile Czech Republic France Greece
Guatemala Hungary Italy Japan Poland Portugal Singapore
South Korea Switzerland Thailand Turkey Ukraine Vietnam

Oxford is a registered trade mark of Oxford University Press
in the UK and in certain other countries

Published in the United States
by Oxford University Press Inc., New York

© Eitan Bar-Yosef 2005

The moral rights of the author have been asserted
Database right Oxford University Press (maker)

First published 2005

All rights reserved. No part of this publication may be reproduced,
stored in a retrieval system, or transmitted, in any form or by any means,
without the prior permission in writing of Oxford University Press,
or as expressly permitted by law, or under terms agreed with the appropriate
reprographics rights organization. Enquiries concerning reproduction
outside the scope of the above should be sent to the Rights Department,
Oxford University Press, at the address above

You must not circulate this book in any other binding or cover
and you must impose the same condition on any acquirer

British Library Cataloguing in Publication Data

Data available

Library of Congress Cataloging in Publication Data

Data available

Typeset by SPI Publisher Services, Pondicherry, India
Printed in Great Britain
on acid-free paper by
Biddles Ltd, King's Lynn, Norfolk

ISBN 0–19–926116–4 978–0–19–926116–1

1 3 5 7 9 10 8 6 4 2

For Shira

Acknowledgements

Although this book is about the Holy Land in Victorian culture, many of the themes, images, and locales discussed in it have been an intimate part of my own experiences. Looking back, I now realize that I began envisioning this project when, as an undergraduate living in Jerusalem, I purchased my first copy of Edward Said's *Orientalism*. I can still remember the thrill of reading it and realizing that nothing about my homeland, Israel, would ever seem the same again. A few years later I learnt that Said actually grew up in the imposing mansion on the corner of (what had become, after 1948) Nahum Sokolow Street, just around the block from my rented flat. Said's family residence now housed the International Christian Embassy, a militant, pro-Zionist fundamentalist organization: so here was a typical Jerusalem streetcorner, which brought together the millenarian dream, the Zionist project, and the Palestinian tragedy.

Officially, however, this book began life as an Oxford D.Phil. dissertation. Working in the Bodleian all those long afternoons, my thoughts would often drift to Thomas Hardy's *Jude the Obscure*: with the golden dome of the Radcliffe Camera filling the huge window beside me, I could certainly see why poor Jude imagined Christminster (that is, Oxford) as a coveted New Jerusalem. What I did not foresee at the time was that, unlike Jude, who lived in a small working-class suburb called 'Beersheba' (that is, Jericho), I would eventually find myself in the actual, literal Beer-Sheba, where Ben-Gurion University of the Negev was kind enough to offer me a Kreitman postdoctoral fellowship, then a job. Just around the block from my house, where this book was completed, is the British War Cemetery, that corner of a foreign field which is forever England. 'Look, Daddy,' cries my 4-year-old daughter as we pass the green lawn, almost dazzling in the desert sun: 'a piece of England!'

In many ways, the movement from Jerusalem to Oxford, to Beer-Sheba, and then back to Oxford again (in the form of a manuscript sent to OUP headquarters in Jericho), epitomizes the kind of journeys this book revels in. The fusion between imaginative and empirical geographies, between the literal and metaphorical Jerusalems, is precisely the stuff that English dreams about the Holy Land were made of.

It is time, then, to thank all those who made my own journey possible, first and foremost the funds and institutions that supported this work: the British Council; the Committee of Vice-Chancellors and Principals of the Universities of the United Kingdom; AVI Foundation; the Harold Hyam Wingate Foundation; the Ian Karten Charitable Trust; St Anne's College, Oxford; the Anglo-Jewish Association; the Palestine Exploration Fund (PEF); the Kreitman Foundation, Ben-Gurion University of the Negev; Yad Hanadiv; and the Israeli Council for Higher Education.

Thanks are due to librarians, archivists, and staff at the Bodleian Library; the British Library; the Imperial War Museum (IWM); the Public Record Office, Kew; University College London; the PEF; the Church's Ministry among the Jews; the SPCK; John Murray Archive; Reading University Library; the Evangelical Library; the Jewish National and University Library; the Weizmann Archive; and the Central Zionist Archives. I am particularly indebted to Ralph Hyde, now retired from the Guildhall Library, London, for allowing me to consult his delightful collection of panorama ephemera; and to Yaakov Wahrman, whose library of Holy Land travel books is one of the finest in the world.

I am grateful to the Trustees of the IWM for allowing me access to their remarkable collection of soldiers' letters and diaries, to Anthony Richards of the Department of Documents, and to the copyright holders for permission to quote from the following collections: Papers of Major V. H. Bailey, Papers of D. H. Calcutt, Papers of R. B. Clark, Papers of Lieut. C. G. Dowding, Papers of Major-General G. P. Dawnay, Papers of Captain P. C. Duncan, Papers of W. N. Hendry, Papers of A. J. Kingston, Papers of W. Knott, Papers of R. Louden, Papers of H. T. Pope, Papers of A. S. Surry, Papers of Captain E. T. Townsend, and Papers of Miss D. Williams. Although every effort has been made to obtain permission, in some cases I have been unable to locate the copyright holders; any information regarding their whereabouts would be appreciated. For permission to reproduce and revise my own material which has appeared elsewhere in print I thank Cambridge University Press, Indiana University Press, and Sage Publications.

The Staff at OUP was wonderful, always kind and helpful: Sophie Goldsworthy, who initiated the publication of this book; Tom Perridge and Jacqueline Baker, who oversaw the production process; and Jean van Altena, who meticulously copy-edited the text. I am grateful to all.

My dissertation was written under the supervision of Robert J. C. Young, who, unlike his restless Middle Eastern supervisee, was always calm and extremely patient: his work taught me that postcolonial criticism can be politically committed, responsible, but also lucid and accessible. The same could be said of my wonderful examiners, Kate Flint and Bryan Cheyette, whose work has inspired me in numerous ways, long before, and much after, the viva.

I would also like to express my thanks to all those scholars who shared their vast knowledge with me, answered queries, or simply listened patiently to my ideas: they include David Bebbington, the Revd Philip B. Cliff, Todd Endelman, David Feldman, J. F. C. Harrison, Ruth Kark, R. D. Kernohan, Sara Kochav, Hugh McLeod, John Moscrop, Michael Ragussis, Tom Segev, Nicholas Shrimpton, John Walsh, Bernard Wasserstein, and Sarah Williams. William D. Rubinstein and Hillary Rubinstein, Nancy Henry, and Bernard Porter were all kind enough to furnish me with manuscripts of their work before publication.

Good friends and colleagues who read different parts of this book and offered helpful advice include Bashir Abu-Manneh, Yoav Alon, Yael Ben-zvi, Oren Meyers, Ilana Pardes, Shany Payes, Gordon Peake, Kevin Rosser, Ido Shahar, Yael Shapira, Relli Shechter, Yaron Toren, Ilan Troen, and—last but certainly not least—Nadia Valman. Dror Wahrman's enthusiasm for the project has been as stimulating as his friendship. Baruch Hochman and Ilana Pardes, my teachers at the Hebrew University, made me realize what studying literature could really be about; I often think of them with gratitude.

For the Victorians, the 'Holy Land' was imbued with a powerful sense of community, family, and home. I feel very much the same way, especially after those long years in England. For their generosity and love, I thank my parents, Daniela and Benni Bar-Yosef, who were always so supportive; my aunt and uncle, Edna and Dan Weiner; and my dear grandmother, Margaret Treumann. But my greatest debt of gratitude is to Shira Zeitak, to whom this book is of course dedicated. Her patience, humour, and love made everything—including Tamar and Talya—not only possible, but worthwhile.

E.B.

Contents

List of Illustrations	xii
List of Abbreviations	xiii
Introduction: Holy Lands	1
1. Christian Walks to Jerusalem: English Protestant Culture and the Emergence of Vernacular Orientalism	18
2. The Land and the Books: High Anglo-Palestine Orientalism and its Limits	61
3. Popular Palestine: The Holy Land as Printed Image, Spectacle, and Commodity	105
4. Eccentric Zion: Victorian Culture and the Jewish Restoration to Palestine	182
5. Homesick Crusaders: Propaganda and Troop Morale in the Palestine Campaign, 1917	247
Epilogue: *The Holy Places* Revisited	295
Index	303

List of Illustrations

1. J. M. W. Turner, 'Jerusalem from the Mount of Olives', 1836 (by kind permission of Edinburgh University Library). — 71
2. 'Pilgrims in the Desert', *Penny Magazine*, 1837 (by kind permission of Edinburgh University Library). — 115
3. 'Christ Delivering the Keys to St. Peter', *Penny Magazine*, 1832 (by kind permission of Edinburgh University Library). — 117
4. 'Elijah in the Desert', *Pictorial Bible*, 1836 (by kind permission of the Jewish National and University Library). — 118
5. 'View of Jerusalem', *Saturday Magazine*, 1833 (by kind permission of Edinburgh University Library). — 123
6. 'The Valley of Jehoshaphat', *Saturday Magazine*, 1839 (by kind permission of the National Library of Australia). — 124
7. 'Jerusalem from the Mount of Olives', *Illustrated London News*, 1862 (by kind permission of the National Library of Australia). — 134
8. 'The Blood Red Knight', programme, c.1850. — 138
9. 'The Market Square', *Jewish Missionary Intelligence*, 1907 (by kind permission of the National Library of Australia). — 152
10. 'Palestine and Eastern Exhibition in Stroud', *Jewish Missionary Intelligence*, 1892 (by kind permission of the National Library of Australia). — 157
11. 'Group of Helpers', *Jewish Missionary Intelligence*, 1912 (by kind permission of the Jewish National and University Library). — 160
12. Bernard Partridge, 'The Last Crusade', *Punch*, 1917 (© Punch, Ltd.). — 248

List of Abbreviations

CMJ	Church's Ministry among the Jews
CZA	Central Zionist Archives
EEF	Egyptian Expeditionary Force
EQA	Eastern Question Association
IWM	Imperial War Museum
ILN	*Illustrated London News*
JC	*Jewish Chronicle*
JJC	John Johnson Collection
LJS	London Society for Promoting Christianity among the Jews
PEF	Palestine Exploration Fund
PEFQSt	*Palestine Exploration Fund Quarterly Statement*
PenM	*Penny Magazine*
PN	*Palestine News*
PRO	Public Record Office
RTS	Religious Tract Society
SatM	*Saturday Magazine*
SDUK	Society for the Diffusion of Useful Knowledge
SPCK	Society for Promoting Christian Knowledge
TNA	The National Archives of the UK
WA	Weizmann Archive

Introduction

Holy Lands

> I will not cease from Mental Fight,
> Nor shall my Sword sleep in my hand:
> Till we have built Jerusalem,
> In Englands green & pleasant Land.[1]

In 1804, William Blake began composing and etching one of his most monumental prophecies, *Jerusalem*. It was a much shorter poem, however, written that same year as part of his Preface to *Milton*, which eventually usurped the title 'Jerusalem' to become Blake's most enduring work: an English institution. Performed every summer, with great pomp and circumstance, at the very end of the Last Night of the Proms, Blake's hymn has come to mean different things to different people. For some, dreaming of a lost rural Eden, the powerful pledge to rebuild Jerusalem offers a glimpse of heaven on earth. For others, it evokes the utopian fantasy of a socialist England, envisaged by artists from William Morris to Morrissey (who often enters the stage, in his concert tours, with 'Jerusalem' thundering in the background). For those stirred more easily by the fading glamour of the Royal Albert Hall, Blake's lines are saturated with the bitter-sweet memory of England's imperial greatness and the patriotic hope that glory is still within reach: which is undoubtedly why 'Jerusalem' was selected as the England football team's official anthem for the Euro 2000 tournament.[2]

---

[1] *The Complete Poetry and Prose of William Blake*, ed. David V. Erdman, comm. Harold Bloom (Garden City, NY: Anchor, 1982), 95–6.
[2] Shirley Dent and Jason Whittaker, *Radical Blake: Afterlife and Influence from 1827* (London: Palgrave, 2002), 88–95.

Not all athletic appropriations of the poem have been as congratulatory. 'Jerusalem' is played throughout Tony Richardson's *The Loneliness of the Long-Distance Runner* (1962), first to signify the thrill of the working-class runner as he roams through the countryside, then as a bitter foil to the dreary images of the English reformatory system or to the dark Satanic mills that dominate northern England's urban landscape. Less poignant but equally critical is Hugh Hudson's *Chariots of Fire* (1981), in which the hymn epitomizes a powerful English Hebraism that excludes, as late as the 1920s, both Anglo-Jews and over-zealous Evangelicals—exactly those minorities whose imagery (or cultural power) English Hebraism has appropriated.[3] The same mythical suggestiveness that made Blake's lines 'the closest thing the English have to an anthem'[4] could also make 'Jerusalem' a symbol of social, denominational, and political contention.

Secular or devout, socialist or nationalistic, all these Jerusalems share at least one common feature: firmly grounded in English soil, they seem to have very little to do with their original namesake in the Middle East. But when we return to Blake's own vision—rooted, as critics have long argued, in 1790s radical culture—we discover that he was imagining the building of Jerusalem in green and pleasant England just as England was moving closer and closer to the actual, territorial Jerusalem in Palestine. Indeed, the same turbulent events which rekindled the hope for a 'Jerusalem' of social justice among radical circles in England—namely, the French Revolution and the Napoleonic wars—were equally instrumental in ushering in a new era in the English involvement in the Holy Land: in June 1799, a Royal Navy frigate joined forces with the Ottoman defenders of Acre in defeating Napoleon Bonaparte's troops; henceforth Britain, anxious to protect the route to India, would be increasingly drawn towards Palestine, with strategic, political, economic, and religious interests always enmeshed.[5] It is typical, for

---

[3] Martyn J. Bowden, 'Jerusalem, Dover Beach, and King's Cross: Imagined Places as Metaphors of the British Class Struggle in *Chariots of Fire* and *Loneliness of the Long-Distance Runner*', in Stuart C. Aitken and Leo E. Zonn (eds.), *Place, Power, Situation, and Spectacle: A Geography of Film* (Lanham, Md.: Rowman & Littlefield, 1994), 69–100.

[4] Jeremy Paxman, *The English: A Portrait of a People* (1998; Harmondsworth: Penguin, 1999), 10.

[5] The British Empire was only one of the European players competing for control over the Holy Land, and its increasing penetration—the establishment of a British consulate in Jerusalem (1838) or of the joint Anglo-Prussian Bishopric (1841)—was

example, that the Palestine Exploration Fund (PEF), established in 1865 to carry out cartographical and topographical surveys of the land, saw clergymen work alongside military officials. The War Office was only too happy to sponsor the Fund's projects: with the inauguration of the Suez Canal in 1869, and the British occupation of Egypt in 1882, Palestine's strategic significance was considerably enhanced.

Britain's gradual penetration—though hardly as premeditated, consistent, or linear as some accounts would have it—culminated in December 1917, when, following a bloody battle in the Judean hills, General Edmund Allenby finally led the triumphant British Army marching into Jerusalem. A few months later, in March 1918, Blake's hymn from *Milton*, set to music by Sir Hubert Parry, received its first great public performance.[6] The occasion was a suffragette rally, and henceforth 'Jerusalem' would become synonymous with the work of the Women's Institute (*vide* the title of its official history, *Jam and Jerusalem*[7]); the venue, incidentally, was the Royal Albert Hall, where the dream of establishing Jerusalem in England would be reiterated year after year.

These two Jerusalems—'here' and 'there', in England and in Palestine, the suffragettes' and the PEF's—are very seldom evoked in the same book, not to mention the same paragraph. British social historians and literary critics have pointed to the significance of Protestant vocabulary in the emergence of the English working-class movement, and, more recently, in the forging of the modern British state; Britain's interests in the Holy Land have been analysed by historians of empire, historical geographers, and—occasionally—by postcolonial critics.

---

swiftly matched by Britain's European contenders. As Alexander Schölch has observed, up until 1917, exclusive control of the Holy Land by a single European power seemed unthinkable: 'The later connection between British imperialism and Zionism, on the one hand, and the elimination (or displacement) of other European rivals, on the other, was based on quite specific conditions. Writing history can easily turn into a historiography of success—the story, that is, of successful movements.' It is with Schölch's warning in mind that this study was conceived and written. See Alexander Schölch, *Palestine in Transformation, 1856–1882: Studies in Social, Economic and Political Development* (1986), trans. William C. Young and Michael C. Gerrity (Washington: Institute for Palestine Studies, 1993), 47.

[6] Charles L. Graves, *Hubert Parry: His Life and Works* (London: Macmillan, 1926), ii. 92–3.

[7] Simon Goodenough, *Jam and Jerusalem* (Glasgow: Collins, 1977).

There has been virtually no attempt, however, to consider the affinity between those diverse fields of inquiry.

This is precisely what the following study sets out to do: to reveal the various cross-exchanges between the imperial project of exploring, representing, and eventually conquering Palestine and between the long tradition of internalizing those central biblical images—'Promised Land', 'Chosen People', 'Zion'—and applying them to England and the English.[8]

Tracing the interplay between metaphorical and literal appropriations of the 'Holy Land' across a series of cultural and social demarcations, my discussion operates on several levels. Most straightforwardly, it reassesses the Victorians' encounter with Palestine, particularly the role played by the Protestant biblical vocabulary in evoking a unique sense of ambivalence towards the imperial desire to possess the land. It shows, in other words, that when the so-called Orientalist drive to the Levant was superimposed on the long-standing religious impulse toward the same geographical terrain—as was the case with British interests in the Holy Land—the discourse that emerged could be much more ambiguous than postcolonial criticism has hitherto acknowledged.[9]

On a broader level, this book joins the ongoing debate about the dissemination of imperial ideology in Victorian England and its signi-

---

[8] Many of these observations hold true for the British isle (if not isles) as a whole. My study excludes other parts of Britain, not simply because Jerusalem is to be built in *England*'s green and pleasant land, but because Scotland, Wales, and Ireland raise questions which simply cannot be explored here. Of course, many eminent Scots and Welshmen (and at least one eccentric Irishman) will form part of this narrative, from Walter Scott to Lloyd George; the letters of some of their lesser-known countrymen, who served in Palestine, will be read alongside those of English Tommies. 'British' will be continuously employed to signify any official, political, or imperial capacities. On Scots in Palestine see R. D. Kernohan, *The Road to Zion: Travellers to Palestine and the Land of Israel* (Edinburgh: Handsel, 1995); on the 'Holy Land' metaphor in Wales see Dorian Llywelyn, *Sacred Place, Chosen People: Land and National Identity in Welsh Spirituality* (Cardiff: University of Wales Press, 1999); John Harvey, *Image of the Invisible: The Visualization of Religion in the Welsh Nonconformist Tradition* (Cardiff: University of Wales Press, 1999), 95–118.

[9] It is precisely the notion of Orientalism 'as heterogeneous and contradictory'—the idea that the binary opposition between Occident and Orient is 'a misleading perception which serves to suppress the specific heterogeneities, inconsistencies, and slippages of each individual notion', as Lisa Lowe has aptly written—that brings me to explore, historicize, and conceptualize that *distinct* strand of Orientalism which might be dubbed 'Anglo-Palestine'. Although French and American attitudes towards the Holy Land are occasionally explored in this study, as a rule, this book is not concerned with other Western variants of Orientalism. See Lisa Lowe, *Critical Terrains: French and British Orientalisms* (Ithaca, NY: Cornell University Press, 1991), 5, 7, and *passim*.

fication. It demonstrates that by drawing on a wide range of sources that go beyond the highbrow, the academic, and the official, we can begin to grasp the limited currency and multiple meanings of the Orientalist discourse in the metropolitan centre. Finally, by mapping out the various points of convergence between Blake's holy city and Allenby's, this study also examines the relationship between the language of class and the language of empire: as such, it presents an interdisciplinary exercise which builds 'Jerusalem' as a bridge between British social history and postcolonial studies.

Although Britain's strategic and cultural involvement in Palestine (particularly during the Mandate years, 1917–48) has generated a mammoth body of work, few have employed the theoretical insights offered by postcolonial criticism. Following Yehoshua Ben-Arieh's *The Rediscovery of the Holy Land in the Nineteenth Century* (1970), members of the 'Historical Geography' school of Israeli academia have produced invaluable work on Western—and very often British—interventions in Palestine. More descriptive than analytical, however, and shaped by an explicitly Zionist–Eurocentric agenda (the land is always a forlorn Ottoman province when 'rediscovered' by the West), these studies have seldom taken serious notice of the recent interest in the discursive constructions of the Orient.

The suspicion towards postcolonial studies which characterized mainstream Israeli scholarship up to the 1990s was probably fuelled by the fact that this burgeoning discipline could be traced back to the publication of one seminal work, Edward Said's *Orientalism: Western Conceptions of the Orient* (1978). Said's academic project was inseparable from his political commitment to the Palestinian cause, which, in turn, stemmed from his own exilic condition as a dispossessed Palestinian. It is precisely this genealogy, however, that makes the absence of Palestine from postcolonial criticism all the more puzzling: the scholarly field which has emanated from Said's ground-breaking work has swiftly moved on to explore other territories, such as the Caribbean, the Far East, Africa, and particularly India, the jewel in the crown of postcolonialism. Britain's imperial ambitions towards Palestine have received scant attention;[10] if mentioned at all in postcolonial literary scholarship,

---

[10] As Jacqueline Rose has noted, the idea that 'the pre- and post-war Jewish question...should seep back into [British] national self-fashioning has gone relatively

for example, nineteenth-century Palestine is depicted, simply and unproblematically as a fraction of a generic 'Orient'.[11] This, surprisingly enough, even applies to Said's own work. The Holy Land is rather marginalized in *Orientalism*; and although he dwells extensively on the nature of Zionist colonialism—most prominently in *The Question of Palestine* (1979)—Said very rarely stops to think about the distinct nature of Western interests in the Holy Land, which might distinguish it from other Orientalist encounters.

To be sure, there has been at least one exception: long aware of the significance of the 'Holy Land' paradigm to the emergence of American national identity, historians and critics working in the field of American studies have been quick to employ the tools refined by postcolonial criticism in their readings of nineteenth-century perceptions of Palestine.[12] Nevertheless, these accounts often approach American Orientalism either analogically (to explain American colonial attitudes in North America) or typologically (as harbingers of twentieth-century American imperialism), and it is not difficult to see why: nineteenth-century American settler-colonial culture was directed primarily westwards, towards the Frontier, rather than eastwards, towards the Middle East. America's cultural investment in Palestine simply lacked the strategic and political impetus that defined the British involvement. And yet, it is the British encounter with Palestine that has been so consistently, and curiously, overlooked.[13]

---

unremarked'. The question of Israel/Palestine, she writes, is one of the '[b]lind spots of our national self-imagining' (*States of Fantasy* (Oxford: Clarendon Press, 1996), 67, 69). For a critique along the same lines, pointing to the marginalization of anti-Semitism in postcolonial studies, see Bryan Cheyette, 'White Skin, Black Masks', in Keith Ansell-Pearson *et al.* (eds.), *Cultural Readings of Imperialism: Edward Said and the Gravity of History* (London: Lawrence & Wishart, 1997), 106–26.

[11] Cf. Patrick Brantlinger, *Rule of Darkness: British Literature and Imperialism, 1830–1914* (Ithaca, NY: Cornell University Press, 1988), 135–71; Daniel Bivona, *Desire and Contradiction: Imperial Visions and Domestic Debates in Victorian Literature* (Manchester: Manchester University Press, 1990), 1–31.

[12] John Davis, *The Landscape of Belief: Encountering the Holy Land in Nineteenth-Century American Art and Culture* (Princeton: Princeton University Press, 1996); Hilton Obenzinger, *American Palestine: Melville, Twain, and the Holy Land Mania* (Princeton: Princeton University Press, 1999); Millete Shamir, ' "Our Jerusalem": Americans in the Holy Land and Protestant Narratives of National Entitlement', *American Quarterly*, 55/1 (2003), 29–60.

[13] The Puritan 'Holy Land' paradigm, so central to American self-fashioning, was of course imported to the New World from England, where it continued to inform both

The omission, far from being accidental, hints at a fundamental problem facing those scholars of British history and culture who have attempted to tackle 'the question of Palestine'. And the problem, I would like to suggest, is that throughout the nineteenth century, English stakes in the Holy Land were shaped by traditions and articulated in ways which cannot be accommodated by Said's model of Orientalism, a model which continues to dominate much of postcolonial criticism today, despite the more nuanced readings suggested by followers and critics alike.

Recall the PEF, in many ways a fine example of Orientalism in action, defined by Said as 'the discipline by which the Orient was (and is) approached systematically, as a topic of learning, discovery, and practice', but also as 'that collection of dreams, images, and vocabularies available to anyone who has tried to talk about what lies east of the dividing line'. Orientalism, Said writes, 'expresses and represents the Orient culturally and even ideologically as a mode of discourse with supporting institutions, vocabulary, scholarship, imagery, doctrines, even colonial bureaucracies and colonial styles'.[14] The PEF was undoubtedly one of these institutions. Its cartographical surveys of western and southern Palestine, conducted in 1871–8 and 1913–14, were carried out by members of the Royal Engineers, among them future imperialist agents like H. H. Kitchener and T. E. Lawrence. The British take-over of Palestine in 1917 would have been much less feasible had it not been for the one-inch map of the country produced by the PEF.

So far, so good. But what seems, ostensibly, to be an exemplary case of Orientalism by the book—Said's book, that is—becomes something quite different when we dig deeper into the Fund's origins and consider, for example, the speech delivered by the Archbishop of York, for many years the PEF's president, when he rose to outline the goals of the new society at its first public meeting, in May 1865:

This country of Palestine belongs to *you* and to *me*, it is essentially ours. It was given to the Father of Israel in the words: 'Walk through the land in the length

---

radical and imperial politics for three more centuries. See Christopher Hill, *The English Bible and the Seventeenth-Century Revolution* (1993; Harmondsworth: Penguin, 1994), 249–50.

[14] Edward W. Said, *Orientalism: Western Conceptions of the Orient* (1978; Harmondsworth: Penguin, 1995), 73, 2. Subsequent page numbers are cited parenthetically in the text.

of it, and in the breadth of it, for I will give it unto thee.' *We* mean to walk through Palestine in the length and in the breadth of it, because that land has been given unto us. It is the land from which comes news of our Redemption. It is the land towards which we turn as the fountain of all our hopes; it is the land to which we may look with as true a patriotism as we do to this dear old England, which we love so much. (Cheers.)[15]

These are words—sentiments, convictions—that Said's model simply cannot accommodate. According to Said, Orientalist knowledge, once accumulated, virtually begs to be translated into a practical plan for conquest and domination. At the beginning of *Orientalism*, for example, he famously analyses Balfour's address to the House of Commons in 1910, in which Balfour justifies British rule of Egypt. 'England knows Egypt,' Said writes; 'Egypt is what England knows; England knows that Egypt cannot have self-government; England confirms that by occupying Egypt' (p. 34). But Palestine presents an opposite case altogether: as the Archbishop makes clear, the accumulation of knowledge is required to facilitate an already *existing* claim to domination, since Palestine 'has been given to us'. As we shall see, this was hardly an eccentric or isolated remark: seeking to justify their nation's interests in Palestine, members of the English élite continually blurred the series of stark oppositions—East/West, self/other—which underlie Said's work: Palestine is a 'there' which is already a 'here'; a land which, like 'this dear old England', belongs, a priori, 'to *you* and to *me*'.

It is certainly not my intention to imply that the British representation of other Oriental spheres could, or indeed should, be reduced to a rigid binary reading. What I would argue, however, is that due to its geographical location, historical heritage, and, most significantly, its scriptural aura, Palestine—the Holy Land, the land of the Bible—offers an exceptionally forceful challenge to the binary logic which Said traces in Orientalism. This resistance to an 'either/or' dialectic can explain why Palestine fits much more comfortably in the slippery dynamic which John Barrell has identified as 'this/that/the other': 'what at first seems "other" can be made over to the side of the self... only so long as a new, and a newly absolute "other" is constituted to fill the discursive space that has thus been evacuated'. The result, an Orientalization of the self

---

[15] PEF Archive, London, PEF/1865/2/8, 'Report of the Proceedings at a Public Meeting', 22 June 1865 (leaflet); italics original.

Introduction 9

which rules out any neat binary rupture, is also visible in the Eurocentric nomenclature of imperialism, which imagines, Barrell writes, 'a treacherous but sometimes manageable "Near East", a terrifying "Far East", and between them an ambiguous and hard to locate "Middle East" '.[16] In view of this geographical layout, it should come as no surprise that Thomas de Quincey, Barrell's subject, attributes his early obsession with the Orient to a childhood habit of sitting in the nursery with his sisters and browsing through an illustrated Bible, with its 'remembered, elegiac landscape'.[17] If the biblical lands, exotic but also strangely familiar, 'terrifying' and yet 'manageable', occupy that ambiguous space between 'this' and 'the other', small wonder that Palestine, the land associated most powerfully with scriptural history—the land whose geopolitical position makes it 'a buffer-state against a further East'[18]—resists any clear-cut division between Orient and Occident.

Striking as it may seem, this biblical component is virtually absent from Said's account: locating the origins of academic Orientalism in mid-eighteenth-century philology, Said, himself a characteristic child of the Enlightenment, constructs Orientalism as a secular, de-Christianized phenomenon; when the Bible does enter *Orientalism*, it is usually in the godless guise of German higher biblical criticism. This is precisely why the PEF's work is so inconsistent with Said's argument: nineteenth-century exploration of the Holy Land, with all its obvious Orientalist and imperialist overtones, was nothing if not a *reaction* against the higher biblical criticism. As Billie Melman has noted, 'the very purpose of scientific interest in Palestine was to corroborate religion, not to undermine it'.[19]

Rather than focus on the process of secularization depicted by Said, other critics have preferred to take up his claim that Orientalism always 'retained, as an undislodged current in its discourse, a reconstructed religious impulse, a naturalized supernaturalism' (*Orientalism*, 121).[20] What I am concerned with, however, is precisely the distance between

---

[16] John Barrell, *The Infection of Thomas de Quincey: A Psychopathology of Imperialism* (New Haven: Yale University Press, 1991), 10, 16.
[17] Ibid. 33, 47.
[18] Ibid. 69.
[19] Billie Melman, *Women's Orients: English Women and the Middle East, 1718–1918* (1992; 2nd edn. London: Macmillan, 1995), 29.
[20] Cf. William Hart, *Edward Said and the Religious Effects of Culture* (Cambridge: Cambridge University Press, 2000), 63 and *passim*.

what Said sees as the fossilized religious birthmarks of Orientalism and the vibrant religious institutions and practices which continued to shape nineteenth-century Orientalist thought in England.[21] To ignore this religious energy, or to claim simply that it had been 'reconstituted, redeployed, redistributed' in a secular framework, is to overlook the extent to which the divine promise—cited by the Archbishop as England's own—defined not only the English encounter with Palestine, but the British imperial ethos as a whole.

The primary objective of this book, then, is to offer a new cultural history of the Victorian fascination with Palestine, which will acknowledge the momentous role played by biblical culture in the construction of Englishness. Years ago, in her remarkably insightful study, Barbara Tuchman coined the phrase 'Bible and Sword' as shorthand for the 'twin motives' that brought Britain to Palestine: religious and political, cultural and imperial, moral and material.[22] But the dichotomy suggested by her title should not obscure the richness of the phenomenon Tuchman describes so well: it is impossible to understand the origins of the Anglo-Palestine Orientalist discourse, and the sort of claims it makes on the land, without realizing that the 'political' vision of 'England in Jerusalem' was in fact shaped by the 'religious' dream of building Jerusalem in England.

Indeed, if the affinity between Bible and sword is central to my discussion, equally significant is the recognition that the Bible made this sword a double-edged one. The same language which could engender a broader imperial claim over parts of the East was also the language employed to resist this imperial quest—*renounce* the distant, Middle Eastern Holy Land in favour of a 'Holy Land' that was 'dear old England, which we love so much'. Always lurking, often as a faint possibility only, in the most unfaltering imperial day-dreams, this ambivalence—in which the metaphorical appropriation of the 'Holy Land' overshadows the literal locus itself—could sometimes run its full

---

[21] Recent historiography has begun to challenge the traditional interpretation of 'the modern as secular' by pointing to the centrality of religion to the Enlightenment and to the project of modernity itself. See the discussion in Dror Wahrman, Jonathan Sheehan, and Dale K. Van Kley, 'Review Essays: God and the Enlightenment', *American Historical Review*, 108/4 (2003), 1,057–1,104.

[22] Barbara Tuchman, *Bible and Sword: England and Palestine from the Bronze Age to Balfour* (1956; New York: Ballantine, 1984), pp. xiii–xiv.

gamut. Nowhere is this more apparent than in the letters and diaries written by the British soldiers who fought with Allenby in 1917. Like the Archbishop of York, they too turned to biblical imagery to define their attitudes towards the land. However, rather than assert their right to walk 'in the length and in the breadth of it', the soldiers employed hymns, scriptural verses, and other Sunday-school idioms to deflate Palestine's sacred aura and construct it as a land that is anything but holy. Worn out by the war, longing to return home, Tommy should hardly be reproached for feeling that Blighty, and not Palestine, was the Holy Land. But in their subversive grouse the soldiers were also re-enacting what was a fundamental principle of popular Protestant culture: the notion that the real Jerusalem is above, or in our hearts, or—as Christian learns in his long journey in *The Pilgrim's Progress*—just around the corner, a Zion in Bedfordshire.

Bunyan's vision marks the starting-point of my narrative, because his allegory typifies the religious culture with which I am concerned here—a common set of practices and beliefs which evolved around the Bible: attending Sunday school, with its scriptural geography classes and magic-lantern slides of Palestine; browsing through the old illustrated family Bible; singing hymns; praying; listening to mother read *The Pilgrim's Progress*. The phenomenon I have in mind is not so much 'popular religion'—a term often set in direct opposition to the official, the institutional, the learned—as a shared vocabulary, a common cultural core. Victorian England, Hugh McLeod has written, 'was overwhelmingly a Christian and a Protestant nation'.[23] Despite the decline in adult church attendance, 'the almost universal exposure of Victorian working-class children to the Sunday school meant that the great majority of the population grew up with a basic acquaintance with the Bible, Christian hymns and Christian doctrine'.[24]

To convey this 'basic acquaintance', I employ the term *vernacular biblical culture*. I emphasize 'biblical', because it is the biblical

---

[23] Hugh McLeod, *Religion and Society in England, 1850–1914* (London: Macmillan, 1996), 2.

[24] Hugh McLeod, *Religion and Irreligion in Victorian England* (Bangor: Headstart, 1993), 35–6. As Sarah Williams has shown in her important work on popular religious culture in south London, undenominationalism was a key feature of the local Sunday-school culture. See S. C. Williams, *Religious Belief and Popular Culture in Southwark, c.1880–1939* (Oxford: Oxford University Press, 1999), 141.

vocabulary and imagery which concern us (and not, for example, Christian morality or rites of passage). 'Vernacular', on the other hand, indicates the historical roots of this culture: it denotes that linguistic register which was shared by the élite and the masses alike;[25] but it also evokes the post-Reformation era, in which the Bible, translated from the sacred Latin, could become almost democratically available. No less significant, 'vernacular' captures the sense of an indigenous world-view which was so central to the appropriation of the biblical vocabulary. 'Vernacular Orientalism', in turn, will be the name given here to what John Barrell has called 'Orientalization of the self': namely, that cultural system in which Oriental paradigms—in our case, 'Holy Land', 'Jerusalem'—are domesticated and internalized, becoming an integral part of the Western (or, in our case, English) self. Set against Said's model of a secularized academic Orientalist discourse, vernacular Orientalism provides an analytical and historical framework which invites us to write Palestine 'back' into postcolonial studies.

By exploring the affinity between Orientalism and Protestant biblical culture, my aim is not simply to reconsider the nineteenth-century English encounter with Palestine, but also to contribute to the recent scholarly interest in the effects of empire on nineteenth-century metropolitan culture. 'British historians have yet to explore in a systematic way colonialism's imprint on metropolitan language, institutions and practices,' writes Susan Thorne in her *Congregational Missions and the Making of an Imperial Culture in Nineteenth-Century England* (1999). That Thorne's study, just like Catherine Hall's *Civilising Subjects* (2002)—or, indeed, my own book—all turn to Protestant Evangelical culture to explore the linkages between empire and metropolis, seems to testify to the enduring influence of E. P. Thompson's *The Making of the English Working Class* (1963). As Thorne rightly notes, Thompson— himself a product of the colonial encounter, born in India to a Methodist missionary who served in Palestine in 1917—never considers empire as one of the factors which shaped his subjects' consciousness of class. And yet it is characteristic of his scholarly accomplishment that his work actually offers the me thodological capacity to explore the

---

[25] Peter Burke, *Popular Culture in Early Modern Europe* (London: Temple Smith, 1978), 28, 270.

connections that his critics chastise him for ignoring.[26] Following Thompson's cue, Thorne's study hinges on the nineteenth-century tendency to liken Britain's labouring poor to the inhabitants of the purportedly uncivilized heathen lands. Hall's journey begins in Kettering, the town where the Baptist Missionary Society was formed in 1792, but also the name of a small Jamaican village established to honour its English namesake—a dual manifestation capturing the array of geographical projections and fantasies which marked the Victorian missionary project.[27]

What Thorne achieves with the metaphor of savages, and Hall with the two Ketterings, my study attempts to accomplish with the multiplicity of Holy Lands which populated the Victorian cultural landscape. Here, too, Thompson's work is vital: as my first chapter will show, Thompson's acute insights regarding the role played by biblical imagery in connecting religious revivalism with radical politics suggests a way of approaching the relationship between the language of class and the language of empire. The ubiquity of the biblical vocabulary, on the one hand, and its elasticity, on the other, explain how images of 'Holy Land' and 'Chosen People' were employed throughout the nineteenth century to articulate working-class grievances *and* to justify Britain's imperial achievement overseas; to signify anything from the aspirations of the Chartist Co-operative Land Company to Matthew Arnold's notion of the 'true life of literature', that 'Promised Land, towards which criticism can only beckon';[28] to envision the colonization of Palestine by Jews, or, indeed, its colonization by the British. Like Blake's 'Jerusalem' today, the Victorian 'Holy Land' could embody an array of conflicting visions about what it means to be English. Rather than denote the geographical terrain only, the title of my book encapsulates the diversity of Victorian Holy Lands—earthly and heavenly, radical and patriotic, secular and sacred, visual and textual, literal and metaphorical.

---

[26] Susan Thorne, *Congregational Missions and the Making of an Imperial Culture in Nineteenth-Century England* (Stanford, Calif.: Stanford University Press, 1999), 3, 1, 175.
[27] Catherine Hall, *Civilising Subjects: Metropole and Colony in the English Imagination 1830–1867* (Cambridge: Polity, 2002), 1–2.
[28] Matthew Arnold, 'The Function of Criticism at the Present Time', in *Essays in Criticism* (London: Macmillan, 1865), 41.

It is this multiplicity of Zions that requires us to go beyond the familiar sources that are usually discussed in this context. In addition to travel accounts, fine art, and three-decker novels, my study explores the work of missionary and educational organizations, which made conscious efforts to reach a broader audience: the Society for Diffusion of Useful Knowledge (SDUK), the Society for Promoting Christian Knowledge (SPCK), the London Society for Promoting Christianity among the Jews (LJS), and the PEF. It thus draws on a variety of cultural forms that were part and parcel of vernacular biblical culture: advertisements, almanacs, exhibitions, hymns, illustrated Bibles, memoirs, penny magazines, state-sanctioned propaganda, Sunday-school textbooks, tracts, and so forth.

The common, even plebeian features of vernacular Protestant culture can perhaps explain why Edward Said's work is not only inattentive to the biblical aspects of Orientalism, but also ignores 'the role or significance of anything that does not correspond to the most traditional notions of culture and literature'.[29] This omission of mass culture raises significant questions concerning the dissemination and circulation of the Orientalist discourse: if Orientalism was 'that collection of dreams, images, and vocabularies available to anyone who has tried to talk about what lies east of the dividing line', we should nevertheless ask—available to whom? How? And in what form? Said asserts, for instance, that travel literature 'contributed to the density of public awareness of the Orient' (p. 192)—a claim that most literary critics still take for granted—but since he never actually discloses any circulation or price figures, this remains a hypothesis only. In fact, as Chapter 2 demonstrates in detail, remarkably high prices, leading to surprisingly low circulation figures (often no more than several hundred copies), meant that only a tiny fraction of society was exposed, directly, to these travel accounts. Similarly, Said mentions 'stabilizing influences like schools, libraries, and governments' (p. 201), but fails to offer any adequate explanation of how these agents actually propagated the Orientalist discourse. Once again, the PEF is a case in point: despite their fervent efforts to mobilize support for the exploration of Palestine, the Fund's leaders found it extremely difficult to make their work known to the public, or to attract

---

[29] Robert J. C. Young, *White Mythologies: Writing History and the West* (London: Routledge, 1990), 133.

public interest; consequently, the Fund remained on the brink of financial collapse until the First World War.

This is not to say that Orientalist imagery depicting the terrestrial Palestine was unavailable: from the 1830s onwards, cheap magazines and itinerant exhibitions did reach a substantial audience. However, the popularization of the learned (or 'academic') Orientalist discourse was subjected to an active process of exclusion and modification, which cannot be taken for granted. As John MacKenzie has rightly remarked, 'a full understanding of Orientalism requires some comprehension of the extensive range of artistic vehicles through which representations of the Orient were projected'.[30] It is by drawing on a variety of sources that are often silenced by the more dominant voices that this study examines how the Orientalist discursive apparatus functions—or, to be precise, malfunctions—in cultural spheres beyond Said's highbrow culture.

My inclination, in this respect, is to agree with those scholars who, either alarmed by the postcolonial tendency to find empire everywhere or simply determined to look beyond the upper-class surface, have attempted to swing the pendulum back, as it were, and point to the vulnerability, rather than the authority, of the imperial ethos. In his superb study of British working-class culture, Jonathan Rose has shown that throughout the nineteenth century, most Brits seemed strikingly unaware of their imperial possessions overseas.[31] Bernard Porter, who has written a whole book about this question, claims that, at least up to the 1880s, 80 per cent of Victorians—or, in other words, the working classes—were kept in ignorance of empire: 'Imperial Britain', he writes, 'was generally a *less* imperial society than is often assumed.'[32]

Porter seems to take his argument a bit too far: relying on an extremely narrow definition, his survey excludes Orientalist, racist, and exotic images that were available to working-class readers and were often congruent with imperial or colonial knowledge; which is exactly why Palestine—though officially not a part of the empire until

---

[30] John M. MacKenzie, *Orientalism: History, Theory and the Arts* (Manchester: Manchester University Press, 1995), 14.
[31] Jonathan Rose, *The Intellectual Life of the British Working Classes* (2001; New Haven: Yale University Press, 2002), 321–64.
[32] Bernard Porter, ' "Empire, what Empire?" Or, why 80% of Early- and Mid-Victorians Were Deliberately Kept in Ignorance of It', *Victorian Studies*, 46/2 (2004), 257; idem., *The Absent-Minded Imperialists: Empire, Society, and Culture in Britain* (Oxford: Oxford University Press, 2004), p. xv.

1922—is central to the debate. As this book will demonstrate, even when popular Orientalist imagery was abundant, different people could understand it in very different ways. Reader response, Rose reminds us, 'depends entirely on the frame of the audience, which in turn depends on their education and their other reading experiences'.[33] As we shall see—and as Rose himself implies in his survey of Sunday-school culture—the context in which the geography of Palestine was taught, the limits of children's geographical imagination, and, most significantly, the flexibility of the biblical vocabulary, all meant that, rather than signify a region 'out there', a region that should be explored and outlined and eventually possessed, rather than broaden their worldview, these scriptural geography lessons reinforced the domestic, inward-looking Bunyanesque fantasy of discovering Jerusalem just around the corner. To understand what the biblical language meant to different Victorians—to appreciate the variety of cultural forms this language could take—is to realize that the imperial discourse was not as monolithic and hegemonic as many postcolonial scholars would like to think.

This, then, is my overarching argument. I begin by demonstrating that the imperial vision of 'England in Jerusalem' was shaped by the vernacular vision of building Jerusalem in England; but I conclude by insisting that it was the vernacular vision which prevailed: metaphorical appropriations of the 'Holy Land', in both domestic and imperial contexts, played a much more dominant role in the English cultural imagination than the literal, geographical Holy Land itself.

The first three chapters concentrate on the myriad ways in which this process was reflected in the cultural politics of metropolitan representation, and especially the interplay between various cultural currents: my narrative explores the meaning of the Holy Land in vernacular biblical culture up to the late 1790s (Chapter 1); outlines the boundaries of the academic Anglo-Palestine Orientalist discourse in such highbrow cultural forms as novels, fine art, and travel writing (Chapter 2); and then considers how the popularization of this academic discourse shaped the representation of the Holy Land in nineteenth-century mass culture (Chapter 3). The discussion then proceeds to read the metaphorical/literal paradigm in the context of Britain's political, commercial, and military involvement in Palestine. Chapter 4

---

[33] Rose, *Intellectual Life*, 322.

works against the Zionist historiographical grain by demonstrating that plans concerning the Jewish restoration to Palestine were very often associated with charges of religious enthusiasm, eccentricity, even madness, all of them categories of differentiation which located the Christian Zionist outside the cultural consensus. Chapter 5 examines the British military campaign in Palestine, 1917–18, and the emergence of the 'homesick Crusader', an image which reflected a negotiated stand between official propaganda and public imagination, but also marked the hesitant mood which characterized Britain's presence in Palestine throughout the Mandate years: the real Promised Land was England.

By emphasizing the pre-eminence of the metaphorical 'Jerusalem' I certainly do not wish to underestimate the role played by British colonialism in reshaping the Holy Land's geopolitical landscape: the tangible repercussions of the Mandate period, with which Israelis and Palestinians are still struggling today, are anything but metaphorical. At the same time, it is only by turning to the metropolitan centre itself and tracing the array of ambiguities, contradictions, and gaps that typify Orientalist culture that we can begin to understand both the sway of Orientalism and its limits.

Finally, a word about geographical terminology. Throughout the nineteenth century, 'Holy Land', 'Palestine', and 'Syria' were often used interchangeably in the West.[34] Palestine and Syria were more easily identifiable: the first usually referred to the southern region, covering present-day Israel, the Israeli-occupied territories, and parts of Jordan; the latter to the northern area, parts of what is today Lebanon, Syria, and northern Israel. 'Holy Land', on the other hand, was a much vaguer term, often denoting the territory associated with the events of the Old Testament and, more significantly, with the life and teaching of Jesus Christ. With Jerusalem at its heart, this is the land with which this study is mostly concerned: a land whose boundaries were not so much geographical as emotional; a land which calls to mind not only bloody battles for domination, but also a peculiar kind of 'mental fight' that will never, Blake assures us, cease.

---

[34] Gideon Biger, 'The Names and Boundaries of Eretz-Israel (Palestine) as Reflection of Stages in its History', in Ruth Kark (ed.), *The Land that Became Israel* (New Haven: Yale University Press, 1990), 1–22.

1

Christian Walks to Jerusalem

English Protestant Culture and the Emergence of Vernacular Orientalism

Let us begin with an image that encapsulates the English fascination with the Holy Land: an image of a reader and a book. Many readers—and many books—come to mind. Consider, for example, Disraeli's Tancred, who, just before embarking on a pilgrimage to Jerusalem, spends many a delightful afternoon with the enchanting Lady Bertie, travelling together through the crisp landscapes of David Roberts's Syrian drawings.[1] Or recall the young Philip, the orphaned hero of W. Somerset Maugham's *Of Human Bondage*, whose dreary Sabbath is suddenly brightened when his aunt brings him an old picture book of the Holy Land, 'a romantic narrative of some Eastern traveller of the thirties, pompous maybe, but fragrant with the emotion with which the East came to the generation that followed Byron and Chateaubriand'.[2] And then there is Clara, the North Yorkshire protagonist of Margaret Drabble's *Jerusalem the Golden*, who finds solace in the words of the Sunday hymnal by envisioning 'not the pearly gates and crystal walls and golden towers of some heavenly city, but some truly terrestrial paradise, where beautiful people in beautiful houses spoke of beautiful things'.[3]

---

[1] Benjamin Disraeli, *Tancred; or The New Crusade* (1847; London: Peter Davies, 1927), 156.
[2] W. Somerset Maugham, *Of Human Bondage* (1915; Harmondsworth: Penguin, 1992), 36.
[3] Margaret Drabble, *Jerusalem the Golden* (1967; Harmondsworth: Penguin, 1969), 32.

Still, to realize how these very different readers imagined their own private Promised Land, it is necessary to summon another, more desperate reader, who first appears in the similitude of a dream:

> I dreamed, and behold *I saw a Man clothed with Raggs standing in a certain place, with his face from his own House, a Book in his hand, and a great burden upon his Back.* I looked, and saw him open the Book, and Read therein; and as he read, he wept and trembled: and not being able longer to contain, he brake out with a lamentable cry; saying, *what shall I do?*[4]

With godly Christian life imagined as a journey to Zion, John Bunyan's *The Pilgrim's Progress* (1678) is a powerful illustration of the new role assigned to the Holy Land in Protestant culture. Working in three parallel channels—repealing the physical pilgrimage, emphasizing the posthumous rewards of the New Jerusalem, and disseminating the Bible in the vernacular—the Reformation drew believers away from the earthly Jerusalem. The land which had been a pivotal destination for pilgrimages and Crusades was now transformed into a metaphor, easily associated with the believer's most intimate experiences, effortlessly literalized in the most familiar of settings.

Employing Bunyan's masterpiece as its starting-point, this chapter explores the cultural process of internalizing the scriptural geography and re-imagining it in, or as, England. My discussion outlines the roles played by different appropriations of the 'Holy Land' in people's lives; it examines how class, education, and ideology might have affected the literality with which the biblical vocabulary was realized, and traces the relationship between these images and the actual Holy Land in the East. I will conclude by revisiting the illustrious careers of Richard Brothers and Joanna Southcott, the two most prominent millenarian prophets of the 1790s, whose teachings demonstrate how a growing awareness of the geographical Holy Land could complicate the Bunyanesque dream of building Jerusalem in England.

Beginnings: 'As ye came from the Holy Land'

In his spiritual autobiography, *Grace Abounding* (1666), John Bunyan recalled a question that troubled him greatly as a boy, 'and that was,

---

[4] John Bunyan, *The Pilgrim's Progress* (1678/84), ed. N. H. Keeble, World's Classics (Oxford: Oxford University Press, 1984), 8. Subsequent page numbers will be cited parenthetically in the text.

Whether we were of the *Israelites,* or no: for finding in the Scriptures that they were once the peculiar People of God, thought I, if I were one of this race, my Soul must needs be happy'.[5] *The Pilgrim's Progress* could be read back to this juvenile anxiety, for it is here that Bunyan imagines a chosen child of God, speaking the language of Canaan, and making his way to the land of milk and honey.

Repeatedly alluding to the Exodus saga, Bunyan's allegory refines the analogy between the Christian spiritual life and the Israelites' journey from Egypt. Christian is taken to the summit of the Hill Clear for a glimpse of the Celestial City (p. 100), just as Moses was shown Canaan from Mount Pisgah; and just like the Israelites, Christian crosses the river to reach the Promised Land. Furthermore, on his way to Mount Zion—a road which was 'cast up by the Patriarchs, Prophets, Christ, and his Apostles' (p. 23)—Christian passes through familiar biblical landmarks: steep Mount Sinai (p. 16) and the Valley of the Shadow of Death, where there was a 'Quagg' into which '*King* David *once did fall*' (p. 51); he observes the 'Pillar of Salt into which *Lot's Wife* was turned' (p. 89), enjoys the Arcadian wonders of Immanuel's Land (p. 97) and the Country of Beulah (p. 126), and all this before entering the Celestial City, Jerusalem.

Although he specifies geographical sites like Sinai and Jerusalem, Bunyan insists that the Holy Land is always a metaphor, even in the Bible: 'By metaphors I speak,' he writes in his 'Apology': 'was not Gods Laws, / His Gospel-Laws in older time held fourth / By Types, Shadows and Metaphors?' (p. 4). Consequently, Bunyan can refer to Christian's destination as 'Heaven', 'Heavenly Country', the 'Celestial City', the 'Paradise of God', and the 'heavenly Jerusalem', but also as 'City of Zion', 'Mount Zion', the 'Land that flows with Milk and Honey', and the 'Promised Land'. The dichotomy between the earthly and the heavenly, the old and the new, collapses altogether. The signifier 'Zion' comes to mean one thing only: the world-to-come.

The use of 'Zion' as a metonym for the city of Jerusalem or as a metaphor for the people of Israel is of course current in the Old Testament; and the shift from the earthly to the heavenly is suggested by Paul's dismissal of the 'Jerusalem which now is, and is in bondage

---

[5] John Bunyan, *Grace Abounding to the Chief of Sinners* (1666), ed. Roger Sharrock (Oxford: Clarendon Press, 1962), 9.

with her children. But Jerusalem which is above is free, which is the mother of us all' (Gal. 4: 25–6).[6] Similarly, Bunyan's representation of Christian life as a pilgrimage can be traced back to the interpretation in Hebrews, which sees the Patriarchs as 'strangers and pilgrims on the earth' who were journeying to 'a better country, that is, an heavenly' (11: 13–16). When, in the second century AD, the literal pilgrimage to Jerusalem emerged as a popular movement, it was in direct opposition to the exegesis of the early Church Fathers, expressed most authoritatively in Augustine's *City of God*. Jerome (d. 420) articulated this official stand when he maintained that access to the court of heaven 'is as easy from Britain as it is from Jerusalem'.[7]

Bunyan's great contribution, then, was not in internalizing the pilgrimage, but in literalizing John's golden vision of the New Jerusalem in the contemporary panorama of English life. The literal/textual landscape of Old Testament Canaan is read typologically, only to be reconstructed as a muddy, poorly signposted seventeenth-century English road. 'Whether by choice or by the fortunate limits of Bunyan's imagination—probably a bit of both—it is all visualised in terms of the contemporary life that Bunyan knew,' C. S. Lewis has written: 'the field-path, seductive to footsore walkers; the sound of a dog barking as you stand knocking at the door; the fruit hanging over a wall which the children insist on eating though their mother admonishes them "that Fruit is none of ours"—these are all characteristic'.[8] Even the glories of the Celestial City must have appeared remarkably familiar to Bunyan's readers. As Christian and Hopeful approach Zion, they hear the bells ringing, as they might have done on a Sunday morning in Bedfordshire (p. 131).[9] The world-to-come is conspicuously similar to this fleeting world. Christian left his home only to find himself back where he began; Jerusalem was just around the corner all along.

---

[6] It was precisely against the earthly, historical city—associated with Jewish tradition and the Jewish Fall—that the Christian heavenly Jerusalem was constructed. See Robert L. Wilken, *The Land Called Holy: Palestine in Christian History and Thought* (New Haven: Yale University Press, 1992), esp. chs. 3–5.

[7] Quoted in J. G. Davies, *Pilgrimage Yesterday and Today* (London: SCM Press, 1988), 80.

[8] C. S. Lewis, 'The Vision of John Bunyan' (1969), repr. in Roger Sharrock (ed.), *Bunyan, The Pilgrim's Progress: A Casebook* (London: Macmillan, 1976), 196–7.

[9] John R. Knott, *The Sword of the Spirit: Puritan Responses to the Bible* (Chicago: University of Chicago Press, 1980), 153.

Whatever future generations would make of it, Bunyan's vision of Jerusalem in England captures a distinct moment in Restoration Puritan culture, in which continuity and change, despair and hope, were interfused. U. Milo Kaufmann has shown that Bunyan follows the Puritan tradition of heavenly meditation: the evocation of scriptural imagery, augmented by the reader's own experiences, is offered as a foretaste of heaven.[10] But *The Pilgrim's Progress* should also be read against the very earthly millenarian expectations which were rekindled by the Civil War.[11] Drawing on the prophetic texts of Daniel and Revelation, which they applied to contemporary events, many Puritans believed that Christ's Second Coming was imminent. Radical sects like the Levellers and the Fifth Monarchy Men took these ideas to their utmost extreme. The Diggers' project of cultivating the common land of St George's Hill in Surrey, for example, was an attempt to institute the New Jerusalem as a collective settlement, here and now. 'If any one say: The glory of *Jerusalem* is to be seen hereafter, after the body is laid in the dust,' the Digger Gerrard Winstanley declared, 'they speak their imagination, they know not what. I know that the glory of the Lord shall be seen and known within the Creation.'[12]

After 1660, however, most Dissenters accepted that Christ's kingdom was not of this world. The consolatory passages in the Bible, used as a call to action just decades before, were now taken to refer to the afterlife.[13] When Bunyan's Atheist asserts that 'There is no such place as you Dream of, in all this world', Christian agrees; Mount Zion, he says, 'is in the World to come' (p. 110). Max Weber has offered *The Pilgrim's Progress* as the best illustration for 'an age to which the afterlife was not only more important, but in many ways also more certain, than all the interests of life in this world'.[14] Perhaps, but Bunyan's

---

[10] U. Milo Kaufmann, *The Pilgrim's Progress and Traditions in Puritan Meditation* (New Haven: Yale University Press, 1966), esp. 151–74.

[11] Peter Toon (ed.), *Puritans, the Millennium, and the Future of Israel: Puritan Eschatology, 1600 to 1660* (Cambridge: James Clarke, 1970).

[12] Gerrard Winstanley, 'The New Law of Righteousness' (1649), in *The Works of Gerrard Winstanley*, ed. George H. Sabine (Ithaca, NY: Cornell University Press, 1941), 153.

[13] Christopher Hill, *The English Bible and the Seventeenth-Century Revolution* (1993; Harmondsworth: Penguin, 1994), 331, 415.

[14] Max Weber, *The Protestant Ethic and the Spirit of Capitalism* (1905), trans. T. Parsons (London: Unwin, 1984), 109–10.

imagination always pictures the world-to-come as the world-that-is. *The Pilgrim's Progress* may reject the millenarian expectation of an imminent, terrestrial New Jerusalem, but it nevertheless shares the millenarian fantasy of reaching a Jerusalem that would adhere to the most familiar and palpable of terms.

This is not to suggest that the literalization of the scriptural vocabulary and the internalization of the biblical landscape were necessarily typical of Puritan, or even Protestant, cultures. Vernacular medieval drama, for instance, often functioned in the same way. *The Second Shepherds' Play*, which begins with the shepherds' complaints about the bleak weather, the taxes, and the gentry's treatment, reallocates the events of the Nativity to the fifteenth-century Yorkshire moors. The landscape depicted in Tasso's *Gerusalemme Liberata* (1581)—the 'silver streams of Jordan's crystal flood'—often brings to mind an eastern Ferrara.[15] In *Paradise Lost* (1667), greatly indebted to Tasso's epic, Milton's invocation of 'Siloa's brook that flow'd / Fast by the oracle of God' conjures up a Delphic stream near 'Sion hill' (1. 10–12).[16] A powerful visual tradition translated images like these to canvas. The Renaissance Italian and Flemish masters depicted biblical scenes in the settings of their native lands: scriptural figures were dressed in contemporary clothes, and Jerusalem was painted overlooking a sea, a lake, or the green Roman Campagna.[17]

By the time Baroque artists were generating similar images, this visual representation must have become a convention, but it was initially embedded in the medieval conception which Benedict Anderson, following Auerbach, has called simultaneity-along-time: 'Figuring the Virgin Mary with "Semitic" features or "first-century" costumes in the restoring spirit of the modern museum was unimaginable because the medieval Christian mind had no conception of history as an endless chain of cause and effect or of radical separations between past and present.'[18] But this temporal conception seems to provide only part of

---

[15] Torquato Tasso, *Jerusalem Delivered* (1581), trans. Edward Fairfax (1600; London: Centaur, 1962), 3. 57. 2.

[16] Although Canaan is occasionally mentioned in Milton's epic—esp. in Book XII, in Michael's description of Adam's descendants—the role played by the 'Holy Land' metaphor is on the whole marginal.

[17] Naomi Shepherd, *The Zealous Intruders: The Western Rediscovery of Palestine* (London: Collins, 1987), 17–19.

[18] Benedict Anderson, *Imagined Communities* (1983; rev. edn. London: Verso, 1996), 23.

the explanation. To what extent, one wonders, were these representations of the Holy Land the result of a geographical sensibility as well? After all, with the dwindling of the Crusading spirit and the rise of the Ottoman Empire in the fifteenth century, European accessibility to Palestine was becoming increasingly limited. This new political and military reality may have enhanced the inclination to imagine the Promised Land in quintessentially local terms.[19]

Of course, even in the heyday of the medieval pilgrimage movement, only the privileged few could afford to visit Jerusalem: 'Good intentions, stout heart, ready tongue, and fat purse' were needed, according to one pilgrim.[20] Travel to the Holy Land was perhaps pilgrimage *par excellence*, the model for all sacred journeys throughout Christendom, but it was also the great exception: most Christian pilgrimage had always been national, if not local.[21] Chaucer's Wife of Bath visited the Holy Land—'And thries hadde she been at Jerusalem; / She hadde passed many a straunge streem' (1. 465–6)—but it is on the way to Canterbury, a much more reachable destination, that we hear her tale.

Since local pilgrimages were domestic re-enactments of the great type itself, many indigenous holy places across Europe, Compostela being the most celebrated, claimed a direct connection to Palestine. According to English legend, the abbey of Glastonbury, the oldest in England, was founded by Joseph of Arimathea, the wealthy Jew who buried Christ and became an apostle to the British Isles. With the Joseph myth, the English could now link themselves directly to the birthplace of their religion.[22] Another tradition was associated with Walsingham, Norfolk.

---

[19] In periods when Jerusalem was governed by Christians, the architecture of the earthly city featured in medieval Christian art, and even contributed to the visualization of the heavenly city. See Bianca Kühnel, *From the Earthly to the Heavenly Jerusalem: Representations of the Holy City in Christian Art of the First Millennium* (Freiburg: Herder, 1987).

[20] Quoted in Jonathan Sumption, *Pilgrimage: An Image of Medieval Religion* (London: Faber & Faber, 1975), 204.

[21] Simon Coleman and John Elsner, *Pilgrimage, Past and Present* (London: British Museum Press, 1995), 93.

[22] D. J. Hall, *English Mediaeval Pilgrimage* (London: Routledge & Kegan Paul, 1966), 45–75. Other myths claimed that the English people were the descendants of Gomer, grandson of Noah; that the ancient Druids were the Phoenicians of Tyre and Sidon; that Jesus had visited England as a boy; or that the empress Helena, who marked the Holy Sepulchre in Jerusalem, was born in England. See Barbara Tuchman, *Bible and Sword: England and Palestine from the Bronze Age to Balfour* (1956; New York: Ballantine,

In 1061, Lady Richeldis de Faverches was carried away, in a vision, to Nazareth. On her return, she instructed carpenters to build an exact replica of Mary's house, which came to be known as England's Nazareth; visitors to the site were called palmers, just like the pilgrims to Palestine.[23] While Glastonbury's aura was based on the presence of an apostle from Jerusalem, Walsingham suggested that England, like Canaan, was sacred terrain: both, after all, boasted their own Nazareths. An old ballad asks,

> As ye came from the holy land
> Of blessed Walsingham
> O met you not with my true love
> As by the way ye came?[24]

Already here we can sense how the geography of Canaan could be reallocated, internalized, domesticated in one's indigenous landscape, creating a 'Holy Land' which was infinitely more attainable, physically and mentally, than its original overseas.

This brings us to the boundaries of the geographical imagination, 'the mechanism by which people come to know the world and situate themselves in space and time'.[25] How did those men and women, who could never have hoped to go there themselves, imagine the Holy Land? One way to approach this question is to suggest that during certain periods, Palestine's existence as a geographical space—a place one could travel to and bring relics from, a place one could conquer and rule—was brought closer to home. When, in November 1095, Pope Urban II marshalled the First Crusade, he initiated such an era. Only a tiny fraction of society actually travelled to Jerusalem, but the enormous effort required to launch Richard I's Crusade in 1191 must have touched the lives of many:

1984), 1–21; Hugh A. MacDougal, *Racial Myth in English History: Trojans, Teutons, and Anglo-Saxons* (Hanover, NH: University Press of New England, 1982), 31–70.

[23] Elizabeth Ruth Obbard, *The History and Spirituality of Walsingham* (Norwich: Canterbury Press, 1995); Hall, *English Mediaeval Pilgrimage*, 104–29.

[24] Thomas Percy, *Reliques of Ancient English Poetry*, ed. Henry B. Wheatley (London: Swan Sonnenschein, 1891), iii. 102.

[25] Joan M. Schwartz and James R. Ryan, 'Introduction: Photography and the Geographical Imagination', in *Picturing Place: Photography and the Geographical Imagination* (London: Tauris, 2003), 6. The term 'geographical imagination' was coined by David Harvey, *Social Justice and the City* (London: Edward Arnold, 1973), 24–7.

the nuns of Swine who bought land to provide money for a crusader; the officials, priests, collectors, and jurymen who managed the Saladin tithe and the taxpayers who paid it; the pig farmers of Warwickshire; the ironworkers of the Forest of Dean; the ship owners of the Cinque Ports and elsewhere; the dairy farmers of Hampshire; the sheriffs who paid excessive amounts for their jobs. All were bound to the enterprise alongside the crusaders themselves.[26]

With a new preaching campaign launched, on a national scale, every decade between 1211 and 1291, few could have remained ignorant of their obligation to the Crusading movement.[27]

But how did this obligation affect the image of the Holy Land itself? According to Norman Cohn, the Continental poor who joined the First Crusade, 'passionately interested in reaching, capturing and occupying Jerusalem', saw it as a symbol of prodigious hope: 'No wonder that—as contemporaries noted—in the minds of simple folk the idea of the earthly Jerusalem became so confused with and transfused by that of the Heavenly Jerusalem that the Palestinian city seemed itself a miraculous realm, abounding both in spiritual and in material blessings.'[28] The significant point here is not so much Jerusalem's miraculousness, as its attainability. This Holy Land, unlike 'the holy land / of blessed Walsingham', was located well beyond the sphere of the familiar; but it was within reach nevertheless.

If the Crusades brought the earthly Jerusalem closer to people's lives, the Reformation accomplished the opposite: Protestant culture presented a new doctrinal framework in which the earthly city was distanced, deferred, or simply neglected. The most obvious change introduced by the Reformers was the discarding of physical pilgrimages and transforming them (or, if we think about the Pauline interpretation, restoring them) into spiritual quests instead. The real Promised Land, Martin Luther explained, is in 'our hearts':

In former times saints made many pilgrimages to Rome, Jerusalem and Compostela in order to make satisfaction for sins. Now, however, we can go on true pilgrimages in faith, namely, when we diligently read the psalms, prophets,

---

[26] Christopher Tyerman, *England and the Crusades, 1095–1588* (Chicago: University of Chicago Press, 1988), 83.

[27] Simon Lloyd, *English Society and the Crusade, 1216–1307* (Oxford: Clarendon Press, 1988), 245.

[28] Norman Cohn, *The Pursuit of the Millennium* (1957; rev. edn. New York: Oxford University Press, 1970), 63, 64–5.

gospels, etc. Rather than walk about holy places we can thus pause at our own thoughts, examine our heart, and visit the real promised land and paradise of eternal life.[29]

Luther's views emanated from his condemnation of the trade in indulgences, but this doctrinal shift neatly corresponded with the new circumstances in the East—the fall of Constantinople in 1453, and particularly the Ottoman conquest of Jerusalem in 1516. The pilgrimage to the Promised Land of eternal life was not merely a purer and safer journey; it was the only journey possible, as the actual Holy Land remained, for decades, virtually inaccessible.

In England, the Ten Articles (1536) did not mention pilgrimages explicitly, but they were accompanied by royal injunctions to the clergy, who were to persuade their parishioners 'that they shall please God more by the true exercising of their bodily labour, travail or occupation, and providing for their families, than if they went about the said pilgrimages'.[30] Subsequently, Article XXII (1571) denounced the 'Romish Doctrine concerning Purgatory, Pardons, Worshipping and Adoration as well of Images as of Reliques, and also Invocation of Saints'.[31] This included local pilgrimage as well; with the suppression of English monasteries and holy places—England's Nazareth, too, was demolished in 1538—Protestantism merely continued the internalization of the Holy Land, this time reallocating the pilgrimage not just to one's own vicinity, but to one's own soul.

There were two closely related doctrines here, working together: on the one hand, the abolition of the physical pilgrimage; on the other, a new stress on the idea of personal judgement and the rewards of a more accessible heaven.[32] As the first was undermining the importance of the earthly Jerusalem in the East, the latter was magnifying the role of its heavenly sister. According to this new Protestant creed, salvation could be attained in the most narrow and restricted of geographical spheres:

---

[29] Table talk 3,588, in *Luther's Works*, ed. and trans. Theodore G. Tappert (Philadelphia: Fortress Press, 1967), liv. 238.

[30] Quoted in Philip Hughes, *The Reformation in England* (London: Hollis & Carter, 1950), i. 354.

[31] *Book of Common Prayer* (Oxford: Oxford University Press, n.d.), 687.

[32] Ulrich Simon, *Heaven in the Christian Tradition* (London: Rockliff, 1958); Colleen McDannell and Bernhard Lang, *Heaven: A History* (New Haven: Yale University Press, 1988), esp. chs. 6–8.

the vertical division in which the medieval pilgrimage to Palestine had been performed (travelling from West to East, North to South, or simply from 'here' to 'there') was transformed into a horizontal divide (from below to 'above') or simply internalized (Jerusalem in 'our hearts'). This Promised Land of eternal life was truly accessible to all believers, just like the text which showed the way there.

Indeed, it was the translation of the Bible into the vernacular—the most remarkable reform of all—which allowed the English to complete this internalization of the Holy Land and imagine it with a new, unprecedented sense of intimacy. The Protestant insistence on *sola Scriptura*, complemented by a thriving print culture, meant that by the late sixteenth century, the Bible was almost everywhere to be found, not merely in the form of a book, but also in everyday artefacts like painted cloths depicting biblical scenes or 'godly tables' for decorating the bare walls.[33] The dissemination of biblical culture led to a close identification with the trials and tribulations of the Old Testament Israelites, which, in turn, gave rise to the idea that the English people themselves (or at least some of them) were God's chosen nation. This conviction had a critical effect on the events of the Civil War and the foundation of the Commonwealth, but it persisted, as we shall see, long after.[34]

The conception of England as Israel could take many forms. Winstanley, who told Thomas Lord Fairfax that he was of the race of the Jews, believed that 'all the prophecies, visions and revelations of scriptures, of prophets and apostles, concerning the calling of the Jews, the restoration of Israel and making of that people the inheritors of the whole earth' referred to the coming utopian society that the Diggers were building in England.[35] But even those who were considerably less literal-minded—those who believed that 'Israel' in Romans 11: 25 ff. referred to the Jews—were quick to recognize the compelling parallels

---

[33] Tessa Watt, *Cheap Print and Popular Piety, 1550–1640* (Cambridge: Cambridge University Press, 1991), esp. chs. 5–6; Margaret Spufford, *Small Books and Pleasant Histories: Popular Fiction and its Readership in Seventeenth-Century England* (London: Methuen, 1981), 194–218.

[34] Hill, *English Bible*, 264–70, 440.

[35] Quoted in Christopher Hill, 'Till the Conversion of the Jews', in *Collected Essays*, ii: *Religion and Politics in Seventeenth-Century England* (Brighton: Harvester, 1986), 277. See also Knott, *Sword of the Spirit*, 85.

between their own experiences and those of the scriptural Israelites.[36] The Geneva Bible (1560), with its blunt Calvinistic commentary, and John Foxe's *Book of Martyrs* (1563) advocated this notion explicitly. The editors of the King James Bible (1611) omitted most of the annotation, desiring 'that the Scripture may speak like itself, as in the language of Canaan, that it may be understood even of the very vulgar'.[37] But with the Bible in the vernacular, the 'language of Canaan' was now English, encouraging Englishmen to think of themselves as Israelites, and of England as their Canaan. Which brings us back to Bunyan's Christian, who 'naturally spoke the Language of *Canaan*' (p. 74), much to the annoyance of the keepers of Vanity Fair.

This internalization of the twin biblical images—'Promised Land' and 'Chosen People'—offered the English, collectively and as individuals, a way of understanding their place in the world. This was true under Charles I, but also under Victoria. Matthew Arnold's celebrated observation in *Culture and Anarchy* (1869) about that 'strength and prominence of the moral fibre' which 'knits in some special sort the genius and history of us English ... to the genius and history of the Hebrew people' is in fact surprisingly reminiscent not only of Bunyan's juvenile yearnings of discovering himself an Israelite, but also of the British–Israelite movement which flourished in the 1870s, advocating the idea that the Anglo-Saxons were the literal descendants of the lost ten tribes.[38] Two centuries after the Diggers had failed to establish Jerusalem in Surrey, a literal-minded interpretation like this was considered bizarre, to say the least. Arnold was no British Israelite, but his discussion in *Culture and Anarchy* brings the racial and the cultural so closely together that it is no longer possible to determine what created this uncanny affinity between the English and the Hebraic, against all racial dictum.

Both the eminent Victorian and the eccentric fringe were employing the very same paradigm; they differed merely in the literality with which

---

[36] Robert M. Healey, 'The Jew in Seventeenth-Century Protestant Thought', *Church History*, 46/1 (1979), 63–79; David S. Katz, *Philo-Semitism and the Readmission of the Jews to England* (Oxford: Clarendon Press, 1982), 9–42.

[37] Quoted in Gerald Bray (ed.), *Documents of the English Reformation* (Cambridge: James Clarke, 1994), 435.

[38] Matthew Arnold, *Culture and Anarchy* (1869), ed. J. Dover Wilson (1932; Cambridge: Cambridge University Press, 1969), 142.

the biblical metaphor was realized. Rather than being presented, categorically, as opposites, literal and metaphorical appropriations of this language should be seen as adjacent points along the same continuum. Seventeenth-century eschatology and even Victorian millenarianism were merely extreme interpretations of what had been a ubiquitous element in English culture, crossing all social, cultural, and denominational divides.

Biblical Culture and Vernacular Orientalism

Writing in 1625, Samuel Purchas seemed to reiterate the established Protestant creed when he explained that the 'best Pilgrimage... is the peaceable way of a good Conscience to that Jerusalem which is above'.[39] Nevertheless, the fact that this admonition appeared in Purchas's successful anthology of travel accounts reminds us that while Protestantism was restricting the geographical theatre in which salvation was to be attained, English explorers were ceaselessly expanding the boundaries of English knowledge, commerce, and supremacy. How was 'Jerusalem in England' imagined against these very different geographical dimensions?

The steady flow of travel accounts and geographical studies throughout the seventeenth century—from George Sandys's *A Relation of a Journey* (1615) to Nathaniel Crouch's *Two Journeys to Jerusalem* (1683)—indicates that Palestine was part of this new culture of exploration. It was curiosity rather than piety, however, that led Englishmen to Jerusalem; and their Protestant scepticism often fed into a sober tone, anticipating some characteristics of the higher biblical criticism.[40] As Thomas Fuller claimed in *A Pisgah Sight of Palestine* (1650), although his studies of scriptural geography 'are not essential to salvation, yet they are ornamentall, to accomplish men with knowledge, contributing much to the true understanding of the History of the Bible'.[41] Commerce, too, was an incentive. In 1581, a group of English merchants

---

[39] Samuel Purchas, *Hakluytus Posthumus or Purchas his Pilgrimes* (1625; Glasgow: Glasgow University Press, 1905), ix. 478.
[40] Tuchman, *Bible and Sword*, 102–20, 151–7; Samuel C. Chew, *The Crescent and the Rose: Islam and England during the Renaissance* (New York: Oxford University Press, 1937), 73–81, 89–99.
[41] Thomas Fuller, *A Pisgah-Sight of Palestine* (1650; London: John Williams, 1662), i. 2.

established the Levant Company, receiving a royal charter to trade in the dominions of the Sultan of Turkey, including Palestine. In 1600, the same group founded the East India Company, which has come to typify the rise of British imperialism and the birth of modern Orientalism.

It is tempting to view this ethos of exploration as the antithesis to the Protestant biblical culture which emerged at the very same period, and which *The Pilgrim's Progress* seems to exemplify. There is a range of possible oppositions here. Bunyan is concerned with the godly, the plebeian, the familiar; this emerging imperial culture is often associated with the worldly, the scientific, the exotic. The explorers use and produce navigation tools, maps, travel narratives; Bunyan relies on the Bible and his imagination alone. Most significantly, this proto-imperial culture was gazing outwards, to the wonders that lay eastwards (and westwards) of England; Bunyan was looking inwards, into the English landscape, if not simply the English soul.

Attractive, certainly, but this dichotomy is also unduly simplified: suffice it to state that all East India vessels carried as reading matter, besides Hakluyt's *Voyages*, copies of the Bible and Foxe's *Book of Martyrs*.[42] Another, less conventional way of problematizing these binary oppositions is to suggest that despite (or is it because of?) its introspective view, *The Pilgrim's Progress* is also an Orientalist text. After all, depicting Christian's journey to the Promised Land and its city of Jerusalem, it offers a distinct way of imagining the East. One could argue, obviously, that the landscape depicted in *The Pilgrim's Progress* does not strive to represent any Eastern reality: but this is precisely the point. The Holy Land envisaged in Bunyan's text is not an attempt to reconstruct the Orient from that 'bundle of fragments brought back piecemeal by explorers, expeditions, commissions, armies, and merchants'; nor is it an attempt to imagine and hence create 'the Orient, the Oriental, and his world'.[43] In fact, the Oriental and his world are of no consequence whatsoever. Instead, the Orient is imagined using nothing but Englishness.

The Pilgrim's Progress could thus be read as a key text of 'vernacular' Orientalism, defined as that cultural process whereby what was initially

---

[42] Hill, *English Bible*, 18.
[43] Edward Said, *Orientalism: Western Conceptions of the Orient* (1978; Harmondsworth: Penguin, 1995), 166, 40.

an Oriental paradigm (in this case, the Holy Land, Israelites) is internalized, localized, made to become an integral part of English self-fashioning, identity, and culture.[44] 'Vernacular' is useful here, because it evokes that historical transition, discussed above, in which the Bible was made available in the language of the people; but also because it conveys this knee-jerk association of the biblical vocabulary with everything that is indigenous and mundane. Moreover, by denoting that linguistic register which was shared by the educated minority and the masses alike, 'vernacular' also provides a cultural model which is more subtle than the crude division between high and low, academic and plebeian; the educated minority alone mastered Latin, but the vernacular was shared by all. Vernacular Orientalism was a way of imagining the common ground that was England; but it was also, simply, common cultural ground.

This vernacular tradition should be set against the learned Orientalism depicted by Edward Said. While the scholarly body of knowledge which emerged in the sixteenth century—geographic, cartographic, ethnographic, and so forth—was both produced and consumed by an extremely limited social stratum, biblical language was available ubiquitously. And whereas Said's academic Orientalism is 'that collection of dreams, images, and vocabularies available to anyone who has tried to talk about what lies east of the dividing line',[45] its vernacular counterpart is conspicuously similar, with the admirable exception that it recognizes neither the 'east' nor the 'line'. Vernacular Orientalism thus upsets the delicate balance on which much of postcolonial studies has been constructed. As Robert J. C. Young has remarked, the creation of the Orient by the West, 'if it does not really represent the East, signifies the West's own dislocation from itself, something inside that is presented,

---

[44] The terms 'vernacular' and 'Orientalism' are employed here because my discussion is concerned with Palestine, and hence with biblical culture. It is certainly possible, however, to construct a broader methodological framework which would encompass similar cultural moments: the most obvious example is the Victorian analogy between the metropolitan urban 'jungle' and its colonial counterpart, as in William Booth's *In Darkest England* (1890). 'Vernacular Orientalism', in other words, can be used to describe the Western domestication of the exotic, or the internalization of the other by the self. For various aspects of the 'Orientalization' of imperial Britain see Julie F. Codell and Diana Sachko Macleod (eds.), *Orientalism Transposed: The Impact of the Colonies on British Culture* (Aldershot: Ashgate, 1998).

[45] Said, *Orientalism*, 73.

narrativized, as being outside'; Orientalism 'represents the West's own internal dislocation, misrepresented as an external dualism between West and East'.[46] But vernacular Orientalism goes even further: far from 'misrepresenting' an internal dualism in a colonial context, it narrativizes something 'outside' as being unequivocally 'inside'.

Several questions come to mind. The core of Said's argument is that Orientalism, 'as a Western style for dominating, restructuring, and having authority over the Orient', virtually begged for knowledge to be translated into colonial control.[47] But vernacular Orientalism always looks inwards rather than to the people and landscapes of the actual East: what, then, are its political and social implications? Does it seek to exercise authority? How? And over whom? Moreover, how did this image of Jerusalem in England affect the representation of other parts of the Orient, which were not internalized in a similar manner? And, finally, how could vernacular Orientalism shape attitudes towards the actual Holy Land in the East?

These issues will be addressed in the following pages and chapters. But we can begin by acknowledging that 'pure' vernacular Orientalism exists as a theoretical construct only; in practice, it should always be considered alongside other cultural influences. Even the Geneva Bible was not immune to the renewed interest in cartography: its various editions included maps of the Holy Land, depicting the Exodus route and the land in Christ's time.[48] We have no way of assessing what common readers made of these maps, but, as Samuel Chew and Nabil Matar have shown, references to the Levant trade, to Islam, to the legacy of the Crusades, and hence to Palestine were not difficult to come by in seventeenth-century England, whether in the form of sermons, captive narratives, mummers' plays, or inn-signs of Saracens' heads.[49] Following their readmission to England in 1655, flesh-and-blood Jews—as opposed to their centuries-old stereotypes—were also becoming

---

[46] Robert J. C. Young, *White Mythologies: Writing History and the West* (London: Routledge, 1990), 139–40.

[47] Said, *Orientalism*, 3.

[48] Catherine Delano-Smith, 'Maps in Bibles in the Sixteenth Century', *Map Collector*, 39 (1987), 2–14.

[49] Chew, *Crescent*; Nabil Matar, *Islam in Britain, 1558–1685* (Cambridge: Cambridge University Press, 1998).

increasingly visible, challenging any straightforward identification between the English and 'Israel'.[50]

With these constant reminders of the actual Orient, an unequivocal internalization of the biblical vocabulary probably required either a remarkably naïve reader or a remarkably devout one; preferably, both. It is hardly surprising, then, that the strict literality which marked the Diggers' interpretation of prophecy was considered exceptional even among their millenarian peers. When Thomas Fuller complained that 'because the New Jerusalem is now daily expected to come down ... these corporall (not to say carnell) studies of this terrestrial Canaan, begin to grow out of fashion, with the more knowing sort of Christians',[51] he was perhaps alluding to the likes of Winstanley, who insisted that all prophecies referred to Jerusalem in Surrey. The great majority of these Christians, however, believed that the terrestrial Canaan played a central role in the eschatological design, and that the restoration of the Jews to their homeland (before or after their conversion, the exact order was much disputed) was an essential harbinger for the Second Coming.[52] Confusion often followed: as James Shapiro has noted, the 'increasing sense of the impossibility of sincere Jewish conversion in the late sixteenth and early seventeenth centuries occurs at precisely the same time that apocalyptic belief in the imminent conversion of the Jews was on the rise, creating a sharp and disturbing division between the two positions'.[53]

Nevertheless, in the two generations before the 1660s, many radical millenarians devised detailed plans to restore the Jews; some cranky, others almost practical. One of the most eloquent is Samuel Gott's utopian tale *Nova Solyma* (1648), which describes the journey of two young Englishmen from Dover to Joppa, by ship, and from there, on horseback, to the New Jerusalem. They arrive on the annual festival celebrating the founding of the city fifty years earlier: the Turks were

---

[50] Frank Felsenstein, *Anti-Semitic Stereotypes: A Paradigm of Otherness in English Popular Culture, 1660–1830* (Baltimore: Johns Hopkins University Press, 1995), 40–57.

[51] Fuller, *Pisgah-Sight*, i. 2.

[52] Hill, 'Till the Conversion'; Katz, *Philo-Semitism*, 89–126; Mel Scult, *Millennial Expectations and Jewish Liberties: A Study of the Efforts to Convert the Jews in Britain up to the Mid-Nineteenth Century* (Leiden: Brill, 1978); Mayir Vereté, *From Palmerston to Balfour* (London: Frank Cass, 1992), 92–101.

[53] James Shapiro, *Shakespeare and the Jews* (New York: Columbia University Press, 1996), 20.

expelled, the Jews converted, and the New Jerusalem—with twelve gates and geometrically planned streets, just as in Revelation—established on the site of the 'old Solyma' from which 'not a vestige remained'. The novel concludes with the signing of a commercial treaty between those two favoured nations, England and Nova Solyma.[54]

It was quite possible, then, for Englishmen to think of themselves as a—or even *the*—chosen people, the true Israel, and yet to manifest an interest in the Jews as the descendants of the ancient Israelites; to imagine the Kingdom of God in England and yet ponder the role designated to Jerusalem in the East. Against Winstanley's indigenous rendering of the 'Jerusalem in England' trope, works like *Nova Solyma* projected the eschatological plan across a broad geographical canvas, looking not only to the Old World of the East, but also to the New World in the West, where a Puritan Zion was being established.[55]

'A land of pure delight': Empire, Class, and Geographical Imagination

Even if we accept that the dissemination of biblical vocabulary crossed all social divisions, whether in its strict millenarian form or in more subtle versions, it is still necessary to ask whether different appropriations of 'Holy Land' and 'Chosen People' corresponded to socio-economic differences. Were members of the rising mercantile classes inclined to apply the millenarian ethos to a broader geographical vision? Were the poor, the illiterate, predisposed to understand biblical imagery in a more personal and indigenous vein, literalizing it not 'out there', halfway across the globe, but 'here', in the most familiar of environments?

---

[54] [Samuel Gott], *Nova Solyma: The Ideal City; or Jerusalem Regained* (1648), trans. and ed. Walter Begley (London: John Murray, 1902), i. 78–9, ii. 216–21.

[55] Hilton Obenzinger, *American Palestine: Melville, Twain, and the Holy Land Mania* (Princeton: Princeton University Press, 1999), 14–23. The North American colonies were soon dotted with Bethels, Canaans, and Goshens. This Puritan nomenclature certainly refined the literalization of the 'Holy Land' metaphor, but the fixed, institutionalized scriptural grid it imposed over the New World topography may have obscured the more personal, or contesting, internalizations of biblical vocabulary which we find in England at the very same period. Similarly, the social homogeneity of the colonies (compared, at least, with Europe) may explain why English appropriations of the 'Promised Land' very often reflected socio-economic aspirations (that are more reminiscent of the African-American slave experience than any social schism we may find within white-settler American society).

Some historians believe that they were. The activist utopian millenarianism of the late 1640s, associated with the Fifth Monarchy Men and the Levellers, was 'preponderantly lower-class', Christopher Hill has claimed.[56] According to Brian Manning, the Digger movement emerged as a protest against the impoverishment of wage labourers and those with little or no land.[57] Over-glorifying the Diggers, Marxist historiography has probably underestimated the 'distinctly middle-class element' discernible in English millenarianism.[58] But surely it would not be far-fetched to assume that literal-minded interpretations of Scripture were more typical of plebeian readers (or, indeed, listeners), who had little opportunity for leisure or travel, who relied on biblical culture as a major source of information and comfort, and who yearned for comfort in the face of ongoing hardship. For them, a Protestant 'Jerusalem', accessible to all, was a powerful symbol of hope.

'Two conceptions of religion were living in England side by side, and the French Revolution compelled a choice between them,' V. Kiernan has written: 'One was of religion as the formulary of an established society, its statement of faith in itself; the other as a catastrophic conversion of the individual, a miraculous shaking off of secret burdens. One was fixed on this world, the other on the next.'[59] The Dissenting minister Isaac Watts was certainly among the latter when he described, in his immensely popular hymn (1715), that 'land of pure delight / Where Saints Immortal reign':

> O could we make our Doubts remove,
> These gloomy Doubts that rise,
> And see the *Canaan* that we love,
> With unbeclouded Eyes.
>
> Could we but climb where *Moses* stood,
> And view the Landskip o're,
> Not *Jordan's* Stream, nor Death's cold Flood,
> Should fright us from the Shore.[60]

---

[56] Hill, *English Bible*, 307.
[57] Brian Manning, *1649: The Crisis of the English Revolution* (London: Bookmarks, 1992), 111.
[58] Yonina Talmon, 'Millenarian Movements', *European Journal of Sociology*, 7/2 (1966), 186–7.
[59] V. Kiernan, 'Evangelicalism and the French Revolution', *Past and Present*, 1 (1952), 46.
[60] Isaac Watts, *Hymns and Spiritual Songs, 1707–1748*, ed. Selma L. Bishop (London: Faith Press, 1962), 230–1.

Throughout the eighteenth century, particularly after the emergence of Evangelicalism in the late 1730s, scores of hymns perpetuated this image of the Promised Land—or Canaan, or Jerusalem—as a coveted afterlife. Wesley's *Collection of Hymns for the Use of the People Called Methodists* (1779), for example, employs Bunyanesque idioms like 'High on Immanuel's land', 'the mountain of God', 'the city above', 'Jerusalem, the saints' abode', 'Our labour this, our only aim, / To find the New Jerusalem', and so forth.[61] The pilgrim metaphor is elaborated to justify, if not glorify, poverty:

> No foot of land do I possess,
> No cottage in this wilderness,
> A poor, way-faring man;
>
> I lodge awhile in tents below,
> Or gladly wander to and fro,
> Till I can Canaan gain.[62]

Rippon's *Selection of Hymns* (1787) for Baptists included Samuel Stennett's own variation on the same theme:

> On Jordan's stormy banks I stand,
> And cast a wishful eye
> To Canaan's fair and happy land,
> Where my possession lie.[63]

The range is enormous: almost every eighteenth-century hymnal contained similar images of heaven. With the rise of the Sunday-school movement in the 1780s, a gush of tracts, magazines, and school-books sought to familiarize children, too, with a detailed knowledge of heaven and with the history of the Old Testament Israelites.[64] 'The old Jewish civilisation became actual and vivid to the men and women who listened to the rhetoric of the new type of preacher,' the Hammonds have observed: 'The Sunday-schools, that spread rapidly over the north of

---

[61] John Wesley, *A Collection of Hymns for the Use of the People Called Methodists* (1779; 3rd edn. London: Paramore, 1802), 69–81.
[62] Ibid. 71.
[63] John Rippon, *Selection of Hymns* ... (1787; 10th edn. London: 1802), hymn 584.
[64] Paul Sangster, *Pity My Simplicity: The Evangelical Revival and the Religious Education of Children, 1738–1800* (London: Epworth Press, 1963), 138 and *passim*; Thomas Laqueur, *Religion and Respectability: Sunday Schools and Working-Class Culture, 1780–1850* (New Haven: Yale University Press, 1976), 160–9.

England and the industrial districts, were primarily institutions for interpreting this civilisation to children brought up in factories and mines.'[65]

Following Halévy's thesis that Methodism, as a stabilizing force, prevented revolution in England in the 1790s, historians have often seen Evangelicalism as an instrument of social control. The factory system, E. P. Thompson has claimed, demanded a worker adapted to the discipline of the machine: 'But how are these disciplinary virtues to be inculcated in those whose Godliness (unless they become overlookers) is unlikely to bring any temporal gain? It can only be by inculcating "the first and great lesson... that man must expect his chief happiness, not in the present, but in a future state".'[66] Thomas Laqueur essentially agrees that 'in inculcating values relating to personal behaviour, Sunday schools appear to have been a remarkably successful agency of bourgeois moral imperialism'. The Bible and *The Pilgrim's Progress* were key texts in this indoctrination,[67] encouraging labouring men and women to think of themselves as God's elect, passing in this world on their way to Zion, Canaan, the Promised Land. 'Jerusalem, my happy home,' asks Joseph Bromehead's unforgettable hymn (1796), 'When shall I come to thee?'

Laqueur's expression 'bourgeois moral imperialism' brings us back to the question of the political and social implications of vernacular Orientalism. What the Hammonds, Thompson, and Laqueur are all in effect asserting is that the 'middle classes' sought to secure a certain image of the Holy Land (primarily as a golden afterlife) and of the chosen people (the workers themselves) which would match the new work ethic required for a stable industrial society. In other words, if Said's Orientalism is a 'Western style for dominating, reconstructing and having authority over the Orient', we could say that eighteenth-century vernacular Orientalism was a middle-class style of dominating, restructuring, and having authority over the lower orders at home.

This, of course, will not do, especially if we bear in mind Gramsci's notion of hegemony, emphasizing the flux and complexity of cultural

---

[65] J. L. Hammond and Barbara Hammond, *The Town Labourer, 1760–1832* (1917; Stroud: Alan Sutton, 1995), 272.
[66] E. P. Thompson, *The Making of the English Working Class* (1963; Harmondsworth: Penguin, 1968), 398, quoting Dr Andrew Ure's *Philosophy of Manufactures* (1835).
[67] Laqueur, *Religion and Respectability*, 170, 160.

formation:[68] dominant forces were able to maintain their authority only through the careful orchestration of an ideological consent among subordinate groups. Indeed, far from being imposed from above, *The Pilgrim's Progress*, as Macaulay has noted, 'is perhaps the only book about which the educated minority has come over to the opinion of the common people'.[69] Similarly, Evangelical Nonconformity could be said to have echoed the aspirations, rather than the despair, of the working classes.[70] As late as 1930, D. H. Lawrence still shuddered at the memory of the Sunday school's fixation with Revelation: 'Long before one could think or even vaguely understand, this Bible language, these "portions" of the Bible were *douched* over the mind and consciousness, till they became soaked in, they became an influence which affected all the processes of emotion and thought.' But even Lawrence found himself admiring the consoling power that the chapel offered its believers:

With nonconformity, the chapel people took over to themselves the Jewish idea of the chosen people. They were 'it', the elect, or the 'saved'. And they took over the Jewish idea of ultimate triumph and reign of the chosen people. From being bottom dogs they were going to be top dogs: in Heaven... It is doctrine you can hear any night from the Salvation Army or in any Bethel or Pentecost Chapel. If it is not Jesus, it is John. If it is not Gospel, it is Revelation. It is popular religion, as distinct from thoughtful religion.[71]

The potential subversiveness contained in the biblical vocabulary recalls Homi K. Bhabha's reading of the ambivalence that pervades the colonial encounter. In 'Signs Taken for Wonders', he considers the imposition of the English book, *the* English book, on the colonized population. The context—a tree outside Delhi, May 1817—transforms the Bible into 'an insignia of colonial authority and a signifier of colonial desire and discipline', but it also generates an array of ambiguous meanings and competing interpretations. Subsequently, instead of describing the fixity

---

[68] Antonio Gramsci, *Selections from the Prison Notebooks*, ed. and trans. Quintin Hoare and Geoffrey Nowell Smith (London: Lawrence & Wishart, 1971), 54–5.
[69] Lord Macaulay, 'John Bunyan', in *Encyclopaedia Britannica*, 11th edn. (Cambridge: Cambridge University Press, 1910), iv. 806.
[70] Alan D. Gilbert, *Religion and Society in Industrial England* (London: Longman, 1976), 83.
[71] D. H. Lawrence, *Apocalypse* (1931), ed. Mara Kalnins (St Albans: Granada, 1981), 1, 6.

of European rule, the Bible empowers the colonized subject with a mode of resistance against oppression: there is an undecidability at the heart of the missionary encounter 'that turns the discursive conditions of dominance into the grounds of intervention'.[72]

It is indicative of Bhabha's project that he makes no reference to the ambiguous meanings that this biblical vocabulary might have had back in England. Indeed, that Bhabha can describe the Bible simply as an 'English book' is in itself testimony to the remarkable process in which a narrative concerned with Semite protagonists and Eastern landscapes had become a quintessential part of Englishness. Just like the Gramscian notions of 'hegemony' and 'subaltern'—which were coined, initially, to describe class conflicts in a European context, before being annexed by postcolonial critics to depict social control in an imperial frame—Bhabha's missionary encounter could be seen as an external playing-out of what was originally a domestic tug-of-war. Long before Delhi, 1817, it was the *vernacular* Orientalist encounter which initially transformed the discursive conditions of dominance into the grounds of intervention: rather than encourage readers to wait, patiently, for their heavenly allotment, Christian's journey to Zion urged new generations of radicals to establish their own Jerusalem in England, here and now. '*Pilgrim's Progress* is, with *Rights of Man*, one of the two foundation texts of the English Working-class movement,' E. P. Thompson has claimed; the connecting notion between religious revivalism and radical politics had always been that of the 'Children of Israel'[73]—and, we might add, the land of Israel.

But hegemony works both ways. Keen to highlight the radical implications, Thompson typically overlooks the fact that 'Chosen People' and 'Promised Land' were also the connecting notions between religious revivalism and nationalist, if not downright imperialist, politics. Linda Colley has recently demonstrated how the Protestant sense of election played a fundamental role in the formation of the modern British state, with its distinctly colonial outlook. The empire, too, was a land of pure delight: when Isaac Watts compiled his best-selling translation of the Psalms in 1719, he was only too happy to replace all references to 'Israel' in the original text with the words 'Great Britain'. *The Pilgrim's Progress* may have inspired generations of radicals, Colley writes, but it also

---

[72] Homi K. Bhabha, *The Location of Culture* (London: Routledge, 1994), 102, 112.
[73] Thompson, *Working Class*, 34, 429.

contributed to a more conventional mass patriotism.[74] Bunyan's Jerusalem in England anticipated the Blakean, Chartist, even Labourite New Jerusalems; but even Kipling's 'The White Man's Burden' (1899) echoes the great burden on Christian's back.[75]

That *The Pilgrim's Progress* informed causes as diverse as radical and imperial politics might suggest that these causes were less diverse than they seem. It certainly confirms the hegemonic status of vernacular biblical vocabulary in English culture. What is particularly significant for our discussion is that throughout the eighteenth century, the various appropriations of biblical imagery, whether at home or overseas, had virtually nothing to do with the geographical Holy Land. In the imperial context, Britain's ambitions were essentially turned either to the Atlantic or to India and the Far East; Palestine was hardly a part of this imperial culture.[76] The fact that the East India Company soon eclipsed the work of its elder sister, the Levant Company, is indicative in this respect of the movement 'from the Dome of the Rock to the Rim of the World'.[77] Active millenarian Puritanism fitted economic expansion and colonization better than did traditional religion; however, while mid-seventeenth-century radical millenarianism attributed a central role to the earthly Holy Land, what remained after the 1660s was a more subtle, secularized form of the millenarian spirit, in which the restoration of the Jews to Palestine played a very minor role, and English commercial enterprise was central.[78] Britain's imperial gaze was aimed well beyond the holy places in Palestine, from which its sense of divine election had originally emerged.

---

[74] Linda Colley, *Britons: Forging the Nation, 1707–1837* (New Haven: Yale University Press, 1992), 30, 28. For a broader perspective see Anthony D. Smith, *Chosen Peoples: Sacred Sources of National Identity* (Oxford: Oxford University Press, 2003); William R. Hutchison and Hartmut Lehmann (eds.), *Many Are Chosen: Divine Election and Western Nationalism* (Minneapolis: Fortress Press, 1994).

[75] The white man must deliver the ungrateful natives to the Promised Land of civilization: 'The cry of hosts ye humour / (Ah, slowly!) toward the light:—/ "Why brought ye us from bondage, / Our loved Egyptian night?" ' (*Rudyard Kipling, The Complete Verse* (London: Kyle Cathie, 1990), 262).

[76] Of the hundreds of maps recorded in Christopher M. Klein, *Maps in Eighteenth-Century British Magazines: A Checklist* (Chicago: Newberry Library, 1989), only four are related to the Mediterranean; there is virtually no mention of Palestine.

[77] Stephen Greenblatt, *Marvelous Possessions: The Wonder of the New World* (Oxford: Clarendon Press, 1991), 26.

[78] Hill, *English Bible*, 433; Hill, 'Till the Conversion', 291.

In the domestic context, on the other hand, whether radical, plebeian, or even patriotic, Jerusalem could be encountered later (in heaven) or established here (in England's green and pleasant land); but the Jerusalem which existed now and there (in the present, in the land called Palestine) was essentially irrelevant. This perception, formulated by Protestant indoctrination, was sustained by material conditions, such as the lack of visual imagery. Bibles, editions of *The Pilgrim's Progress*, and various religious publications were common, but illustrated versions were not. Even in the 1830s, only a few inexpensive books contained cuts or engravings.[79] When religious visual imagery was available—for example, in ballads, chapbooks, or in church stained-glass windows[80]—it was usually an extremely crude or ill-defined replica of standard medieval iconography, in itself a vernacular tradition of imagining the Holy Land. Geographical studies and travel narratives about Palestine—like Richard Pococke's *Description of the East* (1743) or Richard Tyron's *Travels from Aleppo to the City of Jerusalem* (1785)—appeared throughout the century, but were limited, obviously, to affluent readers. Only in the mid-1830s would geographical studies begin to filter down the social scale, and even then, as Chapter 3 will show, the image of the earthly land continued to be obscured by the Protestant emphasis on the Jerusalem which is above.

This brings us back to the question of the 'chain of practices and processes by which geographical information is gathered, geographical facts are ordered and imaginative geographies are constructed'.[81] With few books, hardly any images, and virtually no chance of foreign (or even local) travel, how could people imagine an Eastern city called Jerusalem? Moreover, reading about Jerusalem—if one *could* actually read—was one thing; obtaining a coherent geographical perception was a very different matter. 'I would willingly have taken a Pilgrimage to the holy Land to have beheld you,' cries the studious parson Adams in Fielding's *Joseph Andrews* (1742) when he meets his supposedly generous benefactor. But when the innkeeper asks him about the Levant, it

---

[79] Patricia Anderson, *The Printed Image and the Transformation of Popular Culture, 1790–1860* (Oxford: Clarendon Press, 1991), 16–35.

[80] John Ashton, *Chapbooks of the Eighteenth Century* (1882; London: Skoob, 1962); John Phillips, *The Reformation of Images: Destruction of Art in England, 1535–1660* (Berkeley: University of California Press, 1973).

[81] Schwartz and Ryan, 'Introduction', 6.

seems that the good parson's geography is somewhat muddled: ' "Pray where's the *Levant*?" quoth Adams, "that should be in the *East Indies* by right." '[82] A hundred years on, things remained very much the same—as the author of *Peter Parley's Method of Telling about the Geography of the Bible* (1839) suggests in a somewhat anxious anecdote:

'Was there really such a place as Jerusalem?' said a boy to his father, in my hearing, a short time since. Now this child had been accustomed to read the Scriptures, and was familiar with the New Testament. Why, then, this doubt as to the actual existence of that city in which the principal events occurred which are recorded in the Gospels? It doubtless arose from a want of definite knowledge of the geography of the country in which it was situated.[83]

It was this lack of 'definite' geographical knowledge, fused with the powerful biblical imagery that was everywhere current in this Sunday-school culture, that explains why generations of English boys and girls associated the Holy Land with their own vicinity, community, or daily life: vernacular Orientalism in its most immediate, instinctive, form. A. E. Housman (b. 1859) loved to gaze at the soft hills of the Promised Land of Shropshire from a hilltop which his siblings nicknamed 'Mount Pisgah'.[84] Stanley Spencer (b. 1891) captured this naïve literalization of the biblical tales when he depicted Christ carrying his cross in the narrow streets of Cookham. In the warm community of his Cumberland Methodist chapel, tailor's son Norman Nicholson (b. 1914) grew up believing that

we all belonged to the same country. And that country was the Holy Land. The landscape of the Bible was far more familiar to us than the geography of England. We had news of it twice every service in the lessons; the preachers preached about it; the hymns depicted and extolled it. Jerusalem, Jericho, Bethlehem, Canaan, the Sea of Galilee, Mount Carmel, Mount Ararat, Gilead, Moab, the Brook Cherith and cool Siloam's shady rill—all these seemed no further from home than, say, the Duddon Valley... It was not only that the Bible lands seemed near to home: in some ways they *were* home. And they

---

[82] Henry Fielding, *The History of the Adventures of Joseph Andrews, and of his Friend Mr. Abraham Adams* (1841), ed. Douglas Brooks-Davies, World's Classics (Oxford: Oxford University Press, 1999), 152, 159.

[83] Revd Samuel Blair, *Peter Parley's Method of Telling about the Geography of the Bible* (London: Hodson, 1839), p. v.

[84] Richard Perceval Graves, *A. E. Housman: The Scholar-Poet* (London: Routledge & Kegan Paul, 1979), 24.

looked like home. To me the shepherds keeping watch over their flocks were men like the Watsons of Millom Farm, or the Tysons of Beck Farm, or the Falconers of Water Blean.[85]

Dennis Potter (b. 1935) described a similar sensation:

And for me, of course, the language of the New Testament in particular, but the Bible in general was actually, as it is to a child. I don't know, I suppose even to a child brought up in Pinner or Wembley Park, it must be something similar, but it was the Holy Land—I knew Cannop Ponds by the pit where Dad worked, I knew that was where Jesus walked on water; I knew where the Valley of the Shadow of Death was, that lane where the overhanging trees were. As I said, I was a coward. At dusk I'd whistle, going down that particular lane.[86]

Potter was growing up in the 1940s, as the British were governing Palestine. Imagine, then, the perceptions that children must have had more than a century and a half earlier. And perhaps not just children, considering that even after the introduction of the Bank Holiday in 1871, more than half the population in Britain had never set eyes on the sea.[87] Up to the Second World War, British working people consistently described their mental maps in terms that call to mind a Saul Steinberg cartoon', Jonathan Rose has written: 'The center ground was dominated by the streets where they grew up, drawn to enormous scale and etched in fine detail. Nearby towns hovered vaguely in the middle distance. Foreign countries, if they existed at all, were smudges on the horizon.'[88]

This is not to claim that the working-class geographical imagination in the eighteenth or even the nineteenth century could not accommodate empire, or that biblical culture was the only source of influence and experience. Whereas Bunyan imagines a land of milk and honey just around the corner, the protagonist of the equally popular *Robinson Crusoe* builds a Promised Land far-away, on a tropical island. And against Bunyan's internalization of Oriental paradigms, the *Arabian Nights* introduced the wonders of a distant, exotic Orient. But whereas Egypt and Damascus represented a congruent space in which the

---

[85] Norman Nicholson, *Wednesday Early Closing* (1975), 94–5, quoted in Jonathan Rose, *The Intellectual Life of the British Working Classes* (2001; New Haven: Yale University Press, 2002), 351–2.
[86] Dennis Potter, *Seeing the Blossom* (London: Faber & Faber, 1994), 8.
[87] James Walvin, *Beside the Seaside: A Social History of the Popular Seaside Holiday* (London: Allen Lane, 1978), 75.
[88] Rose, *Intellectual Life*, 342.

fabulous Orient and the biblical lands could overlap, the Holy Land was not Orientalized in a similar manner.

We could say, by way of conclusion, that throughout the eighteenth century, the different appropriations of the 'Holy Land' either fell too short of—or beyond—the actual Holy Land: Palestine was too far away for the radical geographical imagination to consider; for the imperial geographical imagination, not far enough. As a metaphor, the 'Holy Land' was much more accessible, and endlessly more useful, than the geographical place itself.

Towards the end of the century, however, things began to change. In 1799, the British fleet joined the Turkish forces in defending Acre against Napoleon's army, anticipating a century-long British–Ottoman alliance. The emergence of the Eastern Question would gradually bring the earthly Holy Land to the attention of English men and women. The millenarian culture that flourished in England in the 1790s offers a rare glimpse of this transition: torn between the anticipation of a New Jerusalem in England's green and pleasant land, and the growing recognition that the apocalyptic scenario should involve a much wider geographical sphere, the two prominent prophets of the age, Joanna Southcott and Richard Brothers, were forced to accommodate these two very different 'Jerusalems'.

The affinity between popular millenarianism and the rise of socialist movements like Owenism and Chartism has received ample attention.[89] My objective, however, is to examine how the millenarian construction of 'Jerusalem' as a radical utopia was affected by Britain's expanding interests in Palestine. The dissemination and respectability of ideas concerning the Jewish restoration will be discussed in Chapter 4; here, I would like to rely on the extensive work of these two prophets—a poor domestic servant from the west country and a retired navy officer—to map the changing boundaries of the geographical imagination, in or about 1800.[90]

---

[89] Thompson, *Working Class*, esp. 877–87; W. H. Oliver, *Prophets and Millennialists: The Uses of Biblical Prophecy in England from the 1790s to the 1840s* (Auckland: Auckland University Press, 1978), 197–217; J. F. C. Harrison, *The Second Coming: Popular Millenarianism 1780–1850* (London: Routledge & Kegan Paul, 1979), chs. 7–8.

[90] The following section presents the rudiments of my discussion in 'Green and Pleasant Lands: England and the Holy Land in Plebeian Millenarian Culture, *c*.1790–1820', in Kathleen Wilson (ed.), *A New Imperial History: Culture, Identity, and Modernity in Britain and the Empire, 1660–1840* (Cambridge: Cambridge University Press, 2004), 155–75.

The Holy Land in Popular Millenarian Culture, c.1790–1820

English millenarianism did not die out with the Restoration; rather, it persisted throughout the eighteenth century, significant at all social levels.[91] The 1790s, in particular, saw a great millenarian outburst: the French Revolution and the tumultuous wars that ensued were recognized by many as the first in the anticipated series of events which would dispatch the millennium. Within this broad cultural climate, however, two distinct traditions could be outlined. One was respectable, orthodox, learned; the other rooted in popular culture and folk customs.[92]

The academic tradition was associated with eminent scholars like Joseph Priestley, Samuel Horsley, and George Stanley Faber, who,despite obvious denominational and political differences, approached prophecy with a typical scientific sobriety. They tended to be postmillenarian, believing that the Second Advent would follow, not precede, the millennium. Corresponding with the optimistic principles of the Enlightenment, their apocalypse was a peaceful continuation of the present, a result of human effort, epitomized in the notion of the Christian mission.[93] It is telling that the Church Missionary Society (established in 1798), the British and Foreign Bible Society (1804), and the London Society for Promoting Christianity among the Jews (1809) were all established in this period of millenarian upheaval.

As we have seen, the return of the Jews to Palestine and their conversion to Christianity were considered essential phases in the millenarian design. The failure of the Jewish Naturalization Act in 1753 merely reinforced the conviction that, rather than being assimilated, the Jews were awaiting their restitution.[94] Some venerable millenarians believed that England had been providentially chosen to be the agent

---

[91] Oliver, *Prophets and Millennialists*, 17.

[92] Harrison, *Second Coming*, 3–10, 207–8. For some cross-exchanges between the two traditions see Iain McCalman, 'New Jerusalems: Prophecy, Dissent, and Radical Culture in England, 1786–1830', in Knud Haakonssen (ed.), *Enlightenment and Religion: Rational Dissent in Eighteenth-Century Britain* (Cambridge: Cambridge University Press, 1996), 312–35.

[93] D. W. Bebbington, *Evangelicalism in Modern Britain: A History from the 1730s to the 1980s* (London: Unwin Hyman, 1989), 62.

[94] N. I. Matar, 'The Controversy over the Restoration of the Jews in English Protestant Thought: 1754 to 1809', *Durham University Journal*, 87 (1990), 30.

of the restoration. But as Napoleon extended his sway to the Holy Land in 1798–9, the question of whether the Antichrist himself was to restore the Jews acquired a new sense of urgency.[95] A failure to persuade Turkey to give up Palestine and to prepare the Jews for their great migration, warned James Bicheno, 'would prove most fatal to our government and commerce'.[96]

'Academic' millenarianism, then, relied on a clear-cut division between those who were to convert and those who were to be converted; and it operated within a vast geographical theatre in which, amidst the European struggle for dominion over the East, the restoration would take place: Priestley, Horsley, Faber, and Bicheno, all agreed that prophecies about Israel should be applied to the Jews, not to the English,[97] and that the apocalyptic scheme outlined in Scripture was to be re-enacted in the Levant. Drawing on contemporary geographical and philological scholarship, fusing prophetic and imperial calculations, this postmillenarian discourse once again suggests the inadequacy of employing a secularized (if not secular) Orientalism to explain the emergence of Britain's colonial interests in the Middle East.

At the opposite end of the millenarian spectrum were the popular, largely self-educated millenarians: stemming from the radical sects of the Civil War, they were relatively untouched by the logic of the Newtonian cosmos.[98] Whereas the academic tradition provided detached and objectified calculations, popular millenarianism usually centred around the charismatic figure of a prophet who conveyed the heavenly communications directly to the disciples. These tended to be premillenarian: salvation was to be achieved through divine intervention, which would destroy the existing evil order and bring about the millennium. They were much more likely to think of themselves as God's chosen people than set up, or even support, a mission to the Jews.

Revolutionary ambitions often merged, at least discursively, with the millenarian impulse.[99] As Jon Mee has observed, the flexibility of

---

[95] McCalman, 'New Jerusalems', 329–33.
[96] James Bicheno, *The Restoration of the Jews, The Crisis of All Nations*... (London: Bye and Law, 1800), 96.
[97] Oliver, *Prophets and Millennialists*, 62.
[98] Harrison, *Second Coming*, 6.
[99] Clarke Garrett, *Respectable Folly: Millenarians and the French Revolution in France and England* (Baltimore: Johns Hopkins University Press, 1975), 225.

Thomas Paine's political rhetoric is demonstrated by his preparedness to turn to the language of popular religion when he seeks to appeal directly to the disenfranchised reader.[100] We should not, however, confuse the usage of this terminology as a rhetorical device in the service of radical/infidel politics (in itself an indication of the hegemony of biblical imagery) with an authentic inclination to implement the millenarian vision in its most literal terms. This turning of the vision inwards is where popular millenarianism and vernacular Orientalism converge: *we* are the chosen people, and *here* is where our Jerusalem is to be established.

Vernacular Orientalism, as I have said, did not exist in a cultural vacuum. Throughout the eighteenth century, the same sources which could encourage a close identification with the biblical vocabulary—for example, Protestant almanacs[101]—often implied that the earthly Jerusalem 'out there' must also play a pivotal role in the apocalyptic design. A chapbook entitled *The Wandering Jew, or The Shoemaker of Jerusalem* describes how, reaching Hull, the mythical Jew prophesies 'that before the end of the world the Jews shall be gathered together from all parts of the world, and return to Jerusalem, and live there, and it shall flourish as much as ever'.[102] Popular sources like these complicated the almost instinctive urge to envision the apocalypse in indigenous terms. The *Jews* are to return to Jerusalem and live *there*: what, then, is to become of us, and of the Jerusalem here?

In 1799, as news about Napoleon's campaign in Palestine was reaching England, it was probably becoming increasingly difficult to ignore these questions. Yet, the location and appearance of the earthly Jerusalem must have remained obscure to many; first and foremost for Joanna Southcott, the distinguished prophetess herself.[103]

Born in 1750 and brought up in a small Devonshire village, Southcott entered domestic service in the Exeter area, eventually becoming a skilled upholsteress; although she received no formal education, she was

---

[100] Jon Mee, *Dangerous Enthusiasm: William Blake and the Culture of Radicalism in the 1790s* (Oxford: Clarendon Press, 1992), 5.
[101] Colley, *Britons*, 20–2.
[102] *The Wandering Jew, or The Shoemaker of Jerusalem* ([Hull]: Sutton, 1810), 7.
[103] On Southcott see James K. Hopkins, *A Woman to Deliver her People: Joanna Southcott and English Millenarianism in an Era of Revolution* (Austin, Tex.: University of Texas Press, 1982); Harrison, *Second Coming*, chs. 5–6; Thompson, *Working Class*, 420–8, 878–9; *DNB*.

not illiterate. In 1792 her housework was interrupted by a mysterious voice informing her that she was the 'Woman clothed with the Sun' from Revelation 12. At the age of 42, an unmarried household servant, Southcott became a prophetess, ordered by the Spirit to set down the communications she received in writing. In 1802 the Spirit directed Southcott to begin sealing believers: thousands signed a petition calling for the overthrow of Satan, and received the seal with her signature. In 1814 she caused a national sensation by announcing that she herself, a 64-year-old virgin, was to give birth to Shiloh, the new Messiah. She died in December that year, the autopsy revealing no sign of pregnancy.

Although the most significant element in Southcott's teaching was the approach of the Kingdom of God, her teaching did not offer a detailed blueprint of the millenarian utopia.[104] Rather, it depicted the millennium as the ultimate state of blissful existence. Jerusalem represents spiritual regeneration and material prosperity in terms that shift from the sparkling metals and precious stones of Revelation to the organic, Edenic qualities that feature in Old Testament prophecies:

> I told thee I had gold in store,
> To build Jerusalem's ruins here:
> I said my kingdom should come down,
> With every splendor man to crown,
> I said My vines should clusters bring,
> And every happiness should spring...[105]

Or in another passage, this time in prose:

> ...and I will so improve the earth, that it shall be as the Garden of Eden to man, for every barren mountain shall become a fruitful field! And I will throw down and build up, until every house is made pleasant for man: gardens and vine-yards shall join to their houses: ... Such shall Jerusalem and all the borders be new built.[106]

James Hopkins has remarked that the forthcoming 'golden days' are described in terms that would have been easily understood by Joanna's audience.[107] But these were also the terms with which Joanna herself

---

[104] Hopkins, *Woman to Deliver her People*, 145.
[105] Joanna Southcott, *The Second Book of Visions* (London, 1803), 8.
[106] Joanna Southcott, *Answer of the Lord to the Powers of Darkness* (London: E. Spragg, 1802), 112.
[107] Hopkins, *Woman to Deliver her People*, 145.

was most familiar: a roof, good crops, rest, land. These material assurances challenge the Methodist image of the believer as an impoverished yet happy pilgrim, awaiting his portion of the heavenly Canaan. Southcott thus echoes the yearning for land which 'rises again and again, twisted in with the outworker's desire for an "independence", from the days of Spence to the Chartist Land Plan and beyond', as E. P. Thompson has written: 'Land always carries associations—of status, security, rights—more profound than the value of its crop.'[108] This is precisely what Southcott promises her followers, as she transforms the image of the Promised Land to, simply, the promise of land.

When Southcott envisions 'gold of ophir, that shall come / To build Jerusalem up again',[109] the millenarian utopia is not assigned a specific geographical location. Yet it is intimately associated with the fate of her own followers, and therefore with England itself. A hymn, adapted from Southcott's texts for the use of her congregation, declares:

> If to GOD'S VOICE men could hearken,
> And obey His strict command,
> They will find, from what HE'TH spoken,
> This shall be "a happy Land."*
> "A happy Land."

And in case of doubt, the asterisk leads to a footnote that states explicitly: the happy land is England.[110]

The approaching birth of Shiloh, who was to lead the Jews to the Holy Land, made the geographical question more pressing. 'Happy are those that are longing for my coming', the Spirit declared, 'and to see the CHILD born, that I shall set upon my holy hill of Zion.'[111] But where was this Zion? Southcott herself was not quite sure. In *The Third Book of Wonders* (1814) she asserts that the approaching Kingdom of God has no direct relationship to the earthly Jerusalem: 'The new Jerusalem, coming down from heaven, meaneth where the visitation is made

---

[108] Thompson, *Working Class*, 254.
[109] Joanna Southcott, *A Continuation of the Prophecies* (Exeter, 1802), 15, quoted in Hopkins, *Woman to Deliver her People*, 146.
[110] Philip Pullen, *Hymns, or Spiritual Songs, Composed from the Prophetic Writings of Joanna Southcott*... (London: McPherson, *c.*1814), 87.
[111] Joanna Southcott, *Prophecies Announcing the Birth of the Prince of Peace* (London: W. Marchant, 1814), 37.

known: it does not mean Jerusalem where it stood.'[112] In *The Fourth Book of Wonders* (1814), on the other hand, she implies that the old city is fundamental to the eschatological plan: 'for I shall cast out all the heathens for their sakes, and now establish the THRONE OF DAVID for ever in Jerusalem, as I have promised. For, *where I was crucified, I will be exalted; where I died for* MAN, *my* SON *shall reign over* MAN.'[113] Nevertheless, even when she does allude to the earthly Jerusalem, it is always to the ancient city depicted in Scripture: the tension, if it exists, is not so much between England and a present-day reality in the East, but between England and a textual representation that can always be applied, yet again, to the 'happy land'. Clinging to the Bunyanesque, Southcott's formulations always fall back, eventually, on the terms most familiar to both her followers and herself. The Holy Land as a geographical reality that might contradict or complicate her interpretation of prophecy did not seem to trouble her.

This was hardly the case with Richard Brothers.[114] Born in 1757 in Placentia, Newfoundland, Brothers was sent to England to join the Navy. He became a midshipman at the age of 14, fought in several battles, and was promoted to lieutenant. Following the Peace of Versailles, he retired on half-pay, which allowed him to tour the Continent. Since he refused, on religious grounds, to take the oath required for the receipt of his pension, he soon fell into debt, was sent to a workhouse, and later to prison. In 1792, the same year that Southcott first heard the Spirit, Brothers decided to leave England, when he was suddenly notified by God that he was the Prince of the Hebrews and the Nephew of the Almighty, descended from King David through James, one of the brothers of Jesus. In 1794 he published *A Revealed Knowledge of the Prophecies and Times*, which anticipated that the Kingdom of Christ was at hand. Some of the revolutionary aspects of his teaching alarmed the authorities; arrested in March 1795 and examined by the Privy Council

---

[112] Joanna Southcott, *The Third Book of Wonders, Announcing the Coming of Shiloh; with a Call to the Hebrews* (London: W. Marchant, 1814), 16.

[113] Joanna Southcott, *The Fourth Book of Wonders, Being the Answer of the Lord to the Hebrews* (London: W. Marchant, 1814), 51.

[114] On Brothers see Garrett, *Respectable Folly*, chs. 8–9; Harrison, *Second Coming*, esp. ch. 4; Thompson, *Working Class*, 127–9; Cecil Roth, *The Nephew of the Almighty: An Experimental Account of the Life and Aftermath of Richard Brothers, RN* (London: Edward Goldston 1933); John Barrell, 'Imagining the King's Death: The Arrest of Richard Brothers', *History Workshop Journal*, 37 (1994), 1–32; *DNB*.

on suspicion of treason, Brothers was eventually committed to a lunatic asylum, where he continued to develop his millenarian designs. He was released in 1806, residing with a few faithful supporters until his death in 1824.

Central to Brothers's eschatology was the 'departure of the Hebrews from all nations, and their return to Jerusalem', which, he calculated, would take place in 1798.[115] Unlike Southcott, who often insisted that the prophecy of Jewish restoration 'alludes to the restoration of faith',[116] Brothers urged the Jews to 'collect all their property and depart in great haste from all nations to their own land'.[117] He himself would lead them back and undertake the building of the New Jerusalem. 'It is fifteen hundred years since my family was separated from the Jews, and lost all knowledge of its origin,' he explained.[118] Only divine intervention allowed him to discover his real identity, as a descendant of the House of David.

Whereas Southcott follows Bunyan in imagining England as that 'happy land', Brothers's geographical imagination is considerably broader: the New Jerusalem is to be built on the devastation of the present Jerusalem in the Middle East. Consequently, his entire corpus is an elaborate effort to address the endless technicalities demanded by this new Exodus. Relying on travel accounts by Wood and Bruce, who visited the East in the mid-eighteenth century,[119] he points out

> that the whole land of Israel is now quite a desert, and that on entering it, I have first to divide it into numerous portions, then get it cultivated with the plough and the shovel, to sow seed and plant trees; I have harbours to make for shipping, and store-houses for immediately receiving what is landed from them; high roads to make; and water-courses to form; materials to provide, and cities to build...[120]

---

[115] Richard Brothers, *A Revealed Knowledge of the Prophecies and Times* (London, 1794), i. 12, 14.
[116] Joanna Southcott, *The True Explanation of the Bible, Revealed by Divine Communications* (London: S. Rousseau, 1804), 409.
[117] Brothers, *Revealed Knowledge*, ii. 129.
[118] Ibid. i. 78.
[119] Richard Brothers, *A Description of Jerusalem: Its Houses and Streets, Squares, Colleges, Markets, and Cathedrals, the Royal and Private Palaces, with the Garden of Eden in the Centre, as Laid Down in the Last Chapters of Ezekiel* (London: G. Riebau, 1801), 68, 74.
[120] Richard Brothers, *A Letter from Mr. Brothers to Miss Cott... with an Address to the Members of His Britannic Majesty's Council* (London: G. Riebau, 1798), 134.

To accomplish this, Brothers appeals to numerous nations, from Abyssinia to Japan, presenting each with a detailed list of provisions required to establish the new 'Hebrew empire'.[121] Russia, for example, is requested to send 400 shiploads of timber, 6,000 barrels of beef, 40,000 tents 'with kettles and ovens in proportion', in addition to the 300 shiploads of timber, 100 large wagons, 800 wheelbarrows, etc., required from each country. England should donate 100,000 tons of coal, 10,000 tons of beef, 90,000 sacks of flour, and so forth, in endless detail.[122] At first, Brothers's plans seem to reflect the urgency of the project, but the crazed list soon loses all sense of operative meaning and becomes a mere textual construct, mimicking similar biblical inventories.

In some instances, Brothers maintains that prophecy should be understood allegorically. In Revelation 21, John 'is so struck with wonder at being shewn, in a vision, the appearance of this matchless city... that he compares the walls to Jasper, the city itself to fine gold!', but the description 'must be taken in a metaphorical sense'.[123] More often than not, however, Brothers insists on a thoroughly literal realization of prophecy. A typical example concerns the New Jerusalem's 'river of water of life'. In both Ezekiel's and John's visions, there is a wide river flowing through the city, a fact which simply does not correspond with the topographical reality of the old Jerusalem. According to Brothers's *A Description of Jerusalem* (1801), to ensure that 'the great and splendid city' would indeed be built, the 'present form' must be 'altered to a necessary level by sinking the Mount of Olives, or removing it, and by bringing again a good river of water through that ground'.[124] To realize the biblical vision, the existing topography must yield to the biblical text.

Brothers devotes much thought to the transformation of Palestine into a green and pleasant woodland 'in such a manner as will set off the land to appear lively and delightful'.[125] Similarly, his meticulous designs for Jerusalem, based on the descriptions in Ezekiel and Revelation, present a perfectly proportioned city. With a Garden of Eden, a glorified

---

[121] Ibid. 23.
[122] Ibid. 90–1, 89, 123.
[123] Richard Brothers, *A Letter to the Subscribers for Engraving the Plans of Jerusalem* (London: G. Riebau, 1805), 38.
[124] Brothers, *Description of Jerusalem*, 17.
[125] Brothers, *Miss Cott*, 81.

Hyde Park, at its centre, and buildings and streets reminiscent of Nash's work in Regent Street,[126] Jerusalem would easily eclipse the capitals of Europe: 'Look at London and Paris, those two great and wealthy cities, there are no such regular streets in either, or healthy accommodations as in ours.'[127]

These geographical and architectural transformations had their racial equivalent, which brings us to the most remarkable aspect of Brothers's teaching. It was not only Brothers himself who was of Hebrew extraction; many English men and women could boast a similar lineage. Those closest to Brothers were lucky enough to belong to the prestigious house of David; others were the descendants of the lost ten tribes, those Israelites captured by the Assyrians, exiled and eventually scattered throughout Europe, 'having lost all remembrance, either by tradition or genealogical manuscript, of such a distinctive origin'. That they were now 'different in dress, manners and religious ceremonies from the visible Jews' should not deceive the students of prophecy.[128] In short, most of the Hebrews who would be restored by Brothers to Palestine were actually English Christians: 'It is plain that it is not the visible Hebrews that are meant, because they are known as such already; but it is the invisible Hebrews, descended from the old, that are to be singled out and distinguished from the strange people they live amongst.'[129]

The conviction that the English were God's chosen nation goes all the way back to Foxe's *Book of Martyrs*. What is unique about Brothers is his ability to accommodate two contradictory traditions. In his claim that prophecies about 'Israel' refer to the Jews, Brothers joins Faber, Priestley, and their eminent colleagues who see the Jews as the object (and the English as agents) of conversion and restoration. At the same time, by insisting that the 'real' Jews are in fact the English, Brothers shares with Southcott—if not Winstanley and Bunyan—the fantasy of belonging, literally, to God's elected race. Of course, whereas Southcott's interpretation is essentially spiritual, Brothers's argument is genealogical (even though he, too, dismisses the Jewish ritual of circumcision and

---

[126] Roth, *Nephew of the Almighty*, 84.
[127] Brothers, *Description of Jerusalem*, 34.
[128] Richard Brothers, *Wrote in Confinement: An Exposition of the Trinity* (London: G. Riebau, 1796), 25.
[129] Brothers, *Miss Cott*, p. xii.

emphasizes the spiritual aspects of belief instead).[130] Just as he bends the topography of Jerusalem to allow the literalization of prophecy, Brothers develops a racial theory which enables him to literalize the familiar analogy between England and Israel. Brothers can thus voice grievances associated with specific class-oriented aspirations, particularly the want of land, but resolve them by shifting to a colonial framework: 'All the families which I have recognised as of Hebrew extraction, are... entitled, as well as the visible professed Jews, to reside in their native land, whether in city or country, or alternately in both if they like: although the distribution of the land belongs to me, yet as brethren our right of inheritance is general.'[131] While polite millenarians approached the Jewish restoration to Palestine as a project that could benefit British imperialism, Brothers's proto-British Israelism made the 'Hebrew empire' a British colonial project *par excellence*.

From this fusion of millenarian vocabulary, colonial visions, and working-class aspirations, an extraordinary narrative emerges. 'Palestine, 3211 years ago, when the Hebrews entered it from Egypt, abounded with springs and rivers, corn, wine, and oil,' writes Brothers; 'but now all is barren, as if never inhabited by our ancestors.' Nevertheless,

> many of these difficulties [are] easily conquered, by a wise people fortified with courage and perseverance; for it is our own country, and the only one we can live free in. Therefore, every man and woman must call up to their assistance every energy of patience, virtue, and industry, to settle the foundation of all future praise and all future benefit, by putting as many parts of the country as possible into a state of cultivation.[132]

This probably sounds familiar: the barren land restored to its former glory; the appeal for patience and industry; and, above all, the conviction that 'it is our own country, and the only one we can live free in'. Indeed, Brothers's account is conspicuously similar to the official Zionist version which would emerge almost a century later (relying heavily on both millenarian and colonial imagery). Like the Zionists, Brothers explains that the Hebrew empire would initiate a commercial burst of growth, 'so that no one can lose by the change, but, on the contrary, all will materially gain'.[133] But he, too, never stops to consider the fate of

---

[130] Ibid. 76–7.   [131] Ibid. 80.
[132] Brothers, *Description of Jerusalem*, 43–4.
[133] Richard Brothers, *The New Covenant between God and his People* (London: A. Snell, 1830), 6.

the present inhabitants of the Holy Land who are to give way to the colonizers. It is Palestine's indigenous population that remains truly invisible.

Southcott and Brothers, then, imagine very different 'Jerusalems'; but how can we account for these diverse visions? And to what extent do they reflect broader cultural undercurrents?

There is little doubt that the experience which moulded Brothers's perception of the world—and which made him, in many ways, an exceptional figure in popular millenarian circles—was his long service in the Royal Navy. It enabled him to expand his geographical imagination, to translate abstract textual descriptions into topographical detail, and to grasp the practical implications of travel.[134] Only an awareness of Palestine's geographical reality, and a seaman's mentality, can account for his endless inventories of supplies needed to make the desert blossom. In both scholarship and expression, Brothers was much closer to Priestley and Bicheno than to Southcott; what distanced him from the respectable millenarians was his insistence on the personal role assigned to himself (and to the rest of the 'invisible' Jews). Challenged with Palestine's irrepressible existence, Brothers adopted the radical working-class appropriations of 'Holy Land' and 'Chosen People', but transferred them back to the geographical region in which they were initially forged. The result is a pseudo-jingoistic attempt to solve working-class grievances by turning to the colonial framework: the promise of land, Brother explains, is possible only in the Promised Land.

Joanna Southcott, by contrast, never left England. There is little evidence that books, other than the Bible and her aunt's hymnal, affected her development. Her upbringing, education, and occupation all link her to deep-rooted provincial traditions: no wonder she was much less knowledgeable about the outside world. So, although Napoleon looms large over many of her prophecies, the emphasis is always on England's survival and safekeeping, rather than on any imperial vision. Closely associated with English life, customs, and landscape, the immediacy of Southcott's Jerusalem and the soothing familiarity which it evokes—as opposed to Brothers's fantasy in the desert—may explain

---

[134] Marcus Rediker, *Between the Devil and the Deep Blue Sea: Merchant Seamen, Pirates, and the Anglo-American Maritime World, 1700–1750* (Cambridge: Cambridge University Press, 1987), 10, 294.

why her following was considerably larger, and her influence more enduring. The Holy Land was simply too far away to demand any real consideration.

This seems to be true of her followers as well: shocked by Southcott's untimely death, some of them embarked on a journey to Jerusalem. The little that we know about this specific group comes from a sarcastic pamphlet, *An Interesting Account of the Proceedings of the Followers of the Late Joanna Southcott, Shewing the Folly of Their Intended Departure for the City of Jerusalem with a Full Description of That Ancient and Celebrated City, Its Laws, Government, etc.* (1817). The anonymous author mocks these '*chosen few*'—'the High Priest, the Female Secretaries, and the West-Riding Merchant, that plain and undesigning Yorkshireman'—who are making their way to the 'golden city' where they hope to find the newly resurrected Joanna. It is not so much the millenarian folly which annoys the writer, however, as the travellers' inability to grasp the palpable dimensions of Jerusalem. Since 'they have not received accurate information with respect to that important point', some imagine 'that the great waters will be frozen over, so as to afford an *easy* passage', while others 'are in daily expectation of seeing the sky overspread with clouds, from which a plentiful supply of ASSES is to issue'. Presuming that many of Southcott's disciples 'have not, in the course of their reading, paid much attention to the situation of Palestine', the writer finally reaches the real purpose of his work: an accurate topographical description of Jerusalem and the surrounding country, based on the travels of Dr Shaw, who visited Palestine in the 1730s.[135] The pamphlet undoubtedly overplays the Southcottians' confusion (indeed, the entire account might well be fictitious); yet this band of distressed millenarians, anxious to reach the Holy Land but overwhelmed by the corporeal implications of the quest, captures a representational crisis typical of the period.

It would be only appropriate to end with another 1790s prophet, William Blake, and his beautiful lines from *Jerusalem*, a natural sequel to the short poem from *Milton*:[136]

---

[135] *An Interesting Account...* (London: T. Nicholson, 1817), 12, 10–11, 12.
[136] On Blake, Brothers, and Southcott see Morton D. Paley, 'William Blake, The Prince of the Hebrews, and the Woman Clothed with the Sun', in Paley and Michael Curtis Phillips (eds.), *William Blake: Essays in Honour of Sir Geoffrey Keynes* (Oxford: Clarendon Press, 1973), 260–93.

> The fields from Islington to Marybone,
> To Primrose Hill and Saint Johns Wood:
> Were builded over with pillars of gold,
> And there Jerusalems pillars stood.[137]

This, Harold Bloom has noted, is one of Blake's most personal poems, 'an autobiographical epitome of the whole of *Jerusalem*'. The places named in subsequent stanzas—'The Ponds where Boys to bathe delight: / The fields of Cows by Willans farm' (p. 172)—were associated by Blake with his own childhood (p. 935); once again, we encounter the familiar infantile fantasy of discovering the Holy Land in one's own vicinity.

Blake elaborated this theme throughout his adult life. In the prophetic books written during and after 1804, Jerusalem—whether she is thought of as the daughter of Albion, a spiritual presence, or a pillared structure—is associated primarily with Britain. Indeed, as A. L. Owen has shown, between 1797 and 1804 Blake became convinced that Britain, not Palestine, was the original Holy Land.[138] 'All things Begin & End in Albions Ancient Druid Rocky Shore', wrote Blake in his address 'To the Jews' in *Jerusalem* (p. 171). This should be understood in its most literal sense, just like the short poem from *Milton* which means, literally, 'I shall struggle to restore our own lost British Jerusalem'.[139]

What is especially revealing is Blake's vernacular Orientalism. Informing a friend about Blake's new work, Robert Southey described 'a perfectly mad poem called *Jerusalem*—Oxford Street is in Jerusalem'.[140] But Southey was wrong: it was Jerusalem in Oxford Street, never the other way around. Blake's rearrangement of the scriptural geography in the English landscape, the allotment of the British Isles between the twelve tribes, the image of Golgonooza which fuses Ezekiel's vision with the bricks and mortar of London—all these exhibit an ingenious reworking of the Bunyanesque tradition. There is, however,

---

[137] *The Complete Poetry and Prose of William Blake*, ed. David V. Erdman, comm. Harold Bloom (Garden City, NY: Anchor, 1982), 171. Subsequent page numbers will be cited parenthetically in the text.
[138] A. L. Owen, *The Famous Druids: A Survey of Three Centuries of English Literature on the Druids* (Oxford: Clarendon Press, 1962), 233, 225.
[139] Ibid. 235.
[140] Quoted in Ruthven Todd, *Tracks in the Snow: Studies in English Science and Art* (London: Grey Walls, 1946), 46.

a major difference: emerging more than a century later and in a very different intellectual climate, Blake's vision is more a simulacrum than an actual equivalent of Bunyan's. It seems that just like Brothers, whose genealogy affirmed the desire of belonging to God's elect, Blake devised his complex mythology simply to recover the naïve childhood fantasy of Jerusalem standing in the fields from Islington to Marybone. 'The Beauty of the Bible is that the most Ignorant & Simple Minds Understand it Best,' he wrote (p. 667). Blake was not ignorant, and hardly simple-minded, but his prophetic books are a colossal exertion to mimic such a reading.

Blake, it appears, was perfectly aware of the political and military developments of the day. As David V. Erdman has pointed out in *Prophet Against Empire*, the great victory song of Night I in *The Four Zoas* evidently celebrates the British defeat of Napoleon in the eastern Mediterranean, possibly alluding to the Battle of the Nile and the Siege of Acre. The battle areas, Egypt and Palestine, are symbolized by 'the Palm tree' and 'the Oak of Weeping'.[141] Palestine, furthermore, appears in *Jerusalem* as one of the thirty-two nations that will 'dwell in Jerusalems Gates'; it is tenth on the list, following Turkey and Arabia and preceding Persia and Hindostan (p. 227).

The idea that Palestine must return to Albion's Jerusalem, 'as in the times of old', is a pivotal moment in the representation of the Holy Land, for it is here that Blake so unmistakably distinguishes between Palestine (or Canaan) and Jerusalem, two concepts which *The Pilgrim's Progress* applies interchangeably. For Blake, the first is a nation, perhaps a people, a portion of land located between Arabia and Persia; the latter, sometimes a figure of a woman, is primarily a spiritual concept signifying a return to the blissful existence in the Garden of God, a perfect social order: 'Mutual shall build Jerusalem: / Both heart in heart & hand in hand' (p. 173). And it is to be built, needless to say, in England's green and pleasant land. Blake consciously turns away from the geographical city: it is only the social ideal embedded in it which matters.

But this was also true for Southcott—which raises the intriguing possibility that her Jerusalem was not simply a product of a limited geographical imagination and a specific cultural environment, a

---

[141] David V. Erdman, *Prophet Against Empire: A Poet's Interpretation of the History of his Own Times* (1954; 2nd edn. Princeton: Princeton University Press, 1969), 319–20.

'default' vision, as it were. Rather, it may have been a consciously introspective vision, shifting from the imperial to the vernacular; from the marvellous possessions overseas to social justice at home; from 'there' to 'here'. This distinct vision of England and Englishness can later be traced in those offspring of Southcottianism: Owenism, Chartism, Labour. Southcott, too, may have been a prophetess against Empire.

Brothers's work, on the other hand, suggests how the vernacular Orientalist tradition could shape the English claim over Palestine. Indeed, his assertion that 'it is our own country' anticipates the Archbishop of York's claim in his address to the PEF in 1865: 'This country of Palestine belongs to you and to me, it is essentially ours.' As the next chapter will show, while the Blakean 'Jerusalem in England' may have signalled a conscious turning away from the earthly city, the nineteenth-century English encounter with the earthly city had everything to do with the Blakean 'Jerusalem in England'.

2

The Land and the Books

High Anglo-Palestine Orientalism and its Limits

Sometime in 1872, an English couple was journeying from the Dead Sea to Jerusalem. Determined not to give in to the local tribes that forced protection on Westerners, the couple 'attempted the trip without the formality of a Bedouin guard'. Unfortunately, the two were soon 'met and robbed of their baggage, their money, clothes, and valuables': the gentleman had 'to beg of the Bedouin robbers *The Times* newspaper in which to clothe himself and his wife. The husband returned to Jerusalem in this valuable journal, his wife being wrapped up in the supplement.' Hand in hand, all Palestine before them, they take their solitary way: two civilized English travellers—independent, courageous, resourceful—who fully appreciate the value of an English newspaper, the same newspaper which would later print their 'amusing account' as an illustration of the 'peculiar misgovernment of the country'.[1]

The anecdote was probably a yarn, but its light-hearted tone demonstrates that by the 1870s, travel to Palestine had become a commonplace, at least for the editors and readers of *The Times*. Napoleon's 1799 campaign marked the emergence of the Eastern Question, which dominated nineteenth-century diplomacy: how much of the Ottoman Empire had to be preserved, and in what form, to protect the interests of each of the European powers?[2] With its strategic location and religio-cultural significance, Palestine soon became central to this struggle.

---

[1] *The Times*, 18 May 1872, 9; attributed to the *JC*.
[2] Alexander Schölch, *Palestine in Transformation, 1856–1882: Studies in Social, Economic and Political Development* (1986), trans. William C. Young and Michael C. Gerrity (Washington: Institute for Palestine Studies, 1993), 49.

As the Ottoman Empire disintegrated, the European presence in Palestine became increasingly visible through the work of diplomats and missionaries, scholars and soldiers, artists and writers—many of them English—who depicted the land in maps and surveys, paintings and photographs, novels and poems, sermons and travel accounts.[3] The affinity between these cultural forms and the West's economic and military expansion—between 'culture and imperialism'—has been explored by Edward Said and others. The Holy Land, in this respect, was no exception: it is telling that General Allenby prepared for his 1917 offensive by consulting George Adam Smith's *Historical Geography of the Holy Land* (1894), a work which marked the culmination of a century of Holy Land exploration.[4]

Nevertheless, to read this body of knowledge simply as a catalyst for future domination is to ignore the ambiguity which characterized the English encounter with Palestine, and which distinguished it from other colonizable regions. Lytton Strachey's description of General Gordon—wandering about Jerusalem with a Holy Bible under his arm, investigating questions like the location of Gibeon and 'the position of the Garden of Eden'[5]—was parodic, but it captured a truism: the Bible was the map with which Palestine's landscape was scrutinized. It is impossible, in other words, to understand the affinity between the production of Orientalist books and the claim over the land without considering the affinity between *The Land and the Book* (appropriately, the title of one

---

[3] See, among numerous others, Barbara Tuchman, *Bible and Sword: England and Palestine from the Bronze Age to Balfour* (1956; New York: Ballantine, 1984); A. L. Tibawi, *British Interests in Palestine, 1800–1901* (Oxford: Oxford University Press, 1961); Yehoshua Ben-Arieh, *The Rediscovery of the Holy Land in the Nineteenth Century* (Jerusalem: Carta and the Israel Exploration Society, 1970); Neil Asher Silberman, *Digging for God and Country: Exploration, Archaeology and the Secret Struggle for the Holy Land, 1799–1917* (New York: Alfred A. Knopf, 1982); Naomi Shepherd, *The Zealous Intruders: The Western Rediscovery of Palestine* (London: Collins, 1987); John Pemble, *The Mediterranean Passion: Victorians and Edwardians in the South* (1987; Oxford: Oxford University Press, 1988); Billie Melman, *Women's Orients: English Women and the Middle East, 1718–1918* (1992; 2nd edn. London: Macmillan, 1995); Ruth and Thomas Hummel, *Patterns of the Sacred: English Protestant and Russian Orthodox Pilgrims of the Nineteenth Century* (London: Scorpion Cavendish, 1995).

[4] Robin Butlin, 'George Adam Smith and the Historical Geography of the Holy Land: Contents, Contexts and Connections', *Journal of Historical Geography*, 14/4 (1988), 383.

[5] Lytton Strachey, *Eminent Victorians* (London: Chatto & Windus, 1918), 217.

of the century's best-selling studies of scriptural geography).[6] Gordon, that archetypal Christian soldier, has come to epitomize the role played by the Protestant ethos in the exercise of imperial authority over peoples and lands. Yet, in the case of Palestine, at least, Protestant biblical culture shaped an imperial claim which retained a powerful sense of ambivalence, even reluctance, which often went beyond what Mary Louise Pratt has called the 'anti-conquest' impulse.[7]

To suggest, furthermore, that highbrow cultural forms had a ubiquitous effect—to claim, like Edward Said, that travel books shaped the public's perception of the Orient[8]—and yet to avoid questions like dissemination and circulation is either to overlook the material conditions in which discourses operate or to rely on a very narrow definition of 'public'. The image of the couple clothed in *The Times* sums up the linkage between travel, class, and readership; but it also reflects the very palpable dimensions of cultural production: the newspaper as ink and paper. Paraphrasing Pratt's question—'How are metropolitan modes of representation received and appropriated on the periphery?'[9]—we can ask: how were these modes of representation received and appropriated in the metropolitan centre itself?

This chapter considers the question by exploring the production, construction, and consumption of this distinct discourse—'academic Anglo-Palestine Orientalism'. Tracing the representation of the Holy Land in cultural forms like fiction, fine art, and particularly travel literature, it begins by observing the cycles of citation and repetition which generated both a self-contained community of writers and a coherent body of texts. It continues by examining some of the major themes and images which characterized these new, and distinct, Orientalist representations; and concludes by outlining the commercial conditions in which these cultural forms were in fact disseminated.

---

[6] W. M. Thomson, *The Land and the Book; or, Biblical Illustrations Drawn from the Manners and Customs, the Scenes and Scenery of the Holy Land* (London: T. Nelson, 1859). Thomson, it should be noted, was American.

[7] Mary Louise Pratt, *Imperial Eyes: Travel Writing and Transculturation* (1992; London: Routledge, 1998), esp. 7, 38–68.

[8] Edward Said, *Orientalism: Western Conceptions of the Orient* (1978; Harmondsworth: Penguin, 1995), 192.

[9] Pratt, *Imperial Eyes*, 6.

'We read them all!': Social and Textual Interactions

In 1788, when the Irish eccentric Buck 'Jerusalem' Whaley declared that he would walk all the way to Jerusalem, 'some observed that there was no such place at present existing; and others that, if it did exist, [he] should not be able to find it'.[10] So incredible did the idea seem, that a wager of an estimated £15,000 was instantly drawn.[11] Napoleon's Middle Eastern campaign may have directed Europe's attention back to Palestine, but the journey to Jerusalem remained, for decades, an extremely taxing experience. Conditions certainly improved with time: the Egyptian occupation of Palestine in 1832 introduced tough policing measures, which crushed the local population but made the journey much safer for foreigners; and the reforms which followed the Ottoman reconquest in 1840—attained through European support—gave way to Western intervention on an unprecedented scale.[12] Developments in maritime and land transport certainly helped to reduce the cost of travel; nevertheless, as William Bartlett estimated in 1844, a traveller 'with one servant, and three horses, and a guide, will hardly spend *less* than a guinea a day, inclusive of his servant's wages'.[13] Trollope's comment in 1866 that 'Jerusalem and the Jordan are as common to us as were Paris and the Seine to our grandfathers' is most revealing in this respect:[14] those whose grandfathers could not have afforded to visit Paris in 1800, could hardly hope to visit Jerusalem in the 1860s.

Thomas Cook's Eastern Tours revolutionized travel to the Holy Land. Between 1869 and 1882, Cook conducted about 5,000 tourists to Palestine, almost three-quarters of the total number of British and American visitors. By 1891 the number had risen to 12,000.[15] These were impressive figures, but with a trip to Palestine and Egypt priced at £95, and a longer excursion (which included Constantinople and

---

[10] Edward Sullivan (ed.), *Buck Whaley's Memoirs, Including His Journey to Jerusalem*... (London: Alexander Moring, 1906), 34.

[11] Whaley collected the money after a year-long journey, having 'played ball against the walls of Jerusalem', as agreed. See *DNB*.

[12] Shepherd, *Zealous Intruders*, 107–40.

[13] William H. Bartlett, *Walks about the City and Environs of Jerusalem* (London: Virtue, 1844), 219.

[14] Anthony Trollope, *Travelling Sketches* (London: Chapman & Hall, 1866), 92.

[15] Piers Brendon, *Thomas Cook: 150 Years of Popular Tourism* (London: Secker & Warburg, 1991), 135; Pemble, *Mediterranean Passion*, 50.

Athens) at about £180, this hardly amounted to a mass movement.[16] 'It is a great event in one's life to be able to come and see these wonderful places and countries,' Cook wrote in 1872, 'with the Bible in one hand and Murray in the other.'[17] But the actual sale figures for Murray's *Handbook for Travellers in Syria and Palestine* merely illustrate the point. The first edition, 2,000 copies, was printed in April 1858; three years later, there were still 933 copies on hand. With sales of 100–50 copies per annum, the edition had sold out only by June 1867. A new edition was published in June 1868, shortly before the opening of the Suez Canal and the launching of Cook's Palestine tours. Nevertheless, 821 copies of the 2,000 printed were still on hand in 1883. As late as June 1892, there were 297 copies in stock, which were all wasted in order to pave way for a new, revised edition.[18]

Travel to Jerusalem, then, was essentially a middle-class phenomenon, which seldom extended to the lower middle class.[19] When a Cook's tour was joined by a member of the working classes, the event was exceptional enough to attract special notice. In 1875, the American journalist Charles Warner encountered Cook's caravan near Damascus. Among the more typical tourists—a college professor, a student of divinity, 'some indomitable English ladies', a group of young men 'who made a lark of the pilgrimage', and the great library entrepreneur C. E. Mudie—Warner discovered a more humble traveller: 'He was, by his own representation, an illiterate shoemaker from the South of England; of schooling he had never enjoyed a day, nor of education, except as sprung from his "conversion," which happened in his twentieth year.' The poor shoemaker was 'seized with an intense longing to make a pilgrimage to the Holy Land'. He worked hard to save the money, but 'more than thirty years passed before he saw himself in possession of the sum he could spare for the purchase of a Cook's ticket to the Holy Land'. Ironically, the desire to travel to Jerusalem seemed to improve the shoemaker's lot. As Warner notes, 'such industry and singleness of purpose were not without result: his business prospered

---

[16] *Program and Itineraries of Cook's Palestine Tours* (London: Thomas Cook, 1877), 23.
[17] Quoted in J. G. Davies, *Pilgrimage Yesterday and Today* (London: SCM Press, 1988), 148.
[18] See ledgers at the John Murray Archive, London, E.393, F.67, G.137, I.331. The first Baedeker guide to Palestine was published in 1876.
[19] Melman, *Women's Orients*, 35.

and his fund increased'. He now had 'a shop of his own and men working under him', and one of his sons was a college student in London.[20] A Victorian variation on the Protestant ethic, this time it was the vision of the earthly, not the heavenly, Jerusalem which initiated commercial success. The fact that the very same shoemaker is mentioned in at least two other contemporary sources[21] makes him something of a mythical figure, reminiscent of another celebrated travelling shoemaker, the Wandering Jew.

There were, of course, working people who did visit Palestine regularly: sailors, soldiers, and—no doubt the largest group—servants who accompanied their masters. As in the case of the legendary shoemaker, it appears that a journey to Palestine could sometimes improve the servant's financial lot. A report in *The Times* of 10 November 1804 suggests, in passing, that one of the servants who accompanied 'the celebrated Jerusalem Whaley in his trip to the capital of Judea' was now the owner of 'an obscure alehouse, in Dublin'.[22] Perhaps servants were compensated for the hardship of travel. In Disraeli's *Tancred; or The New Crusade* (1847), closely based on the author's visit to Palestine in 1831, the good Tancred de Montacute makes a pledge to his two servants: 'we are in extreme peril; I took you from your homes; if we outlive this day, and return to Montacute, you shall live on your own land.'[23]

Disraeli depicts the servants—the aptly named Freeman and Trueman—as loyal, good-hearted buffoons, who refer to the princely Bedouin as 'niggers' (p. 241) and 'savages' and address them in English, not because they seem to understand, but 'from a mixture of pride and perverseness peculiarly British', as if this was 'striking proof of the sheer stupidity of their new companions' (p. 259). Representing the servants represent the 'savages', Disraeli is clearly ridiculing the only members of the labouring class in a novel otherwise crowded with aristocrats, be they English, Arab, or Jewish. Disraeli's fantasy of eradicating all racial difference between East and West (discussed below) merely reinforces the division between the 'two nations' within England itself.

---

[20] Charles Dudley Warner, *In the Levant* (1876; Boston: Osgood, 1877), 208–9.
[21] John Wilson, *The True Solution of the Eastern Question* (London: Guest, 1877), 30, quoting the *Church of Scotland Missionary Record*, Oct. 1876.
[22] *The Times*, 10 Nov. 1804, 2.
[23] Benjamin Disraeli, *Tancred; or The New Crusade* (1847; London: Peter Davies, 1927), 241. Subsequent page numbers are cited parenthetically in the text.

Unfortunately, Freeman and Trueman could not defend themselves. Servants left little testimony of their travel (if, indeed, their labour could be called that).[24] To paraphrase Said's citing of Marx, since servants did not represent themselves, they had to be represented. Rather than helping to expand the Victorian travel canon, they were written into it—that is, when they were not simply written out. While travel to Palestine was not, in fact, an exclusively middle-class phenomenon, travel writing almost certainly was.

Citation and repetition

On board his P&O steamer, heading eastwards, William Makepeace Thackeray found that all the British excursionists had been battling to read Alexander Kinglake's *Eothen*.[25] 'What the pilgrims said at Cesarea Philippi surprised me with its wisdom,' Mark Twain observed a few years later; 'I found it afterwards in Robinson. What they said when Genessaret burst upon their vision charmed me with their grace. I find it in Mr Thompson's "Land and the Book".'[26] This interplay between texts and real-life experience is typical of all travel, but it is particularly typical of travel writing, as the readers-cum-producers enter the literary tradition which shaped their expectations in the first place. Virtually every travel account or geographical study contained the obligatory list of those celebrated travellers who had visited Palestine previously, as well as long citations from their work. By the 1850s, reviewers were losing their patience: 'Let us suppose we read, say for instance, only a few of these all but daily Oriental productions,' exclaimed *Tait's Edinburgh Magazine* in 1852: 'Alas! We read them all! Yes; there they are; the same Arabs, Camels, deserts, tombs and jackals that we journeyed with, rode on, traversed, dived into and cursed respectively, only a week ago, with some other traveller.'[27] The *Art Journal* complained that 'the subject has

---

[24] James Clifford, 'Travelling Cultures', in Lawrence Grossberg *et al.* (eds.), *Cultural Studies* (London: Routledge, 1992), 106–7.

[25] William Makepeace Thackeray, *Notes of a Journey from Cornhill to Grand Cairo* (1846; Oxford: Oxford University Press, n.d.), 142. Subsequent page numbers are cited parenthetically in the text.

[26] Mark Twain, *The Innocents Abroad* (1869; Harmondsworth: Penguin, 2002), 384. Twain is confusing Thomson with Thompson.

[27] Quoted in Kenneth Paul Bendiner, 'The Portrayal of the Middle East in British Painting, 1835–1860' (Ph.D. thesis, Columbia University, 1979), 6.

been gone over again and again, until the Holy Land is better known in England than the English lakes'.[28]

The number of individuals who were willing to risk their own assets just to have their travel account published (see below) suggests that it was only by joining this endless textual procession that travellers felt they had truly experienced Palestine.[29] The Holy Land was being concretized, but only through a complex process of textualization—which makes that wandering English couple, wrapped in *The Times*, all the more emblematic. Pilgrimage, as Edward Said has noted, is, after all, 'a form of copying'.[30]

What should not be underestimated, however, is the extent to which this textual repetition was the product of other, external repetitions. Most travellers, whose principal destination was Jerusalem, followed the beaten track. Rather than visit the relatively lush Galilee, they spent most of their time in the barren Judean hills and the sand dunes of the coastal plain.[31] Even the more adventurous explorers trod hard on each other's heels, meeting the same peasant communities and guided by the same Bedouin sheikhs as their predecessors. By the 1870s, the peasants, overfamiliar with the questions and answers of the enquiring foreigners, had begun to repeat one geographer's theories to the next.[32]

Social connections, then, were inseparable from textual interactions. Consider, for example, the relationship between Alexander Kinglake and Eliot Warburton, whose books were two of the best-selling travel accounts of the century. Kinglake had twice attempted to write *Eothen* (1844), but only when he addressed the narrative directly to his friend Warburton, did he actually produce a manuscript. When Warburton decided to embark on a pilgrimage of his own, Kinglake furnished his friend with a map marked with his original route and a copy of his

---

[28] *Art Journal*, 6 (1 May 1854), 155.
[29] Cf. Derek Gregory, 'Scripting Egypt: Orientalism and the Cultures of Travel', in James Duncan and Derek Gregory (eds.), *Writes of Passage: Reading Travel Writing* (London: Routledge, 1999), esp. 114–15.
[30] Said, *Orientalism*, 177.
[31] C. Gordon Smith, 'The Geography and Natural Resources of Palestine as Seen by British Writers in the Nineteenth and Early Twentieth Century', in Moshe Ma'oz (ed.), *Studies on Palestine during the Ottoman Period* (Jerusalem: Hebrew University Press, 1975), 92, 94.
[32] Shepherd, *Zealous Intruders*, 47, 58.

journal.[33] Kinglake's chapter on Lady Hester Stanhope cited a long letter from Warburton, describing her death. When Warburton drafted *The Crescent and the Cross* (1845), he decided to borrow whole passages from *Eothen*, among them his own letter, thus quoting Kinglake quote himself. Next, Warburton reviewed *Eothen* in the *Quarterly Review* of December 1844. 'He writes as if addressing this friend,' explained the critic of Kinglake's 'original and brilliant book'.[34] In the following number of the same periodical, it was Kinglake's turn to review *The Crescent and the Cross*: 'The writing is of a kind that indicates abilities likely to command success in the higher departments of literature.'[35]

This, no doubt, was an extreme case, but almost everywhere we look, the travellers, authors, artists, and publishers are linked in unexpected ways. Byron was so moved by the third volume of Edward Clarke's *Travels* (1810–23), that he wrote to Clarke of his desire to visit Palestine himself.[36] James Silk Buckingham, on the other hand, was not impressed. His *Travels in Palestine* (1821) included a harsh critique of Clarke's study and an implicit attack on the *Quarterly Review*, which responded with a vicious article believed to have been written by Buckingham's co-traveller, William Bankes, an old friend of Byron's from Cambridge.[37] Bankes was later to join Irby and Mangles, whose *Travels in Egypt* (1823) was successfully reprinted by Murray (the publisher of the *Quarterly*), who had rejected the manuscript submitted by Buckingham, who, incidentally, sued Bankes and won.[38] In 1844, when Thomas Cook first contemplated the possibility of conducting tours to Palestine, he consulted his friend and fellow temperance campaigner: again Buckingham.[39]

The web of social and professional ties was also a textual web, as notes, letters, and whole passages travelled effortlessly from one publication to another. What was characteristic of first-hand accounts, was true, by definition, of the hundreds of volumes produced by scholars

---

[33] Gerald de Gaury, *Travelling Gent: The Life of Alexander Kinglake* (London: Routledge & Kegan Paul, 1972), 45.
[34] *Quarterly Review*, 75 (Dec. 1844), 51, 54.
[35] *Quarterly Review*, 75 (Mar. 1845), 533.
[36] Silberman, *Digging for God and Country*, 23.
[37] Tuchman, *Bible and Sword*, 169.
[38] Ralph E. Turner, *James Silk Buckingham, 1786–1855: A Social Biography* (London: Williams & Norgate, 1934), 142–55.
[39] Brendon, *Thomas Cook*, 57–8.

like the Revd J. A. Wylie, who compiled detailed studies of scriptural geography based on travellers' eyewitness accounts. Eventually, at the age of 74, Wylie did visit Palestine,[40] but most compilers remained armchair travellers only. Visual imagery was often produced in the same way. The engravings in *Landscape Illustrations of the Bible* (1836), a lavish two-volume quarto album, were based on drawings by J. M. W. Turner and other major artists—none of whom had been to Palestine— who relied on 'on-the-spot' sketches by architects and amateurs.[41] Turner's depiction of the Holy City, for example, includes not only a familiar Turneresque sky, but also an emblematic rainbow added to augment the spiritual effect (see Fig. 1). In 1838, two years after he contributed to this same illustrated album, David Roberts embarked on his first visit to the Bible lands with the purpose of correcting the 'inaccuracies' of the *Description de l'Egypt*, which he knew to exist even before seeing the 'original' it claimed to represent.[42] John Ruskin commended Holman Hunt's painting *The Scapegoat* (1859), by claiming that 'Of all the scenes in the Holy Land, there are none whose present aspect tends so distinctly to confirm the statements of Scripture as this condemned shore. It is therefore exactly the scene of which it might seem most desirable to give a perfect idea to those who cannot see it for themselves.'[43] Ruskin was somehow able to comment authoritatively on the 'present aspect' of the land's scenery, despite the fact that he, too, had never seen it.

What these various ties reveal is the mechanism behind the textual production of a self-contained community; or, from the opposite direction, the creation of a community through the production of self-contained texts. In her study of antiquarians, historians, and archaeologists in Victorian England, Philippa Levine has noted that the make-up of these groups often resembles the notion of an 'invisible college', 'comprising informal networks within a specific area of study, in which collaboration, citation of one another's works and informal communication have been seen as tangible evidences of existence'.

---

[40] 'J. A. Wylie', *DNB*.

[41] Bendiner, 'Portrayal of the Middle East', 6–7.

[42] Timothy Mitchell, *Colonising Egypt* (1988; Berkeley: University of California Press, 1991), 29.

[43] *The Works of John Ruskin*, ed. E. T. Cook and Alexander Wedderburn (London: George Allen, 1904), xiv. 63.

Fig. 1. J. M. W. Turner, 'Jerusalem from the Mount of Olives', in *Landscape Illustrations of the Bible...from Original Sketches Taken on the Spot Engraved by W. and E. Finden* (London: John Murray, 1836).

The relationship between invisible colleges and the formation of élites 'is a palpable one', she writes, since the invisible college is defined by exclusion as much as inclusion.[44]

In many respects, the 'invisible college' model is an extremely useful description of the nineteenth-century community of writers, artists, and scholars who represented Palestine. The term should be employed more loosely here, because the range of work was enormous, shifting from scientific surveys and poems to sermons and Royal Academy paintings. Moreover, unlike historical or antiquarian societies which have left comprehensive records of their membership, our writers, artists, and scholars were not affiliated to any formal organization. A Palestine Association was established in London in 1805 'for the purpose of promoting the knowledge of the geography, natural history, and antiquities of Palestine and its vicinity, with a view to the illustration of the Holy Writings'.[45] However, due to the risky conditions of travel and research, the Association was essentially inactive.[46] Consequently, until the establishment of the PEF in 1865, there was no society or organization committed to the systematic study of Palestine; and even then, the PEF's administration was more reminiscent of a clique than a professional organization.

Although the PEF was, at best, a pseudo-academic society, its work marked the pinnacle of nineteenth-century Holy Land scholarship. One reason was that institutionalized academia was very slow to incorporate the study of geography. As late as the 1850s, George Butler's geography lectures at Oxford were considered a daring novelty. Josephine Butler, who assisted her husband, recalled having drawn a rough map of Europe, including the northern coast of Africa and part of Asia Minor:

The conversation then turned on letters we had just received from Arthur Stanley and Theodore Walrond, who were visiting Egypt. 'Where is Cairo?' someone asked, turning to the map spread on the table. I put the question to an

---

[44] Philippa Levine, *The Amateur and the Professional: Antiquarians, Historians and Archaeologists in Victorian England, 1836–1886* (Cambridge: Cambridge University Press, 1986), 36–7.

[45] *Palestine Association 1805* (London, 1805), 3.

[46] Finally, in 1834, it was absorbed into the Royal Geographical Society. See Fredrick Jones Bliss, *The Development of Palestine Exploration* (London: Hodder & Stoughton, 1906), 255–6.

accomplished College Tutor. His eye wondered hopelessly over the chart; he could not even place his hand on Egypt![47]

It was only during the late 1870s that geography emerged as a distinct academic discipline,[48] but even then, the status of Oriental studies remained problematic. In Paris and Berlin, Oriental languages were taught in universities and special training schools; in late Victorian and even Edwardian Britain, on the other hand, the study of Islamic languages and topics was carried out on an extremely limited scale. Between 1910 and 1914, for instance, Oxford University engaged one professor of Arabic; two teachers, for Arabic and Persian, were subsidized by the government for training civil servants. Apart from the study of languages, no other faculty offered instruction in any Middle Eastern subject.[49] Of course, the study of biblical Hebrew and cognate subjects was widely diffused in the universities, and even more so in other religious educational frameworks. However, for various reasons (explored in the next chapter), religious societies like the Society for Promoting Christian Knowledge (SPCK) and the Religious Tract Society (RTS) were slow to respond to the geographical rediscovery of Palestine. As late as 1835, the SPCK was still reprinting Edward Wells's *Historical Geography of the New Testament* (1708). Even when these societies did support new work—the Revd Henry Baker Tristram, for example, was commissioned by the SPCK in 1863 to study Palestine's flora and fauna—it continued to rely on the 'invisible college' network.

That the writers, artists, and scholars discussed here amount to a splendid assemblage of respectable, middle-class men (and occasionally women) of letters is perhaps inevitable. *A Publisher and his Friends*, the title of Samuel Smiles's account of John Murray's firm, encapsulates the essence of this milieu, which contributed to the exploration and representation of Palestine far more than any formal institution. And it is precisely the absence of any real institutional framework which makes the 'invisible college' so appropriate for our discussion, allowing us to approach this collective body of fiction, travel writing, and paintings as an academic, or high, Orientalist discourse.

---

[47] Quoted in J. N. L. Baker, *The History of Geography* (Oxford: Blackwell, 1963), 38.
[48] Brian Hudson, 'The New Geography and the New Imperialism: 1870–1918', *Antipode*, 9/2 (1977), 12–19.
[49] Albert Hourani, *Islam in European Thought* (Cambridge: Cambridge University Press, 1991), esp. 64–8.

'A sort of patriotism': Themes and Images

In December 1816, while he was visiting Venice, Lord Byron found himself involved in a legal scandal concerning a book of poems, *Pilgrimage to Jerusalem*, which had just been published in London under his own name. Byron was furious. 'The answer to this is short,' he wrote to his publisher, John Murray: '*I never wrote such poems.*' It was not the financial dispute, or even his reputation, which seemed to trouble Byron most. Rather, it was the very idea itself. ' "A Pilgrimage to *Jerusalem*!" How the devil should I write about *Jerusalem*, never having yet been there?'[50]

Still, only a year earlier, Byron had published *Hebrew Melodies*, in which he explicitly pursued biblical and Hebraic themes. 'On the Day of the Destruction of Jerusalem by Titus', for example, begins:

> From the last hill that looks on thy once holy dome
> I beheld thee, Oh SION! when rendered to Rome:
> 'Twas thy last sun went down, and the flames of thy fall
> Flash'd back on the last glance I gave to thy wall.[51]

This certainly demonstrates that Byron, though 'never having yet been there', could—and did—write about Jerusalem. How, then, should we understand his agitation at the idea of writing about a pilgrimage without undertaking it? What makes Byron disclaim *Hebrew Melodies* as a text 'about' Jerusalem?

Byron, to be sure, was thinking about two different cities and, furthermore, two different styles of representation. The Westerners who travelled to Jerusalem from the 1800s onwards were appalled by the discrepancy between the appearance of the city and its depiction in Renaissance and Baroque art.[52] Soon, with the work of artists and writers, many of them Byron's friends, the land of the Bible and its inhabitants would be Orientalized, reallocated from the present-tense landscapes of the West to the exotic past-as-present which was the East. When Byron exclaimed that it was impossible to write about Jerusalem

---

[50] Byron to Murray, 9 Dec. 1816, in *The Works of Lord Byron*, ed. Rowland Prothero (London: John Murray, 1900), iv. 21, 22. The poem in question was written by John Agg and published by Johnson (1817).
[51] *Byron's Hebrew Melodies*, ed. Thomas Ashton (London: Routledge & Kegan Paul, 1972), 168.
[52] Shepherd, *Zealous Intruders*, 17–19.

without having been there, he was referring to the work produced by this new order of artists-travellers-pilgrims, of which he himself was patron saint. By comparison, Byron's own Zion in *Hebrew Melodies* lacks a sense of topographical precision. Rather than anticipate a work like Melville's *Clarel, A Poem and Pilgrimage in the Holy Land* (1876), Byron's fall of Jerusalem seems to look back to Tasso and Milton.

Byron's offhand comment to Murray, then, captures the moment in which a new artistic convention was eclipsing an older one, but it also marks a return to the notion of the pilgrimage as a physical journey to a sacred geographical terrain. Edward Said has observed that 'the Orient was a place of pilgrimage, and every major work belonging to a genuine if not always to an academic Orientalism took its form, style, and intention from the idea of a pilgrimage there'.[53] What Said overlooks is that for Protestants—who had been taught, for centuries, that the road to the Promised Land lies in the heart—the very concept of a pilgrimage entailed an inherent difficulty. 'What a pleasant thing it would be, after all, if in our day we could only believe in a pilgrimage!' sighs Frances Power Cobbe as she chances on some pious Russian pilgrims by the River Jordan. But that is impossible, 'As England's religion admits of nothing of the kind', and she immediately begins to dote on 'glorious old Bunyan'.[54]

Cobbe was not the only English (or, indeed, Protestant) traveller to Palestine whose thoughts turned to Bunyan. A satirical pamphlet mocking Queen Caroline's visit to Palestine was entitled *The New Pilgrim's Progress* (1820); not surprisingly, this was also the subtitle of Mark Twain's travel account, *Innocents Abroad* (1869). Lady Anne Blunt (Byron's granddaughter) based her *Pilgrimage to Nejd* (1879) on Bunyan's text, but only to use the allegory in a Muslim, not a Christian, framework: the Delectable Mountains become Jabal Shammar, and the 'Lord of the Hill' the Emir Ibn Rashid.[55] These texts have little in common, apart from the fact that they all rely on readers' familiarity with Bunyan to achieve their subversive effect. Indeed, regardless of the motive which brought them there—corroboration of Scripture, scientific exploration, missionary work, diplomatic or commercial

---

[53] Said, *Orientalism*, 168.
[54] Frances Power Cobbe, *The Cities of the Past* (London: Trübner, 1864), 135.
[55] Melman, *Women's Orients*, 295–6.

commissions, leisure, curiosity, boredom—English men and women who travelled to Palestine were compelled to establish the affinity between Christian's pilgrimage to Zion and their own excursion. If a pilgrimage to Jerusalem is essentially a spiritual journey, what does a visit to the earthly city signify? Or, more broadly: how can the experience of 'England in Jerusalem' relate to the Bunyanesque concept of 'Jerusalem in England'?

A Protestant pilgrimage

A. P. Stanley, Professor of Ecclesiastical History at Oxford and author of the successful *Sinai and Palestine* (1856), addressed these questions in a sermon delivered in Palestine in 1862. As Dean of Westminster Abbey, a leading Broad Church figure, Stanley worked to tighten the union between church and state.[56] His sermon reads as a conscious effort to articulate a comprehensive English stand.

On the one hand, Stanley adheres to the familiar Protestant creed when he insists that it is 'perfectly possible to be just, and holy, and good, without coming to Palestine. Pilgrimage is not really a Christian duty. Holy places are not really holy in the sight of God, except for the feelings that they produce... It is not the earthly, but the heavenly Jerusalem, which is the "mother of us all".' On the other hand, Stanley acknowledges that 'it is by thinking of what has been here, by making the most of the things we do see in order to bring before our minds the things we do not see, that a visit to the Holy Land becomes a really religious lesson'. To visit the place where Jesus died and rose 'is to give a new force to the sound of [his] name whenever afterwards we hear it in Church or read it in the Bible'. And he concludes:

> We are not pilgrims: we are not crusaders. But we should not be Christians—we should not be Englishmen—we should not, I had almost said, be reasonable beings, if, believing what we do about the events that took place here, we could see Jerusalem and the Holy Land as we would see any other town or country. Even if it were only for the thought of the interest which thousands in former ages have taken in what we shall see... —if only for the thought of the feeling which our visit to these spots awakens in the hearts of thousands far away in our dear homes in England:—we cannot but gather up some good feelings, some more than merely passing pleasure, from these sacred scenes.[57]

---

[56] 'A. P. Stanley', *DNB*.
[57] A. P. Stanley, *Sermons Preached before HRH the Prince of Wales during his Tour in the East* (London: John Murray, 1863), 31, 30–1, 32.

By asserting that a visit to Palestine enables the believer to gain a better understanding of biblical truth, Stanley is reworking the traditional typological relationship between the earthly and the heavenly.[58] Similar strategies were employed by virtually every Western visitor to the land.[59] The contemporary, geographical landscape was always read as a type of—or a metaphor for—something else: past grandeur, future restoration, the real city below the surface, or the better city beyond it. The most intriguing aspect of Stanley's approach, however, is the way in which he incorporates England and Englishness into his typological equation. Indeed, it is their identity as Englishmen—their duty to those 'dear homes in England'—which not only justifies the visit to Palestine, but almost demands it. What Jerusalem is to the New Jerusalem, what the sentiment aroused in the Holy City is to the feeling awakened whenever the name 'Jesus' is heard in church, so is visiting Palestine to being English. Standing in Jerusalem, Stanley's thoughts wander back to England, but England is also the best justification for standing in Jerusalem. As we shall see, this double movement—advancing eastwards but gazing westwards—is typical of the English encounter with Palestine. That Stanley delivered this sermon in his capacity as guide to the Prince of Wales (the future Edward VII) during his 1862 tour of the Holy Land merely accentuates the nationalist impetus behind this notion of the Protestant pilgrimage.

Comments like these were not limited to the English: Chateaubriand's *Travels to Jerusalem* (1811) presents a similar, if not more powerful, French connection (not least because the Frenchman can indulge in the Crusading heritage without distancing himself from its Catholic overtones). Nevertheless, as Said has noted, the English and the French approached the Middle East differently. For the English, to write about 'Egypt, Syria, or Turkey, as much as travelling in them, was a matter of touring the realm of political will, political management, political definition'. For the French, the region echoed with the sounds of French defeats and loss, an 'Orient of memories'.[60]

---

[58] Davies, *Pilgrimage Yesterday and Today*, 140–52.
[59] Yehoshua Ben-Arieh, 'Holy Land Views in Nineteenth-Century Western Travel Literature', in Moshe Davis and Ben-Arieh (eds.), *With Eyes towards Zion III: Western Societies and the Holy Land* (New York: Praeger, 1991), 10–29.
[60] Said, *Orientalism*, 169–70.

But national affiliation was not the only factor: religious difference also shaped the representation of Palestine's landscape. The Protestant unease concerning the physical pilgrimage was most evident in the holy places, particularly the Church of the Holy Sepulchre, which seemed to incarnate the worst defilements of the Eastern and Roman Churches.[61] For an Englishman, Thackeray wrote, jarred and distracted by the 'flaring candles, reeking incense, savage pictures of Scripture story' and the 'din and clatter of strange people', the church seemed 'the least sacred spot about Jerusalem' (p. 208). Even English visitors who did not dismiss the authenticity of the sites were distressed to find that the open landscape had been restyled, roofed, and embellished. Kinglake, weary of the busy crowds surrounding the tomb, sends for horses to ride to Calvary. The Dragoman is amused: 'Mount Calvary, Signor?—Eccolo! it is *upstairs—on the first floor*.'[62] This was a far cry from the Protestant image, perfected in Mrs Alexander's 1848 hymn:

> There is a green hill far away,
> Outside a city wall,
> Where the dear Lord was crucified,
> Who died to save us all.[63]

Edward Clarke, who visited Jerusalem in 1801, was the first in a long succession of British Protestants who were obsessed with unearthing the actual locales of the New Testament events. It is hardly surprising that the Garden Tomb, identified by General Gordon as the real sepulchre, was situated on a bare hill outside the walled city.[64]

The Protestant imagination, then, turned from the holy sites themselves—from the enclosed shrines, but even from the cities and villages—to the open landscape. This is most evident in nineteenth-century visual representations. Only a dozen or so of the 120 plates in David Roberts's *The Holy Land* (1842–9) depict the actual holy places; it is the landscape, not the monuments, which figures prominently.[65]

---

[61] Hummel and Hummel, *Patterns of the Sacred*, 18–35.
[62] Alexander Kinglake, *Eothen* (1844; London: T. Nelson, n.d.), 152–3. Subsequent page numbers are cited parenthetically in the text.
[63] *The Methodist Hymn Book* (London: Methodist Conference Office, 1933), 173.
[64] Sarah Kochav, 'The Search for a Protestant Holy Sepulchre: The Garden Tomb in Nineteenth-Century Jerusalem', *Journal of Ecclesiastical History*, 46/2 (1995), 278–301.
[65] Bendiner, 'Portrayal of the Middle East', 142–3.

Similarly, while French Catholic photographers concentrated on man-made, commemorative sites, their British Protestant colleagues tended to depict the relatively untouched landscape.[66]

This characterized textual representations as well. Describing the Church of the Nativity in Bethlehem, Chateaubriand claimed that 'Nothing can be more pleasing, or better calculated to excite sentiments of devotion, than this subterraneous church':

> on quitting the crypt, where you have met with the riches, the arts, the religion, of civilized nations, you find yourself in a profound solitude, amidst wretched Arab huts, among half naked savages and faithless Mussulmans. This place is, nevertheless, the same where so many miracles were displayed; but this sacred land dares no longer express its joy, and locks within its bosom the recollections of its glory.[67]

A. P. Stanley, by contrast, turns away from the ostentatious shrine to the open landscape surrounding it:

> I have said, one is reminded of the Nativity by the convent. But, in truth, I almost think it distracts one from it. From the first moment that those towers, and hills, and valleys burst upon you, there enters the one prevailing thought that now, at last, we are indeed in the 'Holy Land.'

And elsewhere he asserts:

> The Churches of the Holy Sepulchre or of the Holy House may be closed against us, but we have still the Mount of Olives and the Sea of Galilee; the sky, the flowers, the trees, the fields, which suggested the Parables; the holy hills, which cannot be removed, but stand fast for ever.[68]

The English depiction of the landscape is shaped by this all-engulfing gaze, dismissing the tiny man-made monuments in favour of the panoramic view as a whole. 'Enough for us that on this soil the Saviour laid down his life,' wrote Warburton; 'enough for us that these skies above us received Him, risen, and still bespeak his presence.'[69]

---

[66] Yeshayahu Nir, *The Bible and the Image: The History of Photography in the Holy Land, 1839–1899* (Philadelphia: University of Pennsylvania Press, 1985), 106–7.

[67] François-René Vicomte de Chateaubriand, *Travels to Jerusalem and the Holy Land through Egypt* (1810–11), trans. Fredric Shoberl (3rd edn. London: Henry Colburn, 1835), i. 331–2.

[68] A. P. Stanley, *Sinai and Palestine* (1856; London: John Murray, 1896), 104, 473. Subsequent page numbers are cited parenthetically in the text.

[69] Eliot Warburton, *The Crescent and the Cross* (London: Henry Colburn, 1845), ii. 191. Subsequent page numbers are cited parenthetically in the text.

Little wonder, then, that it was the view from the Mount of Olives—a 'Monarch-of-all-I-survey' scene if ever there was one[70]—which attracted English travellers most.[71] As Edward Clarke noted, 'So commanding is the view of Jerusalem afforded in this situation, that the eye roams over all the streets, and around the walls, as if in the survey of a plan or a model of the city.'[72] Inviting travellers to attain a broad perspective and, at the same time, leave the corrupted and polluted city behind them, the Mount of Olives offered an ideal fusion between Protestant sensibilities, the contemporary passion for the picturesque, and the Romantic Alpine view (which, as M. H. Abrams has observed, was in itself a secularization of the biblical 'Pisgah sight' motif[73]). Like Jane Austen's protagonists in *Northanger Abbey* standing on Beechen Cliff and gazing towards the glories of Bath spread down beneath them, the Mount of Olives offered visitors to Jerusalem a chance to examine 'fore-grounds, distances, and second distances—side-screens and perspectives—lights and shades';[74] but it also allowed them to conjure up some of the most consecrated memories associated with the life of Christ. 'Oh! what a relief it was to quit its narrow, filthy, ill-paved streets for that lovely hill, climbing it by the same rocky path our Saviour and his faithful few so often trod,' wrote Lord Lindsay in 1838.[75] Norman Macleod, editor of the Evangelical journal *Good Words*, spent his last day in Jerusalem there, 'Alone, with no companion but my Bible'.[76]

Tourists were perhaps less at liberty to plan their route, but Thomas Cook composed the narrative for them: 'It is from the summit of the Mount of Olives that Jerusalem, once "the joy of the whole earth" is best seen, and my plan was to let as little of it, on the west side, be seen as possible, until the glorious sight of walls, domes, minarets, flat and

---

[70] Pratt, *Imperial Eyes*, 201–8.
[71] Hummel and Hummel, *Patterns of the Sacred*, 24–6; Shepherd, *Zealous Intruders*, 24.
[72] Edward Daniel Clarke, *Travels in Various Countries of Europe Asia and Africa*, 6 vols., pt. II, sect. I: *Greece, Egypt and the Holy Land* (London: T. Cadell, 1812), 573.
[73] M. H. Abrams, *Natural Supernaturalism: Tradition and Revolution in Romantic Literature* (New York: Norton, 1971), esp. 65–70.
[74] Jane Austen, *Northanger Abbey* (1818), ed. Anne Henry Ehrenpreis (Harmondsworth: Penguin, 1985), 125–6.
[75] Lord Lindsay, *Letters on Egypt, Edom, and the Holy Land* (1838; London: Henry Colburn, 1843), ii. 61.
[76] Norman Macleod, *Half Hours in the Holy Land: Travels in Egypt, Palestine, Syria* (1865, as *Eastward*; London: James Nisbet, 1896), 173.

dome roofed houses, burst at one view on the astonished beholder.'[77] From here, Jerusalem seemed to lose its disturbing palpability and attain an almost ethereal existence: floating, as it were, between heaven and earth, with the golden Dome of the Rock glimmering in the sun, this was the closest the earthly Jerusalem could masquerade as its heavenly sister. At a safe distance, Jerusalem could once more become the 'joy of the whole earth'. 'The distant view', declared one visitor, 'is all.'[78]

A desolate, empty land
Having to define the nature of their pilgrimage was one thing; but English travellers were also impelled to come to terms with Palestine's actual—and often shocking—appearance, very different from the biblical imagery of milk and honey or the Old Masters' green landscapes. Virtually all English visitors commented on Palestine's desolation. 'Those writers, ancient and modern, who have represented [Palestine] as barren, must be understood, however, as referring only to the mountainous districts around Jerusalem,' warned Josiah Conder in his *Modern Traveller* (1823).[79] Nevertheless, the 'burning Sun of Syria' which looms large over the dry landscapes of Walter Scott's *The Talisman* (1825), seems to flare over the greater part of English writing about the land.[80]

One obvious reason for the dissemination of this image was that it corroborated the twin notions of Ottoman despotism and Oriental backwardness. Volney's *Ruins of Empire* (1791) was one of the first texts to promote this argument, which soon became an Orientalist commonplace.[81] The mere presence of a desert, that most non-European feature, signified inefficiency, laziness, and bad government.[82] In his official *Report on the Commercial Statistics of Syria* (1840), the diplomat John Bowring observed that the 'agricultural produce of Syria is far less than might be expected from the extensive tracts of fertile lands and the favourable character of the climate'. This was

---

[77] Quoted in Brendon, *Thomas Cook*, 129.
[78] Quoted in Shepherd, *Zealous Intruders*, 24.
[79] Josiah Conder, *The Modern Traveller*, i: *Palestine* (London: Thomas Tegg, 1823), 11.
[80] Walter Scott, *The Talisman* (1825; Oxford: Oxford University Press, 1912), 1.
[81] Thierry Hentsch, *Imagining the Middle East*, trans. Fred A. Reed (Montreal: Black Rose, 1992), 123–30.
[82] Bendiner, 'Portrayal of the Middle East', 117.

the result of heavy taxation, the conscription for military service, but, most significantly, 'Oriental character': 'No element in the Mussulman character is more opposed to the sound commercial principle than their indifference to the progress of decay.'[83]

Equally responsible for the persistence of the 'barren land' image was the Protestant endeavour to corroborate scriptural truth: after all, it was precisely on the biblical testimonies that travellers based their claim that the land, once flowing with milk and honey, had deteriorated under Muslim rule. Alexander Keith's *Evidence of the Truth of the Christian Religion Derived from the Literal Fulfilment of Prophecy* (1828) was the leading advocate of the argument that Palestine's 'aspect in the present day is the precise likeness delineated by the pencil of prophecy, when every feature that could admit of change was the reverse of what it now is'.[84] There is 'a perfect accordance between the *predicted* and the *existing* state of this country', wrote the Revd J. A. Wylie (1844), and went on to classify the various prophecies under three heads: '1st, The desolation of its soil; 2^{d}, The ruin of its cities; 3^{d}, The expatriation of its people.'[85] Chronologically speaking, this Orientalization of the landscape corresponded with the Orientalization of Scripture, signified by the emerging higher biblical criticism. Ironically, what writers like Keith and Wylie were in fact suggesting was a way of challenging the sceptical biblical criticism using its own tools.[86]

The conviction that Palestine was barren was inseparable from the idea that it was uninhabited. 'The plains are verdureless, these hills are bare, these streets are empty,' Wylie wrote.[87] Beshara Doumani has traced three ways in which native Palestinians were erased from the nineteenth-century Orientalist discourse. First, he points to the fabrication of a historical chronology which emphasized, almost exclusively, the biblical and Crusader periods; the intervening and following centuries, characterized by Muslim rule, were largely ignored. Secondly, the

---

[83] John Bowring, *Report on the Commercial Statistics of Syria Addressed to the Right Hon. Lord Viscount Palmerston* (London: William Clowes, 1840), 9, 28. 'Syria' here denotes an area which includes the Holy Land.
[84] Alexander Keith, *Evidence of the Truth of the Christian Religion* (1828; 38th edn. London: Nelson and Sons, 1861), 98.
[85] J. A. Wylie, *Ruins of Bible Lands* (1844; 14th edn. London: Blackwood, n.d.), 201.
[86] Pemble, *Mediterranean Passion*, 184–5.
[87] Wylie, *Ruins of Bible Lands*, 249.

preponderant number of works about Jerusalem made the history of the city synonymous with the history of Palestine as a whole, even though Jerusalem was hardly a typical Palestinian community. Finally, travel accounts and geographical studies focused primarily on the relationship between Palestine's physical features and the biblical events. All this led to the 'amazing ability to discover the land without discovering the people'.[88] As Billie Melman has shown, the liminal role assigned to English women within their own society often enabled them to develop more subtle Orientalist perceptions. Mary Eliza Rogers's *Domestic Life in Palestine* (1862), for example, depicts a Palestine teeming with wives and daughters, servants and merchants, villagers and nomads: it is anything but empty. This 'domestic' view, in turn, could always be utilized to serve the dominant agenda. Rogers's brother, the British vice-council to Haifa, reminds her that his mission is to report to the council. 'The fact of your being my fellow-traveller', he tells her, 'will perhaps induce people to receive us into their strongholds the more readily and unsuspectingly.'[89]

While the indigenous population was not entirely absent even from the dominant Orientalist discourse, its role was constructed to conform to the English perception of the Oriental space: in the changeless East, the natives functioned as a living museum. When, in 1829, Henry Hart Milman described Abraham as 'the sheikh or Emir of a pastoral tribe, migrating from place to place', a scandal was quick to follow.[90] A few decades later, however, this would become another Orientalist cliché. 'Oriental life has, as it were, been stereotyped,' observed the author of the typically titled *Scripture Manners and Customs; Being an Account of the Domestic Habits, Arts, etc., of Eastern Nations, Mentioned in Holy Scripture, Illustrated by Extracts from the Works of Travellers* (1841).[91] The painter David Wilkie, who claimed that the Arabs 'look as if they had never changed since the

---

[88] Beshara B. Doumani, 'Rediscovering Ottoman Palestine: Writing Palestinians into History', *Journal of Palestine Studies*, 21 (1992), 7–9. See also Issam Nassar, 'In their Image: Jerusalem in Nineteenth-Century English Travel Narratives', *Jerusalem Quarterly File*, 19 (2003), 6–22.

[89] Mary Eliza Rogers, *Domestic Life in Palestine* (1862; London: Kegan Paul, 1989), 216.

[90] Henry Hart Milman, *The History of the Jews* (1829; London: J. M. Dent, n.d.), i. 48.

[91] [Mary Fawley Maude], *Scripture Manners and Customs*...(1841; 19th edn. London: SPCK, [1862]), p. xxxi.

time of Abraham', was one of the first artists to depict biblical characters in the garb of present-day Bedouin.[92] On visiting the land, Wilkie discovered that 'the great mass of Italian Scripture Art is, in backgrounds, costumes, and characters, so purely imaginative, or so completely Italian, that Evangelical Syria is completely unrepresented'. He called for 'a Martin Luther in painting...to sweep away the abuses by which our divine pursuit is encumbered'.[93] William Holman Hunt shared Wilkie's belief that the painting of historically accurate biblical pictures was a distinctly Protestant endeavour.[94] By the mid-nineteenth century, the Old Masters' Holy Land was succeeded by a new set of Orientalist stock images, first in paintings, then in photographs.[95]

It was the figure of the Bedouin which dominated these Orientalist representations. Gibbon, in the famous fiftieth chapter of *Decline and Fall*, had perpetuated the myth of the noble savage, and as early as 1810, 'most narratives of travel in the Levant contained a set piece on the Bedouin in which they were described as independent, faithful and hospitable'.[96] Images varied—recall *The Times* anecdote with which we began—but it was a commonplace to observe that while the 'dwellers in the cities soon become corrupt, and lose the characteristics of their race', the Bedouin 'is today as he was in the days of Ishmael, unconquered, and indomitable', as Warburton noted (ii. 243, 248). To focus, almost exclusively, on the nomadic Bedouin, was another way of erasing the Palestinian presence in the land.

To what extent was this erasure a conscious endeavour? Partly, it was the white male traveller's familiar ability to ignore his subordinates, both European and indigenous. Kinglake exposes this mental mechanism when he writes: 'I had been journeying (cheerily indeed; for the voices of my followers were ever within my hearing, but yet), as it were, in solitude, for I had no comrade to whet the edge of my reason, or wake

---

[92] Quoted in Malcolm Warner, 'The Question of Faith: Orientalism, Christianity, and Islam', in Mary Anne Stevens (ed.), *The Orientalists: Delacroix to Matisse* (London: Royal Academy of Arts, 1984), 32.

[93] Quoted in Wilkie Collins, *Memoirs of the Life of William Collins, Esq., RA* (London: Longman, 1848), ii. 184.

[94] Warner, 'Question of Faith', 33.

[95] Bendiner, 'Portrayal of the Middle East'; Stevens (ed.), *Orientalists*; Nir, *Bible and the Image*.

[96] Kathryn Tidrick, *Heart-Beguiling Araby: The English Romance with Arabia* (1981; London: Tauris, 1989), 22.

me from my noonday dreams. I was left all alone to be taught and swayed by the beautiful circumstances of Palestine travelling' (p. 110). In this respect, Warburton's claim that during the 'greater part of the time I passed at Jerusalem I was as solitary as when I was in the desert' (ii. 193) is most revealing: both in the desert and in the city, the English traveller was always surrounded by an invisible train of attendants.

Nevertheless, what we find so often is not so much the image of an empty land, as the fantasy of it, as if only solitude could allow English travellers to experience Palestine to the full. 'Tancred had fixed upon this hour for visiting Gethsemane, because he felt assured that no one would be stirring,' Disraeli wrote: 'There are moments when we must be alone' (p. 188). For the English, a visit to Palestine was one such very long moment.

A familiar land

In his discussion of *Tancred*, Daniel Bivona writes that 'the dream of abolishing the interior/exterior dichotomy by uncovering the exterior as always already interior is the dream of obliterating all distinctions, including that between the metaphorical and the literal'.[97] Bivona is considering Disraeli's desire for religious and racial reunification—the idea that Arabs are 'only Jews upon horseback' (p. 261)—but his critique also applies to the construction of the Palestinian landscape. The Holy Land was Orientalized, but these new foreign features were swiftly assimilated, allowing the land to be rediscovered as something already known. As Bartlett described the scenery near Jaffa, 'Every object is novel and Oriental in character, and independent of its picturesque beauty, is linked by a delicious association with our earliest dreams of Biblical scenery and incident.'[98]

This explains some of the remarkable comments made by travellers. Consider, for example, Alexander Kinglake, standing on a summit overlooking the eastern shore of the lake of Galilee. An exemplary moment of the Orientalizing mechanism that John Barrell has called 'this/that/the other',[99] Kinglake imagines Palestine as the final frontier

---

[97] Daniel Bivona, *Desire and Contradiction: Imperial Visions and Domestic Debates in Victorian Literature* (Manchester: Manchester University Press, 1990), 22.

[98] Bartlett, *Walks about the City*, 9.

[99] John Barrell, *The Infection of Thomas de Quincey: A Psychopathology of Imperialism* (New Haven: Yale University Press, 1991), 10. Cf. Robert Shannan Peckham, 'The

of civilization, an Orient which is still, just barely, an Occident: 'that farthest shore was the end of the world that belongs to man the dweller, the beginning of the other and veiled world that is held by the strange race whose life (like the pastime of Satan) is a "going to and fro upon the face of the earth."' Kinglake gazes eastwards, only to direct his inner vision westwards. Although conscious of the 'exact train of thought that ought to be suggested by the historical associations of the place', he is nevertheless reminded of a very different set of cultural and geographical co-ordinates: 'the calm face of the lake was uplifted... and instead there came to me a loving thought from over the seas in England, a thought more sweet than Gospel to a wilful mortal like this.' No wonder, then, that the Oriental landscape is suddenly Anglicized: 'There she lay, the Sea of Galilee. Less stern than Wastwater—less fair than gentle Windermere—she had still the winning ways of an English lake' (pp. 121–2).

Harriet Martineau, in her *Eastern Life, Present and Past* (1848), describes a similar experience on her way from Petra to Hebron:

The first thought or impression which I remember as occurring on my entrance into the Holy Land was one of pleasure that it was so like home. When we came to towns, everything looked as foreign as in Nubia: but here, on the open hills, we might gaze round us on a multitude of familiar objects, and remember to whose eyes they were once familiar too.

And elsewhere:

For about two hours after leaving Nazareth, the hills were stony, and scantily clothed... but after that, for about another hour, the scenery became so like that of the outskirts of an English park, as to give us the same home-feeling that we had in meeting familiar weeds on our entrance into the Holy Land.[100]

Martineau's remark that 'It was very like home—like the wilder parts of England, except for our Arab train, and the talk about wild Bedoueens' (iii. 56) illustrates how this uncanny familiarity both depends on, and intensifies, the fantasy of the open, empty landscape.

A. P. Stanley agreed with her. Describing his 'Recollections of the first day in Palestine', he writes:

Exoticism of the Familiar and the Familiarity of the Exotic: *Fin-de-Siècle* Travellers to Greece', in Duncan and Gregory (eds.), *Writes of Passage*, 164–84.

[100] Harriet Martineau, *Eastern Life, Present and Past* (London: Moxon, 1848), iii. 53, 230–1. Subsequent page numbers are cited parenthetically in the text.

And I am struck by what is also noticed by Miss Martineau—the western, almost the English, character of the scenery. Those wild uplands of Carmel and Ziph are hardly distinguishable (except by their ruined cities and red anemones) from the Lowlands of Scotland or of Wales; these cultivated valleys of Hebron (except by their olives) from the general features of a rich valley in Yorkshire or Derbyshire. The absence of palms and the presence of daisies greatly contributes to this result, and added to the contrast of the strange scenery which has been ours for the last month, gives a homelike and restful character to this first entrance which can never be effaced. (pp. 101–2)

All travellers have a tendency to compare their new vicinity with what they already know. This is what Warburton does when he remarks that the scenery on the road to Jerusalem 'resembled that of the wildest glens of Scotland' (ii. 39). And when Robert Curzon points out that 'Windsor Castle multiplied by ten would have very much the appearance of Jerusalem as seen from this point of view',[101] he is probably trying to help his readers visualize the landscape. However, the writers quoted above go beyond this pattern of analogy: they describe an almost eerie sensation of feeling at home. Rather than dismiss the Oriental features, they incorporate them, read them as quintessentially theirs. According to Stanley, it is the absence of palm-trees—'so intimately connected with our associations of Judea' (p. 144) but 'now all but unknown on the hills of Palestine' (p. 121)—which makes the landscape seem so English. Eastern desolation has helped transform the Oriental landscape into an *English* one.

Certainly, for travellers arriving from Sinai or Arabia, Palestine seemed relatively green, and Stanley in particular emphasizes that it is 'unquestionably a fertile land in the midst of bareness' (p. 122). What is significant for our discussion, however, is not whether the Holy Land did, or did not resemble England, but the fact that these English writers felt—or wanted to feel—that it did. What, then, had awakened this sense of home-coming which seems to characterize the depiction of no other Oriental province but Palestine?

On the one hand, it could be traced back to the endless process of citation and repetition which conditioned the travellers' expectations. The fact that 'the subject has been gone over again and again, until the

---

[101] Robert Curzon, *Visits to Monasteries in the Levant* (1849; London: Humphrey Milford, 1916), 193–4.

Holy Land is better known in England than the English lakes', as the *Art Journal* complained, no doubt helped Kinglake perceive in the Sea of Galilee the winning ways of an English lake.

But there is a deeper current here, which brings us back to Stanley's assertion that a pilgrimage to the Holy Land evokes something intimately connected with the idea of England and Englishness: 'We still experience a sort of patriotism for Palestine,' writes Warburton: 'Narrow as are its boundaries, we have all a share in the possession: what a church is to a city, Palestine is to the world... The first impressions of childhood are connected with that scenery; and infant lips in England's prosperous homes pronounce the names of forlorn Jerusalem and Galilee with reverence' (ii. 54). The first impressions of childhood: this is why Martineau could claim that the places she visited in Palestine were 'familiar to my mind's eye from my youth up' (iii. 118); Bartlett could associate the Oriental objects with 'our earliest dreams of Biblical scenery'; and Henry Baker Tristram could feel in Jerusalem as if 'revisiting a father's grave, or the house of one's youth'.[102]

This powerful nostalgic association of the Holy Land with one's childhood, one's Sunday school, churchyard, family Bible, home, is precisely where vernacular Orientalism—the internalization of the Holy Land in English culture, the notion of 'Jerusalem in England'— fed into the actual encounter with the land and, subsequently, into the emergence of the academic Orientalist tradition. The question is, of course, what sort of claim does this sense of familiarity make on the landscape?

Strategies of dispossession

Drawing on the work of Edward Said, Paul Carter, and Timothy Mitchell, the geographer Derek Gregory has outlined several 'strategies of dispossession' which highlight the linkage between the colonial project, the construction of space, and various modalities of power–knowledge.[103] The first, 'dispossession by othering', follows Said's

---

[102] H. B. Tristram, *Pathways to Palestine* (London: Sampson Low, 1881), 25. For very similar responses among American travellers to Palestine—particularly the references to the figure of the mother—see John Davis, *The Landscape of Belief: Encountering the Holy Land in Nineteenth-Century American Art and Culture* (Princeton: Princeton University Press, 1996), 16–17.

[103] Derek Gregory, *Geographical Imaginations* (Oxford: Blackwell, 1994), 168–74.

model of Orientalism, which, as we have just seen, fails to account for the English tendency to imagine Palestine as a quintessential self, not 'other'.

A second strategy, 'dispossession by naming', is exemplified through Paul Carter's *The Road to Botany Bay* (1987). Rejecting the idea that 'the newcomers travelled and settled a land *which was already there*', Carter traces the origins of Australian 'spatial history' in the act of naming, by which 'space is transformed symbolically into a place, that is, a space with a history', 'something that could be explored and read': space 'was a text that had to be written before it could be interpreted'. Carter goes on to discuss at length the etymology of place-names deriving from either the 'language of feeling' or the 'language of description'. He concludes: 'The country did not teach [the traveller] how to read. Rather, he found there what he was looking for.'[104]

The colonization of Australia demanded a textual construction which permitted travellers to discover something already familiar, already English. Palestine, too, was to be read like a book, but in this case, there was no need to develop a complex linguistic/spatial strategy which would sanction the colonial project. The book was already available: the Bible. The British obsession with matching biblical place-names with actual geographical sites stands in stark contrast to the conscious act of naming which characterized the encounter with Australia. Consequently, the Holy Land was perceived as a space which encouraged, rather than resisted, assimilation. It is indicative, for example, that the Palestine Association established in London in 1805 aspired to explore 'the knowledge of the geography, natural history, and antiquities of Palestine and its vicinity' by 'imitating as closely as possible the meritorious exertions made by THE AFRICAN ASSOCIATION'. But it was in order to promote 'biblical and historical knowledge', 'with a view to the illustration of the Holy Writings', that this project—'a pursuit worthy the attention of Christians'—was to be carried out.[105] Even when Palestine was approached as if it were a *terra incognita*, it was only to enhance its pre-eminence as a *terra sancta*.

---

[104] Paul Carter, *The Road to Botany Bay* (London: Faber & Faber, 1987), pp. xxi, xxiv, 67, 41, 349.
[105] *Palestine Association 1805*, 3, 7, 4.

Naturally, the Bible lands present a more complex case. A third strategy proposed by Gregory, 'dispossession by spatializing', relies on Timothy Mitchell's *Colonising Egypt* (1988), which sets forth a distinct machinery of representation—'the world-as-exhibition'—in which the world is set up like an object on display, to be viewed, experienced, and investigated: 'Europeans in general arrived in the Orient after seeing plans and copies—in pictures, exhibitions and books—of which they were seeking the original.' So the 'real' Orient became a place that one 'already knew by heart' on arrival—hence Kinglake's excitement at observing the Pyramids, whose form was familiar to him from the days of early childhood: 'I had no print, no picture before me, and yet the old shapes were there; there was no change: they were just as I had known them.' Accordingly, he strives to persuade himself that these 'angles... were of harder stuff and more ancient than the paper pyramids of the green portfolio' (p. 219). As Mitchell concludes:

> The Orient was something one only ever rediscovered. To be grasped representationally, as the picture of something, it was inevitably to be grasped as the reoccurrence of a picture one had seen before, as a map one already carried in one's head, as the reiteration of an earlier description... To describe the Orient, which refused to provide a point of view and to represent itself, became more and more a process of redescribing these representations.[106]

This certainly addresses some aspects of the English 'rediscovery' of Palestine, but it does not go far enough in explaining that unique cultural condition, in which the Holy Land mirrored England mirroring the Holy Land. As Kinglake suggests, the English encounter with Egypt could also awaken memories of bygone childhood days. But although they were commodified and domesticated, reduced to fit the 'green portfolio', Kinglake's miniature paper pyramids nevertheless function as symbols of a remote geographical area, beyond the familiar and the easily accessible, tiny fragments of 'there' that populated one's nursery. Palestine, on the other hand, stirred up a powerful identification with 'here': the 'old shapes' and 'pictures' which English travellers saw before their eyes when they visited the Holy Land were an English lake, an English church, an English home, Bunyan. It is no coincidence that the *Arabian Nights*, which were continuously evoked in accounts of

---

[106] Mitchell, *Colonising Egypt*, 28, 30.

The Land and the Books 91

Oriental travel, were seldom mentioned by English visitors to Palestine; and while Jaffa could still remind Thackeray of a 'famous and brilliant scene of the *Arabian Nights*' (p. 188), by the time he embarked on the road to Jerusalem, the Bible had become his sole source of reference. Egypt, like Mesopotamia, had its own share of biblical associations which located it within that manageable sphere between 'this' and 'the other';[107] but these were eclipsed by a dazzling, often alarming array of Oriental images which lacked the soothing reassurance of an already familiar plan. As Mitchell shows, it was precisely this lack of a 'plan' which generated the colonial project of making sense of the landscape, making it 'become readable, like a book'.[108] In Palestine—already a land with a book, *the* land with *the* book—no such process was necessary.

The association between the Orientalist gaze and childhood was certainly not limited to Palestine or even the Bible lands. Analysing the British experience in Africa (Hegel's 'land of childhood') through a reading of Haggard's imperial romances, Gail Ching-Liang Low has observed that 'because childhood presents a world of innocence uncorrupted by age and civilisation ... the boy child is necessarily the only figure capable of inheriting or founding, this blank new (colonial) world'.[109] G. A. Henty's late Victorian juvenile tales—primarily *Winning His Spurs: A Story of the Crusades* (1882) and *At Aboukir and Acre: A Story of Napoleon's Invasion of Egypt* (1899)—demonstrate how Palestine's backward, desolate scenery could make it an ideal site for the imperialist infant (or infantile) hero. Swarming with fearless Englishmen and proud Bedouin, justifying Western intervention and yet mourning the gradual modernization of the never-changing East, Henty's novels suggest that the encounter with Palestine, like other colonial encounters, could be saturated with a melancholic 'imperialist nostalgia'.[110] My point, however, is that in the Holy Land, this imperial longing was reinforced—but also, as we shall see in a moment,

---

[107] Cf. Frederick N. Bohrer's notion of 'exoticism' in *Orientalism and Visual Culture: Imagining Mesopotamia in Nineteenth-Century Europe* (Cambridge: Cambridge University Press, 2003).
[108] Mitchell, *Colonising Egypt*, 33.
[109] Gail Ching-Liang Low, *White Skins/Black Masks: Representation and Colonialism* (London: Routledge, 1996), 45.
[110] Renato Rosaldo, 'Imperialist Nostalgia', *Representations*, 26 (1989), 107–22.

negated—by a more 'vernacular' (or literal) form of nostalgia: one's longing for the Sunday school, the chapel, parents, *home*.

Palestine, in other words, defies Gregory's three 'strategies'. This is not to imply that, had the English image of Palestine been less ambiguous, Allenby would have conquered Jerusalem earlier. But by recognizing that the same elements which made the Holy Land so familiar also complicated its construction as a 'colonizable' space, we come closer to understanding the nature of this distinct Orientalist desire, epitomized so powerfully in the favourite English vista of Jerusalem from the Mount of Olives: to gaze at the Holy City from this safe distance is to penetrate and withdraw—to claim and discard—at the very same time. This ambivalence, as Stanley's sermon shows, is based on a careful balance between the literal pilgrimage and the metaphorical pilgrimage; between 'England in Jerusalem' on the one hand and 'Jerusalem in England' on the other.

This balance, however, could easily tip either way. An obvious example is the PEF, established in 1865 to explore Palestine's archaeological remains, its geography, topography, botany, and zoology. 'No country should be of so much interest to us as that in which the documents of our Faith were written, and the momentous events they describe enacted,' declared the Prospectus. Its founders maintained that a work 'is urgently required which shall do for the Holy Land what Mr. Lane's *Modern Egyptians* had done for Egypt'; they promised to identify 'ancient towns of Holy Writ with the modern villages which are their successors'; and they explained the significance of a topographical survey, 'which when we *advance inland* should give the position of the principal points throughout'.[111] The Fund's object, the Archbishop of York stated at the annual meeting in 1875, 'is to know Palestine through and through . . . ; and our reason for turning to Palestine is that Palestine is our country. I have used that expression before, and I refuse to adopt any other . . . England is my country, I know it and feel it, but Palestine also is my country.'[112]

The Archbishop's expression illustrates once again how vernacular biblical culture could provide the impetus for the academic Orientalist project. In the case of the PEF, this project had a distinctly imperial

---

[111] PEF Archive, London, PEF/1865/2, 'Prospectus', 1865 (leaflet); my italics.
[112] *PEFQSt*, July 1875, 115.

The Land and the Books 93

outlook: the Fund co-operated closely with the War Office, which provided both surveyors and equipment. As John Moscrop has claimed in his history of the Fund, the PEF 'doubled up as a research body and learned society, a tool for extending British imperial influence and as a cover for obtaining strategic information to support British military interests'.[113]

The PEF demonstrates how this a priori sense of familiarity could easily be yoked to a practical form of military and colonial expansion: why would one devise 'strategies of dispossession' for a land that was one's inheritance to begin with? Yet, it was also possible to understand the encounter with the Holy Land in very different terms: to gaze back homewards rather than 'advance inland'. Since the high Anglo-Palestine Orientalist discourse already contained this interpretation within it— since the same vocabulary which encouraged imperial ambitions could also be employed to resist them—all that was needed was a certain reading of the biblical text which would upset the balance between 'England in Jerusalem' and 'Jerusalem in England'.

It seems that the further we withdraw from the highly determined circuits in which the 'bourgeois, scientific, commercial, aesthetic' travellers were moving,[114] the more likely we are to see this balance overturned. As I've already suggested, this is demonstrated most poignantly in the experiences of British soldiers in Palestine during the First World War. However, even Victorian working-class travellers, who were often described as possessing an exceptional knowledge of Scripture, tended to approach the Holy Land in a more Bunyanesque frame of mind. 'I was pained to think', writes Warner in his account of the poor shoemaker,

> that the reality of the Holy Land might a little impair the celestial vision he had cherished of it for forty years; but perhaps it will be only a temporary obscuration; for the imagination is stronger than the memory, as we see so often illustrated in the writings of Oriental travellers; and I have no doubt that now he is again seated on his bench, the kingdoms he beholds are those of Israel and Judea, and not those that Mr. Cook showed him for an hundred pounds.[115]

Similarly, Norman Macleod quoted a sea captain of a Newcastle collier who visited Jerusalem:

---

[113] John J. Moscrop, 'The Palestine Exploration Fund, 1865–1914' (Ph.D. thesis, Leicester, 1996), 7.
[114] Clifford, 'Travelling Cultures', 107.
[115] Warner, *In the Levant*, 210.

'I knows and believes as well as you do the Scripturs, and knows that all them places are in the Bible; but don't let any of them guides come it over me so strong with their lies, and tell me that that hill is the Mount of Holives, and that other place the Holy Sepulchre, and Calvary, and all that sort of thing. I won't believe them Jews: I knows them far too well; you don't!'

Macleod concluded: 'Whether the captain was ever able to square the actual Jerusalem with his ideal one, I know not.'[116]

What these readings suggest is an inability—or, perhaps, a reluctance—on the part of more humble visitors to 'square' these two Jerusalems and thus adhere to the hegemonic reading of the 'proper' relationship between the land and the book. The biblical imagery translated by the PEF into a passionate claim for possession is applied here to signify a more explicit turning away from the geographical Holy Land to its metaphorical appropriations. Of course, these accounts tell us a great deal more about middle-class perceptions of the working class than about working-class perceptions of the Holy Land (the fact that it was only a relative of Macleod's who had actually met the captain did not keep the writer from quoting the good skipper verbatim). Working men and women simply did not participate in the construction of the Anglo-Palestine Orientalist discourse. And not only its construction: as we shall now see, for a very long time, the various cultural forms through which the Orientalist discourse was propagated remained unattainable to all but the very few.

'Like gas and water': Dissemination and Readership

Let us now return to Tancred, who, on the eve of his journey to the East, visits his friend Lady Bertie, another Palestine devotee:

The enamoured Montacute hung over her with pious rapture, as they examined together Mr. Roberts' Syrian drawings, and she alike charmed and astonished him by her familiarity with every locality and detail.... It was calculated that by these means, that is to say three or four visits, they might perhaps travel through Mr. Roberts' views together before he left England. (p. 156)

Roberts's work was published in twenty parts, ranging from a guinea (cheap covers) to £2. 2s. ('coloured and mounted as originals, in

---

[116] Macleod, *Half Hours in the Holy Land*, 114.

portfolios') each.[117] The complete work, issued between 1842 and 1849, was priced at £21–42; among the 634 subscribers were Queen Victoria, the archbishops of York and Canterbury, the Austrian Emperor, and the Russian Tsar.[118] Just like the actual journey which it had supposedly supplanted, this 'travel through Mr. Roberts' views' was also confined to a very limited social circle. By looking closely into the prices, sales, and circulation of travel books—the genre which is so often credited with the distribution of Orientalist imagery—we can grasp how the market-place defined the dissemination of the discourse.

The Victorian presses, John Pemble has written, 'plied the reading public with *Sketches, Notes, Diaries, Gleanings, Glimpses, Impressions, Pictures, Narratives,* and *Leaves from Journals* about *Tours, Visits, Wanderings, Residences, Rambles* and *Travels*' to the Mediterranean.[119] Listing first-hand accounts published between 1500 and 1915, Richard Bevis's bibliography includes almost 3,000 English books about the Middle East, most of them issued in the nineteenth century.[120] Robert Davies's analysis of Bevis's data shows that in the fifty years between 1775 and 1825, 181 books about Palestine, Syria, Egypt, and Arabia were written and published in English, and 39 translated from other languages; in 1825–76, the figure leaps to 870 English books and 82 translated; and in 1877–1914, 930 in English and 39 translated. A dramatic increase in publication could usually be linked to specific political events: 1801–3 (Napoleon's campaign), 1837–42 (the Ottoman reconquest), 1850–7 (the Crimean War), or 1882–4 (the British conquest of Egypt). Of these different Middle Eastern areas, Palestine and Egypt were the most popular, particularly after 1869. Fifteen to thirty new titles on Egypt and Palestine were published in twenty-seven out of the forty-four years

---

[117] *The Holy Land, Egypt, Arabia, and Syria by David Roberts, ARA, The Historical and Descriptive Notices by the Rev George Croly* (London: Moon, 1840), 4.
[118] Yehoshua Ben-Arieh, *Painting Palestine in the Nineteenth Century* (Tel-Aviv: Yad Izhak Ben-Zvi, 1992), 99, 102 [Hebrew].
[119] Pemble, *Mediterranean Passion,* 7.
[120] Richard Bevis, *Bibliotheca Cisorientalia: An Annotated Checklist of Early English Travel Books on the Near and Middle East* (Boston: G. K. Hall, 1973). Reinhold Röhricht, *Bibliotheca Geographica Palaestinae* (Berlin: Reuther, 1890), lists more than 5,000 publications about Palestine, many in English, issued by 2,000 European writers between 1800 and 1877.

between 1870 and 1914; there were only two years (1892 and 1914) when the figure dropped below ten.[121]

These figures are somewhat misleading. Since he records first-hand reports only, Bevis overlooks the vast number of secondary volumes which were compiled on the basis of eyewitness accounts. These compilations, moreover, were very often classified in Victorian catalogues under 'Religion' rather than 'Geography, Voyages, and Travel'. Together, these two categories covered almost 40 per cent of the entire market during the first half of the nineteenth century.[122] So the number of titles dealing with Palestine was probably much higher than the already impressive figure put forward by Bevis.

The number of titles was only one indicator; we must also consider prices, editions, sales, and profit.[123] Wallace Cable Brown has found evidence that at the beginning of the nineteenth century virtually any travel book, especially about the East, sold well.[124] However, the actual number of copies printed was quite low. Out of the ten new titles relating to Syria and Palestine, published by Bentley in 1829–50, only one—a translation of Lamartine's *A Pilgrimage to the Holy Land* (1835)—went through three editions, totalling 2,000 copies.[125] An average edition was around 750 copies,[126] but not all copies printed were sold. For example, in 1829–31, each of the twenty travel books

---

[121] Robert Davies, 'Warriors and Gentlemen: The Occidental Context of the Arabian Travel Narratives of Burton, Blunt and Lawrence' (Ph.D. thesis, Loughborough, 1991), 136-7, 122.

[122] Simon Eliot, 'Some Trends in British Book Production, 1800–1919', in John O. Jordan and Robert L. Patten (eds.), *Literature in the Marketplace: Nineteenth-Century British Publishing and Reading Practices* (Cambridge: Cambridge University Press, 1995), 37.

[123] The following figures are based on the archives of three leading Victorian publishers of Middle East travel books: the John Murray Archive, London; the Longman Archive, Reading University; and the Bentley Papers, the British Library. In all three archives I have relied mostly on the divide ledgers, and occasionally on the commission ledgers. Since all these entries are well catalogued, I have allowed myself to omit any direct references, except in special cases.

[124] Wallace Cable Brown, 'The Popularity of English Travel Books about the Near East, 1775–1825', *Philological Quarterly*, 15 (1936), 70–80. See also Nigel Leask, *Curiosity and the Aesthetics of Travel Writing, 1770–1840: 'From an Antique Land'* (Oxford: Oxford University Press, 2002), 11–13; William St Clair, *The Reading Nation in the Romantic Period* (Cambridge: Cambridge University Press, 2004), esp. 555–60.

[125] British Library, Bentley Papers, MSS Add. 46,637.

[126] Richard D. Altick, *The English Common Reader: A Social History of the Mass Reading Public, 1800–1900* (1957; 2nd edn. Columbus, Oh.: Ohio State University, 1998), 263.

published by the partnership of Colburn and Bentley sold an average of 661 copies per title.[127]

Speaking in 1852, Thomas Longman admitted that in the late 1820s 'every new book of travels, history, biography, and even every poem of pretension, was published in quarto, and at a high price'.[128] The average retail price of the fourteen Palestine-related titles published by Bentley in 1829–50 was about 31s.: the cheapest was John Carne's *Travels in the East* (1829), which sold for 10s. 6d.; the most expensive—a lavish quarto reprint of Buckingham's *The Arab Tribes* (1830)—priced at a ludicrous 73s. 6d.[129] Clearly, as Altick has noted, there was more profit in selling small editions at higher prices.[130] An illuminating example is Burckhardt's *Notes on the Bedouins*, which was published by Bentley twice in two years. The first edition (1830) included 250 one-volume quarto copies, which sold for the costly price of 52s. 6d. A year later, 500 copies were issued, this time in a two-volume octavo edition, which sold for 28s. However, while the expensive edition sold out immediately, 324 copies of the cheaper edition remained in stock, and were eventually sold off.[131]

The costly prices meant that the number of potential consumers was quite limited. Henniker's *Notes During a Visit to Egypt...Mount Sinai and Jerusalem* (Murray, 1822) was printed in 750 copies, which sold at a relatively cheap 12s. and brought the author a profit of £48. 7s. 6d. A second edition, two years later, sold only 87 out of the 500 printed, and resulted in a loss of £88. 14s. 7d. Even when demand was high, the costs sometimes made a second edition unwelcome. The first edition of Thomas Legh's *Narrative of a Journey in Egypt, Nubia, the Holy Land* (1816), published by Murray at 21s., all but sold out, bringing the writer and the publisher a profit of £136. 15s. 11d. each. A year later, Murray bought the copyright for £50, invested an additional £31 in new plates, and printed a second, cheaper edition (the wholesale price was dropped from 13s. to 7s.). This extra expenditure meant that

---

[127] Royal A. Gettmann, *A Victorian Publisher: A Study of the Bentley Papers* (Cambridge: Cambridge University Press, 1960), 134.

[128] *The Times*, 18 May 1852, 8.

[129] All these are the *listed* retail prices. As Altick and others have noted, the actual price was usually somewhat lower; but this does not affect my basic argument.

[130] Altick, *English Common Reader*, 261.

[131] British Library, Bentley Papers, MSS Add. 46,674, fol. 49; 46,637, fols. v, xii.

although all 750 copies were purchased, Murray lost £49. 1*s*. 6*d*. on the second edition.

The widespread practice of printing high-priced books in small editions persisted up to the late 1820s. From 1827 onwards, with the introduction of cheap imprints like Constable's Miscellany, the SDUK's Libraries of Useful and Entertaining Knowledge, or Colburn and Bentley's Standard Novels (6*s*.), there was a significant decline in the price of books and reprints.[132] By 1835, medium-priced books (ranging from 3*s*. 7*d*. to 10*s*.) became the largest single group.[133] Irby and Mangles's *Travels in Egypt . . . and the Holy Land* (1823), for example, was reprinted by Murray's Colonial and Home Library in 1844, priced at 2*s*. 6*d*.[134] Similar titles could be found in other series.

The reduction in prices may explain why travel books published after the 1850s were generally less profitable.[135] In 1897, just prior to the sale of Richard Bentley and Son, the ledgers were scrutinized, and the appraisal revealed that many travel accounts had resulted in deficits.[136] Once again, due to the cost of paper, printing, and advertising, even large sales at lower prices did not guarantee profit. Between May 1847 and January 1853, Longman printed, and eventually sold, 30,000 copies of Walter Macleod's popular *Geography of Palestine*, but the company was still £43. 11*s*. 7*d*. short of any earnings. Only in June 1867, after publishing a more expensive edition—the wholesale price went up from 9*d*. to 1*s*. ½*d*.—did Longman actually recover the loss.

In order to profit, then, a book had to sell several thousand copies at a relatively high price (above 10*s*.). Layard's *Nineveh and its Remains* (Murray), 2 volumes for 36*s*., was such a case. Between December 1848 and June 1849, 5,250 copies were published and sold out, bringing the author and the publisher a handsome profit of £1,800. 6*s*. 11*d*. each. The fourth edition, of 2,000 copies, sold out as well. 'Murray announces a steady continual sale for the book,' wrote the delighted Layard, 'which will place it side by side with *Mrs. Rundell's*

---

[132] James J. Barnes, *Free Trade in Books* (Oxford: Clarendon Press, 1964), 111.
[133] Eliot, 'Some Trends', 39.
[134] Angus Fraser, 'John Murray's Colonial and Home Library', *Papers of the Bibliographical Society of America*, 91/3 (1997), 398.
[135] Davies, 'Warriors and Gentlemen', 124.
[136] Gettmann, *Victorian Publisher*, 133.

Cookery.'[137] Another publishing success was A. P. Stanley's *Sinai and Palestine* (Murray). Between March 1856 and June 1858, five editions were published, amounting to 8,000 copies which sold at 16s. During that period alone, Stanley grossed more than £850 in profits. By December 1868, an additional 10,200 copies had been published and sold, with the price reduced only to 14s.[138]

However, these seem to be the exceptions. The archives of the big publishing houses seem to be filled with accounts of low sales and deficits. Woodcock's *Scripture Lands* (Longman, 1849) sold only 279 copies out of the 1,000 printed; Kennard's *Eastern Experience* (Longman, 1855), 276 out of 750; Lewin's *Jerusalem, a Sketch of the City* (Longman, 1861), 161 out of 500; his next book, *Siege of Jerusalem* (Longman, 1863), 172 out of 500; and so on. Most of these books were priced around 10s., and in many cases, the authors—who commissioned the presses to publish their books for them—were obliged to reimburse the firm for the loss. The remaining copies were usually undersold to cheap booksellers or coffee-houses, shipped to the colonies, or simply wasted.

Among this unhappy lot are a striking number of well-known authors, whose work is often discussed by historians of Palestine exploration. William Allen's *The Dead Sea* (1855)—which boldly proposes to connect the Mediterranean and the Dead Sea—was printed by Longman at 25s. Two years after publication, only 301 copies out of 750 were sold. Eventually, 405 copies were undersold, with a final loss of £157. 12s. 11d. James Fergusson, a prominent PEF member, advanced his ideas regarding the holy places in *Notes on the Site of the Holy Sepulchre* (Murray, 1860). Out of the 500 copies published, 49 were sent to be reviewed, 178 were kept by the author, and only 31 were actually sold in the twelve months following publication. In 1866, the remaining 132 were wasted. His next study, *The Holy Sepulchre* (Murray, 1865), must have seemed a splendid success: 309 copies of the 500 were sold, with a humble loss of £20. 7s. 11d. By 1878, there was actually a profit of about £6. Four years after the publication of Richard Burton's *Gold Mines of Midian* (Kegan Paul, 1878), there were still 44 copies of the

---

[137] Quoted in George Paston, *At John Murray's: Records of a Literary Circle, 1843–1892* (London: John Murray, 1932), 78.
[138] John Murray Archive, E.371, E.334, F.87, 88.

original 500 left. Isabel Burton's *Inner Life of Syria* (H. S. King, 1875) sold only 220 copies between May 1875 and the end of 1882. Kegan Paul was nevertheless willing to issue a new edition in 1884, maybe because Captain Burton's works were usually quite profitable.[139]

Ironically, low sales that led to underselling meant that the book could actually reach a wider audience. At the same time, the financial risk—and the fact that the market was 'already overwhelmed with little volumes about palm-trees and camels'[140]—meant that publishers were reluctant to annoy their readers. Murray refused to print Martineau's *Eastern Life*, which he had initially commissioned. The book was seen as a 'conspiracy against Moses', Martineau complained, and Murray's 'clerical clients interfered to compel him to resign the publication'.[141] Murray also failed to recognize the potential of *Eothen*—just like nineteen other publishers.[142] After its great success, Murray admitted to Kinglake that he feared that the 'wicked spirit of jesting at everything, which forms the essence of the book' would have 'raised a clutter and proved for my Colonial Library a place on the list of prohibited books'.[143] Thackeray did not require a publisher's rejection to rewrite his chapter on Jerusalem. His mother sent him 'a letter so full of terror and expostulation, and dread of future consequence for my awful heresy that I have to cancel it and begin afresh'.[144] This is how commercial considerations helped shape the thematic homogeneity of the genre.

Significantly, even with the decrease in prices, travel books were still beyond the reach of most people. John Chapman, a fierce advocate of underselling, explained in 1852 that 'novels, narratives of voyages and travels, and indeed nearly all the most entertaining books' were stretched 'to fit the publisher's Procrustean bed of three volumes per octavo', simply because the publisher knows 'that books of this class *will* be had at almost any price by the few; and in face of the difficulties he has to encounter from the high price and advertising, he finds it easier

---

[139] Davies, 'Warriors and Gentlemen', 134.
[140] Curzon, *Visits to Monasteries*, 5.
[141] Harriet Martineau, *Autobiography* (1877; London: Virago, 1983), ii. 295; Paston, *At John Murray's*, 75–6.
[142] Gettmann, *Victorian Publisher*, 185.
[143] Quoted in de Gaury, *Travelling Gent*, 47.
[144] Thackeray to Charlotte Ritchie, Aug. 1845, in Gordon N. Ray (ed.), *The Letters and Private Papers of William Makepeace Thackeray* (Oxford: Oxford University Press, 1945), ii. 209.

and more profitable to sell 500 copies of a work at a guinea and a half per copy, than 5,000 at half a crown, or 50,000 at a shilling'.[145] As Altick makes clear, the 'benefits of this reduction continued to be limited to the relatively prosperous minority—a steadily expanding minority, but still only a fraction of the population'.[146]

This is also reflected in the price of some of the books we have considered: even though a process of constant reduction is visible, the books—including the half-crown volumes—were still limited, almost exclusively, to middle-class readers.[147] *Eothen* was first offered to the public at 12*s.*, and was later reduced to 5*s.* (1847) and 2*s.* 6*d.* (1851); Thackeray's *Journey from Cornhill* at 6*s.*; Disraeli's *Tancred* cost the standard 31*s.* 6*d.*, later reduced to 15*s.* (1849); altogether it sold a little more than 2,300 copies.[148] Having purchased her house with the first year's proceeds of *Eastern Life*, Martineau urged her publisher, Moxon, to use her share of future profits to cheapen the book: 'I had an earnest desire that it should circulate widely among the less opulent class who were most likely to sympathise with its contents.'[149] The new edition of *Eastern Life* was reduced from 31*s.* 6*d.* to 10*s.* 6*d.* (1850), but this was still an impossible price for working-class readers. It would take years before these texts would become widely available: Altick estimates that only the 1890s saw the ultimate victory of the cheap-book movement.[150]

Of course, even during the 1850s, the greater part of middle- and even upper-middle-class readers did not purchase books. The *Reviews*— the *Quarterly, Edinburgh, Monthly, Critical*, and so forth—dedicated many columns to travel literature, quoting at such length that reading the actual book could seem pointless. Nevertheless, the circulation figures for these quality periodicals seldom passed 10,000, and was often much lower.[151] But most readers did not purchase books simply because they borrowed them. Travel, history, geography, and antiquities had long been favourites with middle- and upper-middle-class library

---

[145] John Chapman, *Cheap Books, and How to Get Them* (London: John Chapman, 1852), 8.
[146] Altick, *English Common Reader*, 286.
[147] The following figures rely on Sampson Low (ed.), *The British Catalogue of Books Published from October 1837 to December 1852* (London: Sampson Low, 1853).
[148] Robert Blake, *Disraeli* (London: Eyre & Spottiswoode, 1966), 193.
[149] Martineau, *Autobiography*, ii. 295–6.
[150] Altick, *English Common Reader*, 316.
[151] Ibid. 392–4.

subscribers.[152] Travel and adventure books accounted for about 16 per cent of volumes acquired by Mudie's circulating libraries between 1853–62;[153] and Mudie's catalogue for 1858 includes nearly all of the travel accounts and geographical studies mentioned here. However, membership of these lending libraries was limited to those who could afford the annual guinea subscription. In 1872 the *Spectator* estimated that the number of 'really comfortable families', those who could afford Mudie's guinea, cannot exceed '60,000 out of the 4,600,000 within Great Britain'.[154]

There are several trends, then, operating simultaneously. On the one hand, the undeniable overflow of Palestine-related titles did not necessarily result in an equally proportionate number of copies. Either because the publishers continued to produce small and expensive editions, or simply because of low, unsatisfactory sales, the number of actual copies in circulation was certainly much less impressive than might have been expected, or indeed, than was believed. Part of this fallacy derives from the fact that up to 100 copies of each new book were sent to journals, periodicals, and newspapers for reviews: as far as the reviewers were concerned, the market must have seemed flooded. Furthermore, unlike novels, travel accounts and geographical studies had a more limited potential to begin with. Even successful studies seldom sold more than 20,000 copies. On the other hand, the reduction in the price of books throughout the first half of the century, and even much later, was of immediate benefit only to an extremely limited stratum of society; and it was precisely this audience which had access to the volumes distributed by the new network of libraries. All this makes travel literature a middle-class genre *par excellence*.

It would be wise to qualify some of these assumptions. As the century progressed, working-class readers found it easier to gain access to borrowed books. It is estimated that by 1850, there were 610 Mechanics' Institute Libraries in England, 4,000 church and chapel libraries established by the SPCK and the RTS, and countless other parish, village, Sunday-school, factory, artisan, and working-men's

---

[152] Paul Kaufman, 'Some Reading Trends in Bristol, 1773–84', in *Libraries and their Users: Collected Papers in Library History* (London: Library Association, 1969), 28–35.
[153] Davies, 'Warriors and Gentlemen', 123.
[154] Guinevere L. Griest, *Mudie's Circulating Library* (London: David & Charles, 1970), 79.

libraries for which no adequate statistics exist.[155] However, as we have seen, the SPCK and the RTS—which supplied the core stock of most church, parish, and school libraries—were slow in adjusting their publications to the geographical exploration of the Holy Land. Of the many books suggested by an 1833 guidebook, outlining the organization of circulating libraries issued by the RTS, only *Manners and Customs of the Jews*, *Scripture Illustrations*, and Keith's *Evidence of the Truth of Prophecy* reflected the new discursive preoccupations.[156]

There were some exceptions. Volney's *Ruins of Empire* was popular among artisans during the 1790s, and its fifteenth chapter, the vision of a 'New Age', was frequently circulated as a tract.[157] Keith's *Evidence* also enjoyed a remarkable success; reprinted more than forty times throughout the century, it was said to be found 'in almost every home and known as a household word throughout the land'.[158] Generally speaking, however, before the 1840s—and probably much afterwards—working men, women, and their children simply did not have access to the books, articles, studies, or paintings representing Palestine as a geographical, Oriental space.

Nowhere is this better illustrated than in Eliot Warburton's preface to the eighth edition of *The Crescent and the Cross*:

The 'cheap excursions' that now open new sources of interest and information to the labouring classes are not confined to mere locomotion on the railroad or the river. Excursions of thought, not less useful, may be made by the artisan, without leaving his own fireside: there seated, in relaxation of physical toil, he may explore Egypt with Belzoni, and Nineveh with Layard, or perform pilgrimage to the Holy Land, as his fathers did in the old times before him. The knowledge and material for thought that were formerly secluded among philosophers and travellers, are now 'laid down,' as it were, like gas and water, at almost every poor man's door.[159]

---

[155] Elizabeth Nicholson, 'Working-Class Readers and Libraries: A Social History, 1800–1850' (MA thesis, University College London, 1976), 1, 32, 101.
[156] *Religious Circulating Libraries, of the RTS* (London: RTS, 1833).
[157] E. P. Thompson, *The Making of the English Working Class* (1963; Harmondsworth: Penguin, 1968), 107–8.
[158] 'Alexander Keith', *DNB*.
[159] Warburton, 'Dedicatory Preface to the 8th edn.', in *The Crescent and the Cross* (16th edn. London: Hurst & Blackett, 1860), pp. iii–iv.

Warburton's book, when first published in 1845, cost 25*s*. By the time this passage was written, in 1850, it was slightly cheaper, available either as a two-volume work (21*s*.) or as one (10*s*. 6*d*.). In this respect, Warburton's analogy between texts and 'gas and water' is most appropriate: the same people who could afford running gas and water were also those who could purchase Warburton's book. That these consumers were the 'poor' seems highly unlikely.

Most English men and women, then, were not exposed, at least not directly, to the language and imagery of this evolving—and highly ambivalent—Anglo-Palestine Orientalist discourse. The only Holy Land available to them was the golden land of pure delight or Bunyan's Jerusalem. If these new representations of the Holy Land as a geographical reality, as a desolate, Oriental, yet strangely familiar space, were to acquire a hegemonic status; if these images were to filter down the social ladder and become truly accessible; if visual and textual travel accounts could really function as a substitute for travel—it was only through the dissemination of cheap, attainable, cultural commodities. And it is only by turning to these popular forms that one can realize the full scope, as well as the limits, of the Orientalist discursive apparatus.

3

Popular Palestine

The Holy Land as Printed Image, Spectacle, and Commodity

Sitting on a roof-top, his eyes fixed on the twilight mist, young Jude Fawley catches his first sight of Christminster's dreaming spires. 'The Heavenly Jerusalem,' murmurs the boy as he gazes at the ancient town of lore; henceforth, through the 'solid barrier of cold cretaceous upland to the northward he was always beholding a gorgeous city—the fancied place he had likened to the New Jerusalem'.[1]

Thomas Hardy's *Jude the Obscure* (1895) depicts a world embedded in biblical and Christian imagery: dashing home, still overwhelmed by his Pisgah sight, the anxious Jude tries not to think of 'Apollyon lying in wait for Christian' (p. 17). Yet, rather than signify the pilgrim's otherworldly aspirations, Jude's New Jerusalem represents a very practical progress: education, cultivation, self-help. Christminster, which acquires 'a tangibility, a permanence, a hold on his life' (p. 18), is the Promised Land of social mobility.

Of course, as with the earthly Jerusalem, the distant view is often deceptive. When he finally settles in Christminster—as a stonemason, not a scholar—Jude visits an 'itinerant exhibition, in the shape of a model of Jerusalem', to which schools were admitted 'at a penny a head in the interests of education'. Jude's cousin, Sue, who is there with her schoolchildren, is not impressed. 'How does anybody know that

---

[1] Thomas Hardy, *Jude the Obscure* (1895), ed. Patricia Ingham, World's Classics (Oxford: Oxford University Press, 1985), 16, 18. Subsequent page numbers are cited parenthetically in the text.

Jerusalem was like this in the time of Christ?,' Sue wonders, just as she discovers Jude, 'his form being bent so low in his intent inspection of the Valley of Jehoshaphat that his face was almost hidden from view by the Mount of Olives.' 'I got so deeply interested that I didn't remember where I was,' blushes Jude when he recognizes his cousin: 'How it carries one back, doesn't it!' (pp. 108–9).

Hinging on the interplay between the two holy cities, this scene is a bitter reminder of Jude's futile quest: obscured by a diminutive Mount of Olives, Jude is no more 'in' the New Jerusalem of Christminster than he is 'in' the Old Jerusalem of Christ. Ironically, the only language in which Jude can imagine his salvation is the language of his oppression: 'Jerusalem' signifies Jude's hope of transcending his designated role within the fixed social order, but it also signifies that fixed social order itself, that moral 'Hebraic' code symbolized here by the educational model. 'I fancy we have had enough of Jerusalem,' Sue proclaims, although—or is it *because*?—she can skilfully draw in chalk 'a perspective view of Jerusalem, with every building shown in its place' (pp. 109–10). A variation on this theme is found later in the novel, when, in the farcical riot that follows Phillotson's dismissal from his school, 'a blackboard was split', 'three panes of the school-windows were broken', and 'a church-warden was dealt such a topper with the map of Palestine that his head went right through Samaria' (pp. 260–1). The comedy derives from the gap between the Holy Land's unmistakable moralistic aura and the Lilliputian proportions of its reproduction. It is as if the narrow-mindedness of the religious code imposed on Phillotson, Sue, and Jude is epitomized by the tiny dimensions of the map of Palestine or the model of Jerusalem, the very tools with which the Church seeks to propagate its control.

Jude's visit to the model of Jerusalem not only typifies the ubiquity and flexibility of biblical language, but also illustrates how the academic Anglo-Palestine Orientalist discourse would eventually become available to a wider audience: 'made after the best conjectural maps, based on actual visits to the city as it now exists' (p. 108), travelling exhibits like Jude's model provided cheap, accessible images of the Holy Land. Whereas the previous chapter has dealt with the cross-fertilization between vernacular traditions and the emergence of academic Orientalism, this chapter moves on to explore academic Orientalism in the context of nineteenth-century mass culture. The first section will look at the cheap illustrated press of the 1830s, particularly the *Penny Magazine* and the *Saturday Magazine*, publications that are now considered to be among the first British mass-market periodicals. I will then turn from textual, two-dimensional, privately consumed representations to visual, three-dimensional, public representations: the panoramas, dioramas, models, and exhibitions of mid and late nineteenth-century culture. Shifting pace and methodology, the third section will focus on the PEF as a case-study highlighting Victorian efforts to popularize the Anglo-Palestine academic discourse. Underlying my analysis is the conviction that this popularization demanded an active process of selection, exclusion, and interpretation, which was shaped by a complex web of religious, social, and commercial interests: just like *The Pilgrim's Progress* or Watts's hymns, these new images of Palestine could mean various things to different people.

What this chapter traces, then, is the creation of a 'universal Holy Land visual literacy', in John Davis's useful phrase.[2] It is precisely the 'universality' of the discourse, however, that I wish to reconsider. As we shall see, representations produced for working-class consumption always stood at one remove behind those available to their betters. In 1847, when Brunetti's celebrated model of ancient Jerusalem was exhibited at the Model Gallery, Piccadilly, thousands flocked to see it; however, with an admittance fee of 1*s.*—6*d.* for children and schools—it was only the more prosperous sector of the middle class that could afford to gaze at the model. Ten years later, those who visited Brunetti's model could purchase a stereoscope and admire Holy Land views in the leisure of their own abode. By the time Hardy was writing *Jude the Obscure*—by the time a model of ancient Jerusalem was available to the schoolchildren of Oxford at a penny a head and the stereoscope was no longer a novelty—the well-to-do were touring Jerusalem with Thomas Cook.

This belatedness meant that the poorer man's and woman's Promised Land continued to be forever deferred. Yet, this deferral was typical of the popular appropriation of the academic discourse as a whole, since, by definition, it could never offer more than a Pisgah sight. 'I have caused thee to see it with thine eyes,' Moses was told on Pisgah as he was

---

[2] John Davis, *The Landscape of Belief: Encountering the Holy Land in Nineteenth-Century American Art and Culture* (Princeton: Princeton University Press, 1996), 73.

gazing at the Promised Land, 'but thou shalt not go over thither' (Deut. 34: 4).[3] Rather than simply denote a geographical Palestine 'out there', these new mass-produced images fed back into the vernacular biblical tradition, and the Holy Land continued to be associated, first and foremost, with the family Bible, the Sunday school, and home.

Penny Palestine: Cheap Magazines and Sunday-School Literature

In 1838, as he was passing through Derbyshire, the radical journalist George Holyoake met a young innkeeper who 'appeared never to have seen a paper with pictures'. Short on cash, Holyoake offered to pay with some copies of the *Penny Magazine*, which 'proved as valuable as glass-beads in dealing with Indians'.[4] Indeed, the *Penny Magazine* (1832–45), edited and published by Charles Knight for the SDUK, offered its readers a remarkable commodity: a rich variety of well-executed wood-cuts for an exceptionally low price. With a peak circulation of 200,000 copies per week, and an estimated readership of one million, the *Penny Magazine* was the first British mass-market periodical.[5]

Confident that these textual glass beads would lure Britain's savages, the SDUK's governing body believed that the dissemination of morally improving and politically innocuous pictorial material was necessary to counteract the disruptive influence of the radical press.[6] It remains unclear whether members of the working class actually read the *Penny Magazine*.[7] One thing, however, is certain: the magazine was *aimed* at the broadest audience possible. That is why the SDUK resolved 'with obvious prudence, to avoid the great subjects of religion and government, on which it was impossible to touch without provoking angry

[3] On the 'Pisgah sight' in Victorian culture see George P. Landow, *Victorian Types, Victorian Shadows: Biblical Typology in Victorian Literature, Art, and Thought* (London: Routledge & Kegan Paul, 1980), esp. ch. 7.
[4] G. J. Holyoake, *Sixty Years of an Agitator's Life* (London: Unwin, 1892), i. 70.
[5] Richard D. Altick, *The English Common Reader: A Social History of the Mass Reading Public, 1800–1900* (1957; 2nd edn. Columbus, Oh.: Ohio State University Press, 1998), 332–9; Patricia Anderson, *The Printed Image and the Transformation of Popular Culture, 1790–1860* (Oxford: Clarendon Press, 1991), 50–83; Scott Bennett, 'Revolutions in Thought: Serial Publications and the Mass Market for Reading', in Joanne Shattock and Michael Wolff (eds.), *The Victorian Periodical Press: Samplings and Soundings* (Leicester: Leicester University Press, 1982), 225–57.
[6] Bennett, 'Revolutions in Thought', 226; Anderson, *Printed Image*, 46.
[7] Patricia Anderson, '"Factory Girl, Apprentice and Clerk"—The Readership of Mass-Market Magazines 1830–60', *Victorian Periodicals Review*, 25/2 (1992), 67.

discussion'.[8] Since religious controversy would have limited the *Penny Magazine*'s readership, religious themes were carefully avoided.

A throng of competing publications soon followed. One of the *Penny*'s main rivals, the *Saturday Magazine* (1832–44), was published by the SPCK, whose directors were determined not to leave 'a constant, direct and extensive influence over the minds and feelings of the reading multitude in the hands of those who are . . . either indifferent to religion or hostile to its institutions'.[9] Both the *Penny Magazine* and the *Saturday Magazine* sought to provide cheap, instructive illustrated non-fiction. However, while the former was eager to avoid all religious polemic, the latter employed an unequivocal Anglican tenor. It is precisely this clear-cut ideological distinction between Britain's two pioneering mass-market magazines—and the Societies that produced them—that makes a comparative reading of their depiction of the Holy Land so appropriate to our analysis.[10]

The *Penny Magazine*, the SDUK, and Charles Knight

Two weeks after it commenced publication, the *Penny Magazine* printed a woodcut of a palm-tree as an illustration for an almanac that noted the approach of Palm Sunday, celebrated to commemorate 'the peaceful entry of Christ into Jerusalem'. 'The date-palm', explained the text, 'is in many respects one of the most valuable trees of the East, affording sustenance to its immense population, and cheering a sterile region by its beauty.'[11] That the East needs cheering up is of course a typical Orientalist cliché, but the date-palm soon proved a valuable tree for the *Penny Magazine* as well. With this illustration, the magazine—always keen to discuss issues of travel, history, or geography[12]—offered its visually illiterate readers a key; hereafter, the palm-tree would function

---

[8] *Address of the Committee of the SDUK* (London: Charles Knight, 1846), 4.

[9] SPCK Archive, London, SPCK Committee Minutes, 21 May 1832. The magazine sold 80,000, and occasionally even 95,000 copies per week; see Minutes, 3 June 1834, 5 July 1836.

[10] My analysis of the *Penny Magazine* includes all numbers published between 1832 and 1840; the analysis of the *Saturday Magazine* includes all numbers published between 1832 and 1844.

[11] *PenM*, 1 (14 Apr. 1832), 20.

[12] Taken together, articles dealing with travel, history, antiquities, geography, and anthropology accounted for more than 30 per cent of the texts published in the *Penny Magazine*. See Scott Bennett, 'The Editorial Character and Readership of the *Penny Magazine*: An Analysis', *Victorian Periodicals Review*, 17/4 (1984), 133–4.

as a signifier for all things exotic, its instantly recognizable silhouette towering over locales in the Mediterranean, Africa, the Far East, or South America. So, what begins as a commemoration of a Christian festival, Palm Sunday, is quickly harnessed to serve the magazine's secular and scientific agenda: the accumulation of useful facts. Initially associated with Christ's entry into Jerusalem, the image of the palm-tree swiftly becomes an all-inclusive emblem of 'otherness'.

This strategy is typical, as a whole, of the representation of the Holy Land in the *Penny Magazine*: given that references to the 'Holy' were unwelcome, what remained was merely 'Land'. As an article on 'The Pilgrimage of the Middle Ages' stated: 'The Pilgrimage to Palestine, the scene of the sacred history, had the most important influence on the religious spirit of the middle ages, and was sanctioned by the most rational motives. In the present day the Holy Land may properly be regarded as one of the most interesting portions of the globe which a traveller can visit.'[13] To dwell excessively on the land's holiness is to maintain a medievalist logic, a frightful thought for any sensible utilitarian. With its sacred aura denied, Palestine was permitted to function in the *Penny Magazine* simply as one of those 'interesting portions of the globe', often brightened by an occasional palm-tree.

Perhaps the most striking example of this de-sanctification of Palestine is an excerpt from Edward Clarke's travel account (published 1810–23). Clarke, as we have seen, had much to say about the authenticity of the holy places and the view from the Mount of Olives; nevertheless, it is a scene witnessed by him on his way from Jerusalem to Bethlehem that the *Penny Magazine* quotes for its readers:

> Upon the road ... we met an Arab with a goat, which he led about the country for exhibition, in order to gain livelihood for itself and owner. He had taught this animal, while he accompanied its movements with a song, to mount upon little cylindrical blocks of wood, placed successively one above the other.

'Nothing', concludes the editor, 'can show more strikingly the tenacious footing possessed by this quadruped.'[14] And nothing, we might add, says more about the editorial policy of a magazine which invokes the road between the Nativity and Calvary merely to exemplify the marvels of zoology. As this passage indicates, up-to-date Orientalist texts about

---

[13] *PenM*, 5 (11 June 1836), 229.   [14] *PenM*, 1 (9 June 1832), 101.

Palestine were available to the *Penny Magazine*'s editorship; yet, these texts were very seldom employed to inform the readers about the history, geography, or present condition of the Holy Land, a striking exclusion considering the magazine's professed interest in travel and antiquities.

Indeed, the *Penny Magazine* made very few direct references to Palestine in its first few years of publication: Mount Sinai, it seems, was the closest it was willing to go. In 1835, the magazine printed a series of articles based on Burckhardt's *Travels in Syria and the Holy Land* (1822). Dealing with the history of St Catherine's Monastery or the botanical features of the wild Sinai palm-tree, the articles are painstakingly sober and scientific: God is mentioned only once, and in connection with the beliefs of the Arabs; no reference is made to Sinai's religious or even sentimental meaning for the British reader.[15] Significantly, a week after the publication of the first instalment, the magazine included a somewhat peculiar piece entitled 'Popular Prints'. The article informed the readers that 'Wood-cutting is an art which employs whole villages in Russia; but it is of the coarsest and most uncouth description':

> Among others, we have seen a representation of Mount Sinai at the moment of the delivering of the tablets to Moses, but so full of matter, that we must not attempt to describe it. In fact, there is scarcely a single occurrence or character of importance in the Old Testament which is not attempted; and, to crown the whole, we are favoured with a sun-beam, striking straight through Mount Sinai, and darting upon St. Catherine's tomb.

These illustrations are typical of an 'ignorant and superstitious race; any attempt to break in upon them would be but "cutting blocks with a razor"', concludes the writer.[16]

This article, attributed to the *Quarterly Journal of Education* (a more élitist SDUK publication), conveys the Society's suspicion of religious topics. Clearly, attentive readers of the *Penny Magazine* need only compare this account with the previous (or the following) week's woodcut illustration of Mount Sinai, to discern that these are topics that one should handle with great care if one is to avoid displaying ignorance and superstition. Cultivation is hardly to be attained by sketching the events, landscapes, and characters of the Old Testament.

---

[15] *PenM*, 4 (7 Nov. 1835), 433–5; (21 Nov. 1835), 449–52; (5 Dec. 1835), 473.
[16] *PenM*, 4 (14 Nov. 1835), 443.

And if Mount Sinai is to be engraved at all, it must be done in *Penny Magazine* fashion: scientific, sceptical, secular. Lingering in the abundant wilderness of useful information, and refusing to tread Palestine's *terra sancta*, the *Penny Magazine* was offering its mass readership a Pisgah sight only.

The omission of Palestine from the first five volumes of the *Penny Magazine*, far from being accidental, was dictated by the SDUK's specific ideological orientation. It certainly did not represent Charles Knight's own interests: in 1835, Knight was busy preparing his *Pictorial Bible* for publication (1836–8), with John Kitto as editor. Issued in weekly numbers or monthly parts, the *Pictorial Bible* was published by Knight independently, and not in his capacity as the SDUK's official publisher. This fact is significant, because the idea of publishing a cheap illustrated Bible was initially entertained by the SDUK. In August 1832, Lord Brougham, the Society's indefatigable chairman, stated that 'the Publication of a Bible with Notes illustrative of the History, Manners, Natural History and Arts of the period alluded to in that volume, would be eminently useful and consistent with the objects of the society'. He suggested that the work 'might be published in Penny Weekly numbers'.[17] The Committee commissioned three specimen chapters that would demonstrate how 'a store of useful and most interesting information was essentially to be derived from the study of the Bible, by (copious) illustration of accounts of ancient and modern manners, from Natural History, and from the narratives of recent travellers'.[18] Typically, rather than employ recent Orientalist surveys to highlight the truth of Scripture, the SDUK was proposing the opposite: to derive useful information from the Bible by employing it in the service of recent Orientalist study. This, after all, was precisely the logic that would inform Edward Lane's *Account of the Manners and Customs of the Modern Egyptians*, subsidized and published by the SDUK in 1835.[19]

---

[17] University College London, SDUK Papers, General Committee Minutes, 8 Aug. 1832.

[18] SDUK Papers, 'Special Topics' [52] (Penny Bible), memorandum by Brougham, 12 Sept. 1832.

[19] Published as part of the SDUK's Library of Entertaining Knowledge, Lane's study was issued in two volumes at 4*s*. 6*d*. each. Books published in the SDUK's Library of Useful Knowledge usually cost only 6*d*. each.

Mr Penrose, who submitted the three sample chapters to the SDUK's Committee members, was baffled by their 'implied opinion' that any reference to elementary Christian teaching should be excluded: 'It cannot be their meaning to bring forward a Bible which can be *justly* liable to the charge of coldness of poverty either of thought or feeling,' he protested.[20] But this, of course, was precisely their meaning. In his memoirs, Knight observed that Brougham's Penny Bible 'was given up as impracticable, and not in accordance with the principles upon which the Society was established'.[21] This proto-popularized form of higher biblical criticism was unacceptable in the 1830s; and a godly Bible simply did not figure in the SDUK's plans.

As a result, Knight had to undertake the enterprise alone. His *Pictorial Bible* contained its fair share of useful information, with fine wood engravings 'representing the historical events, after celebrated pictures', 'landscape scenes', and 'subjects of natural history, costume, and antiquities, from the best sources'.[22] The links between Knight's Bible and his work for the SDUK were also manifested visually, as woodcuts travelled freely from the *Penny Magazine* to the *Pictorial Bible*. However, with a consistent Evangelical tone (Kitto had travelled to the East twice as a missionary),[23] and with the weekly numbers priced at 6*d*., the *Pictorial Bible* was not the popular penny publication that Brougham had envisaged.[24] Knight's private project—with its wealth of contemporary Holy Land imagery—thus stood, both commercially and thematically, outside the mass-produced discourse generated by Knight for the SDUK.

Knight and Kitto continued to collaborate, independently of the SDUK, in the publication of *The Pictorial History of Palestine* (1839), *Palestine: The Physical Geography and Natural History of the Holy Land* (1841), and *The Pictorial Sunday Book* (1845). Kitto went on to become one of the great popularizers of scriptural geography. His numerous

---

[20] SDUK Papers, 'Special Topics' [52], 'Extract from the letter accompanying the three specimen chapters'.
[21] Charles Knight, *Passages of a Working Life* (London: Bradbury & Evans, 1864), ii. 252.
[22] John Kitto (ed.), *The Pictorial Bible* (London: Charles Knight, 1836–8), i. p. i.
[23] 'John Kitto', *DNB*.
[24] The monthly parts were priced at 2*s*., the first volume at 17*s*. 6*d*., the second and third at 20*s*.; Altick (*English Common Reader*, 283) is thus correct in claiming that the Bible was limited to the fairly well-to-do.

publications varied in scope, illustration, and price. At least one of them, *The History of Palestine*, became a standard Sunday-school textbook; three others were published by the RTS. Passages from Kitto's biblical works were sometimes published in the *Penny Magazine*, especially after 1837, when, following a decline in circulation, Knight made some editorial changes. The magazine now ventured into the Holy Land more often, though never forsaking its ardent pursuit of useful information.

The cover of number 344, for example, boasted a woodcut of 'Pilgrims in the Desert', who 'have lost their way in that "waste and howling wilderness!" ' (see Fig. 2). The text included excerpts from Tasso, Chateaubriand, and Lamartine which illustrated the difficulties facing those unhappy pilgrims who travel the 'long and circuitous journey from Europe to Jerusalem'. Still, rather than depict the geography of Palestine or reveal the truth of scriptural prophecy, the article employs these excerpts to demonstrate the terrible effects of heat and thirst on the human body. The point is neither theological nor geographical, but simply physiological. And perhaps it is not even that: 'We may now be enabled', explains the text, 'in some measure, to enter into the spirit of the design which heads the present article.' The writer concludes by providing a moving account of the unfortunate pilgrims in the engraving, 'from a beautiful lithographic print, after a picture by Stilke,—one of the ornaments of the modern German school of painting'.[25] By this stage it becomes clear that all this useful information had been accumulated simply to convey the mental and physical state of the helpless figures in the print, and thus develop the readers' capacity to share the rewards of aesthetic experience.

This brings us to the one method of representing Palestine on which there was no disagreement between Knight and the SDUK: the reproduction of the Old Masters' biblical works. As Patricia Anderson has shown, replicas of high art, often accompanied by detailed discussions of aesthetic theories and art history, were considered an exceptionally wholesome ingredient in the *Penny Magazine*'s recipe for self-improvement.[26] In December 1832, for example, with the publication of 'Christ Delivering the Keys to St. Peter', the magazine launched a series of woodcuts based on Raphael's biblical cartoons, allowing the 'thousands

---

[25] *PenM*, 6 (12 Aug. 1837), 305–7.   [26] Anderson, *Printed Image*, 67–78.

THE PENNY MAGAZINE

OF THE

Society for the Diffusion of Useful Knowledge.

344.]　　　PUBLISHED EVERY SATURDAY.　　　[August 12, 1837.

PILGRIMS IN THE DESERT*.

[Pilgrims in the Desert.]

THE long and circuitous journey from Europe to Jerusalem, by Constantinople, through Asia, frequently adopted by pilgrims in the earlier ages, was one of extraordinary toil and danger. After the occupation of Palestine by the Crusaders, it became comparatively an easy task to visit Jerusalem—the pilgrims had only to take shipping for one of the sea-ports; and it was for this reason, amongst others, that the Crusaders held so tenaciously the sea-coast of Palestine. When no longer masters of Jerusalem, they made Acre, which is about seventy miles distant from it, their capital. The fall of Acre was the final loss of the Holy Land. "A motive of avarice or fear," says Gibbon, "still opened the holy sepulchre to some devout and defenceless pilgrims, but a mournful and solitary silence prevailed along the coast which had so long resounded with the world's debate."

Another route was to cross the sandy and generally sterile country which lies between Egypt and Palestine, and which constitutes a portion of the Great Desert of Egypt or Arabia. This desert extends as far into Palestine as close to the walls of Jaffa (the ancient Joppa), the coast-line being covered with sandy hills. The journey from Cairo to Jaffa is calculated as occupying from twelve to fifteen days. With proper care this journey, though attended with some privations, is not a dangerous one. Indeed, Burckhardt says that accidents or misfortunes arising from the want of water, that most grievous of all calamities in "a dry and thirsty land where no water is," must, in general, "arise from a want of proper precaution." But Burckhardt speaks as a hardy and seasoned traveller. Cases must

* A general view of the "Pilgrimages of the Middle Ages" has been given in No. 269 vol. v., of the 'Penny Magazine.'

VOL. VI.　　　　　　　　　　　　　　　　　　　　　　　　2 R

of persons who have never seen the original, or even engravings of them, to judge of the grandeur and beauty of these noble compositions' (see Fig. 3).[27] According to the *Penny Magazine*, it was the ability to recognize grandeur and beauty—not Christian truth or even scriptural history and geography—which was the key to moral and social advancement.

Images of the Holy Land were thus once again employed to encourage the cultivation of industriousness and frugality; whereas Methodist hymnology imagined the Promised Land as a glorified afterlife, the *Penny Magazine* offered its readers visual depictions of the biblical landscape. Nevertheless, by choosing to mass-produce these Renaissance representations of the Holy Land, and, at the same time, suppress the contemporary imagery of Palestine's scenery which appeared in the new travel accounts, this was a belated visualization only. State-of-the-art printing technology was employed to evoke the artistic ethos of bygone generations. The *Penny Magazine*'s readers were encouraged to visualize the Holy Land in terms long obsolete, as one vernacular Orientalist vision was replaced by another.

The *Pictorial Bible* presents a more complex case. Knight spared no expense in reproducing dozens of works by Great Masters, past and present, including Raphael, Veronese, Rubens, Poussin, Reynolds, and many others. The protagonists of the Old Testament are shown to dwell in wooden cabins, and the landscape is unmistakably European. Michelangelo's 'Elijah in the desert', for example, shows the old prophet musing by a waterfall, in a leafy forest, with not a palm-tree in sight (see Fig. 4). In sharp contrast to the *Penny Magazine*, however, art reproductions in the *Pictorial Bible* appeared alongside contemporary illustrations of Palestine's landscape, adapted from the work of early nineteenth-century travellers like Cassas or Forbin. In a later work, *The Gallery of Scripture Engravings* (1846), Kitto explained that the Old Masters simply had no access to accurate representations of the Holy Land:

> The best course that remains to us is, therefore, to take the sacred historical pictures in which the ANCIENTS excelled, and the sacred landscapes in which WE excel—or rather, which we alone possess—and exhibit them together under some such combination as that which the present work affords.[28]

---

[27] *PenM*, 1 (1 Dec. 1832), 348, 350.
[28] John Kitto, *The Gallery of Scriptural Engravings* (London: Peter Jackson, 1846), i. 1.

Fig. 3. 'Christ Delivering the Keys to St. Peter', engraving after Raphael, *Penny Magazine*, 1 December 1832.

Fig. 4. 'Elijah in the Desert', engraving after Michelangelo, in *Pictorial Bible* (London: Charles Knight, 1836–9).

This sort of stereoscopic mental projection was quite a demanding exercise, suitable, perhaps, for those readers who could afford the *Gallery*, published in three volumes at 21*s*. each. Indeed, as we have already seen, readers of the *Penny Magazine* were not advised to take a similar route, not least because the magazine did not provide any images of the 'sacred landscapes in which WE excel'. With the imagery of the geographical Holy Land deferred, their pennyworth view was merely a Pisgah sight.

On the one hand, then, the *Penny Magazine* demonstrates the discursive diffusion of academic Orientalism. By citing the works of Chateaubriand, Clarke, and their fellow travellers, the magazine introduced its million readers to the language employed to discuss the East, with topics ranging from an article about Bedouin Arabs who 'are robbers by profession' to the 'Palace of Ibrahim Pasha as seen from the River Nile'.[29] However, this flow of ideas from the élite to the street was far from unmediated. Since the SDUK was determined to shun all religious subject-matters, the Holy Land had to be divorced from the sentimental and religious spheres and reinvented as 'useful'—either scientific or aesthetic—knowledge. The fact that the *Penny Magazine* did not abound with representations of Palestine suggests that this discursive dislocation was not easily feasible. The Holy Land seldom surfaced in the contemporary Orient that the magazine was charting for its readers; and Jerusalem, the heart of the land, was never illustrated in the *Penny Magazine*, either textually or visually.

The *Saturday Magazine* and Sunday-school curriculum

In many ways, the *Saturday Magazine*'s depiction of the East was not very different from that of its utilitarian rival: it reproduced works of high art that represented biblical themes (though more inclined towards the huge contemporary canvases of Francis Danby and John Martin);[30] it often employed the image of the never-changing East, forever preserving biblical customs and costumes;[31] and it showed a curious fascination with the date-palm tree.[32]

---

[29] *PenM*, 3 (14 June 1834), 227; 5 (16 Jan. 1836), 17.
[30] Cf. *SatM*, 3 (5 Jan. 1833), 1–2; 6 (14 Mar. 1835), 97.
[31] See, *inter alia*, 'The Water Bottles of the East', *SatM*, 1 (4 Aug. 1832), 44; 'Eastern Hand-Mills for Grinding Corn' (25 Aug. 1832), 65.
[32] Cf. *SatM*, 2 (May 1833), 201; 4 (15 Mar. 1834), 102.

Committed to the dissemination of 'useful' information, the *Saturday Magazine* was nevertheless concerned above all with the promotion of Christian knowledge; and whereas the SDUK was reluctant to enter the Holy Land, the SPCK trod it happily, offering its readers a broad range of images and texts which described the present appearance of Palestine, from Mount Tabor and the Sea of Galilee to Bethlehem and the Dead Sea.[33] The emphasis was always on scriptural history and geography, often citing recent travel accounts which testified to the fallen state of the land. In some cases, an effort was made to link up current events. In November 1840, for example, following the British bombardment of Mohammed Ali's rebel forces in Beirut and Acre, the magazine embarked on a series of articles about the Syrian coast, a topic which 'can only be appreciated by the classical scholar, or the Biblical or historical student'.[34] It is hardly surprising, then, that the first distinct visual image of the Holy Land that appeared in the *Saturday* was the one so painstakingly avoided by the *Penny*: the cover of the September 1833 supplement showed a panoramic view of Jerusalem, with all eight pages of that number devoted exclusively to the Holy City.[35] The article is well worth exploring, for it manifests many of the features that characterize the popularization of the high Orientalist discourse in the *Saturday Magazine* and, broadly speaking, in the work of the SPCK and other religious societies until the early 1850s.

Following a lengthy historical account, the article turns to discuss the 'Present Appearance and Condition of the City'. Its description of the glorious view from the Mount of Olives captures the inevitable anxieties awakened by the English encounter with the earthly Jerusalem: the common disappointment with the appearance of the city, which 'is found, on entering its streets, to be badly built, and to present all those signs of poverty which mark the united reign of tyranny and superstition', and the Protestant abhorrence of the Catholic Holy Sepulchre, 'the result of gross superstition'.[36] It is only by distancing oneself from the ill-paved streets and Catholic shrines, claims the *Saturday Magazine*, that the traveller can overcome these theological and aesthetic trials; the Pisgah sight is much preferable to the site itself. This spatial withdrawal is then enhanced by a temporal one, since 'it is not with the

[33] Cf. *SatM*, 4 (3 May 1834), 171; 9 (10 Dec. 1836), 230.
[34] *SatM*, 17 (7 Nov. 1840), 180.
[35] *SatM*, 3 suppl. (Sept. 1833), 121.   [36] Ibid. 126, 127.

city, as it now exists, that the observer has any real concern'. In other words, the article sets out to describe the 'present appearance and condition of the city', only to renounce them as irrelevant, if not distracting. It claims that in order to be appreciated properly—indeed, to be appreciated at all—the city should always be perceived typologically, as a reflection of either the past or the future; either as 'the hallowed cradle of [our] faith' or the 'allowed prophetic type of that Eternal City, in which the glorious anticipations of devout hope will have their perfect consummation', as the first paragraph points out.[37] At the same time as it professes to carry them closer to the actual, geographical Holy Land, the *Saturday Magazine* constantly distances its readers from it. The earthly Jerusalem is offered, only to be instantly denied.

Of course, by insisting on these spatial and temporal withdrawals, the magazine was merely rehearsing the standard tactics devised by the travellers themselves, from Clarke's claim, back in 1801, that it is only when viewed from a distance that Jerusalem presents a truly rewarding view, to A. P. Stanley's assertion that it is the heavenly Jerusalem which is 'the mother of us all'. We should not forget, however, that Clarke delivered his verdict as he was making his way towards the city, or that Stanley's exegesis was in fact an apologia, aimed to justify his own presence in the earthly Jerusalem as guide to the Prince of Wales. It was one thing to read the landscape typologically when one was actually there; and, as I have suggested in the previous chapter, this sort of withdrawal could in fact lead to an altogether broader claim over the land. But when the readers of the *Saturday Magazine* were denied a proper view of the earthly Jerusalem, it was not merely the view of the actual city in the East—which they could never have hoped to visit in the first place—but of their pennyworth account as well. It is telling that parallel to travel accounts of the Holy Land, the *Saturday Magazine* often printed hymns and short passages which continued to imagine a Jerusalem of golden promise, a Canaan beyond the clouds and beyond the tomb, which simply cannot be visualized: 'Dreams cannot picture a world so fair—/ Sorrow and death may not enter there,' in the words of Mrs Hemans.[38]

---

[37] Ibid. 126, 122.
[38] *SatM*, 2 (23 Mar. 1833), 107. Michael Wheeler has noted that from the 1850s onwards, there was a growing tendency, especially in urban communities, to embrace the idea of heaven as a rural space. Other interpretations, influenced by Swedenborg, emphasized the hope of a family reunion, or a heaven of cheerful children. Nevertheless,

The question of visualization is significant, because the magazine's reluctance to allow its readers that extra mile—from the Mount of Olives to the actual city, or, typologically speaking, from the heavenly Jerusalem to the earthly Jerusalem—was reflected in its selection of illustrations. Apart from the large engraving on the front cover, and two smaller woodcuts on the back (depicting the pool of Bethesda and the Holy Sepulchre), the September 1833 supplement included six full pages of densely packed text. The cover illustration, furthermore, showing a view of the city from the Mount of Olives, is false both topographically and architecturally, as it aggrandizes the Church of the Holy Sepulchre to overshadow the Mosque of Omar (see Fig. 5).[39] This was more than just an isolated case. All in all, illustrations of Palestine in the *Saturday Magazine* were often crude or simply inaccurate. The engraving of the 'Valley of Jehoshaphat', for example, depicts the Jaffa Gate, at the opposite side of the city, and throws in a dramatic crag, adorned with palm-trees (see Fig. 6).[40]

The *Saturday Magazine*'s readers were probably not aware of these errors or embellishments, and there is little reason to suspect that this knowledge would have shaken their fundamental belief in the tangibility of the earthly Jerusalem. After all, the visual representation, erroneous or not, rendered the Holy Land a geographical place, as 'real' as any of the numerous countries and regions illustrated in the magazine. Nevertheless, it is difficult to believe that the editors and writers—who were no doubt acquainted with the latest travel accounts and geographical surveys—were unaware of these distortions. These inaccurate, blurred, or second-rate woodcuts of Palestine could well have been the result of negligence or financial constraints, but they were also the graphic equivalents of the conviction that an encounter

---

images of the afterlife as Promised Land, celestial city, or simply 'Jerusalem' persisted well through the century. 'Jerusalem the Golden', one of the most popular Victorian hymns, was written in 1858 (trans. by John Mason Neale from Bernard of Morlaix's 1046 original). See Michael Wheeler, *Heaven, Hell and the Victorians* (Cambridge: Cambridge University Press, 1994), 130–1. See also Frances Knight, *The Nineteenth-Century Church and English Society* (Cambridge: Cambridge University Press, 1995), 57–60.

[39] The engraving is based on a work by Luigi Mayer (1755–1803), published in Britain in 1804. See Yehoshua Ben-Arieh, *Painting Palestine in the Nineteenth Century* (Tel-Aviv: Yad Izhak Ben-Zvi, 1992), 17, 19 [Hebrew].

[40] *SatM*, 15 (21 Sept. 1839), 112.

Fig. 5. 'View of Jerusalem', *Saturday Magazine*, September 1833.

THE VALLEY OF JEHOSHAPHAT.

This ancient burying-place of the Jewish people possesses much interest, on account of its vicinity to and connection with Jerusalem, and also for the very general belief of the Jews to this day, that here the prophecy of Joel (chap. iii, 2—12) concerning the final judgment of all nations, will be literally fulfilled. The followers of Mahomet are also looking for the appearance of their prophet in this identical spot; and it is even said that they have prepared for him a seat on the ledge of a rock, from whence they expect to receive sentence at his hands. This valley has been for ages the favourite burying-place of the Jews, who at the present time will give a large sum of money for permission to inter their dead in the tomb of their fathers. The valley of Jehoshaphat is also called in Scripture "the valley of Shaveh," "the Kings' dale or valley," and "the valley of Melchizedek." It is a deep and narrow glen, on the east of Jerusalem, having on one side Mount Moriah, on the other the Mount of Olives.

The aspect of the valley is sad and desolate: the brook Cedron flows through it from north to south, and shows, by the dull red tint it assumes, that it has partaken of the nature of the soil over which it passes. The name of this brook, and of the neighbouring Mount of Olives, recall to mind the most touching event of all which are recorded in the sacred writings, viz., the bitter suffering and anguish of soul endured by the Saviour of men on the night previous to his crucifixion, an anguish little to be understood by those who, not being partakers of his sinless nature, cannot possibly conceive of the extent of suffering induced by the imputation of the sins of a whole world, and the wrath of an offended God. The Mount of Olives is barren and sombre in its appearance: here and there a few black and withered vines may be seen on its sides; there are also several tufts of stunted olive-trees, while ruins of chapels, oratories, and mosques, increase the air of desolation with which these scenes are marked.

Among the tombs of the valley of Jehoshaphat, there is one of extraordinary size, which is called "the sepulchre of the Blessed Virgin." It is the largest of all the caves in the vicinity of Jerusalem, and was doubtless hewn out for the burial of some person of distinguished rank, or of high estimation among the people. The traveller Pococke thinks it likely to have been the burial-place of Melisendis, queen of Jerusalem; for the authorities for assigning it to the Virgin Mary are very questionable, and it appears improbable that the early Christians should have had it in their power to erect so magnificent a tomb to her memory. In this cave the Christian sects have each an altar, and even the Turks have an oratory. There are also appropriate chapels in the same cave, to mark the supposed tombs of Joseph, the husband of Mary, and of her parents, Joachim and Anna.

The descent to the cave is by a flight of fifty marble steps, each step being twenty feet wide. These are supposed by Dr. Clarke to be of equal antiquity with the cave itself, though no era can be fixed on with certainty as the date of their construction. There are other sepulchres, said to be those of Jehoshaphat, Absalom, St. James, Zachariah, &c., some of them adorned by columns, which appear to support the edifice, but are in fact hewn out from the solid rock into architectural forms. That of Absalom exhibits twenty-four semi-columns of the Doric order, not fluted; six on each front of the monument. The sepulchre of Jehoshaphat, said to have been prepared by order of that king, as the place of his own interment, and from which the valley takes its name, is a grot, the door of which is finely executed, and is its chief ornament.

Across the brook Cedron is a bridge, of a single arch, called St. Stephen's, which is, however, unnecessary during the greater part of the year; for the Cedron dries up, and leaves a perfectly dry channel, excepting after the fall of heavy rains. The barrenness of the whole scene, the silence of the neighbouring city of Jerusalem, the ruinous state of the tombs, with the remembrances connected with this spot, are indeed sufficient to excite a melancholy interest in the valley of Jehoshaphat.

The general desire for education, and the general diffusion of it, is working, and partly has worked, a great change in the habits of the mass of the people. And though it has been our lot to witness some of the inconveniences necessarily arising from the transition state, where gross ignorance has been superseded by a somewhat too rapid communication of instruction, dazzling the mind, perhaps, rather than enlightening it, yet every day removes something of this evil. Presumption and self-sufficiency are sobered down by the acquirement of useful knowledge, and men's minds become less arrogant in proportion as they better informed. There cannot be a doubt, therefore, but that any evils which may have arisen from opening the flood-gates of education, if I may so say, will quickly flow away, and that a clear and copious stream will succeed, fertilizing the heretofore barren intellect with its wholesome and perennial waters.—BISHOP RYDER.

LONDON:
JOHN WILLIAM PARKER, WEST STRAND.
PUBLISHED IN WEEKLY NUMBERS, PRICE ONE PENNY, AND IN MONTHLY PARTS, PRICE SIXPENCE.

with the Holy Land demands a constant process of withdrawal; that the distant view is all.

So, while the magazine's cheap visual imagery undoubtedly contributed to the concretization of the Holy Land, it was nevertheless a representation vague enough to allow 'Jerusalem' to remain an ambiguous concept, at the very least. 'I have caused thee to see it with thine eyes, but thou shalt not go over thither': the readers of the *Saturday Magazine*, who, unlike Moses, were gazing not at the land itself but at a textual/visual reconstruction of it, were often encouraged not to look at all. Perhaps this is why eighty weekly numbers of the *Saturday Magazine* were issued before Jerusalem was finally reached, and why Egypt figured much more prominently in the magazine. One wonders, furthermore, whether the difficulty in illustrating the Holy Land could help explain why the SPCK was equally frustrated in its attempts to publish 'in Parts and Numbers, an Edition of the Holy Scriptures, in the most cheap and popular form, with notes and illustrations': first entertained in 1832, the idea was finally abandoned in 1840, probably due to doctrinal disagreements regarding the 'proposed commentary for the poor'.[41]

This reluctance to allow believers to indulge in the scenery of the earthly land, and the complementary conviction that they should direct their attention to the heavenly city instead, were certainly not limited to the *Saturday Magazine*, or even to the SPCK. Consider, for example, John Kitto's *The Land of Promise* (1851), published by the RTS, which provides a detailed *Topographical Description of the Principal Places in Palestine... Embracing the Researches of the Most Recent Travellers*. 'It is impossible not to feel a deep interest in that land,' Kitto admits in his 'Concluding Observations', before radically changing his tune: 'Palestine is not *now* a favoured land. It is not now nearer to God than England, nor is Jerusalem than London.' What had once been 'the Lord's chosen land' had lost its distinction. 'Those who find their religious emotions greatly quickened by the contemplation of, or a visit to, any place or external object, have much need to pray,' Kitto cautions. The lesson is crystal-clear: 'To every true believer in Jesus belongs a "new Jerusalem," a "heavenly Jerusalem," a "Jerusalem coming down from heaven"... That is "the city of the Great King";... and

---

[41] SPCK Archive, London, SPCK Committee Minutes, 2 Oct. 1832, 1 Jan. 1833.

our concern is comparatively small indeed with the town of el-Kuds—that high seat of Moslem worship among the mountains of Judea.'[42]

It is impossible to determine whether Kitto was mechanically rehearsing the obligatory conventions of Protestant narratives, or whether he was driven by a genuine religious impulse. What is important is Kitto's inability to produce a popular rendering of the high Orientalist discourse without returning, eventually, to the vernacular Orientalist position, with its insistence on an accessible, domesticated Jerusalem, to which the Holy City in the Middle East is wholly irrelevant. Kitto was all too happy to designate the earthly city 'el-Kuds', and thus distinguish it from 'Jerusalem'. Appropriately, he ended his book with the hymn 'Jerusalem, My Happy Home'.

The same impetus informed at least some aspects of the Sunday- and day-school curricula, manifested in a wide array of works across the educational spectrum. In 1825, for example, the Sunday-school periodical, *Teacher's Offering*, organized an essay competition on the subject of 'Sacred Geography'. Master Robert Fletcher, age 15, concluded his prize-winning essay with the words:

> let our thoughts and imaginations follow him from *this land of promise on earth* to the *new Jerusalem*—the *Heavenly Canaan*, which he had gone before to prepare for us. Keeping this new and better country in prospect, 'whither the forerunner has for us entered,' let us trace his footsteps, that we, with all the redeemed, may enter into '*that rest*, which remaineth for the people of God.'[43]

By a happy coincidence, young Master Fletcher was the son of one of the contest's referees, which may explain his remarkably dutiful dismissal of the earthly city.[44]

'Sacred Geography' was becoming a substantial item on the Sunday-school syllabus.[45] Mrs Trimmer's crude biblical prints, popular in the 1780s, were still being reissued in 1840; but they were gradually supplemented, and eventually replaced, by a range of works which drew on contemporary travel accounts, from John Hewlett's *Concise History of the Jews . . . With a Map of Palestine for the Use of Schools* (1813)

---

[42] John Kitto, *The Land of Promise* (London: RTS, 1851), 317–19.
[43] Revd H. F. Burder (ed.), *Juvenile Essays which Obtained the Prizes Proposed by the Proprietor of the* Teacher's Offering (London: Francis Westley, 1825), 61.
[44] Ibid. p. viii.
[45] Peter Gordon and Denis Lawton, *Curriculum Change in the Nineteenth and Twentieth Centuries* (London: Hodder & Stoughton, 1978), 98–106.

to Thomas Applegate's *Sacred Geography and History* (1839). Few teachers would have disagreed with William Lunday, author of the *Geographical Class Book of Palestine* (1849), when he stated that 'there is no branch of learning more calculated to induce the youthful mind to cherish respect and veneration for the Sacred Writings, than the proper unfolding of Scripture Geography'.[46]

This, however, was easier said than done. In 1840, for example, the Revd Edward Field, a school inspector for the National Society, noted in his 'Report on the State of Parochial Education in the Diocese of Salisbury', that the 'geography of the Holy Land is beginning to be pretty commonly studied by means of maps, so far at least as to distinguish the places referred to in the Gospels'. He was sorry, however, to observe that while the 'history of the Bible is always considered to a certain extent in reading it', he found 'very few instances of an attempt to enlarge the study beyond the mere elementary outline of great changes and events'.[47] Scriptural geography was very often taught independently of any broader geographical or historical context.[48] Consequently, even when a map of Palestine was available, it was not altogether clear how the child was to be shown—as the author of *Peter Parley's Method of Telling about the Geography of the Bible* (1839) had insisted—that 'Jerusalem still exists'.[49]

In his *Biblical Reading Book for Schools and Families* (1849), John Beard advised teachers to have their children 'draw Maps on their slates, first by the eye, and finally by memory. Draw for them first, on a large black board, a blank or outline Map. Direct them to put in, first the rivers, then the hills, and then the chief towns. For success in this, they must go over the exercise many times.'[50] This method was perhaps dull, but undoubtedly effective. James Bonwick—who, in 1823, at the age of

---

[46] William Lunday, *Geographical Class Book of Palestine, for the Use of Sabbath and Day Schools* (London: A. Hall, 1849), p. iii.

[47] *Twenty-Ninth Annual Report of the National Society for Promoting the Education of the Poor...* (London: Rivington, 1840), 127.

[48] Jonathan Rose, *The Intellectual Life of the British Working Classes* (2001; New Haven: Yale University Press, 2002), 341–52.

[49] Revd Samuel Blair, *Peter Parley's Method of Telling about the Geography of the Bible* (London: James S. Hodson, 1839), p. iii.

[50] John R. Beard, *A Biblical Reading Book for Schools and Families* (London: Simpkin, 1849), p. vi.

6, was sent to a school in Southwark 'where biblical instruction had the first place of importance'—recalled how even

> Lord Brougham, when at our Annual Examination, was struck with this feature, and afterwards narrated his experience before the House of Lords, saying, 'I saw a boy take a slate, without having any copy, and, solely from memory, trace upon it the outline of Palestine and Syria, marking out all the variations of the coast, the bays, harbours and creeks, inserting the towns and rivers, and adding their ancient as well as modern names....'.[51]

Bearing in mind the Oxford don who could not point to Egypt, this is a remarkable feat indeed. At the same time, it is impossible to guess what this cartographic image actually meant to the boy, considering that no attempt was made to position Palestine within a more comprehensive framework. 'We learned what happened to a small but partially civilized nation two or three thousand years ago,' Bonwick himself noted, but 'of Egypt, Assyria, India, Greece, Rome, or even England, we knew nothing.'[52] How, then, could children be made to understand the topographical reality of a foreign land? David Stow, author of the *Manual for Sabbath School Teachers and Parents* (1838) addressed this problem when he explained that

> [p]icturing out in words is one great object and end in view, in conducting Bible Instruction. It is to give the children a clear perception of the subject of the lesson in the variety of its shades, mentally, in words, as if they saw it before their bodily eyes, in a picture, or by objects.... In Scripture history or geography, objects such as the following require to be pictured out—Zion Hill, Lake of Gennesaret, Brook Kedron, &c. We cannot bring a mountain, or a lake, river, or brook, into the class-room, as objects; but every child, however ignorant, must have seen a hill, or rising ground, a pool of water, and a running stream, with which those may be compared, in their mental vision.

'The real object, in many cases, when presented to the eye may assist, but is limited,' Stow concludes: 'whereas picturing out in words is expansive, and as unlimited as language itself.'[53]

---

[51] James Bonwick, *An Octogenarian's Reminiscences* (1902), quoted in John Burnett, *Destiny Obscure: Autobiographies of Childhood, Education, and Family from the 1820s to the 1920s* (1982; London: Routledge, 1994), 172.

[52] Bonwick, *Octogenarian's Reminiscences*, quoted in Rose, *Intellectual Life*, 346.

[53] David Stow, *Bible Training: A Manual for Sabbath School Teachers and Parents* (1838; 9th edn. Edinburgh: Thomas Constable, 1859), 207–8.

Whether Stow's method was exceptionally effective or influential is difficult to assess. It does, however, expose the limits and limitations of the geographical imagination. 'Peter Parley' urged teachers to introduce the pupils to 'the hills, mountains, rivers, and valleys where Christ and his disciples met, or preached, or journeyed';[54] but it seems, according to Stow, that the pupils could only picture the hills, mountains, rivers, and valleys that they themselves had seen. Claiming that pictorial evidence is effective to a restricted degree only, what Stow is essentially suggesting is imagining the topography of Palestine by employing the features of local topography, imagining the Oriental by using the vernacular. Which begs the question: if even geography lessons were dependent on this sort of manœuvre, how could children picture Mrs Alexander's 'green hill far away' in terms other than their own familiar, neighbouring, green and pleasant hills?

A delightful anecdote suggests what could happen when the perspective was reversed. Visiting Jerusalem in 1855, Mary Eliza Rogers enjoyed the company of Constance Finn, young daughter of the British consul. Born and bred in Jerusalem, the girl had never left her home; little wonder that her mental image of England was conspicuously similar to the Palestinian landscape: 'I showed to Constance an engraving of an English sea-side view, and she immediately said, pointing to a castle, "There's the tower of David; and again, pointing to the bathing machines, exclaimed, "These are the tombs of the kings, and there is the Dead Sea," the only sea which she had ever seen.'[55]

A political pilgrim's progress

Given the unabashed civilizing ethos which inspired organizations like the SDUK and the SPCK, their representations of the Holy Land could be understood as an exercise in 'social control', which rephrases—or suppresses, or obscures—the high Orientalist discourse in order to inculcate virtue, whether in the form of 'useful' knowledge or Christian values. Nevertheless, it is important to note that throughout this period, radical writers, precisely those who seemed most in need of a wholesome pictorial pamphlet, employed the very same imagery, and in very much

---

[54] Blair, *Peter Parley's Method*, p. v.
[55] Mary Eliza Rogers, *Domestic Life in Palestine* (1862; London: Kegan Paul, 1989), 22–3.

the same way, though for very different political ends. Writing in the Owenite journal *New Moral World* in 1839, John Finch described life in Harmony thus:

> On the estate, the land tax is redeemed and the tithes are commuted, there are no giants or anakims there, the Philistines are driven out, and the Lord hath given this goodly land to his people Israel. It is a land of hills and vallies, of wells and springs, of trees, fruits, flowers, grain, sheep, cattle, and is flowing with milk and honey. Arise, therefore, my beloved brethren, leave this Egypt, wherein your lives have been made bitter with hard bondage in brick, stone, mortar, iron, flax, wool, cotton, and all manner of service in the field, pass over this Jordan (Thames) and go up and possess this goodly land.[56]

This Bunyanesque vision of Jerusalem in England was also envisaged by Thomas Doubleday, author of *The Political Pilgrim's Progress*. Published by the *Northern Liberator* in 1839, the narrative describes Radical's laborious journey to the 'City of Reform', where the people 'enjoyed to the full all the fruits of their own labour and skill'. Having suffered many hardships, Radical and his family reach the Delectable Mountains, where the kind shepherds indulge him with a view of the city, 'which he distinctly saw, though at a great distance'. Resisting Political Apollyon, Vanity Fair, and even an evil Jew at Usury-Row, Radical—'like Bruce, when he reached the sources of the Nile; like Lander, when he sailed down the embouchure of the Niger'—finally beholds 'the lofty and noble towers and glittering spires of the city with a sensation of awe and rapture'.[57]

A less allegorical, though equally utopian pilgrimage is found in 'The Charter and the Land' (1847), a short story published in the Chartist periodical *The Labourer*, which follows William Wright, a disillusioned Stockport weaver who becomes converted to O'Connor's land scheme. Renouncing the pub, the diligent Wright now saves a shilling a week, which he invests in the Chartist Co-operative Land Company. Years pass, and eventually the happy day arrives when William, his wife Betsy, and their three children travel 'by the third class train' to their allotment in Watford. Joined by 'many new comrades upon the same mission to

---

[56] John Finch in *New Moral World* (1839), quoted in Edward Royle, *Robert Owen and the Commencement of the Millennium: A Study of the Harmony Community* (Manchester: Manchester University Press, 1998), 6.

[57] [Thomas Doubleday], *The Political Pilgrim's Progress from the Northern Liberator* (Newcastle: Northern Liberator, 1839), 5, 24, 66.

the Holy Land', 'emancipated slaves' like themselves, they finally reach 'the entrance to Holy Land', where they are 'conducted to their respective abodes, all anxiously inspecting their castle and their labour-field'. 'God bless LAND and the CHARTER', exclaims the good Betsy.[58] Note how different this earthly vision is from Bessy Higgins's heavenly outlook in Mrs Gaskell's *North and South* (1855): 'But it's not for me to get sick and tired o' strikes. This is the last I'll see. Before it's ended I shall be in the great City—the Holy Jerusalem.' Here, in Gaskell's middle-class version, the Holy Land is safely located in the afterlife.[59] Even Charles Kingsley's *Alton Locke, Tailor and Poet* (1850), sympathetic as it is to working-class aspirations, prefers to imagine the workers' 'Promised Land' in typological, rather than territorial, terms.[60]

Differing in tone, style, and political context, radical texts like these made use of the vernacular image of a Promised Land just around the corner (or, by the late 1840s, just a train's ride away), an English Canaan of social reform, flowing with milk and honey, to which the actual Palestine is of course not relevant (even if the sources of the Nile, for some reason, are).[61] The role of religion in the emergence of British socialism has been widely recognized; images of the Promised Land or Jerusalem were still employed to articulate working-class aspirations well into the twentieth century.[62] But surely it is remarkable that a similar strategy of withdrawal—which continues to imagine the 'Holy Land' in terms that are divorced from the actual locus itself—was also adopted by the writers who were popularizing the high Orientalist discourse for a mass readership. One could argue, of course, that whereas Kitto directed his gaze to the Jerusalem above, the Owenites envisioned a Jerusalem below, earthly and accessible. Still, both the popularized Orientalist discourse and the radical text presented their

---

[58] 'The Charter and the Land' (1847), repr. in Ian Haywood (ed.), *The Literature of Struggle: An Anthology of Chartist Fiction* (Aldershot: Scolar Press, 1995), 193–4.

[59] Elizabeth Gaskell, *North and South* (1855), ed. Angus Easson, World's Classics (Oxford: Oxford University Press, 1982), 132.

[60] Landow, *Victorian Types*, 208–10.

[61] On biblical rhetoric and Chartism see Jamie L. Bronstein, *Land Reform and Working-Class Experience in Britain and the United States, 1800–1862* (Stanford, Calif.: Stanford University Press, 1999), 63–7; on the 'Promised Land' as a golden English mythical past see Patrick Joyce, *Democratic Subjects: The Self and the Social in Nineteenth-Century England* (Cambridge: Cambridge University Press, 1994), 190–1.

[62] Cf. H. T. Muggeridge, *The Labour Pilgrim's Progress* (London: Independent Labour Party, 1916).

readers with Promised Lands which were equally removed from the Promised Land in the Middle East.

This similarity is indicative of the ubiquity of the biblical vocabulary and its ability to contain multiple meanings, both hegemonic and counter-hegemonic. But it also suggests that it was difficult to popularize the high Anglo-Palestine Orientalist discourse without falling back on the vernacular tradition. Indeed, as we have seen in the pedagogical approaches to scriptural geography, even when it was prescribed in the context of a strictly geographical inquiry, Palestine was still imagined as—or at least associated with—the familiar, the domestic, the indigenous.

Prints, photographs, and stereoscopes

It is necessary, at this point, to broaden our perspective. By the 1850s, the dramatic rise in the mass production and dissemination of cheap illustrated material naturally affected the representation of the Holy Land. The lavishly illustrated *Cassell's Family Bible*, for example, triumphed where both the SDUK and the SPCK had failed: issued in penny numbers from 1859 onwards, it sold 350,000 copies in six years.[63] The publishing boom meant that the SPCK, too, was forced to polish its collection of glass beads. In 1855, the Society introduced some vigorous changes to its catalogue; by 1864, it included cheap volumes like *Pilgrimage through Palestine, Holy Week in Jerusalem*, and *Happy Land*. The 'Prints' section boasted a set of six 'Scenes in the Holy Land, Printed in Colour, After Recent Photographs' (6*d*. each, 1*s*. 8*d*. in cheap frames); a cheaper set of twelve 'Scenes in the Holy Land' (6*d*. each, in glazed frames); thirty prints 'Illustrative of the Fulfilment of Prophecy'; and sets of illustrations depicting Scripture history, places, manners, and customs or prophetic sites.[64]

A typical SPCK set, for example, included thirty superb woodcuts (¾*d*. plain, 2*d*. coloured) by Josiah Whymper, one of the leading Victorian wood-engravers. The compositions, showing tiny Eastern figures eclipsed by colossal ruins and complemented by short texts, depicted biblical sites like Ashkelon ('There never was a more striking verification

---

[63] Altick, *English Common Reader*, 303.
[64] *Report of the SPCK* (London: SPCK, 1864), Catalogue H (Books, Prints, Maps, etc.).

of prophecy than the utter desolation of this formerly important and wealthy town'), Jericho ('contains about 200 inhabitants, who are ndolent and dishonest'), Gaza ('the inhabitants are praised for their cleanliness and personal neatness, qualities which are rare in modern Palestine'), as well as the Dead Sea, Bethlehem, Nazareth, Hebron, the Jordan, and of course the obligatory view of Jerusalem from the Mount of Olives.[65] Reproducing the same landscapes of Palestine—the same sites viewed from the same angles, or simply the very same woodcuts—these cheap commodities offered an accessible repertoire of standard images. Similar artefacts, including holiday greeting cards, stamp albums, prize books, reward cards, pamphlets, and magic-lantern slides were issued by the RTS and other publishers from the late 1850s onwards, always employing this familiar stock of images. Following the Education Acts of 1870 and 1880, as secular instruction was gradually assigned to the day-school, the Sunday-school unions published hundreds of graded lesson plans and courses of study on biblical geography and history.[66] When the *Art Journal* jested in 1854 that the Holy Land was better known in England than the English lakes, it was perhaps speaking on behalf of a very narrow stratum of society; but three decades later, images of the Holy Land must have been available to the great majority of people.

This was still a Pisgah sight only, but the view was now much grander, more focused, occasionally coloured, and, most significantly, increasingly accessible—so accessible, that when the *Illustrated London News* printed a view of Jerusalem from the Mount of Olives, it assured its readers that the engraving was based on a photograph taken by Francis Bedford, who accompanied the Prince of Wales's 1862 Oriental tour (see Fig. 7). 'Nothing can be more interesting than this inevitably truthful view of Jerusalem,' mused the *ILN*:

A 'Turner' version of Dover Castle and cliffs, full of the best poetry of art, is very charming; but Jerusalem is a subject not to be tampered with, even by a Turner. It is the naked, unadorned reality that we seek in a representation of a site made forever sacred as the centre around which all the events in the life of the Saviour

---

[65] Bodleian Library, Oxford, John Johnson Collection [JJC], 'Religion' [16], Holy Land prints (London: SPCK, *c.*1870).

[66] Thomas Laqueur, *Religion and Respectability: Sunday Schools and Working-Class Culture, 1780–1850* (New Haven: Yale University Press, 1976), 250.

Fig. 7. 'Jerusalem from the Mount of Olives', engraving after a photograph by Francis Bedford, *Illustrated London News*, 22 November 1862.

were enacted. Photography alone would give us that absolute reflex of the scene in which nothing is added and nothing taken away.

The photograph—and, apparently, even a rough engraving of one—conveyed a 'truthfulness' which a standard illustration simply lacked (although it was not so much the clear-cut definition that made this photograph so accurate, as the camera's ability to capture the 'soft, Oriental haze' of the city).[67] Photographs, unlike illustrations, offered an unprecedented air of documentary verisimilitude.[68] The publication of Francis Frith's *Egypt and Palestine, Photographed and Described* was hailed in the *Art Journal* in 1858 as an experiment 'of surpassing value', 'for we will *know* that we see things exactly as they are'.[69] The stereoscope, developed and perfected in the 1850s, added an additional dimension to this sense of truthfulness: depth. Frith was the first to produce stereoscopic images of the Holy Land, and from the 1860s onwards, Palestine became one of the most favourite topics for stereoscopic photography.[70]

Photographs of the Holy Land undoubtedly restricted the possible play between the earthly and the heavenly, which could still exist in illustrated or textual accounts. Nevertheless, the photographic image—just like printed illustrated images before it—became truly disseminated only decades after the technology was made available. The London Stereoscopic Company (established in 1854) alone sold 500,000 viewing instruments in its first two years of existence; but while the stereoscope was priced at a very moderate 2*s*. 6*d*., the price of a single stereographic print varied from 1*s*. to 1*s*. 6*d*., and often reached 3*s*. or even 7*s*. 6.*d*. each. 'A Stereoscope for every home' was the Company's slogan, but it was only in the late 1880s, if at all, that the stereoscopic

---

[67] *ILN*, 41 (22 Nov. 1862), 550, 552.
[68] On 'visual conditioning' see Estelle Jussim, *Visual Communication and the Graphic Arts: Photographic Technologies in the Nineteenth Century* (1973; New York: Bowker, 1983).
[69] *Art Journal*, 10 (Jan. 1858), 30. See also Yeshayahu Nir, *The Bible and the Image: The History of Photography in the Holy Land, 1839–1899* (Philadelphia: University of Pennsylvania Press, 1985); Issam Nassar, *Photographing Jerusalem* (Boulder, Colo.: East European Monographs, 1997).
[70] Dan Kyram, 'Stereoscopic Photography of the Holy Land', *Cathedra*, 68 (June 1993), 161–87 [Hebrew]. See also Jonathan Crary, *Techniques of the Observer: On Vision and Modernity in the Nineteenth Century* (Cambridge, Mass.: October Books, 1990), 116–34; William C. Durrah, *The World of Stereographs* (1977; Nashville: Land Yacht Press, 1997).

experience could became truly attainable.[71] Similarly, regular use of photographs in magazines began only in the 1890s, with the perfection of the halftone process for facsimile reproduction. However, even if we accept that by the 1900s the photographic image of the Holy Land had become widely disseminated, the question nevertheless remains: to what extent did these developments necessarily concretize the Holy Land, make it a more 'real', more geographically tangible space?

I will return to this question later in my discussion. For now, it is enough to state that while these printed representations, produced for private consumption, were made accessible to a wider public than ever before, other images, endlessly more exciting and spectacular, were still available to a select audience only. As the next section will demonstrate, the masses were offered a closer glimpse of the Holy Land, only because the few—or, at least, the fewer—were always several steps ahead. For a penny, viewers in the 1850s could enjoy a woodcut Pisgah sight. For a shilling, they could enjoy Pisgah itself.

'Palestine has come to them': Panoramas, Models, and Exhibitions

On 2 July 1835, William Gladstone noted in his diary: 'saw panorama of Jerusm [*sic*]: disagreeable to the eye but, all say, very veracious.'[72] Gladstone, unfortunately, did not explain why he found the display of the Holy City so unpleasant. Could it have been, one wonders, its blunt veracity, dispelling, once and for all, that hazy aura of ambiguity in which the earthly and the heavenly were still interfused? Possibly. But Gladstone, not for the last time in his life, was in the minority. 'The visions which our ancestors saw with the mind's eye, must be embodied for us in palpable forms,' sighed William Bodham Donne, the Examiner of Plays, in 1857: 'all must be made palpable to sight.'[73] The nineteenth-century 'taste for spectacle', as Michael Booth has aptly termed it, has been well documented.[74] The following account will explore

---

[71] Durrah, *World of Stereographs*, 3–4, 45–52. For prices see the Catalogue appended to David Brewster, *The Stereoscope: Its History, Theory, and Construction* (London: John Murray, 1856).

[72] *The Gladstone Diaries*, ed. M. R. D. Foot and H. C. G. Matthew (Oxford: Clarendon Press, 1968–94), ii. 179.

[73] Quoted in Michael Booth, *Victorian Spectacular Theatre, 1850–1910* (London: Routledge & Kegan Paul, 1981), 2.

[74] Ibid. 1–29; Robert D. Altick, *The Shows of London* (London: The Belknap Press of Harvard University Press, 1978); Thomas Richards, *The Commodity Culture of Victorian*

some of the methods employed to make a Palestine 'palpable to sight'; to make a spectacle of the Holy Land.

Much recent scholarship has approached the spectacle as a colonial institution, not only because pageants and exhibitions were often staged to celebrate empire, but because the techniques of accumulation, organization, and representation which were applied to stage these spectacles were analogous to—and often metonymic of—the disciplinary apparatus which facilitated the implementation of colonial order.[75] My discussion will challenge, or at least complicate, this view by highlighting the cross-exchanges between the public display of the Holy Land and the vernacular Orientalist tradition. After all, just like Bunyan, the Palestine panorama also offered true believers the prospect of Jerusalem in England.

'They always ask for the Sepulchre'

Gladstone's diary entry referred not to Robert Burford's celebrated panorama of Jerusalem—which was attracting crowds to Leicester Square from March that year[76]—but to *The Siege of Jerusalem*, a clamorous equestrian spectacle teeming with knights and Saracens, presented at Astley's Royal Amphitheatre.[77] Similar shows, like *The Blood Red Knight*, were staged there from as early as 1810, and at least up to the 1850s (see Fig. 8). This may account for Gladstone's annoyance, but it also shows that by mid-century, the word 'panorama' often served as a generic name for all pictorial shows.[78] Originally, however,

---

England: Advertising and Spectacle, 1851–1914 (Stanford, Calif.: Stanford University Press, 1990), 17–72.

[75] Paul Greenhalgh, *Ephemeral Vistas: The Expositions Universelles, Great Exhibitions and World's Fairs, 1851–1939* (Manchester: Manchester University Press, 1988); Richards, *Commodity Culture*; Timothy Mitchell, *Colonising Egypt* (1988; Berkeley: University of California Press, 1991), 1–33; Annie E. Coombes, *Reinventing Africa: Museums, Material Culture and Popular Imagination in Late Victorian and Edwardian England* (New Haven: Yale University Press, 1994); Tim Barringer and Tom Flynn (eds.), *Colonialism and the Object: Empire, Material Culture and the Museum* (London: Routledge, 1998); Peter H. Hoffenberg, *An Empire on Display: English, Indian, and Australian Exhibitions from the Crystal Palace to the Great War* (Berkeley: University of California Press, 2001).

[76] *The Times*, 31 Mar. 1835, 2.

[77] *Gladstone Diaries*, ii. 179 n.

[78] Altick, *Shows of London*, 174. See also Bernard Comment, *The Panorama* (London: Reaktion, 1999); Stephen Oettermann, *The Panorama: History of a Mass Medium* (London: Zone, 1997); Ralph Hyde, *Panoramania! The Art and Entertainment of the*

THE BLOOD RED KNIGHT,
OR,
THE WARRIORS OF PALESTINE.

A Grand Romantic Spectacle, in Two Acts, as performed originally at Astley's Royal Amphitheatre.

CONCLUDING TRIUMPH OF THE CRUSADERS

DRAMATIS PERSONÆ.

Sir Roland (the Blood-red Knight)........Mr. J. Howard	Isabella (Alfonso's wife) ....Miss Love
Alfonso (the Pilgrim champion).......Mr. D. W. Broadfoot	Ebra (the miller's wife) ....Miss E. Terry
Gog (a miller)............................Mr. Yarnold	Edith ....Miss J. Coleman
Peter Witlack (warder to the castle)........Mr. Hudspeth	Tabitha Witlack..........................Miss M. Terry
Wolfgang } the Blood Red Knight's myrmi- } Mr. Smith	
Ruthwold } dons...................... } S. Balls	
Edgar } Crusaders, disguised as holy } Mr. Craddock	Priests, Crusaders, Pilgrims, &c.
Egbert } Palmers.................. } Mr. S. Balls	

TO COUNTRY MANAGERS.—The entire Acting Copyright of every Drama published in the "PENNY PICTORIAL PLAY, is vested in the Proprietors, who are willing to give a written permission (pursuant to the Dramatic Authors' Act), upon moderate terms, which may be known upon application to the Publisher.

[NO. VII.]

Fig. 8. 'The Blood Red Knight, or, the Warriors of Palestine', programme, *c.*1850.

the panorama—invented by Robert Barker, an Edinburgh portraitist, in 1788—was a huge circular painting, depicting an entire 360-degree view, with the spectators gazing at a round, unbroken sequence. The 'diorama' was a flat picture with an illusion of depth; the audience, sitting in complete darkness, would see it as the far end of a tunnel. The 'moving panorama' was an extremely long canvas, rolled between two poles, usually dramatizing an extended journey; and the 'moving diorama' was a series of large dioramic paintings, displayed in succession.

Since the mystical Greek root '-orama' (sight) was used quite liberally by the proprietors, it is not always easy to determine the precise nature of an exhibition. But even when they differed in scope and technique, displays like the Palestine panorama exhibited in Fleet Street in 1816, the Shrine of the Nativity presented in 1839 at the Regent Park Diorama, or the tour of the Middle East shown in Charles Marshall's 'Kineorama' in 1841, all shared one common objective: to overwhelm the spectator by creating a world as vivid and realistic as possible.[79] Programmes, pamphlets, and advertisements assured visitors that these displays were based on 'faithful' and 'authentic' sketches, made 'on the spot' by celebrated artist-travellers, men like Joseph Bonomi, Fredrick Catherwood, and William Bartlett, who were members of the 'invisible college' which constructed the high academic Orientalist canon.[80] Through the agency of these commercial ventures, their work—copied and enlarged by professional artists—reached a considerably broader audience: the massive canvases of the panoramas were sometimes viewed by hundreds of thousands.[81] These crowds included people who could not always afford to purchase Bartlett's illustrated books, as well as people who had no wish to purchase them; people who could not always appreciate Catherwood's pioneering cartographical work in Jerusalem, but were happy to enjoy its magnified transformation into an awe-inspiring panorama. In other words, just like the printed images discussed above, these displays could be seen as popularized extensions of the high Orientalist discourse. However, whereas the pennyworth

---

'All-Embracing' View (London: Trefoil, 1988); Scott Wilcox, 'The Panorama and Related Exhibitions in London' (M.Litt. thesis, Edinburgh, 1976).

[79] Wilcox, 'Panorama', 59; *The Shrine of the Nativity of Bethlehem* (London: Regent Park Diorama, 1839); *Art-Union*, 3 (Apr. 1841), 68.

[80] See programmes, pamphlets, and press clippings in JJC, 'Dioramas' [1–3].

[81] Wilcox, 'Panorama', 210.

images of Palestine and the East were circulated vertically, down the social ladder, these mid-century displays, with their standard 1*s*. fee, disseminated the high Orientalist discourse horizontally, across an increasingly broad, yet limited, social stratum.

Much of the initial success of the panoramas derived from their topicality. Presenting recent events which the literate public could only read about in the newspapers, panoramas were the 'newsreels of the Napoleonic era'.[82] Thanks to their size, colour, and detail, panoramas continued to function as a popular form of journalistic reportage even after the emergence of the illustrated press. In 1841, for example, Burford reopened his old Jerusalem panorama in Leicester Square, accompanied by a new panorama of the *Bombardment of St Jean D'Acre*, which depicted the joint British–Austrian–Prussian attack on the rebellious Mohammed Ali, only three months after the battle took place.[83] Likewise, Telbin's diorama of the Holy Land was exhibited in 1863, 'after the Prince of Wales's tour had roused a new interest in the historic sites and scenes of the East'.[84] Nevertheless, panoramas of the Holy Land remained in constant demand regardless of their topicality. In 1889, when asked by the *Pall Mall Gazette*'s reporter about his most popular piece, Mr Poole—'the Panoramist, the Stereoramist, the Dioramist, and all the other "ramists" '—replied:

'They always ask for the Sepulchre of the Holy Saviour in Jerusalem. That began our prosperity. To-day it is still popular, with other subjects. Our public soon forgets. I used to show Gordon in Khartoum, and he always got a rousing cheer. Now he's no good—no good!,' sighed Mr. Poole. 'He's dead.' 'And Stanley?' 'He's down too. Dead or out of sight—out o'mind too. Yes. The panorama business takes the pride out of us. Once under the sod, and who cares for yours truly?'[85]

Images of Palestine were expected to fascinate and entertain. One London display, for example, offered 'Five Exhibitions in One': a model of the Holy Land, a model of the North Pole, living animals from Hindostan, an enchanted Lyre, and an invisible girl who answered 'the questions of the visitors, either in English or French'.[86] As a rule, however, the Holy Land was seen as the one subject that could attract

---

[82] Altick, *Shows of London*, 136.
[83] See *The Times*, 30 Jan. 1841, 5; 20 Aug. 1841, 5.
[84] *ILN*, 43 (19 Sept. 1863), 294.
[85] JJC, 'Dioramas' [1], *Pall Mall Gazette*, 5 Sept. 1889.
[86] JJC, 'Dioramas' [3], pamphlet (*c*.1820).

even the most austere of Evangelicals; which explains why the Palestine panorama continued to do well while interest in the imperial escapades of Gordon and Stanley seemed to fade. The *ILN* remarked, for example, that Telbin's diorama of the Holy Land 'will probably be visited by many persons who would object to attend a theatre for the purpose'.[87] Indeed, George Mogridge's *Old Humphrey's Walks in London* (1843)— which listed attractions for Christians 'without hampering them in their earthly duties, or hindering them on their way to heaven'—urged readers to visit the panorama of Jerusalem, the model of Palestine, and the diorama of the Shrine of the Nativity.[88]

All this meant that the Holy Land was one of the most favourite topics for pictorial shows throughout the century. It was certainly the single most popular topic for panoramas and dioramas in 1851, when millions flocked to London to visit the Great Exhibition. At least three competing entrepreneurs offered views of Palestine. 'A Grand Moving Diorama of the Holy Land', illustrating the 'Exodus of the Israelites', opened in the Egyptian Hall in March. Based on Bonomi's drawings, it carried the spectators from Egypt, via Mount Sinai and Edom, to the city of Jerusalem.[89] The 'New and Magnificent Diorama of Jerusalem and the Holy Land', based on Bartlett's sketches, opened a month later at St George's Gallery, Hyde Park Corner.[90] These two shows soon embarked on a bitter feud; and while the former never tired of boasting that it was 'the original', the latter christened itself the 'largest sacred' diorama.[91] Once St George's Gallery added a choir and an organ ('to give grander effect and reality to various scenes'[92]), the Egyptian Hall retaliated by importing a company of 'musicians, singers and performers from Syria and the Holy Land', whose singing 'is unlike any that we have heard in this country', as the *Theatrical Journal* noted with wonder.[93] Finally, Burford re-installed his old Jerusalem panorama at Leicester Square (or at least a reproduction of it; the original was probably

---

[87] *ILN*, 43 (19 Sept. 1863), 294.
[88] George Mogridge, *Old Humphrey's Walks in London and its Neighbourhood* (London: RTS, 1843), p. iv. Subsequent page numbers are cited parenthetically in the text.
[89] JJC, 'Dioramas' [1], pamphlet and advertisements.
[90] *A Pilgrimage Through the Holy Land, Explanatory of the Diorama, etc.* (London: St George's Gallery, 1851). See also *The Times*, 3 Mar. 1851, 4.
[91] Wilcox, 'Panorama', 135.
[92] JJC, 'Dioramas' [1], advertisement.
[93] *Theatrical Journal*, 12 (27 Aug. 1851), 283. See also Wilcox, 'Panorama', 135.

destroyed in a fire in 1842 when exhibited in New York).[94] The late 1850s saw the decline of 'panoramania', even though Holy Land panoramas were displayed until the end of the century.

Due to their technical specifications and sheer size, panoramas and dioramas were inevitably an urban form of entertainment. They were not, however, restricted to the capital. A diorama of the Holy Land presented in Exeter in 1850 boasted 'a scale of grandeur hitherto unattempted in the Provinces';[95] the 1851 moving diorama from St George's Gallery arrived at Birmingham in May 1855;[96] and its Egyptian Hall rival was probably exhibited in Glasgow as late as 1860.[97] Once available for travel, displays were also duplicated. This was particularly true for models. The programme for Brunetti's model of ancient Jerusalem, displayed in London in 1847, warned that a 'base attempt has been made to pirate the work by a servant formerly in Mr. Brunetti's employ, who is probably at this moment deceiving the public in the provinces with a spurious copy of a great original'. Brunetti, despite his earlier reluctance, was 'obliged, in self-defence, to construct a second model... for the provinces, to defeat this dishonest attempt to deprive him of his hard-earned honours'.[98] Consequently, no fewer than three identical models were being exhibited, concurrently, around the country.

Panoramas, too, were sometimes replicated. For example, *Laidlaw's Panorama of Jerusalem*, exhibited in Hull in 1837, was identical to Burford's 1835 London panorama.[99] Since the original was then on display in North America, this panorama, despite its immensity, must have been reproduced. The fact that people in Hull and those in New York could have visited the same display simultaneously suggests that

---

[94] JJC, 'Dioramas' [3], pamphlet; Davis, *Landscape of Belief*, 226 nn. 17, 18.
[95] Ralph Hyde collection of panorama ephemera, press clipping from *Exeter Flying Post*, 17 Jan. 1850.
[96] Hyde collection, pamphlet.
[97] *The Great Original Grand Moving Diorama of the Holy Land, etc.* (Glasgow: William Gilchrist, 1860).
[98] *Description of the Model of Ancient Jerusalem, Illustrative of the Sacred Scriptures and the Writings of Josephus* (London: Chapman, n.d.), p. ii.
[99] Robert Burford, *Description of the View of the City of Jerusalem and the Surrounding Country, Now Exhibiting at the Panorama, Leicester Square* (London: T. Brettell, 1835); *Description of the View of the City of Jerusalem, Now Exhibiting at the Panorama (Laidlaw's) in This Town, etc.* (Hull: John Hutchinson, 1837).

the panorama was a hybrid of high art and mass entertainment, a bridge between the huge 'panoramic' biblical canvases of Roberts and Martin, displayed from the 1820s to the 1850s, and the rise of cinema in the 1890s. Nevertheless, a visit to the circular panorama was an experience unlike anything offered by other two-dimensional visual forms, in that it was total: the spectators were offered not simply an image or representation of Jerusalem. Rather, they were offered Jerusalem itself.

'The Holy Land is warmed!'

This somewhat preposterous pledge to obliterate all distinction between representation and reality rested, first and foremost, on the visual illusion. Barker's original patent included a circular building, with lighting admitted exclusively from the top, and several obstructions, to prevent the observer from looking above (at the source of light), below, or too near the painting.[100] For the illusion to succeed, it had to be complete and sustained. The eye could not be allowed 'to shift "outside the frame" and compare the artistic illusion with the real surroundings'.[101] The visitors were conveyed through a dark passage, until they emerged from below to the centre of a large rotunda. 'On entering the exhibition room we find ourselves in the centre of a landscape,' explained the *Leisure Hour*: 'Below us is a real foreground with bushes and trees, and facing us is what we know is a picture, but which looks so lifelike that we have great difficulty in persuading ourselves [the] scene is not real.'[102] Visitors to Burford's 1835 panorama discovered themselves on the terrace of the house of the Aga, the governor of Jerusalem, with a splendid view of the Dome of the Rock, the Church of the Holy Sepulchre, and the Mount of Olives. Slightly below the spectators were some Turks, a sheikh and his sons, servants making coffee, Bedouin women, and even a robber about to be flogged. There was nothing to remind the spectators of the London—or Hull, or New York—they had left behind them. The panorama purported to be 'reality itself, enwrapping the spectator on all sides. The fact that the "reality" existed only on painted canvas was obscured by the absence of anything *besides* the canvas.'[103]

---

[100] Altick, *Shows of London*, 129.   [101] Oettermann, *Panorama*, 50.
[102] JJC, 'Dioramas' [1], 'Panoramas and Dioramas', *The Leisure Hour* (n.d.).
[103] Altick, *Shows of London*, 188.

It was precisely on this paradoxical interplay between reality and representation, 'here' and 'there', that the success of the panorama rested; this allowed the proprietors of the St George diorama to declare in 1851 that 'the Holy Land is warmed!'—meaning that heating was installed in the building (*Punch*, quick to react, predicted that soon 'we shall be informed' that the 'Arctic Regions are heated by gas' and 'The Nile is kept dry with hot air'[104]). On the one hand, the *raison d'être* of the panorama was that it depicted a real place, a geographical Jerusalem which existed outside the panoramic space; and the advertisements cited qualified travellers who could testify to the accuracy of the reproduction. On the other hand, the public had to believe that this was not a painting, but the real thing; after all, the entire technical apparatus was constructed to obscure any hint that the Holy Land could exist anywhere else but here, in the rotunda.

I will return to this paradox shortly. It is important, in the meantime, to recognize that the illusion of reality also emerged from an unprecedented sense of control (which was absent, for example, from the moving panorama, in which the spectator's gaze was fixed to the screen, and both the motion and the narrative were manipulated by the artist). The visitor to the circular panorama, Foucault has observed, 'occupied exactly the place of the sovereign gaze'. Indeed, when designing his perfect inspection house, the *Panopticon*, Jeremy Bentham was probably aware of the panoramas that Barker was constructing in the late 1780s.[105] To gaze at this landscape was to master it; yet, as art historian John Davis has noted, like all varieties of the sublime, 'this situation also came with a measure of discomfort, a sense of self-loss in the face of spatial infinitude and the corresponding desire to confront that loss.'[106] Since the panorama was a perfect simulacrum, to view it was to simulate the encounter with the landscape, with all the bewilderment and confusion which followed. Indeed, just like the 'tourist gaze',[107] the panoramic 'sovereign gaze' cannot be enjoyed unconditionally: 'it makes its own demands on the viewer. First among these is the need for order; the

---

[104] *Punch*, 21 (29 Nov. 1851), 242.
[105] Michel Foucault, *Discipline and Punish: The Birth of the Prison* (1975), trans. Alan Sheridan (London: Penguin, 1991), 195–228, 317 n.
[106] Davis, *Landscape of Belief*, 61.
[107] John Urry, *The Tourist Gaze: Leisure and Travel in Contemporary Societies* (London: Sage, 1990), esp. 1–15.

space *must* be governed by an active eye. The surrounding void of the darkened panorama rotunda thus forced its viewer to make choices, to turn, pivot, and construct a narrative, to marshal the full expanse of a 360-degree prospect.'[108] This is precisely what Old Humphrey must do when he visits the panorama of Jerusalem: he must stare 'yonder' (p. 100), 'look all around' (p. 102), 'turn [his] face' (p. 103), and stand 'gazing on the interesting scenes' around him (p. 105). Horrified to discover that he has been, 'for a moment, led away by Mohammedan splendour', the Christian visitor's thoughts 'soon return to more interesting inquiries. He feels an affectionate reverence stealing over him; he yearns to gaze upon the spot whence the Redeemer entered Jerusalem' (p. 99). And Humphrey immediately gratifies this yearning for Christ by diverting his gaze to that favourite spot, the Mount of Olives.

Apart from securing additional profits, the lectures, guided tours, and programmes which accompanied these shows assisted spectators who were overwhelmed by the huge landscape around them; but they also attempted to impose a distinct interpretation on the scene. Old Humphrey's account sounds very much like Kitto's *Land of Promise* (both were published by the RTS) when he claims that it is impossible to understand the scene, a 'confused pile of yellowish-white stone walls', without having a proper knowledge of the Bible (p. 95). And like Kitto, he concludes his tour with a typological reading of the landscape around him: 'Oh, how poverty stricken is this earthly Jerusalem to that heavenly city with the golden gates...!' (p. 105). Whereas Humphrey's outlook was essentially Anglican, the official souvenir programme which accompanied Burford's panorama introduced a more daring Orientalist view. It made no mention of the heavenly city at all, and instead delighted in the 'vast assemblage' of mosques and domes, which 'excite curiosity, and, being mostly of white stone, sparkle, under the rays of a glorious eastern sun, with inconceivable splendour'.[109]

Nevertheless, neither of these narratives was intrinsic to the panorama itself. The all-engulfing visual image seemed to exist independently of any textual construction; spectators could appreciate the view, and devise their own narrative, without having to attend the lecture or consult the programme. When the writer of an article on Burford's 1841 panorama of the bombardment of Acre described the sight of

[108] Davis, *Landscape of Belief*, 62. [109] Burford, *Description of the View*, 2.

Mohammed Ali's soldiers—'It is evidently all over now. *Mash Allah!* The Prophet is great! they seem to say, as they turn a stupefied look upon the wreck of the town'[110]—he was performing the conventional Orientalist trick of speaking on behalf of the natives. But this certainly was not present in the panorama itself, a painted canvas which spoke for no one. An Egyptian spectator, had he travelled to London in 1841, would have probably come up with a completely different interpretation. Indeed, it was precisely the possibility of absorbing the scene irrespective of any external ideological framework—except, of course, one's own—that forced the anxious Old Humphrey to explain what Jerusalem was 'really' about.

Three-dimensional representations often operated in the same way. Old Humphrey, visiting a model of Palestine exhibited in Somerset House, asserted that the 'eye of the spectator takes in, at one view, the whole of the land of Palestine' (p. 175). Nevertheless, Jude's face behind the Mount of Olives shows that even a model forced the spectator to make choices, pivot, and turn. In a companion to his model of Jerusalem (1846), the Revd John Blackburn explained: 'in order to view this model aright, and obtain just impressions of the real scene... it will be necessary to bring the eye down to the level of its horizon.' Blackburn regarded his work typologically, claiming that 'the Jerusalem which now is, is set forth as *a model* and type [to] the Jerusalem which is above'. Pleased with his pun, he concluded with 'Jerusalem, My Happy Home'.[111] But it is precisely his anxiety about viewing the model 'aright' which implies that there were as many views as there were viewers. Jude, for one, regarded the model as a type of the Jerusalem which is below, the happy home of a Christminster college. The panorama, which enwrapped the spectator on all sides, merely magnified this sense of the spectator's volition.

This is not to suggest that panoramas either represented, or were presented in, an ideological vacuum. Obviously, in its choice of theme (the defeat of an Eastern ruler), the context in which it was displayed (in London, three months after the event), and, most significantly, its composition and depiction of the characters (which, unfortunately,

---

[110] JJC, 'Dioramas' [1], unidentified press clipping, 'Burford's Panorama of the Bombardment of St. Jean D'Acre' (n.d.).
[111] John Blackburn, *Hand-Book Round Jerusalem; or Companion to the Model* (London: Rivington, 1846), 3, 124, 127.

have not survived), Burford's panorama of the bombardment of Acre was an exercise in Orientalism. Likewise, with its clustered crowd of archetypal Turkish and Arab figures, Burford's Jerusalem panorama invited viewers to gaze down and take the whole picture in, without ever having to turn their heads—a quintessential Orientalist perspective. My point, rather, is this: textual accounts, printed visual material, and even photographs always enclosed the image of the earthly Jerusalem within a specific medium, an enclosure which accentuated the fact that the image was also being projected through political, religious, and commercial filters (and, in the case of the stereograph, through actual oculars). The panorama, on the other hand, with its claim of obliterating the medium altogether, offered not so much an unmediated and unabridged version of the earthly city, as an illusion of one.

It was this fundamental claim to verisimilitude that distinguished the spectacle from the two-dimensional, privately consumed artefact. As we have seen, the penny magazines and cheap publications, issued up to the 1850s, deferred—or at least obscured—the image of Jerusalem as a palpable geographical locale, existing at the present moment, in the Middle East. The panorama, on the other hand, and even the diorama and the model, presented a Jerusalem that was visibly and undeniably present. One of the most original aspects of Burford's Jerusalem panorama was that it positioned the spectator not on the Mount of Olives, but on the governor's terrace, near the Mosque of Omar, at the very heart of the city, gazing from the inside out. This was the topographical equivalent of carrying the spectator beyond the conviction that 'the distant view is all', which the popular magazines both preached and practised.

Nevertheless, as I have already suggested, this view did not come without a price: 1*s.*, to be exact, which was the standard admission fee to all pictorial exhibitions throughout the century; and since these displays usually utilized daylight, it was almost impossible for working people to attend them.[112] This, once again, is the familiar pattern in which, representationally speaking, images available for working-class consumption continued to stand one Pisgah behind those available to their betters. It was only towards the very end of the century, after the novelty of the panorama had long faded, that spectacles like these could

---

[112] Hyde, *Panoramania!*, 39–40; Wilcox, 'Panorama', 208.

be enjoyed by a much broader portion of society.[113] In their heyday, however, from the 1830s to the 1860s, these shows catered to middle-class needs. The panoramas were the bourgeois substitute for the Grand Tour:[114] 'The truth seems to be that the love of illustration is greatly on the increase,' noted *The Times* in 1851, 'and that the middle and humbler classes'—not too humble to spare a shilling, though—'who cannot afford to travel, will readily patronize the means by which remarkable scenes and places may be realized to them'.[115] The advertisements explained that panoramas and dioramas were equal to the original, if not better. *The Times*, for example, noted that Burford's panoramas conveyed to the mind 'a completeness and truthfulness not always to be gained from a visit to the scene itself'.[116] They certainly offered the pleasures of travel without its costs or hardships. James Neil, who organized Holy Land exhibitions—a series of 'Splendid, Realistic Spectacles, Beautiful beyond Description'—promised that

> those who attend the POPULAR PALESTINE TALKS, and see the various sights that will be shown and popularly explained each day for a fortnight, will have by far a clearer knowledge and realization of the life of the Holy Land, especially in its immensely important bearing on the Bible that any ordinary traveller could possibly acquire by a seven months' visit to Palestine itself, at the cost of many hundreds of pounds, if he had not spent at least a year in thorough and elaborate studies before he started, and if he has not enjoyed altogether exceptional opportunities of seeing the country when there.

One such exhibition, held at Brixton Hall in the 1880s, was open from 2.30 to 5.30 (1*s*.), and from 7 to 10 (6*d*.). 'Many have long desired to visit the Holy Land,' proclaimed the pamphlet: 'but now, through MR NEIL's magnificent display, Palestine has come to them.'[117]

'As good as a visit to Palestine'

The assurance that Palestine could 'come to them' generated a truly impressive project, a series of similar exhibitions organized by the Revd

---

[113] By the 1900s, model making had become a regular part of Sunday-school activities. Cf. Charles W. Budden, *Model-Making for the Sunday School* (London: Sunday School Union, [1914]).
[114] Altick, *Shows of London*, 180–1.
[115] *The Times*, 27 Dec. 1851, 3.
[116] *The Times*, 27 Dec. 1861, 6.
[117] JJC, 'Dioramas' [1], pamphlet.

Samuel Schor, who, born in Jerusalem to converted Jewish parents, became affiliated to the London Society for Promoting Christianity among the Jews (LJS). The first of these Palestine Exhibitions was held in August 1891 in Felixstowe, where Schor was curate. In November that year, exhibitions were held in Harwich and Stroud; in 1892, in Woodbridge, Plymouth, Croydon, Norwich, Clifton, Tunbridge Wells, Cambridge, Cheltenham, and Bath; by 1900, at least sixty exhibitions had been held all over the country; from 1900 to 1914, at least ninety more.[118] The biggest event was the 'Palestine in London' exhibition, held at the Islington Agricultural Hall in June–July 1907: attracting more than 350,000 visitors, it earned the London Jews Society some £12,000.[119] Three years later, in 1910, the Society celebrated Schor's ten-thousandth lecture on Palestine: it was calculated that he had delivered more than one lecture every day, for twenty-seven years.[120]

With its East London headquarters situated in a square called 'Palestine Place', the London Jews Society was associated with the more fervent Evangelical circles; it seems reasonable to presume that many of the visitors to the exhibitions sympathized with its missionary, if not prophetic, agenda. Still, the number of exhibitions, their broad geographical distribution, and the outstanding value they offered for 1*s.* (6*d.* after 4 o'clock), suggest that the Palestine Exhibition must have appealed to a much broader audience, including those who cared little for the Society's proselytizing project. It is telling, for example, that the Mayor of Liverpool, who opened the Palestine Exhibition in his city in 1907, seemed genuinely astonished when he learnt, from a Jewish rabbi, that the proceeds would 'be applied towards turning Jews from their religion to that of Christianity. Had I known', explained the Mayor,

---

[118] The exhibitions were resumed after the First World War, and were still being held in the late 1950s. Some of the original exhibits have since then been incorporated into the Bible Exploration Centre, St Albans, managed by the London Jews Society (or, in its modern title, the Church's Ministry among the Jews (CMJ)); in addition to the permanent display, the Centre still operates an itinerant exhibition.

[119] These figures are based on W. T. Gidney, *Missions to Jews: A Handbook of Reasons, Facts and Figures* (11th edn. London: LJS, 1914), 73; idem., *The History of the London Society for Promoting Christianity Amongst the Jews, from 1809 to 1908* (London: LJS, 1908), 500–1, 580–1; and the collection of Palestine Exhibition handbooks kept at the CMJ, St Albans.

[120] *The Origin and History of Palestine Exhibitions to Commemorate Rev. Samuel Schor's 10,000th Lecture on Palestine* (London: LJS, 1910), 16.

'nothing would have tempted me to preside at the opening, and thus give my official sanction to such an object.'[121]

Schor's vision was an ambitious one. 'Let it at once be understood', proclaimed the *Palestine in London* official handbook, 'that this Exhibition is no mere bazaar, with just a few photographs and curios to interest the learned, but a popular and realistic representation of the actual life of Palestine to-day.'[122] The present state of the Holy Land was of interest to anyone who looked forward to the Jews' restoration to their homeland; but its importance lay, first and foremost, in the fact that it allowed visitors to gain a better understanding of Scripture. The exhibition, in other words, depended on the Orientalist cliché that 'the actual life of Palestine to-day' reflected the actual life of Palestine thousands of years ago. 'They all knew that the East did not change, and that it was just as it was centuries ago,' noted the Archdeacon of Gloucester when the exhibition reached his diocese in 1905: 'Therefore when their Bibles had so much that was of Eastern origin in it, those living so far away needed some knowledge to help them to appreciate some of its meaning.'[123] 'It is this Eastern atmosphere which the promoters of the exhibition seek to create and which proves so fascinating to the visitor,' explained the *Palestine in Birmingham* handbook: 'The East in the West, the very life of Palestine, with its age-old customs and manners, is set before you the moment you enter the doors.'[124]

The dimensions of the local town hall defined the size of the exhibition, but its structure never changed. There were various models, topographical (modern Jerusalem), miniaturized (the Tabernacle in the desert) or full-sized (a tomb with a rolling stone, a Bedouin encampment, and a Bethany cottage), exhibited alongside hundreds of authentic items from the East, ranging from Babylonian bricks, water-

---

[121] *Jewish Missionary Intelligence*, Dec. 1907, 187.
[122] *Palestine in London: Official Guide* (London: LJS, 1907), 33. This passage demonstrates how the 'bazaar' has been domesticated in English culture. By asserting that the Palestine Exhibition is no 'mere bazaar', Schor of course meant that it was intended to look like a 'real' Oriental market, and not like a typical charitable church sale. Likewise, the Executive Committee of the 'Palestine in Glasgow' exhibition stated in 1906 that it 'decided to make the sale as "Eastern" as possible', meaning that 'No goods were to figure on the stalls which are generally found at the typical bazaar. Goods were therefore ordered from Palestine direct.' See *Jewish Missionary Intelligence*, June 1906, 92.
[123] *Gloucestershire Echo*, 23 Nov. 1905, 1
[124] *Palestine in Birmingham: Official Guide* (Birmingham: LJS, 1921), 1–2.

skins, and ancient tools to locusts, dried flowers, mysterious charms, and a crown of thorns. Among these was a notable collection of costumes of the 'various inhabitants of Palestine', including those of an Arab sheikh, a Jewish bride, a shepherd lad with sling and staff, and the coat of many colours. Finally, there were numerous two-dimensional representations, including photographs, paintings, and, after 1907, cinematic images as well. All these were arranged in a series of courts: Agriculture, Music and Furniture, Eastern Dress and Ornaments, Natural History and Botany, Court of the Holy Temple, and so forth. In addition to the many lectures which followed the display, a series of 'Realistic Scenes of Eastern Life' employed the models and costumes to depict such themes as 'Life in a Jerusalem Home', 'The Life of an Eastern Shepherd', 'Scenes in the Market Place', and 'A Picnic in Palestine'.[125] Refreshments and commodities—olive-wood souvenirs, Eastern sweets, palm branches, and postcards—were sold in stalls located behind façades of Eastern houses, arranged to represent a street in Jerusalem. As a Bolton local paper explained in 1902, as soon as the visitors enter, they 'find themselves surrounded by the grey city walls of Jerusalem. On the left hand side there is a facsimile of the entrance to the Church of the Holy Sepulchre, whilst on the right is the Golden Gate and the great Tower of David.'[126]

Compressing the Holy City into the local town hall, packed with numerous representations of Jerusalem—illustrated, photographed, sculptured, projected—it was this mock Oriental bazaar, the backbone of the exhibition, which was expected to transform the familiar space into 'Palestine' (see Fig. 9). Like the early nineteenth-century panoramas, the Palestine Exhibition presented itself as a convenient alternative to travel. 'There are not many of us to whom the opportunity comes of seeing with our own eyes Jerusalem and Bethlehem, Calvary and the Mount of Olives,' noted a local newspaper when the exhibition reached Grantham in 1906:

Hence we should be thankful and grateful to those who have brought the Holy Land to us, for seeing the pictures, costumes, and realistic Eastern scenes, explained as they are by competent guides, is almost equivalent to a personal

---

[125] *Palestine in Brighton* (Brighton: LJS, 1909), 51, 53.
[126] *Bolton Chronicle*, 25 Oct. 1902, 8.

Fig. 9. 'The Market Square' in the 'Palestine in London' exhibition, *Jewish Missionary Intelligence*, August 1907.

visit to Palestine. Not quite, of course, but it is infinitely more convincing than the reading of even the most lavishly illustrated book.[127]

This last reservation was often forgotten in the excitement of it all: if the representation of Palestine was 'not quite' realistic, visitors were nevertheless encouraged to believe that it was realistic enough. 'The mountain will not come to Mahomet, therefore Mahomet must go to the mountain,' exclaimed *The Windsor and Eton Express* in 1906, slightly muddling its Oriental imagery: 'Everybody cannot go to the Holy Land, therefore Mr. Schor seeks to bring Palestine scenes to us.'[128] Schor was the first to endorse this image of miraculous relocation. Opening the 'Palestine in London' exhibition in 1907, he said:

Here you all are in Palestine, enjoying, I hope, the Palestine heat which we have provided for you. The reason why we have brought Palestine to your doors is... because you cannot all go to Palestine. I expect some of you would like to go there, but you cannot, either because you cannot spare the time, or because you cannot spare the means. And so we have simply touched it, shall I say with a wizard's wand? And have brought the whole land and concentrated it within these walls.[129]

To appreciate the distinctiveness of Schor's project, it is useful to compare it with other popular Holy Land exhibitions which flourished towards the end of the century, especially in the United States. Consider, for example, Chautauqua's 'Palestine Park'. Situated beside a lake in western New York, Chautauqua was established in 1874 as a summer gathering for Sunday-school teachers; it soon became a year-round educational enterprise, offering study programmes, lectures, and eventually a network of travelling tent shows. Palestine Park, one of the most celebrated features of the original centre, was a huge topographic model, 75 feet wide by 170 feet long, complete with miniature plaster cities, built on the shores of the lake, which doubled for the Mediterranean coastline.[130] The (mistaken) belief that the small mountains were made of soil and timber transported from Palestine reinforced the conviction that the Park was holy terrain. To complete the experience, visitors to

---

[127] *Grantham Journal*, 14 July 1906, 4.
[128] *Windsor and Eton Express*, 20 Oct. 1906, 5.
[129] *Jewish Missionary Intelligence*, Aug. 1907, 118.
[130] Burke O. Long, *Imagining the Holy Land: Maps, Models, and Fantasy Travels* (Bloomington, Ind.: Indiana University Press, 2002), 7–41.

the Park, but also local residents, often walked around dressed in Oriental garb.[131]

Like Palestine Park, the Palestine Exhibition also offered its visitors a 'purified and miniaturized' Palestine, 'rid of the problematic elements that compromised a visit to the actual Holy Land'.[132] There were, however, some crucial differences: whereas Chautauqua was a Lilliputian version of the land, easily captured within one's gaze, the Palestine Exhibition, teeming with numerous 'Palestines', made a much greater claim on the visitor's attention. And whereas Palestine Park soon became a popular destination for pilgrims, Schor's project reversed the roles: travelling from one town to the other, it was the Palestine Exhibition itself which was embarked on a pilgrimage—each time to a different holy land.

This last point in particular epitomizes the difference between Schor's Jerusalem street and the Oriental replicas that dominated the landscape of the World's Fairs, replicas like the Egyptian bazaar constructed at the 1889 *Exposition Universelle* in Paris (and, subsequently, in many other international exhibitions): an exact duplicate of a winding Cairo alley, the display included not only façades of houses, shops, and a mosque, but also fifty Egyptian donkeys, imported from Cairo together with their drivers and grooms.[133] Jerusalem, too, was transferred to the West in a similar fashion: the massive, 11-acre 'Jerusalem' constructed at the 1904 St Louis World's Fair included full-scale reconstructions of the Holy Sepulchre, the Wailing Wall, and the Dome of the Rock, as well as twenty-two streets, 300 buildings, and 1,000 indigenous Jerusalemites who were brought over from Palestine.[134] Notwithstanding the neighbouring Ferris wheel which loomed in the background, this was intended to be 'Jerusalem itself', as the *Prospectus* explained: 'When the visitor enters the gates of the city he shall be made to feel as though he were in actual Jerusalem.'[135]

Studying these huge replicas—which took up, and enhanced, the panorama's two-dimensional claim to verisimilitude—Thomas Mitchell

---

[131] Davis, *Landscape of Belief*, 92–4. [132] Ibid. 91.
[133] Mitchell, *Colonising Egypt*, 1–3.
[134] Lester I. Vogel, *To See a Promised Land: Americans and the Holy Land in the Nineteenth Century* (University Park, Pa.: Pennsylvania State University Press, 1993), 213–15.
[135] Quoted ibid. 215.

has pondered the affinity they created between representation and reality:

> The very scale and accuracy of the model assure the visitor that there must exist some original of which this is a mere copy. Such techniques persuade one not that the representation is necessarily exact, but that there is a pure reality out there, untouched by the forms of displacement, intermediation, and repetition that render the image merely an image.[136]

This process, Mitchell claims, both typified and empowered the colonial project: fresh from the spectacles of the World Exhibitions, Westerners who travelled to Egypt insisted on trying 'to grasp the world as though it were a picture or exhibition', and, failing, tried to impose a political and cultural framework that would reorder Egypt 'to appear as a world enframed'.[137]

Mitchell's argument is largely persuasive, but since his interest lies in the effects of this 'gaze' on the lives of the indigenous people of the East, he never stops to consider what this sort of realism could have meant for those spectators who did not travel to the East, and hence could not apply their 'world-as-exhibition' sensibility to the 'pure reality out there'; and it was precisely on these spectators, of course, that the commercial success of the exhibitions depended. Indeed, since the 'pure reality'— say, Jerusalem—was never made accessible to the great majority of visitors who travelled to St Louis to see 'Jerusalem', all that remained was a self-referential loop in which the interplay between representation and reality could never go beyond the representational sphere. Rather than denote a reality 'out there' that would double for the replica, the division between East and West, reality and representation, could only be pursued and encountered within the replica itself.

For the great majority of visitors, then, the Orientalist implications of the Oriental replica could prove much more ambivalent than Mitchell assumes. This, to be sure, may have characterized the representation of all foreign locales, but the Palestine Exhibition accentuated the ambivalence. One reason was its extraordinary mobility: the exhibition travelled not only to the large cities in which other colonial and missionary exhibitions were held, but also to provincial towns, sometimes even villages. 'No place is too small,' the organizers often boasted.[138] One

[136] Mitchell, *Colonising Egypt*, p. xiii.   [137] Ibid. 24, 33.
[138] *Jewish Missionary Intelligence*, Nov. 1915, 130.

had to travel to the World exhibition, usually held in the capital—already a 'there' for most people—to gaze at the huge Oriental replica. The Palestine Exhibition, on the other hand, was always closer to home. It was, in fact, *at* home, especially after 1900, when the 'Palestine and Oriental Exhibition' was renamed 'Palestine in...', the name adjusted to suit the locale. Referred to in the north London newspapers as 'Palestine in Islington', it was even possible to imagine 'Palestine in London' as a parochial event.

Held at a central hall which was undoubtedly frequented by most members of the community, the Palestine Exhibition was thus constructed as a self-sufficient Holy Land, familiar rather than alien, indigenous rather than foreign. Visitors to the Indian Palace Courtyard, an Oriental bazaar reconstructed in South Kensington as part of the Colonial and Indian Exhibition (1886), claimed that the display conveyed 'a sense of repose which cheats one into the belief of being far away from the rattle and bustle of London'. 'At a single step', wrote *The Times*, 'the visitor is carried from the wild, mad, whirl of the individual struggle for existence to which civilisation has been reduced in the ever changing West, into the stately splendour of the unchanging antique life of the East.'[139] The Palestine Exhibition, by comparison, by the very nature of its itinerancy, never allowed its visitors to forget the ever-changing West they had left behind them. The original features of the local hall were always easily perceptible behind the mock Oriental façades (see Fig. 10), indicating that, unlike the huge replicas that were built in the great colonial exhibitions, the Palestine Exhibition could not—and, indeed, did not purport to—offer a perfect replica. Nowhere was this more visible than in the multitude of models and photographs which welcomed the visitor: rather than reconstructing Palestine, these seemed to exhibit an almost frantic attempt to compensate, in typical Victorian excessiveness, for the lack of a basic, unified, one-to-one simulacrum.

The fact that visitors could nevertheless revel in the idea that the experience was all-engulfing and complete—that Palestine 'has come to us'—suggests that visiting the exhibition involved a collective fantasy in which this thinly disguised West was imagined as an authentic slice of

---

[139] Quoted in Hoffenberg, *Empire on Display*, 230.

Fig. 10. 'Palestine and Eastern Exhibition in Stroud', *Jewish Missionary Intelligence*, January 1892.

the East, a collective fantasy in which this England was imagined as the Holy Land:

> When the turnstile has clicked behind you, and the folds of the heavy draught-preventing curtains have parted, your eyes gaze upon what has been aptly called Palestine in Plymouth. But of this we are sure—that all thoughts of Plymouth will soon be banished from your minds. It is Palestine now. Never before have we seen the great bare Drillhall assume so homely an appearance.[140]

To enjoy the experience, Plymouth had to be forgotten and remembered at the very same time; it was by masquerading as 'Palestine' that the bare local hall became all the more homely, all the more recognizable. The exhibition's long-standing success merely enhanced this self-referential sense of intimacy: as a commentator noted in 1924, 'We are apt sometimes to forget how familiar we at home have become with Palestine models and costume lectures.'[141]

While the principle that 'no place is too small' allowed the bringing of Palestine to every corner of the United Kingdom, this, in itself, does not account for the visitors' ability, or will, to suspend disbelief and identify so closely with the objects on display. It is telling, for example, that the 'Orient in London' exhibition, organized by the London Missionary Society in the Islington Agricultural Hall in 1908, did not seem to evoke a similar response, even though photographs of that event look very much like those taken at the Palestine Exhibition.[142] The explanation, it seems, lies in the unique role played by the Holy Land in English Sunday-school culture: whereas the 'Orient' signified absolute otherness, the Holy Land always evoked a powerful sense of familiarity and domesticity. Rather than stretch the Orientalist imagination to its exotic extreme, the success of the Palestine Exhibition seemed to depend on the limits of this imagination.

That the exhibition did not really aim to offer a perfect simulacrum is clear when we observe how this unique geographical displacement was matched by the exhibition's handling of race. Some of the craftsmen on display—just like the odd camel, present in larger venues—were imported directly from Palestine, but most of the 'natives' were mem-

---

[140] CMJ, 'PE' [4], unidentified press clipping, 'The Palestine Exhibition: A Layman's Impressions' (13 Feb. 1908).
[141] *Jewish Missionary Intelligence*, Sept. 1924, 140.
[142] Coombes, *Reinventing Africa*, 174–86.

bers of the community, and the 'Realistic Scenes' were re-enacted by Schor, his wife, 'and a company of ladies and gentlemen, boys and girls, in Eastern Dress' (see Fig. 11).[143] In the first exhibition, in Felixstowe, 'Mr George Elliston looked a giant as David clad in sheep skins, with his club, sling, and stone. Mr Sidney Elliston was a perfect Bethlehem gentlemen, and Mr Crawford a Bedouin chief. Mrs A. Hicks was a splendid Egyptian lady, and Miss Crawford a notable Galilean bride, while Miss Walton and Miss Ethel Walton were charming dancing girls.'[144] Schor's ahistorical fusion of biblical Israelites and present-day Muslims, of the Semitic and the Anglo-Saxon, was an attempt to literalize—albeit temporarily—the metaphor of 'Chosen People', not on a broad national basis, but in a truly local sense. Having built Jerusalem in *our* green and pleasant land, the Palestine Exhibition seemed to imply, *we* are its elect.

This, too, marked the difference between the Palestine Exhibition and other colonial and missionary shows, where the pageants often produced a comical effect, the press criticizing 'the number of stall-holders whose oriental garb cannot disguise the fact that they are stolid, spectacled British matrons, on whom the gorgeous robes of the East do not sit well'.[145] Schor, by comparison, made little effort to conceal the thespians' unmistakably English features. Indeed, part of the excitement was caused by the ability to recognize the white face behind the Semitic mask. As the visitor to the Plymouth exhibition wrote, 'sometimes the Rabbi, sweeping by with stately step is the genuine article, with nothing artificial about him except his broken English—whilst at other times he is possibly your own schoolmaster or even your churchwarden!'[146]

'The Bible is an Eastern Book,' wrote James Neil, 'as much an Eastern book, be it said reverently, as the *Arabian Nights*—a work indeed fully inspired by the Holy Spirit, but, as to its human side, written in the East, by Easterners, and for Easterners.'[147] The Palestine exhibitions demonstrate how this truism—inspired by the higher biblical criticism, and amplified by the academic Orientalist project—could in fact feed

---

[143] CMJ, 'PE' [2], pamphlet ['York, November 1900'].
[144] *Jewish Missionary Intelligence*, Oct. 1891, 155.
[145] Quoted in Coombes, *Reinventing Africa*, 180.
[146] CMJ, 'PE' [4], unidentified press clipping.
[147] James Neil, *Strange Scenes, Part I: Joppa; or, Discoveries on Stepping Ashore* (London: Simpkin, 1894), 2.

Fig. 11. 'Group of Helpers' in the 'Palestine in Blackheath' exhibition, *Jewish Missionary Intelligence*, July 1912.

back into vernacular biblical culture, Orientalizing it, but, at the same time, enhancing the association with one's own vicinity. Unlike Bunyan's Jerusalem, Schor's Promised Land was no longer imagined in quintessentially English (or Western) terms, and its Israelites were now clothed in typical Eastern dress. Yet, just like the vision presented in *The Pilgrim's Progress*, the Palestine Exhibition also offered its visitors an intimate, cosy Zion in England. The actual territory in the East was thus not only inaccessible to the great majority of people, but also, to a certain extent, wholly superfluous. Once again, this cultural projection was by no means limited to Palestine; but in the case of the Holy Land, it reinforced a powerful sense of familiarity which was already current. 'How it carries one back, doesn't it!' exclaims Jude, having examined the model of Jerusalem (p. 109); and by 'back' he refers not so much to the geographical sphere of the old East, as to his own childhood days, to the Jerusalem of his fancy.

The result was a remarkable discrepancy between the official goals of the London Jews Society and the ways in which these were presented by the Palestine Exhibition and experienced by the public. Paradoxically, while the leaders of the Society hoped that the exhibition would bring the English people closer to the Jews, and thus bring the Jews closer to the Christian faith, the exhibition itself was staged in such a way that presented the English themselves as Jews; and while the Society's work in the Holy Land and its open support for the Zionist cause helped secure British imperial interests in the Middle East, the exhibition itself seemed to convey a very different message: it seemed to indicate that the Holy Land that mattered was 'here', not 'there'. Against the 'world-as-exhibition' view, proposed by Mitchell, we should perhaps add the complementary notion of 'exhibition-as-home': instead of turning overseas, the exhibition looked inwards, imagining Palestine in and as one's own community.

My point is that the 'Holy Land'—even when presented as a purely geographical, Oriental space—could continue to inform the vernacular impulse. Of course, the ability to toy with a compressed Palestine, to shift it endlessly between one town hall and another and omit all reference to its Arab inhabitants by assuming their roles, was in itself a form of proto-colonial appropriation. At the same time, we simply cannot ignore the context in which these images were produced and consumed. The Orientalist representation of the East as a never-changing, backward sphere was no doubt crucial in shaping Britain's colonial outlook; but in the metropolitan centre itself, these images could have different meanings. It was one thing to 'obliterate' the East when one was actually there; it was quite another when one had not left England, had not left one's own town hall.

That a visit to the Palestine Exhibition was not, in fact, 'better' than a journey to the actual East is indicated by the fact that the Revd Schor also conducted private tours to Palestine, offered to parties of 'ladies and gentlemen'.[148] In May 1908, addressing the audience of a Palestine Exhibition at the Drill Hall, Basingstoke, Lord Curzon explained how a visit to the Holy Land changed his perception of the Bible. Since he went there, he said,

---

[148] CMJ, 'PE' [4], pamphlet.

whenever I hear the old Testament read, I recall the scenes I have visited, I place the figures in their surroundings, and this makes the narrative more vivid and personal to myself. And although you will not feel this in the same degree, not having been to the country, yet in a small way, from what you will see here and from what you will be told in the addresses and lectures, I hope that the Old and New Testaments, the Scriptures of your faith, may become a little more real to all of you, both in church on Sundays and in your everyday life.[149]

It is not so much the Oriental native—employed to vitalize Curzon's scriptural readings—who is being patronized here, as the native people of Basingstoke, who are encouraged to make their biblical images 'a little more real', but in a 'small way' only. This 'small way', with its inward-looking vision, should be set against the 'larger truth' that only visitors to Palestine can encounter. And it is this 'small way' that suggests that the 'world-as-exhibition' view was not necessarily oriented overseas, seeking to impose a colonial-like order on a blurred reality out there. Instead, it imagined a tiny, self-contained Palestine.

In England's green and pleasant Hyde Park

It is once again necessary, in this context, to expand our perspective. Palestine was one of the most popular topics for Victorian spectacles, but Rome and Paris, the USA and the Far East were equally popular. Moreover, while strict Evangelicals continued to flock to Palestine shows, others were deterred by the pious and didactic tone. Albert Smith—whose *Ascent of Mont Blanc* opened at the Egyptian Hall in March 1852—explained that 'there was a great danger of instruction becoming a bogie to frighten people away rather than attract them'.[150] His own show, one of the biggest hits of the entire Victorian era, was a moving panorama combined with an entertaining routine of impersonations, anecdotes, and songs. Upstairs, he found 'as a second-floor lodger a very respectable panorama of the Holy Land, which had long ceased to stimulate public curiosity'. The Palestine panorama now found itself playing to full houses made up of patrons who could not secure a ticket for Smith's show: 'those who failed ascending Mont Blanc', remarked *The Times*, 'consented to endure a pilgrimage to

---

[149] Earl Curzon of Kedleston, *Subjects of the Day* (London: George Allen & Unwin, 1915), 176.
[150] *The Times*, 18 Sept. 1854, 10.

Palestine'.[151] Seeing no reason why someone else should profit, Smith rented the room himself and, taking advantage of the Crimean War, replaced the Holy Land with a panorama of Constantinople.[152]

These defeats of the Holy Land, first by Mont Blanc, then by the Crimean War, are extremely ironical, considering that the Romantic Alpine view was a secularized, typological version of the Mount Pisgah motif. Likewise, the Crimean War was initially triggered by struggles over the holy places in Jerusalem and Bethlehem, and the Russian intervention on behalf of the Orthodox Church. Both the nineteenth-century fascination with the Alps, then, and the outbreak of war in 1853, could be 'traced back' to the Holy Land.

This is indicative, once again, of the degree to which the literal significations of the biblical vocabulary continued to be overshadowed by its metaphorical appropriations. Indeed, the most coveted Promised Land in that extraordinary summer of 1851 was not that of Bartlett's, Bonomi's, or Burford's panoramas, but the Crystal Palace itself. The feeling of national triumph generated by the Great Exhibition reinforced the notion that the British were a chosen nation. As H. W. Burrows, Canon of Rochester, exclaimed: 'The erection of the splendid temple—that palace which was for God, not for man—was a visible proof to the Jews that they were in a very different state from what they had been in a few years before, ere the Victories of David.' These achievements—'A united people, a gifted monarch, peace and plenty, a pious undertaking, long contemplated and at last happily finished, stamped with God's approval'—were clear signs of providential election, in biblical times for Solomon's subjects, and now for Victoria's.[153]

The sense of religious rapture was everywhere. Commenting on the opening ceremony of the Great Exhibition, the Queen wrote: 'One felt—as so many did whom I have spoken to—filled with devotion, more so than by any service I have ever heard';[154] and Charles Kingsley said, 'it was like going into a sacred place'.[155] But the analogy between

---

[151] *The Times*, 3 Feb. 1854, 10. [152] Altick, *Shows of London*, 476.
[153] H. W. Burrows, *The Great Exhibition: A Sermon Preached on Sunday, May 4th, 1851* (London: Skeffington, 1851), 3, 5.
[154] Quoted in Patrick Beaver, *The Crystal Palace, 1851–1936: A Portrait of Victorian Enterprise* (London: Hugh Evelyn, 1970), 40.
[155] Quoted in Max Schulz, *Paradise Preserved: Recreations of Eden in Eighteenth- and Nineteenth-Century England* (Cambridge: Cambridge University Press, 1985), 185.

the Crystal Palace and Jerusalem was often made even more explicitly. With its palm-trees and fountain, the shining glass and visual profusion, the gathering of nations and sense of utopian triumph, no wonder the Crystal Palace was continuously depicted as Revelation's New Jerusalem, a small-scale heaven on earth, a type of things to come. Many preachers used this analogy to urge believers to prepare themselves for 'the Great Exhibition of the Last Day'.[156] In a sermon delivered in Hull in 1851, Charles Overton declared:

> When you come to the entrance... [and] see the lofty trees with all their green honours, stretching their gigantic boughs in full liberty beneath that mighty dome; there you see the sparkling fountains, and hear the distant music, and gaze upon the honour and the glory of the nations, and the multitudes that are gathered together within those shining walls, you are reminded of *Christian's* entrance into the celestial city.[157]

The Holy Land was incorporated into the Victorian spectacle, but it was the spectacle itself which was becoming the most coveted holy land. Bunyan's New Jerusalem was now a paradise of commodities: for the middle-class imagination, the Great Exhibition was a new kind of Eden, a 'cornucopia of manufactured goods to guarantee the good life'.[158] The Palestine panoramas, with their spectacular dimensions and overflow of detail, were also part of this new ethic and aesthetic of superabundance; but why visit a panoramic reproduction of the earthly city when its celestial counterpart was now established in London?

Even after it was relocated in Sydenham, the Crystal Palace continued to function as a type of heaven—as one children's book proclaimed, 'He says that the Palace, so lovely, so nice / Makes him dream in his sleep that he's in Paradise'[159]—if not simply as an accessible Holy Land. When William Holman Hunt returned from Palestine with an incomplete *Christ in the Temple*, he finished the Temple's background by

---

[156] Revd Henry Birch, *The 'Great Exhibition' Spiritualized* (London: John Snow, 1851), 47. See also, among many others, [Charles Stanley], *The Great Exhibition Tracts* (London: Witherby, 1851); Revd C. T. Davies, *The Crystal Palace and the Crystal City* (2nd edn. Northampton: R. Harris, 1852).
[157] Quoted in Percy M. Young, *George Grove 1820–1900: A Biography* (London: Macmillan, 1980), 55.
[158] Schulz, *Paradise Preserved*, 190.
[159] George H. Robinson, *Peter's Paradise: A Child's Dream of the Crystal Palace* (London: Simpkin, 1890), 2.

travelling regularly to the Alhambra court at the Crystal Palace.[160] The idea that Jerusalem could be established in Sydenham's green and pleasant land was, undoubtedly, yet another metamorphosis of the 'Jerusalem in England' theme, but this time, with a unique middle-class twist. This Promised Land should be set alongside the Chartists' dream of Holy Land, Jude's New Jerusalem of self-improvement, perhaps even William Morris's *Earthly Paradise*. The actual city in the East could hardly compete with these visions; the metaphor shone much more brilliantly than the actual Mediterranean sun.

The PEF, the Public, and the 'Popular'

So far we have examined the work of cultural agents—publishers, editors, preachers, painters—who popularized the academic Orientalist discourse by filtering, adapting, or repressing it. The Palestine Exploration Fund, however, is a somewhat different case, one in which the process of appropriating the academic discourse for mass consumption had been considerably condensed. The Government subsidized the Fund's projects by lending surveyors and equipment, but since it could not support the work directly (or even pay for the surveyors' expenses), the PEF had to rely on donations. The Queen, patron of the Fund, gave £150; the University of Oxford sent £500; but it soon became clear that only a regular flow of subscriptions would allow the Fund to operate. The PEF was forced to turn directly to the public for financial support.[161]

The interaction here, in other words, was not between consumers and mediating cultural agents, but between consumers and the academic élite itself. These were not the amateurs who produced entertaining travel accounts, water-colour paintings, or even geographical textbooks, but skilled scholars and explorers, honorary dons in the 'invisible college' who were involved in a systematic study of Palestine's geography and history. An inability to adapt the discourse to public expectations— or an inability to adapt public expectations to the discourse—could have brought the Fund's work to a standstill. The PEF's attempts to secure public support, then, offer us a final insight into the mechanism

---

[160] Diana Holman-Hunt, *My Grandfather, His Wives and Loves* (London: Hamish Hamilton, 1969), 169.
[161] PEF, *Fifty Years' Work in the Holy Land* (London: PEF, 1915), 28–30.

of popularizing Palestine; and its failures highlight the discursive limits of the academic Orientalist discourse.

Approaching the masses

All historians of the PEF agree that its first years were fraught with financial calamities.[162] When, in 1867, the young lieutenant Charles Warren was given £300 to finance the cost of his excavations in Jerusalem, he was not aware of the fact that this was the Fund's entire capital: as a result, Warren went into a personal debt of some £1,000, and it took months before he was reimbursed.[163] Dismissing these difficulties as birth throes, historians have often remarked, cheerfully, that after these early years of struggle, the society was 'eagerly followed, and supported, by people all over Britain'.[164]

If the PEF was followed, it was certainly not supported. In its first few years, the Fund relied on appeals: it raised £1,438 in 1865, £1,033 in 1866, and a staggering £4,557 in 1867. This donation level was never achieved again before 1918, and in 1869 the PEF Committee was forced to introduce a subscription.[165] Nevertheless, between 1865 and 1914, the Fund's membership never exceeded 1,000, and for most of that time, it had fewer than 800 members. In 1869, Walter Morrison, the Fund's treasurer, noted that while the annual subscription secured about £3,000, at least £5,000 was required to continue operations.[166] In 1872, for instance, the income from subscriptions and donations amounted to little more than £2,450, and in 1880 to £1,454 only.[167] To increase its revenue, the PEF sold publications and photographs, offered lectures and established local societies, but that was never

---

[162] The most authoritative account to date is John J. Moscrop, 'The Palestine Exploration Fund, 1865–1914' (Ph.D. thesis, Leicester, 1996), later revised and published as *Measuring Jerusalem: The Palestine Exploration Fund and British Interests in the Holy Land* (Leicester: Leicester University Press, 1999). See also PEF, *Our Work in Palestine* (London: Bentley, 1873); Neil Asher Silberman, *Digging for God and Country: Exploration, Archaeology and the Secret Struggle for the Holy Land, 1799–1917* (New York: Alfred A. Knopf, 1982).

[163] Charles Warren, *Underground Jerusalem* (London: Richard Bentley, 1876), 4–5. Subsequent page numbers are cited parenthetically in the text.

[164] Naomi Shepherd, *The Zealous Intruders: The Western Rediscovery of Palestine* (London: Collins, 1987), 205.

[165] Moscrop, 'Palestine Exploration Fund', 227.

[166] *The Times*, 25 June 1869, 10.

[167] See balance sheets, *PEFQSt*, Oct. 1872, Oct. 1880.

enough. As John Moscrop has shown, up to the First World War, the Fund was continuously on the brink of collapse, and it was only thanks to the support of the War Office that the Fund survived at all.[168] Letters and reports on behalf of the PEF read like one long, desperate plea.

To be sure, Victorian exploration societies could depend on a limited constituency only. In 1865, for example, the Royal Geographical Society (established in 1832)—the leading institution of its kind—enjoyed receipts of almost £5,500 and a membership of 2,100: healthy figures, but hardly vast.[169] One must bear in mind, however, that the PEF's agenda was as much Christian as it was geographical. In his opening address in 1865, the Archbishop of York declared that the work 'should be carried out on scientific principle', and that the PEF 'should not be started, nor should it be conducted, as a religious society'.[170] But the Archbishop's own speech—just like the prayer with which he opened the proceedings, and indeed, his very presence there—all suggested the exact opposite. By 'religious' he had simply meant 'sectarian'; which is undoubtedly why 260 of the 700 subscribers in 1882 were clergy, most of them Anglican.[171]

It is this obvious religious affiliation which makes the Fund's failure so puzzling. In its heyday, the PEF had about 120 local societies in the UK, with an average of ten members per society; and the *total* receipts from 1865 to 1914 were £138,650.[172] By comparison, the British and Foreign Bible Society (established in 1804) had, by mid-century, 460 auxiliaries, 373 branches, and almost 2,500 local associations, with an *annual* revenue of well over £100,000. Even smaller organizations, like the RTS, had membership lists in the thousands;[173] the income of the London Jews Society for 1859–60, for example, was £32,451.[174] Clearly the Victorians had capital to bestow on religious institutions: if the Holy Land was, as the good Archbishop insisted, 'our country',

---

[168] Moscrop, 'Palestine Exploration Fund', 2, 134. I am indebted to John Moscrop for these figures and estimations.
[169] *Journal of the Royal Geographical Society*, 36 (1866), pp. v, xi.
[170] PEF, *Fifty Years' Work*, 18.
[171] Moscrop, 'Palestine Exploration Fund', 81.
[172] PEF, *Fifty Years' Work*, 170–2; Moscrop, 'Palestine Exploration Fund', 79.
[173] Ian Bradley, *The Call to Seriousness: The Evangelical Impact on the Victorians* (London: Cape, 1976), 137–8.
[174] Gidney, *History*, 268.

why were not the people of England—landlords of Palestine—hastening to support the work of the PEF?

This is not a question posed in retrospect only. Members of the Fund were acutely distressed by this enigma, and it is evoked, again and again, in articles, pamphlets, and letters from the late 1860s onwards. 'For it cannot be alleged that we, as a people, are indifferent to the Bible', exclaimed a correspondent to the *Malvern News*:

> The greater part of a million sterling per annum is subscribed by us to the Church, the Wesleyan and the Non-conformist Missionary Societies, the Tract, and the British and Foreign Bible Societies.
>
> Yet while all these societies are based on a belief in the Bible... and while it is quite within the range of probability that many of the Biblical traditions will be solved by the operations of [the PEF], even in the course of a very few months, yet the total amount contributed to its funds by the British public between the 1st of July and the 31st of December 1868, was only £987. 15s. 1d.!

The conclusion was clear. 'There is no possible explanation of the fact that this association is languishing for lack of funds except this: That the British public is unaware of its very existence.'[175] The *Saturday Review*, which thought it 'a disgrace that this enterprise has received so little public encouragement', was also convinced that the PEF's managers had failed to make the Fund known:

> Whatever may be the cause, it is not to be denied that the Fund has never taken any real or tenacious hold upon the public mind. Much of this failure may, in our view, be attributed to a lack of the peculiar arts by which the public is, in technical phrase, to be got at. Is it owing to the fastidiousness or proper pride, or simply to the guilelessness and ignorance of the means of raising the *popularis aura*, or propitiating the powers that be?[176]

This is a bold suggestion, considering that one of the PEF's founders and its first Honorary Secretary was George Grove. An engineer by training, a biblical scholar, editor of *Macmillan's Magazine*, a self-taught musician who later became director of the Royal College of Music and whose *Dictionary of Music* still bears his name today, Grove was the tireless secretary of the Crystal Palace Company from 1851 to 1873.

---

[175] PEF Archive, London, PEF/1865/2 [press-clippings album], *Malvern News*, 8 June 1869.
[176] PEF/1865/2, *Saturday Review*, 29 Aug. 1868.

His series of popular concerts—like the Handel Festival which attracted tens of thousands—suggests that if ever there was a Victorian who mastered that peculiar art by which 'the public' was 'to be got at', that Victorian was George Grove.

But who, then, was the 'public'? An editorial published in *The Times* in December 1867 declared that no subject was 'more interesting to the popular mind than the Holy Land': 'Palestine is to thousands of Englishmen the only country whose history they have ever read.... The recollections and the hopes of multitudes are bound up with that little province at the corner of the Mediterranean hemmed in between the desert and the sea.' *The Times* was convinced, therefore, that in this 'wealthy, educated, and religious country', Grove's appeal 'ought to excite in the educated public a zeal like his own'. But surely the 'popular mind' and 'the multitudes' were not synonymous with the 'wealthy' and the 'educated': whom, then, must the Fund approach? 'We feel sure that when the objects and the methods of the Association are well understood, they will no longer suffer for lack of funds', concluded the editorial.[177] But how did one go about explaining these objects? This was exactly the dilemma that Grove and his colleagues were facing.

Grove often conducted his PEF correspondence on Crystal Palace stationery,[178] but there is little to suggest that he exploited the Crystal Palace's popularity to promote the cause of Palestine exploration. In 1868, an advertisement for the PEF was printed on the wrappers of 40,000 pamphlets announcing the Handel Festival, but the Fund was charged a total of £75, paid to the Crystal Palace Company.[179] With a remarkably tight budget, Grove preferred to make use of his excellent contacts in the press to publish letters in the *Daily Telegraph*, the *Morning Post*, and occasionally, the *Manchester Guardian*.[180] His main efforts, however, were always aimed at *The Times*. Between 1865 and 1869, Grove sent dozens of letters to the Editor, in which he informed readers on the prospects of the Fund, announced recent discoveries, recorded the names of donors and subscribers, and always appealed for help.[181]

---

[177] *The Times*, 13 Dec. 1867, 8.
[178] Cf. PEF/1865/1/38, printed circular of 12 May 1865.
[179] PEF Committee Minutes, 25 Feb. 1868.
[180] Moscrop, 'Palestine Exploration Fund', 50.
[181] Consider, e.g., the first few months of 1866: letters from Grove were published in *The Times* on 6, 17 Jan.; 12, 21 Feb.; 3, 9, 23 Apr.; 21 May; 27 July.

The circulation of *The Times* in the 1860s was about 60,000.[182] It was read by the élite and the upper middle class, perhaps by the people who would attend the Crystal Palace's Handel festival but definitely not by the 'masses'.[183] Grove may have believed that only the readership of *The Times* combined a broad enough, yet prosperous enough, audience; but was he at all capable of approaching a different audience?

It is telling that even Grove's critics, who protested that his many responsibilities left him little time to make appeals on behalf of the PEF, did not fare better. In his account of the Jerusalem excavations of 1867, Charles Warren described the PEF under Grove's management as 'feeble and imperfectly organised', operating 'spasmodically by fits and starts' (p. 2). Labouring in Jerusalem, increasingly immersed in both gravel and debt, Warren decided to take action himself: 'to whom was I to look? To the public. Fortunately for me and my work, it was to the public I instinctively turned from the commencement, and it was through the public interest excited that I was enabled to proceed' (p. 17). Ironically, what Warren has in mind here is the 'public who passed through Jerusalem' and 'had been down the shafts' (p. 8), and the 'enthusiastic reception by the public which I met with on my return, by the hundreds assembled in the Royal Institution, and the number of letters I have received from persons with whom I previously had no acquaintance' (pp. 17–18). This was a very restricted 'public' indeed.

Similarly, Warren praised the novelist Walter Besant, who succeeded Grove as Secretary in June 1868 (Grove remained Honorary Secretary for ten more years), for 'appealing to the masses who love the Lord and the Book' and 'bringing the good work to the knowledge of the people' (p. 3). It is certainly true that Besant extended his appeals to a broad range of provincial newspapers and denominational periodicals, from the *Primitive Methodist Advocate* and the *Greenock Advertiser* to the *Freemasons' Magazine* and the *Jewish Chronicle*.[184] Warren is also right to credit Besant with introducing the annual subscription and the *Quarterly Statement* which was dispatched to all subscribers, the local

---

[182] Altick, *English Common Reader*, 394.
[183] 'The orchestral programmes of the Palace were never "popular" in the sense that the Palace itself was popular' (Michael Musgrave, *The Musical Life of the Crystal Palace* (Cambridge: Cambridge University Press, 1995), 119).
[184] PEF/1865/2, numerous press clippings.

societies, and the Ladies' Association, established in 1875 to bring the 'work we are doing in Palestine before those who can best be reached by drawing room meetings'.[185] Besant's passionate philanthropic work probably made him, more than any of his colleagues, attentive to the needs of the 'people'. His vision of a 'Palace of Delight', a cultural centre which would cure the joyless monotony of East End life, was finally realized in 1887, when the Queen opened the People's Palace at the Mile End Road.[186] Nevertheless, Warren's assertion that these arrangements 'made the society take such a strong position in the country' seems absurd, considering that his book was published just after one of the Fund's greatest crises (a gush of unpaid bills which threatened to ruin Besant's honeymoon).[187] The fact was that Besant, despite his zealous efforts and good will, rarely touched 'the people'. If he did succeed in bringing the good work to the attention of 'the masses who love the Lord and the Book', the masses offered little support.

There was, in other words, an almost ridiculous gap between the frequent allusions to the 'public'—the 'masses', the 'people', the 'multitudes'—and the Fund's actual patronage. This is more than simply a rhetorical formula or (as in the case of Warren) wishful thinking; rather, it reflects the frustration which marked the PEF's enterprise: a conviction that the exploration of the Holy Land was a topic which must appeal to the widest audience possible, the men and women, as *The Times* had written, whose 'recollections and hopes' were bound up 'with that little province'; but, at the same time, an inability to reach these people, inform them of the Fund's projects, and receive their help.

In the main, this was simply a problem of creating, or adopting, a suitable apparatus; even with the emergence of a printed mass culture, there was still no single medium which could bridge social and regional rifts. A possible solution was to utilize existing networks. Besant not only relied on the denominational press, but also appointed several lecturers who travelled from church to chapel to schoolhouse, offering free lectures, with a collection that went to the PEF. In a typical lecture,

---

[185] *PEFQSt*, 1877, quoted in Billie Melman, *Women's Orients: English Women and the Middle East, 1718–1918* (1992; 2nd edn. London: Macmillan, 1995), 41. See also Walter Besant, *Autobiography* (London: Hutchinson, 1902), 153–68.
[186] 'Walter Besant', *DNB*.
[187] Besant, *Autobiography*, 166.

at the Rehoboth School-Room at Morley, the Revd John James declared that the PEF committee was anxious to raise its funds, 'not by the hundreds or thousands of a few, but by the pounds, shillings, and pence of the many'. After all, 'the working and the middle class of this country took quite as much interest in the Bible and Palestine as the upper ten thousand, and perhaps more—some of them at least'. Still, the audience at Morley was described as 'moderately large' and 'respectable'.[188] Reaching the 'masses' demanded an exceptionally elaborate network, like the one devised by the London Jews Society and the indefatigable Revd Schor. The fact that the full PEF membership cost a guinea suggests that the Fund, in effect, had abandoned hope of enlisting the working class.

On a more fundamental level, the problem of approaching the masses was not merely logistical, but cultural. 'A great deal has been said of late of the working man,' the celebrated archaeologist, A. H. Layard, MP, declared in 1865:

> Let me say this, that if there is any subject in which the working man takes an interest, it is one connected with the illustration of the Holy Scriptures. I speak this after some experience. I am in the habit of giving lectures and discourses to working men—my constituents in Southwark, amongst others—and I have generally chosen some such subject,—for instance, my own journeys in the East, my incidents illustrating Eastern life, manners, and art, as bearing upon the Bible,—and I have always found that such subjects command the largest audiences of working men, and excite the greatest attention.... Therefore, though the Government may not be inclined to help us,—leaving such things, as usual, to private enterprise,—I think upon the score of the public utility, and the interest which the people at large take in researches of this kind, we might almost fairly appeal to it for its sympathy, aid, and support.[189]

Apart from repeating the customary conviction that the Bible is dear to working men, Layard does not really indicate how this appeal is to be made. What is particularly notable about his address, however, is the 'experience' which allows him to describe the life, manners, and art of his constituents in Southwark. Just like the knowledge of the East with which he commanded large audiences of working men, Layard's know-

---

[188] PEF/1865/2, unidentified press clipping, 'Lecture at Morley' (c.1868).
[189] PEF/1865/2/8, 'Report of the Proceedings at a Public Meeting', 22 June 1865 [leaflet].

ledge of working men is embedded in a framework of social dominance and subordination; and it is this colonial-style framework which reveals the distance between Layard, and his peers at the PEF, and the 'masses' they were so eager to approach. Consider Charles Warren's extraordinary career: in 1886, following his appointment as Chief Commissioner of the London Metropolitan Police, Warren undertook to militarize the force. His violent suppression of working-class rallies at Trafalgar Square in the summer of 1887 and, the following year, his complete mismanagement of the Ripper murders in Whitechapel suggest, yet again, that Warren's definition of 'the public' was very limited indeed.[190] As E. P. Thompson has shrewdly noted, Warren was a symbol of 'the feedback of imperialism—its experience and its consequences—to the streets of the imperial capital itself'.[191]

The Fund, then, failed in its attempts to obtain the pence of the 'multitudes'; but what about the shillings and pounds of the readers of *The Times*, and, after 1868, of the numerous other publications which reported regularly on the Fund's progress? It was not enough, of course, to reach an audience: the Fund's objectives needed to be construed in a way that would yield sympathy and support. In 1869, for example, Besant secured the consent of the Evangelical *Christian World* to introduce a shilling subscription scheme: 'Let the shillings of our readers find their way [to Palestine] in thousands.' But months later, the '*Christian World* List' had 'not yet realised the sum we hoped, probably from the natural unwillingness of people interested in the fund to pay money, so to speak, in the dark'.[192]

Rob Roy's biscuits and Joseph's mummy

Grove, in his Crystal Palace office, was the first to recognize that to gain a wide following, the PEF's undertaking could not remain 'in the dark'. The Fund's goals and achievements had to be visualized, made 'palpable to sight', incorporated into the contemporary culture of the spectacle. Only findings, Grove knew, would guarantee an income. In his book,

---

[190] 'Charles Warren', *DNB*; Judith Walkowitz, *City of Dreadful Delights: Narratives of Sexual Danger in Late-Victorian London* (Chicago: University of Chicago Press, 1992), 197.
[191] E. P. Thompson, *Writing by Candlelight* (London: Merlin, 1980), 155–6.
[192] PEF/1865/2, *Christian World*, 18 June 1869.

the disgusted Warren cited Grove's demand in 1867: ' "Give us results, and we will send you money!" was the inspiring cry which reached me in Palestine; in vain I replied, "Give me tools, materials, money, food, and I will get you results." The answer was, "Results furnished, and you shall have the money!" ' (p. 3). Once again, Warren decided to act alone. 'The public who passed through Jerusalem *saw* what was going on, *saw* the difficulties I had to contend with,' Warren explained. On returning to England, 'They could speak, for they had *seen* the work, had been down the shafts, had traversed the sub-structures: the work was for the public, and I took measures to allow the public, both English and Foreign, to *see* all that was going on, and the result was an enthusiasm which no appeal by itself could have raised' (p. 8, my italics). But this was precisely Grove's point: it was only by being allowed to gaze directly at the findings, to *see* the work, that the 'public' (in this case, tourists in Jerusalem) could be persuaded to support it.

As early as 1866, the PEF Committee resolved 'to form a Museum of Biblical objects in the South Kensington Museum'.[193] Difficulties ensued, although an exhibition was finally opened in the summer of 1869 at the Dudley Gallery, Egyptian Hall. It included 350 photographs, models of the Holy Sepulchre and of the ancient city, maps and plans. 'But, after all', as the *Record* noted, 'the chief interest lay in the mementoes of the past—though they be but broken fragments of pottery and stone.'[194] There were ancient vases, jewels, oil lamps, mosaics, catapult balls, and some curious tear bottles; but even the *Christian Times* was forced to admit that of all the articles in the display, 'the greatest interest of the greatest number will be directed to that in which the canoe stores employed by "Rob Roy" during his recent voyage in the East are included. In it are his medicine chest, his toilet implements, a spirit lamp, and some bread and biscuit, which are described as "unconsumed stores" of various exploring expeditions.'[195]

Just a few months previously, 'Rob Roy' (John MacGregor) had sailed a canoe down the River Jordan, to the Dead Sea. The great interest aroused by his supplies—the canoe itself was absent—testifies to MacGregor's growing celebrity. It also suggests, however, that the

---

[193] PEF Committee Minutes, 16 July 1866.
[194] PEF/1865/2, *Record,* 11 Aug. 1869.
[195] PEF/1865/2, *Christian Times,* 13 June 1869.

archaeological findings themselves simply failed to excite the visitors. Indeed, the exhibition was a not a success: only 6,000 people came to see it.[196] A 'strange and inexplicable barrenness', wrote the *Saturday Review*, seemed to 'wait upon all efforts in what would otherwise be beyond doubt the most popular and stirring of all departments of research'.[197] Even Grove himself, in one of his many letters to *The Times*, confessed that 'discoveries of the kind I have named are barren and uninviting to the majority of the readers, even to many who are keenly interested in the Holy Land and Holy Writ'.[198] The *Saturday Review* remarked, tongue in cheek, that with a little more ingenuity, tact, and the good luck of the 'irrepressible Cole' (of the South Kensington Museum), 'neat artistic cases and cabinets would have borne the inviting label of Jewish Antiquities, and in due time might have exhibited to the astonished eyes of cockneys, among other sensational marvels of the place, such undoubted relics as Pharaoh's chariot wheel from the Red Sea, or the identical sword with which Balaam meant to kill his ass'.[199] But such astonishing discoveries were not to be found. 'We did not bring home the ark', wrote Claude Conder, one of the Fund's excavators of the 1870s, 'or the salves of Dan, or Ahab's ivory house, or Joseph's mummy.'[200] Disillusioned with the relics, the Royal Engineers had no problem convincing the PEF Committee in 1869–70 that it was necessary to turn from archaeological to cartographical work.[201] This was even less likely to excite the masses, but at least it guaranteed the backing of the War Office.

In fact, as the *Saturday Review* explained, Joseph's mummy was not necessary: even a crock of Jewish gold, a vessel or two of the Temple, or a stone 'incised with some undoubted Scriptural name' would have acted like a prophet's rod 'in letting forth the waters of public munificence'. The journal recognized, furthermore, that the problem was not simply the dull findings, but the dull representation: 'Much might have been done had some graphic and fluent pen been employed to put into a

---

[196] Silberman, *Digging for God and Country*, 98.
[197] PEF/1865/2, *Saturday Review*, 29 Aug. 1868.
[198] *The Times*, 14 Nov. 1867, 10.
[199] PEF/1865/2, *Saturday Review*, 29 Aug. 1868.
[200] Quoted in Shepherd, *Zealous Intruders*, 193.
[201] Moscrop, *Measuring Jerusalem*, 84.

piquant and attractive form such bits of real information as have come home to us in the comparatively dry and technical shape of Mr Warren's reports of progress.'[202] This was the crux of the matter: how could the dry, technical style of the scholarly discourse be popularized without compromising its scientific principles? Other Palestine exhibitions attracted considerable crowds. Why could not the PEF stage a similar event? The fact that Rob Roy's biscuit relics were on display demonstrates that the exhibition's organizers sensed that the cult of celebrity could help their cause. In 1869, for example, the *ILN* followed Warren's excavations in a series of articles, concentrating less on the studious and more on the adventurous nature of his archaeological work; the celebrated war artist, William Simpson, illustrated the underground shafts.[203]

As a rule, however, unlike the London Jews Society, with its Eastern masquerades, the PEF did not attempt to render its work exciting or amusing; nor could it, according to *The Times*:

> The general public requires everything to be put before it in a popular manner. It is strange with what unwillingness and distaste even well-informed people approach anything which comes before them in an abstract or scientific form or in the guise of learned research. Now, the Exploration of Palestine is necessarily a dry subject. Its promoters do not seek to make it popular. The country has been overrun with ordinary bookmakers, and they have added little enough to the store of knowledge. Mr. Grove and his friends have undertaken a task which, if completed, will be an honour to this country. They desire to survey the whole face of the country, with the view of determining, if possible, the sites of all places of historic interest. They desire to present a truthful picture of the land geographically and geologically... It will easily be understood that these purposes do not readily take the popular mind... But, unfortunately, it is difficult to invest topographical details with interest, or even make them intelligible... Mount Zion and Mount Moriah, the Valley of Jehoshaphat, and the brook Kedron, are like household words, but they give but a vague picture to the mind's eye.[204]

But this is precisely where *The Times* was wrong. The problem was not that these 'household words' gave a vague picture to the mind's eye, but

---

[202] PEF/1865/2, *Saturday Review*, 29 Aug. 1868.
[203] See illustrations in Edward Bacon, *The Great Archaeologists* (London: Secker & Warburg, 1976), 41–2.
[204] *The Times*, 13 Dec. 1867, 8.

rather the complete opposite: the picture they gave was so vivid that it overshadowed the reality itself. As we have seen, these were precisely the locations which appeared again and again in illustrations, exhibitions, and photographs, exactly like the photographs sold by the PEF for 1*s*. 9*d*. (1*s*. 3*d*. for subscribers) in the hope of increasing its meagre income. Broken fragments of pottery and stone did not seem to relate, in any way, to these stirring images of Palestine; and the scholarly style in which the Fund's reports were written seemed equally removed from the sentimental, pious tone with which the Holy Land was usually imagined. 'No country more urgently requires illustration,' declared the PEF Prospectus, but the country presented in Warren's technical reports and shattered pottery was a far cry from the illustrations already available in Bibles and popular geography books, not to mention the ethereal quality of the 'green hill far away' or 'Jerusalem the Golden'.

Underground Jerusalem

It is here, I think, that we can begin to sense the deeper reasons behind the Fund's failure. The many logistical difficulties, the administrators' inability to reach the target audience that they had aimed for, and their unwillingness to compromise the scientific principles on which, they believed, their work rested—all these contributed to the Fund's predicament. But this failure cannot be grasped without recognizing that the Holy Land which the PEF offered simply could not compete with the Holy Land of the 'mind's eye'. The many commentators who were puzzled by the public's indifference were correct in their assertion that the Bible held a paramount position in English culture, and that the 'Holy Land' was one of the most interesting subjects to the 'popular mind'. What they overlooked, however, was the distance between the literal reading of the biblical vocabulary and its metaphorical appropriations. The Fund abandoned the archaeological excavations in the late 1860s, and turned to cartographical surveys, because it preferred to depend on the limited, yet reliable, subsidy offered by the War Office, rather than appeal to the 'multitudes'. But this shift could also suggest that the multitudes were simply not interested in the overtly imperial project of mapping the land.[205] The Holy Land—as the following

---

[205] Moscrop, 'Palestine Exploration Fund', 133–4.

chapter will discuss in detail—was not part of the popular imperial ethos; but it was, as we have seen, intimately associated with the institutions and the traditions of a domestic, inward-looking culture. Many English men and woman may have believed, like the good Archbishop, that the Holy Land was 'their country'; but theirs was the Holy Land of social mobility, the Holy Land of future life, or, most probably, the Holy Land of the Sunday school, the hymns, the illustrated Bible, and the model of Jerusalem.

Indeed, when the Fund's administrators tried to depict their goals in a more accessible manner, they, too, tended to defer the earthly Jerusalem. As early as the PEF's first public meeting in 1865, the Archbishop of York had declared that 'there can be little doubt that under the sacred city, monuments of the greatest value and importance would be found in every foot deep of the ground'.[206] The idea that the 'real' Jerusalem was not the city which appeared on the surface, but rather the one hidden beneath it, underground, soon became current, manifested in titles like Warren's *Underground Jerusalem* (1876) or George St Clair's *The Buried City of Jerusalem* (1887). Where were the walls of the city, the site of the Temple, the sepulchre of Christ, 'and the many other spots whose names ring in the ears of the student of the sacred story?', Grove asked (the readers of *The Times*), and immediately replied: 'Why, all, without any reasonable doubt, hidden below the modern city, and recoverable by energy, tact, and perseverance.'[207] In an article published in *Good Words*, A. P. Stanley claimed that 'the hills, the valleys, the springs of old Jerusalem lie thirty or forty feet below the surface. The very rock from which it was hewn ... the very fountains from which it was fed, have vanished from our view. These, the still living witnesses of those great events, we can still recover; we can still, if we go deep enough, arrive at the streets where David trod.'[208]

This concept was adopted enthusiastically by the Fund's speakers: it justified the poor results of the excavations by explaining that it was all a matter of depth; it sought to unearth a Judaeo-Christian reality beneath the Muslim present, while gratifying the Protestant suspicion of the Catholic holy places; and it echoed the fascination with other buried cities, typical of the Victorian preoccupation with roots, origins, and

---

[206] PEF/1865/2/8, 'Report'.   [207] *The Times*, 15 Aug. 1865, 10.
[208] *Good Words*, 1 Mar. 1868, 175.

beginnings.[209] Significantly, it proposed to do all this by deferring, yet again, the visible, earthly city. Like the heavenly Jerusalem, the Jerusalem in one's heart, the view from the Mount of Olives, or the Palestine Exhibition, 'Underground Jerusalem' continued to avoid the 'larger truth' out there. This fabrication suggests that even an imperial body like the PEF, which brought England closer to Palestine than ever before, could not popularize its scholarly work without eclipsing the 'real' Jerusalem. That it failed to convince the 'public' suggests that even this fabrication was not enough.

'I never want to go to Palestine'

Drawing on a wide array of cultural forms, which extend from the 1830s to the First World War, this chapter has traced some of the major trends in the popularization of the academic Orientalist discourse. It has suggested that rather than amplify the existence of the earthly Holy Land as a geographical space—a place which must be explored and made known and eventually conquered and possessed—these popular images fed back, in fact, into the vernacular Orientalist tradition, the same tradition which, in a way, had bred them in the first place: as we saw in the previous chapter, one cannot understand British imperial stakes in the Holy Land without considering the meaning and significance of the vernacular biblical vocabulary; these popular cultural forms merely retrieved, and accentuated, what had already been present, all along, in the academic Anglo-Palestine Orientalist discourse.

On one level, this was due to the ideological framework in which these popular forms were produced. For various theological or pedagogical reasons, editors and writers thought it best to defer the earthly Jerusalem and offer a Pisgah sight only. At the same time, this was also due to the conditions in which cultural forms like these were consumed. Since the actual East was not available, as an external signified, for comparison, these representations—Oriental or even Orientalist as they were—became associated with the local environment in which they were read, gazed at, or experienced. There is no reason to assume

---

[209] Kate Flint, *The Victorians and the Visual Imagination* (Cambridge: Cambridge University Press, 2000), 139–66.

that when other parts of the world were represented in the metropolis, the effect was necessarily more realistic. However, since the Holy Land was already such a suggestive metaphor, an image so intrinsic to Victorian culture, so real and yet unreal at the very same time, the association with 'Home' was immediate. Moreover, because the Holy Land was almost always represented within a religious context, it is not difficult to see why it became so closely identified with vernacular religious institutions, both official and unofficial.

It was the Sunday school which stood at the heart of this biblical culture. With its scriptural geography classes and magic-lantern shows, the singing of hymns and the reading of Bible stories, the occasional visit to the model of Jerusalem or even to the Palestine Exhibition, the Sunday school introduced the Holy Land to its young pupils. Consequently, just like the school itself, the Holy Land became imbued with a powerful sense of nostalgia, a yearning towards tradition, communal identity, and family: Jerusalem, my happy home.[210]

Rather than evoke the actual Palestine, this biblical Sunday-school culture depended, to a certain degree, on the *suppression* of the real place. In an essay entitled 'Hymns in a Man's Life' (1928), D. H. Lawrence has written:

> O Galilee, sweet Galilee
> Where Jesus loved so much to be,
> O Galilee, sweet Galilee,
> Come sing thy songs again to me!

To me the word Galilee has a wonderful sound. The Lake of Galilee! I don't want to know where it is. I never want to go to Palestine. Galilee is one of those lovely, glamorous worlds, not places, that exist in the golden haze of a child's half-formed imagination. And in my man's imagination it is just the same. It has been left untouched. With regard to the hymns which had such a profound influence on my childish consciousness, there has been no crystallizing out, no dwindling into actuality, no hardening into the commonplace. They are the same to my man's experience as they were to me nearly forty years ago.

---

[210] On the Sunday school and nostalgia see S. C. Williams, *Religious Belief and Popular Culture in Southwark, c.1880–1939* (Oxford: Oxford University Press, 1999), 126–62; Susan S. Tamke, *Make a Joyful Noise unto the Lord: Hymns as a Reflection of Victorian Social Attitudes* (Athens, Oh.: Ohio University Press, 1978), 75–90.

And again: 'I loved "Canaan's pleasant land." The wonder of "Canaan," which could never be localized', just like Moab and Kedron, 'those places that never existed on earth.' Lawrence concluded with the assertion that Nonconformist hymns were a 'clue to the ordinary Englishman';[211] they are also a clue to the ordinary Englishman's Holy Land.

---

[211] D. H. Lawrence, 'Hymns in a Man's Life' (1928), in *Phoenix II: Uncollected, Unpublished and Other Prose Works by D. H. Lawrence*, ed. Harry T. Moore (London: Heinemann, 1968), 597, 599, 600, 601.

4

Eccentric Zion

Victorian Culture and the Jewish Restoration to Palestine

Addressing the members of the Jewish Historical Society of England in 1925, David Lloyd George spoke candidly about the origins of the Balfour Declaration, that short, typed letter dated 2 November 1917, in which 'one nation solemnly promised to a second nation the country of a third'.[1] 'It was undoubtedly inspired by natural sympathy, admiration, and also by the fact that, as you must remember, we had been trained even more in Hebrew history than in the history of our own country,' Lloyd George said: 'On five days a week in the day school, and on Sunday in our Sunday schools, we were thoroughly versed in the history of the Hebrews ... We had all that in our minds, so that the appeal came to sympathetic and educated—and, on that question, intelligent—hearts.'[2]

This is a well-known passage, often cited by historians who evoke Lloyd George's pious Nonconformist education not only to explain his role in Britain's embracing of the Zionist cause during the First World War, but also as an illustration for a much broader cultural claim.[3] Indeed, following the insights of Zionist historians from as early as 1917, and particularly Nahum Sokolow's influential *History of Zionism*

---

[1] Arthur Koestler, *Promise and Fulfilment: Palestine 1917–1949* (1949; London: Macmillan, 1983), 4.
[2] David Lloyd George, 'Afterword' to Philip Guedalla, *Napoleon and Palestine* (London: George Allen & Unwin, 1925), 47–9.
[3] Cf. William D. Rubinstein and Hilary L. Rubinstein, *Philosemitism: Admiration and Support in the English Speaking World for Jews* (London: Macmillan, 1999), 167–8.

(1919), it has become a commonplace to see the Balfour Declaration as the culmination of a rich tradition of Christian Zionism in British culture: a tradition which emerged in the seventeenth century, slumbered in the eighteenth, and re-emerged, with a vengeance, in the nineteenth. Even scholars who have emphasized the immediate political objectives that generated the Declaration—the hope that an appeal to American Jewry would enhance American involvement in the War, or that by reaching the Russian-Jewish proletariat a Bolshevik revolution would be averted—even they have frequently pointed to the wider religious impetus behind the Declaration.[4]

The argument, essentially, has been twofold: first, that an impressive gallery of Victorian individuals and institutions promoted, sometimes vigorously, the Jewish colonization of Palestine; and secondly, that these eminent Christian Zionists were men and women of their time, and that their restorationist views were somehow characteristic of a more prevalent cultural climate. Exactly how prevalent, however, is a question frequently asked, but seldom answered. While it is clear, for example, that the millenarian logic of the restoration was associated with the more zealous Evangelical circles, it has proved extremely difficult to assess the actual circulation or influence of these ideas.[5] Nevertheless, the assumption has often been that nineteenth-century ideas about the restoration of the Jews to Palestine somehow paved the way towards Britain's wartime policy. Consequently, accounts of Christian Zionism often read like a dot-to-dot drawing, connecting Lord Shaftesbury,

---

[4] See, *inter al.*, A. M. Hyamson, *British Projects for the Restoration of the Jews* (Leeds: Petty, 1917); Nahum Sokolow, *History of Zionism 1600–1918* (London: Longman, 1919); Franz Kobler, *The Vision Was There: A History of the British Movement for the Restoration of the Jews to Palestine* (London: World Jewish Congress, 1956); Norman Bentwich and John M. Shaftesbury, 'Forerunners of Zionism in the Victorian Era', in John M. Shaftesbury (ed.), *Remember the Days: Essays on Anglo-Jewish History Presented to Cecil Roth* (London: Jewish Historical Society of England, 1966), 207–39; Michael J. Pragai, *Faith and Fulfilment: Christians and the Return to the Promised Land* (London: Valentine Mitchell, 1985); Michael Polowetzky, *Jerusalem Recovered* (Westport, Conn.: Praeger, 1995); Paul Charles Merkley, *The Politics of Christian Zionism, 1891–1948* (London: Frank Cass, 1998). Numerous anti-Zionist accounts merely take up the Zionist narrative; cf. Regina Sherif, *Non-Jewish Zionism: Its Roots in Western History* (London: Zed Books, 1983). For a rare but useful critique (despite the fact it makes no reference to nineteenth-century culture) see Nabil I. Matar, 'Protestantism, Palestine, and Partisan Scholarship', *Journal of Palestine Studies*, 18/4 (1989), 52–70.

[5] Revd W. J. Conybeare, 'Church Parties', in *Essays Ecclesiastical and Social; Reprinted, with Additions, from the Edinburgh Review* (London: Longman, 1855), 57–164.

George Eliot, and Laurence Oliphant with some of their lesser-known contemporaries, only to reveal, in due course, a neatly sketched draft of the Balfour Declaration. And if we were to indulge in this metaphor further, we might say that the empty space between the lines has been coloured with a vague form of philo-Semitism, what Lloyd George has called 'natural sympathy' and 'admiration'.

As this chapter will demonstrate, what the conventional Zionist interpretation failed to take into account is the fact that throughout most of the nineteenth century, projects concerning the Jewish restoration to Palestine were continuously associated with charges of religious enthusiasm, eccentricity, sometimes even madness—all of them categories of differentiation which located Christian Zionism beyond the cultural consensus. This is the consensus not as it surfaces in retrospect, but as it was understood and practised at the time: no one was more aware of the marginality of their beliefs than the Christian Zionists themselves. That some of them were venerable members of society merely added to their predicament: even their respectability did not allow them to propound these views freely, as they would have liked. Contrary to the rosy picture painted by Zionist historians, Christian Zionism was a desire very reluctant to speak its name.

Concentrating on the period up to the early 1880s—before the emergence of an established 'Jewish' Zionism—this chapter will ask: Why was it that Christian Zionists were so often unwilling to express their ideas in the open? How, as a result, did they seek to articulate their restorationist projects? To what extent was the Jewish colonization of Palestine part of the Victorian imperial vision? And if Christian Zionism was indeed a marginal cultural phenomenon, what should we make of George Eliot's 'Zionist' novel, *Daniel Deronda*? Of Lloyd George's Sunday-school reminiscences? Or, indeed, of the Balfour Declaration itself?

I will begin by charting the political and theological forces which located ideas concerning the Jewish restoration to Palestine in the discursive margins of Victorian culture. As we shall see, the distance between centre and fringe, between respectability and eccentricity, was very often the distance between a literal interpretation of the biblical text and a more flexible, metaphorical one. The relationship between these mainstream and peripheral articulations hinged, in other words, on the multiple, often contradictory, meanings that the biblical imagery could hold for different constituencies. This assertion will then be examined by looking more closely at two specific episodes: the public debate surrounding the Eastern Question in the late 1870s, and the reception of *Daniel Deronda*. I will conclude by suggesting that even after the emergence of the Jewish Zionist movement in the late nineteenth century, the restoration of the Jews to Palestine remained an ambiguous, if not liminal, issue in Edwardian culture and literature.

Christian Zionism and the Boundaries of Cultural Consensus

Mary Seddon, of a respectable Wigston family, had been keenly interested in the return of the Israelites to their old homeland. Finally, in 1823, she gathered some Jews, bought a white donkey, and started off for Jerusalem. She reached Calais—some claim, Paris—before being abandoned by the little assemblage. Her husband had to cross the Channel and fetch her back to England, where he committed her to a lunatic asylum. One of her granddaughters, Georgina Meinertzhagen, remembered visiting the 'remarkable old lady' who studied Hebrew and music, 'full of fun and kind-hearted to a degree, but withal peculiar and flighty'. Still, in her detailed family history, Meinertzhagen omitted the reason for her grandmother's confinement. As her younger sister, Beatrice Webb, candidly explained, the whole affair 'was always referred to as a slur on our birth'. Seddon was eventually released, 'sane on all but one subject—her special mission to lead the Jews back to Jerusalem'. But she never returned to her husband, 'whom she could not mention without a shuddering memory of the horrors of an old-fashioned lunatic asylum with its penal discipline'.[6]

Years later, in 1862, the Seventh Earl of Shaftesbury, the great Evangelical reformer, narrated an anecdote 'to show that eminent men sometimes formed their opinions as to the sanity of a patient on very flimsy evidence':

Once when he was sitting on the [Lunacy] Commission as Chairman the alleged insanity of a lady was under discussion, and he took a view of the case opposite to that of his colleagues. One of the medical men who was there to give

---

[6] Georgina Meinertzhagen, *From Ploughshare to Parliament: A Short Memoir of the Potters of Tadcaster* (London: John Murray, 1908), 191, 200, 223; Beatrice Webb, *My Apprenticeship* (1926; 2nd edn. London: Longman, 1946), 13; *The Diary of Beatrice Webb*, ed. Norman and Jeanne MacKenzie (London: Virago, 1982), i. 305–6.

evidence, crept up to his chair and, in a confidential tone, said, 'Are you aware, my lord, that she subscribes to the Society for the Conversion of the Jews?' 'Indeed!' replied Lord Shaftesbury; 'and are you aware that I am President of that Society!'[7]

The expectation that the Jewish people would return one day to Palestine was central to the work of the Society. After all, both conversion and restoration—the exact order of events was much disputed—were a necessary prelude to the Second Coming.[8] Shaftesbury himself, according to his biographer, 'never had a shadow of doubt that the Jews *were* to return to their own land, that the Scriptures were to be literally fulfilled, and that the time was at hand'.[9] 'Our lot is cast in very wonderful times,' Shaftesbury wrote in an article about the 'State and Prospect of the Jews', published in the *Quarterly Review* in 1839: 'We have reached, as it were, Mount Pisgah in our march; and we may discern from its summit the dim though certain outlines of coming events.'[10] A year later, in the wake of the Damascus Affair and the international crisis concerning the future of Syria, he felt that the restoration of the Jews to the Holy Land was at last imminent. 'Everything seems ripe for their return to Palestine,' he wrote in his diary on 31 July 1840: ' "the way of the Kings of the East is prepared." '[11] He then famously urged Palmerston—his stepfather-in-law—to encourage the Jewish colonization of Palestine as a policy that would benefit both the Ottomans and the British.[12] One might imagine a delighted Mary Seddon, following the developments from her confined room.

Was Shaftesbury mad? According to his friend Henry Fox, his character seemed 'quite unintelligible and can only be accounted for by a dash of madness'. Florence Nightingale thought that, had Shaftesbury not devoted himself to reforming lunatic asylums, he would have been

---

[7] Edwin Hodder, *The Life and Work of the Seventh Earl of Shaftesbury, KG* (London: Cassell, 1886), iii. 139.

[8] D. N. Hempton, 'Evangelicalism and Eschatology', *Journal of Ecclesiastical History*, 31/2 (1980), 179–94.

[9] Hodder, *Life and Work*, ii. 477.

[10] *Quarterly Review*, 63 (1839), 166. The essay was essentially a review of Lord Lindsay's *Letters on Egypt, Edom, and the Holy Land* (1838).

[11] Quoted in Jonathan Frankel, *The Damascus Affair: 'Ritual Murder', Politics and the Jews in 1840* (Cambridge: Cambridge University Press, 1997), 303.

[12] Ibid. 302–10; Isaiah Friedman, *The Question of Palestine; British–Jewish–Arab Relations 1914–1918* (2nd edn. New Brunswick, NJ: Transaction, 1992), pp. xi–xxix.

in one himself.[13] Lady Palmerston told Shaftesbury that her friends regarded him 'certainly as an honest man, but as a fanatic, an extravagante'.[14] Shaftesbury narrated his little anecdote to demonstrate that patients were sometimes locked up 'on very flimsy evidence'; but the anecdote also suggests that very weighty 'evidence' was sometimes required—lineage, wealth—to allow a madman to remain outside the gates of Bedlam. Back in 1795, Richard Brothers told Lady Hester Stanhope that 'she would one day go to Jerusalem, and lead back the chosen people'.[15] The eager Stanhope, Pitt the Younger's niece, travelled to the East, where she became the most celebrated eccentric of the day. Brothers, we remember, was locked up.

Of course, chairing the Jews Society, or even advancing a political plan for the Jewish colonization of Palestine, was still a far cry from purchasing a donkey and heading for the Holy Land. Nevertheless, Shaftesbury himself was the first to sense that even sober projects concerning Jewish restoration were perilous. When, in 17 August 1840, *The Times* published a leader on his plan 'to plant the Jewish people in the land of their fathers', Shaftesbury was far from pleased. He described his feelings in his diary: 'half satisfaction, half dismay; pleased to see my opinions and projects so far taken up and approved;—alarmed lest this premature disclosure of them should bring upon us all the charge of fanaticism.' And again: 'we must pray for more caution. Those gentlemen who have now got access to the columns of the *Times* will, by over-zeal, bring a charge of fanaticism on the whole question.'[16] To be labelled a fanatic—someone 'characterized, influenced or prompted by excessive and mistaken enthusiasm, especially in religious matters'[17]—meant to have one's voice excluded from the public arena, locked away from the political, and even religious, consensus.

To be sure, restoration plans were very often ridiculed because they seemed amazingly far-fetched. In the 1840s, half a century before the emergence of Theodor Herzl's political Zionism, when Jews showed

---

[13] Geoffrey B. A. M. Finlayson, *The Seventh Early of Shaftesbury, 1801–1885* (London: Eyre Methuen, 1981), 22, 600.

[14] Shaftesbury's diary, 3 Sept. 1840, quoted in Frankel, *Damascus Affair*, 308.

[15] The Duchess of Cleveland, *The Life and Letters of Lady Hester Stanhope* (London: John Murray, 1914), 206, 209.

[16] Shaftesbury's diary, 24 Aug. 1840, quoted in Hodder, *Life and Work*, i. 311.

[17] *OED*. 'Fanatic' was still employed at this period to denote both 'mad person' and 'religious maniac'.

little inclination to participate in a mass migration to Palestine—and no inclination to convert—these grand visions of restitution and conversion could well seem preposterous. This was true in 1840, but it was still true in the early 1880s, when Laurence Oliphant, a self-acclaimed eccentric, was advancing his own colonization plans. 'It is somewhat unfortunate that so important a political and strategical question as the future of Palestine should be inseparably connected in the public mind with a favourite religious theory,' Oliphant complained in *The Land of Gilead* (1880), adding, 'so far as my own efforts are concerned, they are based upon considerations which have no connection whatever with any popular religious theory upon the subject'.[18] Still, Oliphant's strict Evangelical upbringing and his long association with the cult led by the American prophet Thomas Lake Harris support his biographer's suspicion 'that he had really more interest than he gave himself credit for even in the religious view of the question'.[19]

Oliphant's attempt to distance himself from the religious aspects of his project suggests that the ridicule with which these plans were often received was rooted not only in their political impracticability, but in the religious climate from which they emerged. The affinity between lunacy and an over-zealous study of prophecy could be traced back to the late seventeenth century, when their aversion to the pious emotionalism of the radical Protestant sects led some members of the ruling-class élite to equate enthusiasm with 'delusion, obsession, madness'.[20] This diagnosis was later imposed institutionally. The author of *Observations on the Religious Delusions of Insane Persons* (1841), for example, maintained that madness could originate in religious excessiveness, such as the 'terror inspired by fanatical preaching' and the 'perplexity of mind from studying controverted subjects, or endeavouring to unravel the mysterious parts of the sacred writings; or the misapplication of particular texts'.[21]

---

[18] Laurence Oliphant, *The Land of Gilead* (Edinburgh: Blackwell, 1880), pp. xxxii–xxxiii.

[19] Margaret Oliphant, *Memoir of the Life of Laurence Oliphant* (Edinburgh: Blackwood, 1892), 287. Biographer and subject were not related.

[20] Roy Porter, 'The Rage of Party: A Glorious Revolution in English Psychiatry', *Medical History*, 27/1 (1983), 39; Andrew Scull, *The Most Solitary of Afflictions: Madness and Society in Britain, 1700–1900* (New Haven: Yale University Press, 1993), 176–7.

[21] Nathaniel Bingham, *Observations on the Religious Delusions of Insane Persons* (London: Hatchard, 1841), 117–18.

A survey of Victorian doctoring of madness is well beyond our scope; it is enough to state that literal interpretations of prophecy were often associated with different forms of mental instability. Ernest Sandeen has observed that some aspects of the London Jews Society appear 'lunatic in retrospect';[22] perhaps not only in retrospect, as Shaftesbury's little anecdote has already implied. Between 1816 and 1825, the Society's enterprise provoked outrage against what was seen as '*the English madness*', or '*this mania of conversion*'.[23] In his well-known analysis of 'Church Parties' (1853), the Revd W. J. Conybeare spared little effort in mocking the May meetings of the Society: 'Their bill of fare includes the immediate approach of the Red Dragon; the achievements of Gog and Magog; a fresh "discovery" of the Lost Tribes...; a new and accurate account of the battle of Armageddon; and a picture of the subversion of Omar's Mosque by an army of Israelites marching from the Seven Dials.' The Society was just one of the many 'extravagances' of that 'extreme party', the 'eccentric offspring' or 'exaggeration' of the old Evangelical school, 'sometimes called the Puritan, sometimes, from its chief organ, the Recordite party'. It was this 'Recordite extravagance', Conybeare stormed, which was 'most directly guilty of driving half-educated men into Atheism'.[24]

Enthusiastic, extravagant, exaggerated, eccentric, fanatic, manic, mad: all these were categories of difference which banished pious Evangelicals to the cultural perimeter. The Society's rivals were not offering a medical diagnosis; religious fanatics were not simply locked up in an asylum (though some, like Marry Seddon, were). However, as fanatics—located somewhere on the scale between harmless eccentrics and unfortunate lunatics—they were placed outside the boundaries of the acceptable, the proper, the sayable.

This is not to claim that the restorationist-millenarian discourse was invisible or inaudible. Far from it: the nineteenth century saw a continuous overflow of books, pamphlets, and sermons all obsessed with

---

[22] Ernest Sandeen, *The Roots of Fundamentalism: British and American Millenarianism, 1800–1930* (Chicago: University of Chicago Press, 1970), 11.

[23] Quoted in Michael Ragussis, *Figures of Conversion: 'The Jewish Question' & English National Identity* (Durham, NC: Duke University Press, 1995), 18, 20–1.

[24] Conybeare, 'Church Parties', 94, 74, 100. On the growing split between 'moderate' and 'extreme' Evangelicalism see Boyd Hilton, *The Age of Atonement: The Influence of Evangelicalism on Social and Economic Thought, 1785–1865* (Oxford: Clarendon Press, 1988), 10–19.

prophetic calculations concerning the exact date and course of the Jewish restoration to Palestine, tirelessly citing Orientalist clichés from travel accounts to make their point: the land is barren, empty, awaiting cultivation. References to these restoration plans were sometimes made in the leading newspapers and periodicals, though very often in a mocking tone, exactly the tone so dreaded by Shaftesbury. In January 1877, for example, the *Morning Post* discussed rumours that the crisis concerning the Ottoman Empire might be solved by the colonization of Jews in Palestine. 'It may be desirable from a romantic point of view to re-establish Palestine,' the *Morning Post* wrote, but it would be unkind of the Jews to ruin England by leaving all at once. Besides,

> we venture to put it to the Jews, would it be prudent to do so? Would it be good speculation? Is there anything to be done with Tyre or Sidon nowadays, or is Jericho a place with a great commercial future before it?...Then what about the language of the returned exiles? How would they communicate with each other? And are such terms as 'charter-party,' 'bill of lading,' 'policy of insurance,' &c., capable of being translated into the language of the prophets?...How would bargains be made, leases entered into, and stocks quoted in the market of the New Jerusalem?

The ultra-Evangelical magazine *The Rock*, which quoted this piece, was appalled: 'enough of this blasphemous persiflage, which we should have hesitated to quote had we not deemed it right that our readers should know what sort of aliment is prepared for the readers of "fashionable papers."'[25] As articles like this make clear, speculations concerning the Jewish restoration certainly made their way in to the 'fashionable papers'; nevertheless, they were very often presented as no more than curiosities or entertaining anecdotes.

I do not wish, in other words, to claim that Christian Zionist ideas were not in circulation. Nor am I suggesting that advocates of millenarian ideas could not be considered esteemed members of society. In his seminal work on the origins of the Balfour Declaration, Leonard Stein has claimed that most of them were little known, 'and their voices did not carry far'.[26] This does not seem to be the case at all: as one anti-restorationist reluctantly acknowledged, the doctrine of Israel's literal

---

[25] *The Rock*, 19 Jan. 1877, 40.
[26] Leonard Stein, *The Balfour Declaration* (London: Valentine Mitchell, 1961), 15.

restoration to Palestine is 'favoured by some of the wisest, most learned, and best men in the Church of Christ'.[27]

Indeed, the social demarcation which sustained the distinction between the two late eighteenth-century millenarian traditions—one intellectual, the other plebeian—was slowly disappearing. The first half of the nineteenth century saw an increasingly visible portion of the respectable middle class involved in institutionalized premillenarian activities, a practical preparation for the Second Advent which would have astounded a sober postmillenarian like Priestley just a few decades earlier. The premillenarian societies which mushroomed in the first half of the nineteenth century—the London Jews Society (1809), the Society for the Investigation of Prophecy (1826), the Albury Park Conferences (1826–30), the British Society for the Propagation of the Gospel among the Jews (1842), and so forth—were all founded and governed by some of the most eminent aristocrats, businessmen, and clergymen of their day; and most subscribers belonged to the more prosperous strata of the middle class.[28] Many of those 'who have been carried away by this false spirit of interpretation', it was claimed in 1864, 'are not ignorant enthusiasts, but belong in considerable numbers to the respectable and educated classes of society'.[29] David Bebbington has suggested that premillenarianism was a symptom of the infiltration of Romanticism into Evangelical religion. As such, it appealed to the better educated, and gathered far more Anglicans than Nonconformists, at least until the 1870s.[30] Consequently, class was no longer a decisive factor in determining the dissemination of these literal, highly personal interpretations of prophecy. It is perhaps telling that by the time John Timbs was compiling his amusing *English Eccentrics and Eccentricities* (1866), Edward Irving (1792–1834), a friend of Carlyle's and a fashionable London preacher, could be listed alongside Richard Brothers and

---

[27] Edward Swaine, *Objections to the Doctrines of Israel's Future Restoration to Palestine, National Pre-eminence, etc.* (2nd edn. London: Jackson & Walford, 1850), p. viii.

[28] Interest in prophecy was not confined to these social circles alone. On premillenarian imagery in nineteenth-century popular almanacs see Maureen Perkins, *Visions of the Future: Almanacs, Time, and Cultural Change, 1775–1870* (Oxford: Clarendon Press, 1996), 89–122.

[29] Patrick Fairbairn, *The Interpretation of Prophecy* (2nd edn. 1865; London: Banner of Truth Trust, 1964), p. vii.

[30] D. W. Bebbington, 'The Advent Hope in British Evangelicalism since 1800', *Scottish Journal of Religion*, 9/2 (1989), 104–5.

Joanna Southcott: his mind, Timbs explained, 'through its prophetic studies, had *lost its balance*'.[31] Irving's congregation was highly respectable, but his swift expulsion from the ministry is indicative of the suspicion with which this extreme form of Adventism was viewed, regardless of the social affiliation of its adherents.

Zionist historiography, then, seems correct in its assertion that Christian Zionist ideas were in constant circulation throughout the nineteenth century, and that many of those who circulated these ideas belonged to the social élite. The crucial point, however, is that *despite* their favoured social position, and *despite* the fact that these views enjoyed such wide visibility, Christian Zionism did not exist—at least until the 1880s—within the cultural, religious, or political mainstream. Of course, the 'mainstream' was not (and is not) monolithic: as a set of hegemonic trends, it was (and is) continuously open to negotiation, as different groups sought to interpret, challenge, or re-define prevalent cultural and theological conceptions. Still, while some of the beliefs and practices associated with Evangelicalism became part and parcel of Victorian culture, Christian Zionism did not. The numerous charges of fanaticism, the derision, and the mockery could be said to reflect the contest between competing parties over the definition of and inclusion in the mainstream; but nothing testifies more to their liminal position within Victorian culture than the Christian Zionists' self-awareness of this liminality; their own understanding of what cannot, or should not, be articulated openly.

This is why Shaftesbury was so distressed by the discussion in *The Times* of his restoration plan. Similarly, this is why the leaders of the London Jews Society were impelled to deny the restorationist expectation, which was, after all, the *raison d'être* of the Society. As early as 1810, the Society announced that a 'charge of enthusiasm has been made by some persons concerning the views of the Society; and it has been asserted that your Committee are influenced by foolish and Utopian expectations'. The Committee members admitted that they

> are aroused to exertion by the signs of the times. Nevertheless, they are not determined to any measures which they adopt by visionary and uncertain calculations. They wish to distinguish between the restoration of Israel to their own country, and the conversion of Israel to Christianity. If nothing

---

[31] John Timbs, *English Eccentrics and Eccentricities* (London: Bentley, 1866), i. 205.

peculiar appeared in the aspect of the times—if neither Jews nor Christians believed the future restoration of Israel—if no exposition of prophecy had awakened attention or excited expectation in men's minds—if it were possible to place things as they stood many centuries ago—still your Committee would urge the importance and propriety of establishing a Jewish mission.[32]

It is typical of the period that while the missionary conversion of the Jews was considered a legitimate cause, still within the safe boundaries of the Victorian consensus, their restoration to Palestine was not. A similar ambivalence characterized the work of the British Society for the Propagation of the Bible among the Jews. The first editorial of the Society's journal, the *Jewish Herald*, informed its readers in 1846 that all questions of prophecy, strategy, and chronology, all matters concerning the restoration and conversion of the Jews, were to be treated as open questions.[33] Thomas Raffles, a Liverpool Congregational preacher, was certainly conforming to the official line when he declared in 1848 that the Society 'simply seeks the conversion of the Jew, as you would seek the conversion of any other man.... It proposes no expedition to Palestine, nor colonization society for the Holy Land. All these things it eschews, as a Society, leaving them to men's private judgements and personal and individual interpretations and opinions.'[34] As Clyde Binfield has explained, 'they preferred to leave prophecy to fend for itself, aware that the nuances of their stance would be evident to close students of form without alarming chance subscribers or casually interested hearers.'[35]

A petty passage to India

This brings us to the complex relationship between the millenarian and the imperial. After all, many Christian Zionists, whose interest in the restoration was essentially doctrinal, were quick to point out that it was in Britain's strategic interest to see Palestine, the gateway to the East, in the friendly hands of the Jews. 'Britain! rejoice!' exclaimed the author of

[32] W. T. Gidney, *The History of the London Society for Promoting Christianity amongst the Jews, from 1809 to 1908* (London: LJS, 1908), 35.
[33] Clyde Binfield, 'Jews in Evangelical Dissent: The British Society, the Herschell Connection and the Premillenarian Thread', in Michael Wilks (ed.), *Prophecy and Eschatology* (Oxford: Blackwell, 1994), 239.
[34] Revd John Dunlop (ed.), *Memories of Gospel Triumphs among the Jews during the Victorian Era* (London: Partridge, 1894), 305.
[35] Binfield, 'Jews in Evangelical Dissent', 239.

The Final Exodus (1854): 'it is for you to lead back to their beautiful land the long-dispersed members of Judah's neglected race, and by planting in their native country a colony of whose attachment to its protectors there could be no doubt, to thrust another obstacle in the path of the threatened invader.'[36] In arguments like these it was virtually impossible to separate millenarian from strategic considerations, because the existence of Britain's empire was seen a priori as a sign of divine election. What is particularly noteworthy, however, is how the imperial language could double the millenarian, cover it up, contain it. Note how Shaftesbury, in 1840, tried to persuade Palmerston to adopt his plan for the colonization of Palestine by the Jews:

August 1.—Dined with Palmerston. After dinner left alone with him. Propounded my scheme, which seemed to strike his fancy; he asked some questions, and readily promised to consider it. How singular is the order of Providence! Singular, that is if estimated by man's ways! Palmerston has already been chosen by God to be an instrument of good to His ancient people; to do homage, as it were, to their inheritance, and to recognize their rights without believing their destiny. And it seems he will yet do more. But though the motive be kind, it is not sound. I am forced to argue politically, financially, commercially; these considerations strike him home; he weeps not like his Master over Jerusalem, nor prays that now, at last, she may put on her beautiful garments.[37]

By employing strictly the political/strategic vocabulary, Shaftesbury could rephrase his 'fanatic' aspiration and reinvent himself as an ambitious statesman. His straight face has certainly convinced some historians. Isaiah Friedman, for example, writes: 'Whatever might have been [Shaftesbury's] private views on the conversion of Jews to Christianity, not a trace of them can be found in his official memorandum of September 1840.... Solving the Syrian Question concerned him, not the conversion of Jews.'[38]

Palmerston himself knew better. In accepting Shaftesbury's plan, his objective, as always, was to preserve Ottoman integrity, but he was well aware of the secret millenarian subtext—of his own role as God's 'instrument'—and he was determined to employ it for his own domestic

---

[36] *The Final Exodus; or, The Restoration to Palestine of the Lost Tribes* (London: Hope, 1854), 14.
[37] Shaftesbury's diary, 1 Aug. 1840, quoted in Hodder, *Life and Work*, i. 310–11.
[38] Friedman, *Question of Palestine*, p. xxvi.

purposes. 'Pray don't lose sight of my recommendation to the Porte, to invite the Jews to return to Palestine,' he wrote to the British ambassador in Constantinople on 4 September: 'You can have no idea how much such a measure would tend to interest in the Sultan's cause all the religious party in this country, and their influence is great and their connexion extensive.'[39] These issues 'excite a very deep interest in the minds of a large number of persons in the United Kingdom and the Sultan would enlist in his favour the good opinion of numerous and powerful classes in the country'.[40] Palmerston here demonstrates his attentiveness to the affinity between the political centre-stage and the religious fringe; it was precisely the fact that the imperial language could stand for the secret millenarian desire that he found so appealing. His assessment of the extraordinary power of the restorationist lobby may have been far-fetched. Nevertheless, this merely reinforces my argument: despite its power—social, political, financial—the Evangelical lobby could not employ the millenarian vocabulary in the open.

Shaftesbury's plan marked the first moment in which the Jewish colonization of Palestine was pursued, albeit briefly, as an official British policy.[41] The fact that more than seventy years would pass before British leaders would once again embrace the Zionist cause suggests that Shaftesbury was an exceptional figure: it was his privileged social and familial status that allowed him to transform millenarian fantasy into practical politics. As a rule, however, the Christian Zionist restoration plans that emerged in the wake of Crimean War, during the Eastern Question crisis of the 1870s, and at least until the 1880s, continued to follow the same cultural pattern: flourishing only on the political and religious perimeter, and often provoking the accustomed charges of eccentricity, fanaticism, even madness.

This begs the question: could not—and indeed, did not—the idea of the Jewish colonization of Palestine function as a purely imperial question, free from any millenarian, or even religious, association?

It seems that it could not. Without its millenarian backbone, resting, as it were, on an imperial basis only, the strategic logic behind the Jewish

---

[39] Quoted in Charles Webster, *The Foreign Policy of Palmerston, 1830–1841* (London: Bell, 1951), ii. 762.
[40] Palmerston to Ponsonby, 24 Nov. 1840, quoted in Frankel, *Damascus Affair*, 310.
[41] Barbara Tuchman, *Bible and Sword: England and Palestine from the Bronze Age to Balfour* (1956; New York: Ballantine, 1984), 201–2.

colonization of Palestine seemed flawed and insufficient. The imperial vocabulary could perhaps eclipse the millenarian madness, but the eclipse was never full; and the Christian Zionists themselves were the first to sense this. Of course, one of the main threads of this study has been the idea that Britain's imperial ethos was embedded in the Protestant vocabulary of 'Chosen People' and 'Promised Land'. By envisioning the colonization of Palestine, and working to define Britain's imperial ambitions regarding the Holy Land, the discourse fell back, as it were, on its initial birthplace; and compared to the elaborate metaphor, the original was found wanting. This testifies not only to the nature of premillenarian thought, but also to the imperial context in which it was operating. We have seen how Richard Brothers strove to construct a colonial plan that would coincide, perfectly and literally, with the millenarian scheme as laid out in Scripture. Fifty years on, it was the opposite that was troubling the premillenarians: how to construct a practical millenarian plan that would correspond with Britain's imperial objectives.

The first challenge was to delineate Palestine's position within Britain's imperial ideological, commercial, and political setting. The purchase of Suez Canal shares in 1875 (allowing Britain controlling interest), the annexation of Cyprus in 1878, and the occupation of Egypt in 1882, both reflected and enhanced the strategic significance of the area. The question of 'significance', however, was always open to interpretation. As far as the premillenarians were concerned, Palestine's religious and historical weight, especially in relation to the apocalyptic scenario, was paramount. 'We must look to the end,' wrote the Revd Samuel Bradshaw in 1884: 'Egypt is but the beginning.... The main artery is Palestine. From thence it is that all good must flow.'[42] But this seemed to contradict the conventional wisdom—the mainstream interpretation—that Empire was first and foremost about India. True, Cyprus, Egypt, and Palestine were all significant, but only because they safeguarded the Suez Canal; and the Canal was important, but only because it provided the shortest and cheapest route to India. The cartographical project carried out by the PEF (and sponsored by the War Office) demonstrates that the British government recognized

---

[42] Samuel Alexander Bradshaw, *The Trumpet Voice; Modus Operandi in Political, Social, and Moral Forecast Concerning the East* (London: C. Poplett, 1884), 9.

Palestine's strategic importance from as early as the 1860s. Nevertheless, it was only much later, during the First World War, that it became imperative to secure Palestine under direct British control.

The result was a disconcerting gap between Palestine's pivotal importance in the millenarian design and its somewhat petty imperial role as a passage to India. The Holy Land could well have been a glittering gem in Britain's imperial crown; but it was certainly not the jewel. Responsible premillenarians struggled to resolve this incongruity. As Henry Edwards admitted in his 1846 colonization plan, the greatest service Palestine could perform was 'as a sort of half-way resting place, toward our Indian territories', 'forming a bulwark against the progress of Russia, invited by the weakness of Turkey'.[43] The Revd Hollingsworth employed the exact same phrase to denote not only the military, but the spiritual objective as well: 'Palestine is our half-way resting place, in the transmission of our religious thoughts, our imperial intentions, and our missionary efforts, whilst we sit at home and plan the evangelization of India, and the farthest East. We want such a place now. We shall need it still more every year.'[44] In terms of its imperial value, the Promised Land had to be presented not as an end to itself, but merely as the means of attaining an altogether greater promise.

This raised a second difficulty. If the only consideration was imperial, not religious, why was it necessary to encourage the migration of Jewish colonizers, especially as the Jews showed little inclination to migrate? Would it not prove more advantageous to colonize Palestine with British citizens? In fact, alongside plans for Jewish restoration, there was a parallel trend of projects envisioning the British colonization of Palestine. In 1841, for example, Sir William Hillary proposed 'again to plant the Banner of the Cross in the land of the Redeemer'—that is, to restore the Latin Kingdom to Jerusalem, this time in a modern, enlightened version. Hillary, a member of the Crusader Order of St John of Jerusalem, believed that the Orderly tradition could resolve incompatible European interests in Palestine. Still, Hillary maintained that Britain's role in restoring Palestine to the Turks secured her a 'leading part' in the negotiations over a lasting settlement, 'in order to have her future

---

[43] Henry Edwards, *The Colonisation of Palestine* (London: Ebenezer Palmer, 1846), 11.
[44] Revd A. G. H. Hollingsworth, *The Holy Land Restored* (London: Seeley, 1849), 248.

interests secured'.[45] In 1868, Yussif Howad, a 'Native of Nazareth', published *Palestine, a New Field for Emigration* (1868), to 'create a feeling in favour of colonizing portions of Palestine with intelligent, enterprising, and industrious Englishmen'.[46]

Schemes like these, however, were rare; and while several German, American, and Swedish colonies were established in Palestine in the second half of the century, there was no parallel British project.[47] The fact that Palestine was never seriously considered a 'New Field' for British emigration merely highlighted the anomaly of a British colonization project which involved non-British citizens. The premillenarians were very troubled by this. Hollingsworth's categorical claim—'We cannot possess the coasts of Syria ourselves. The Jew alone has a right'—rested on the scriptural promise alone.[48] Others struggled to produce more empirical explanations. The Revd James Neil listed 'a variety of reasons why emigration to Palestine by English people cannot possibly be undertaken with any hope of success, in the same way as emigration to the United States or to a British colony'. Among these were their lack of familiarity with Eastern customs and the heat.[49] Only the Jews might function as a civilizing force, and yet endure the sun. Henry Edwards envisioned the migration of a select group of British capitalists, 'six gentlemen only waiting the sanction of Government to go out with fifty thousand pounds each'. However, the 'settlers, who would soon feel constrained to join them, would be Jews, who can live and thrive almost anywhere, upon anything'.[50] This certainly agreed with the construction of 'the Jew' as a hybrid—white, but not quite, and hence ideal for the colonization of a land situated between East and West, an Eastern land that is to be Westernized.[51]

---

[45] Sir William Hillary, *An Address to the Knights of St. John of Jerusalem, on the Christian Occupation of the Holy Land, as a Sovereign State under their Dominion* (London: Mortimer, 1841), 15; idem, *Suggestions for the Christian Occupation of the Holy Land* (London: Mortimer, 1841), 7.

[46] Yussif Howad, *Palestine, a New Field for Emigration* (London: William Macintosh, 1868), 2.

[47] Ruth Kark, 'Millenarianism and Agricultural Settlement in the Holy Land in the Nineteenth Century', *Journal of Historical Geography*, 9/1 (1983), 47–62.

[48] Hollingsworth, *Holy Land Restored*, 248.

[49] James Neil, *Palestine Re-peopled* (3rd edn. London: Nisbet, 1877), 34–5.

[50] Edwards, *Colonisation of Palestine*, 10.

[51] Bryan Cheyette, *Constructions of the 'The Jew' in English Literature and Society: Racial Representations, 1875–1945* (Cambridge: Cambridge University Press, 1993), esp. 106–26.

In the premillenarian scheme, this hybridity seemed to enhance the need for conversion: it was only by embracing Christianity that the Jew could become a true agent of civilization. *Judah's Lion* (1843), Charlotte Elizabeth Tonna's conversionist novel, follows the fortunes of Alick, a young British Jew who travels to Palestine only to discover the truth of Christianity and the shared destinies of England and Israel. In his final speech, a happily converted Alick declares: 'I ask you to watch; to seize every occasion of facilitating our return; not for our sakes, but for your own. God's purposes towards us cannot fail, though the whole world were banded together against us; but I love England, I desire to see her noble lion supreme among the nations; and to insure this, I would see him ever closely allied to the Lion of Judah.'[52] By constructing the colonizing Jew as a loyal British/Christian subject, Tonna was trying to blur the demarcation separating the literal chosen people from their metaphorical brethren, thus presenting the Jewish colonization of Palestine as a quintessentially British project.

It was possible to take this even further. The British Israelites, who began to prosper in the 1870s—seventy years after Richard Brothers first advanced his racial theories—also believed that Israel (Britain) and Judah (the Jews) were to be restored together.[53] The Israelites were exiled from their land long before the preaching of Christ and hence, unlike their Judean brothers, took no part in the persecution of the Messiah. The British nation, in other words, was the rightful owner of the land; the Jews' birthright was seen as a necessary evil. 'The house of Judah can return not one moment before the house of Israel, and when the two houses return TOGETHER, they do so as joint heirs,' explained 'Philo-Israel' in the British Israelite organ, *Nation's Glory Leader*.[54] Rather than follow the philo-Semitic tradition, this form of Christian Zionism reflected a strong anti-Semitic impulse, offering a way of cleansing Europe of its Jewish population.

In 1874, the British Israelites sponsored the Syrian and Palestine Colonization Society, led by John Gawler, Keeper of the Crown Jewels

---

[52] Charlotte Elizabeth [Tonna], *Judah's Lion* (London: Seeley, 1843), 432.

[53] John Wilson, 'British Israelism: The Ideological Restraints on Sect Organization', in Bryan R. Wilson (ed.), *Patterns of Sectarianism: Organization and Ideology in Social and Religious Movements* (London: Heinemann, 1967), 345–76; idem, 'The History and Organization of British Israelism' (D.Phil. thesis, Oxford, 1966).

[54] *Nation's Glory Leader*, 19 Jan. 1876, 402.

at the Tower of London.[55] The Society's object, he explained, 'is one which must prove of the greatest benefit to mankind, and to England in particular, viz., *to initiate a fund to promote the colonization of Palestine by persons of good character (especially Jews)*. If it will open a good field for immigration; and if it will improve the revenues of Turkey and help her to pay some of the interest of her bonds; it furnishes sufficient grounds for an appeal to *Englishmen*.'[56] 'Syria', he declared, 'from its positions and capabilities, surpasses any of our colonies as a field for immigration.'[57] Gawler's insistence on a joint, Jewish–British colonization of Palestine reflected his efforts to reconcile the millenarian vision with the normative imperial ethos. Paradoxically, it was precisely the attempt to render the restoration plan all the more acceptable that made it seem even more eccentric.

This paradox was representative of the movement as a whole. On the one hand, perhaps more than any other subculture considered in this chapter, the British Israelites were unmistakably located on the fringe of Victorian culture. The movement's journals, always with an injured tone of wonder, never tired of citing the derogatory references to their work, from the Margate vicar who called them 'a craze—unchristian—silly' to the *Leisure Hour*'s suggestion they were 'ingenious lunatics'.[58] Some of the most zealous critics were actually premillenarians who were aggravated by the movement's rapid success. 'It is not difficult to understand why this theory should seem very inviting to many minds,' wrote *Israel's Watchman (and Prophetic Expositor)*: 'it is extremely flattering to our national vanity and arrogance, never more full-blown than at the present time. "*We* are Israel and *we* possess the land,"—this will be news to Turkey, Russia, and France!'[59] It is telling that the 1870s saw the swift decline of the 'Teutonist' branch of the movement (advocating the idea that other European nations, too, were descendants of the ten tribes) and a growing support for the more

---

[55] Galya Yardeny-Agmon, 'John Gawler and his 1874 Plan for the Colonization of Palestine', *HaTzionut*, 1 (1970), 84–120 [Hebrew]. On Gawler's eccentric father, who advanced his own resoration plans in the 1840s and 1850s, see also Eitan Bar-Yosef, 'Christian Zionism in Victorian Culture', *Israel Studies*, 8/2 (2003), 32–3.
[56] *JC*, 31 Dec. 1875, 637.
[57] *JC*, 14 Jan. 1876, 668.
[58] *Banner of Israel*, 7 Mar. 1877, 91; *Nation's Glory Leader*, 17 Nov. 1875, 331.
[59] *Israel's Watchman*, Nov. 1878, 366.

exclusive Anglo-Israelite branch.[60] Indeed, the movement's appeal was rooted in its ability to intermingle a scientific racial theory with popular patriotic nationalism. As the *Nation's Glory Leader* explained, 'Our identity with Israel enables us to see why, comparatively speaking, the other Nations of the earth are not in possession of Colonies, and why we alone have them to any appreciable extent.'[61] Their imperial commitment not only made the British Israelites the most ardent supporters of the colonization of Palestine in the nineteenth century, but also gave them a fashionable, cutting-edge allure. So, while the movement was considered bizarre even by its premillenarian peers, it was very much attuned to the political and cultural mainstream. Instead of being defined clinically, their distance from the centre should be defined semantically, as the distance between the literal and the metaphorical. It is the distance between the assertion that Britain's imperial success is a sign of providential election and the conviction that this prosperity makes Britain the *literal* Israel; between Matthew Arnold's observation concerning the Hebraic origins of English culture and the assertion that the English *are* Hebrew.

Incidentally, in 1872, Arnold issued *A Bible-Reading for Schools; The Great Prophecy of Israel's Restoration (Isaiah, Chapters 40–66); Arranged and Edited for Young Learners*, a Sunday-school extension of his insights in *Culture and Anarchy*. 'Only one literature there is, one great literature, for which the people have had a preparation—the literature of the Bible,' he wrote.[62] Arnold praised the historic and poetic value of Isaiah's prophecy; but for the premillenarians there was much more at stake: as far as they were concerned, Isaiah's prophecy held numerous keys to the great restoration that was still to come. Whereas Arnold was longing for the 'true life of literature'—that 'Promised Land, towards which criticism can only beckon'[63]—the British Israelites were frantically devising plans to enter the actual, literal Promised Land. It was one thing to recite 'great passages from the prophets and the Psalms', as Lloyd George did, absorb, and make them part 'of the best in the Gentile

---

[60] Wilson, 'History and Organization', 50–1.
[61] *Nation's Glory Leader*, 10 May 1876, 165.
[62] Matthew Arnold, *A Bible-Reading for Schools* (London: Macmillan, 1872), p. x.
[63] Matthew Arnold, 'The Function of Criticism at the Present Time', in *Essays in Criticism* (London: Macmillan, 1865), 41

character'.[64] But it was something quite different to expect the literal realization of prophecy, to pray daily—like the young Edmund Gosse, son of a fundamentalist Plymouth Brother—for 'the restitution of Jerusalem to the Jews'.[65] It was the difference between what Frank Kermode has called 'the sense of an ending' and the sense of *the* ending.

The Eastern Question, Disraeli, and Daniel Deronda, *1875–8*

So far, I have outlined the cultural currency of Christian Zionism in Victorian England, up to the 1880s. The following account will complement this analysis by looking more closely at the cross-exchanges between centre and fringe in a specific historical and cultural context. The Eastern Question of the late 1870s is an ideal episode, for reasons which will soon become clear. We must begin, however, by briefly sketching the international and domestic developments which constituted this complex affair.[66]

Eastern Questions

In July 1875, the Turks were confronted by a Christian nationalist uprising in Herzegovina, which quickly spread to Bulgaria. The Great Powers convened at Constantinople in December 1876 to persuade the Porte to accept foreign supervision of its rule in Europe; following the failure of the conference, in April 1877, Russia declared war on Turkey. The British government announced its neutrality, but in December, as Russian forces began moving closer to Constantinople, the prospect of a British armed conflict with Russia seemed imminent. On 3 March 1878, a peace treaty was signed at San Stefano, but the concessions exacted by the Russians from the Ottomans were so considerable as to merely deepen the crisis. The Cabinet accepted Disraeli's gamble to order troops from India to Malta; the Foreign Secretary, Derby,

---

[64] Lloyd George, 'Afterword', 48.
[65] Edmund Gosse, *Father and Son* (1907; Harmondsworth: Penguin, 1972), 36.
[66] The following account is indebted to R. W. Seton-Watson, *Disraeli, Gladstone and the Eastern Question* (1935; London: Frank Cass, 1971); Robert Blake, *Disraeli* (London: Eyre & Spottiswoode, 1966); Richard Shannon, *Gladstone and the Bulgarian Agitation, 1876* (2nd edn. Hassocks: Harvester, 1975); Richard Millman, *Britain and the Eastern Question, 1875–1878* (Oxford: Clarendon Press, 1979); Ann Pottinger Saab, *Reluctant Icon: Gladstone, Bulgaria, and the Working Classes, 1856–1878* (Cambridge, Mass.: Harvard University Press, 1991).

resigned in protest. The question was eventually brought before the Congress of Berlin, where the map of the Balkans was redrawn, limiting Ottoman control in Europe, but not in Asia. The *coup* was arranged by the new Foreign Secretary, Salisbury: a secret agreement with the Porte allowed Britain to occupy Cyprus and potentially oversee Asiatic Turkey. On returning to London, Disraeli told the cheering crowds that he had achieved 'peace with honour'.

These were the main international developments, but the British handling of the crisis was shaped primarily by the domestic debate which broke out in June 1876, when the *Daily Mail* published an account of slaughter and rape perpetrated by a Turkish irregular militia on helpless Bulgarian Christians; 20,000 innocents were said to have been murdered. The news aroused a huge public outcry; Disraeli's insistence that the affair must be handled as a question of *realpolitik* alone merely reinforced the protest.[67] Sermons, press exhortations, and charitable relief committees all contributed to a public controversy, 'the extent of which has rarely ever been seen in Britain'.[68] The National Conference on the Eastern Question convened in St James's Hall, London, on 8 December 1876; a loose coalition of Nonconformists, High Churchmen, secular working-class radicals, and agricultural labourers 'created a climate of indignation strong enough to limit substantially the government's options in the ensuing crisis in the East'.[69]

The agitation brought Gladstone back to public life. In September 1876, he published his pamphlet, *Bulgarian Horrors and the Question of the East*, which sold 200,000 copies by the end of the month.[70] 'Let the Turks now carry away their abuses in the only possible manner, namely by carrying off themselves,' Gladstone famously stormed, 'one and all, bag and baggage, shall, I hope, clear out from the province they have desolated and profaned.'[71] Beneath the rhetoric, the substance of Gladstone's programme remained moderate;[72] rather than calling for any radical change in Ottoman territorial integrity, the demonization of the

---

[67] Anthony S. Wohl, ' "Dizzi-Ben-Dizzi": Disraeli as Alien', *Journal of British Studies*, 34/3 (1995), 384; Blake, *Disraeli*, 594–5.
[68] Millman, *Britain and the Eastern Question*, 164.
[69] Saab, *Reluctant Icon*, 1.
[70] Blake, *Disraeli*, 598.
[71] W. E. Gladstone, *Bulgarian Horrors and the Question of the East* (London: John Murray, 1876), 61–2.
[72] Shannon, *Gladstone and the Bulgarian Agitation*, 110.

Ottomans in Gladstone's melodrama served to unite the agitation movement.[73] The atrocities provided a symbolic grievance, a cause that allowed the demonstrators to protest against religious intolerance, the persecution of Christianity, and the corruption and unresponsiveness of the government, 'without ever having to deal with cases familiar enough to bring out their deep and well-founded disagreements'.[74] The international affair merely reflected the domestic scene, with the agitators cast as the oppressed Christian subjects, crushed under the despotic rule of their Oriental tyrant, the (conveniently) Jewish Disraeli. The fact that most prominent English Jews, traditionally devout Liberals, shifted their support to Disraeli, allowed the agitators to elaborate on the racial and religious affinity between Ottomans and Jews, and to claim that Oriental forces, antithetical to Christianity, had taken over England's foreign policy.[75] 'The English people', Gladstone wrote, 'decided the Eastern Question in a Christian sense.' He claimed that the agitation was 'pre-eminently a Christian revolution'.[76]

Historians have recognized two phases in the public debate in Britain. In 1876, attention focused on the moral problem of British support of the Ottomans. But in 1877, with the threat of a new Crimean War, 'the centre of gravity of public interest shifted away from the direct question of Turkish misrule towards the issues and fortunes of the war'. This time, the peace movement was confronted by an effective Russophobe opposition of jingoists, who advanced their own form of populist, music-hall demagogy.[77] The jingoistic attack distilled the bitter division between the two camps. Salisbury remarked that no question had within the memory of man 'so deeply excited the English people, moved their passions so thoroughly and produced such profound divisions and such rancorous animosity'.[78] In other words, while the agitation undoubt-

[73] Patrick Joyce, *Democratic Subjects: The Self and the Social in Nineteenth-Century England* (Cambridge: Cambridge University Press, 1994), 204–12.
[74] Saab, *Reluctant Icon*, 63.
[75] Wohl, ' "Dizzi-Ben- Dizzi" '; see also Ann Pottinger Saab, 'Disraeli, Judaism, and the Eastern Question', *International History Review*, 10 (1988), 559–78; David Feldman, *Englishmen and Jews: Social Relations and Political Culture, 1840–1914* (New Haven: Yale University Press, 1994), 94–120.
[76] W. T. Stead, *The MP for Russia; Reminiscences & Correspondence of Madame Olga Novikoff* (London: Andrew Melrose, 1909), i. 340, 293.
[77] Shannon, *Gladstone and the Bulgarian Agitation*, 239–40; Saab, *Reluctant Icon*, 192–3.
[78] Quoted in Seton-Watson, *Disraeli*, 2.

edly evoked an array of pivotal political and cultural questions, on a more fundamental level it represented a struggle over the definition, and hence control, of the political centre. 'Lord Derby would appear still to be of the opinion that the last word in the Eastern Question is, "who is to occupy Constantinople?",' raged the *Nonconformist* in September 1876: 'Public feeling now recognizes first and last and midst all, one question only, "What is to become of unarmed Christians at the mercy of Mohammedan savages?" '[79] More than anything else, the Eastern Question agitation was about the right to interpret the Eastern Question.

The intensity of the crisis meant that there was perhaps no other moment in nineteenth-century British cultural life—not even the Crimean War—when Britain's imperial objectives concerning the future of the Ottoman Empire and the Middle East came under such public scrutiny; when the question of Muslim rule fed into an Orientalist polemic concerning Britain's identity as a Christian empire; and, most significantly, with Disraeli as premier, when representations of 'the Jew' became so central to a public debate. Empire, Protestantism, Orientalism, Jews: this was the stuff that restoration dreams were made of. The range, diversity, and sheer scale of the reaction make it a remarkably visible manifestation of the boundaries of public consensus. Surely, if there was an episode in Victorian cultural history in which Christian Zionism could emerge as a mainstream affair, this was it.

As far as the premillenarian fringe was concerned, there was no doubt whatsoever as to the meaning of the Eastern Question; the purchase of Suez Canal shares, the prospect of a bloody war with Russia over Eastern spoils, and in particular the annexation of Cyprus and the protectorate over Ottoman Asia, all these were seen as unequivocal signs, pointing to the imminent restoration of the Jews to their land and the Second Coming.[80] In March 1877, for example, *Israel's Watchman (and*

---

[79] *Nonconformist*, 13 Sept. 1876, 918.
[80] This assertion relies on an extensive reading of the premillenarian and extreme Evangelical press: *Banner of Israel, Christian Globe, Christian Herald and Signs of Our Times, Christian World, Hebrew Christian Witness and Prophetic Investigator, Israel's Watchman (and Prophetic Expositor), Jewish Herald, Jewish Intelligence* (later *Jewish Missionary Intelligence*), *Nation's Glory Leader* (originally *Leading the Nation to Glory*), *The Record*, and *The Rock*.

Prophetic Expositor) commented on the failure of the Constantinople Conference:

> The 'Conference,' from which such great things had been expected, has met and separated, and the 'Eastern Question' is *not* settled. Viewing it from the standpoint of prophetic Scripture, not of diplomacy, we are neither surprised nor disappointed at this result... Fully stated, it is not the 'Eastern Question,' but, 'The Eastern Question and the Jewish People.' For, the two cannot be separated; and the last decisive scene of the great drama begun at Constantinople will be played out in Jerusalem. Whether men acknowledge or deny prophecy, confessedly, the question around which ultimately all will turn is that of the *East*—and the East has been, is, and ever will be, indissolubly connected with Israel.

And the journal concluded: 'The "Eastern Question," which *began* in the Crimean War with the dispute about the so-called Holy places in *Jerusalem*, will assuredly also *end in Jerusalem*.'[81]

Numerous editorials, articles, letters, and schemes, all perpetuating an interpretation along these lines, appeared throughout the crisis in the premillenarian press. The Revd Burlington B. Wale, writing in the *Christian Herald and Signs of Our Times*, summed up this future scenario when he explained that the 'solution of the Eastern Question, whenever it comes, will be the overthrow of Turkey. The overthrow of Turkey will be the liberation of Judea. The liberation of Judea will mean its colonization by its own people. And the restoration of the Jews will mean the imminent nearness of the Second Advent of Christ.'[82] The British Israelite *Nation's Glory Leader* was even more concise: 'the solution of the Eastern Question must clearly bring out the possession of the Holy Land by the British.'[83] In a 'Prophetic Conference' held in Mildmay Park in February 1878, the Revd John Wilkinson proclaimed that the Jews 'shall have every inch the Lord has promised' and that 'the Eastern Question is settled by the Lord Jesus himself in Palestine'.[84]

Wilkinson's career illustrates some of the trends and strains that characterized the premillenarian milieu in the second half of the century. In 1851 he became a missionary for the British Society for the Propagation of the Gospel among the Jews, a task he pursued for the

---

[81] *Israel's Watchman*, Mar. 1877, 1, 4.
[82] *Christian Herald*, 26 Apr. 1877, 228.
[83] *Nation's Glory Leader*, 24 July 1878, 295.
[84] *Israel's Watchman*, Apr. 1878, 176.

next twenty-five years. In 1875, excited by international events, he warned that 'the time of the Jews' sojourn amongst us may soon terminate by restoration to Palestine'. In May 1876, anxious about the Society's lack of readiness, Wilkinson resigned: 'In prospect of the near dissolution of Turkey and the probable restoration of the Jews, I wished to devote more time to preaching to the Jews all over our land,' he explained. He then established the Mildmay Mission to the Jews.[85] Wilkinson was also one of the most distinguished opponents of the British Israelite school. His pamphlet, *Englishmen not Israelites*, ignited a bitter feud: the *Banner of Israel* retorted by claiming that since Wilkinson's restoration plans did not take into account the ten lost tribes, his 'method of "Restoring the Jews," therefore, is opposed to God's!'[86]

It is important, then, to note that the restorationist response to the Eastern Question was by no means uniform. Rather, it reflected the familiar array of premillenarian views. When, in August 1876, the *Jewish Herald* (organ of the British Society) began serializing the Revd James Neil's *Palestine Re-peopled*, the editor was forced to admit that the topic was a delicate one, and that it was only the author's long experience of life in Palestine, combined with his 'calm, reverent, and hopeful' approach to prophecy, that made his material publishable.[87] Likewise, in response to a reader's query concerning the 'Return of the Jews to Palestine', in December 1875, the editor of the ultra-Evangelical weekly, *The Rock*, replied: 'We do not want a discussion as to whether the return of the Jews will be national or only partial up to the time of the Lord's second advent, as it is clear that the plenary restoration of Israel and Judah will *not* take place until after that supreme event.'[88] *The Rock*'s most explicit attacks were aimed at the Revd Dr John Cumming, who was notorious for his somewhat disastrous tendency to identify specific dates for the Second Advent.[89] The British Israelites, too, were drawn to explicit calculations: the *Banner of Israel* estimated that the 'time for Israel's "Return," with Judah, to their own inheritance... cannot be delayed beyond AD 1881'.[90]

---

[85] Samuel Hinds Wilkinson, *The Life of John Wilkinson, The Jewish Missionary* (London: Morgan & Scott, 1908), 117, 120.
[86] *Banner of Israel*, 22 Aug. 1877, 281.
[87] *Jewish Herald*, Aug. 1876, 116; Jan. 1877, 14.
[88] *The Rock*, 3 Dec. 1875, 923.
[89] *The Rock*, 14 Jan. 1876, 24; 8 Mar. 1878, 212.
[90] *Banner of Israel*, 3 Jan. 1877, 1.

In other words, there were certainly shades and colours to the premillenarian understanding of the political events. Despite their doctrinal and political differences, however, these disparate groups were bound by a common interpretation of the Eastern Question, viewing it first and foremost as a matter of prophecy. Like the *Nonconformist* and a range of other publications and pressure groups which took part in the agitation, the premillenarians also attempted to explain what the Eastern Question was all about. As the *Israel's Watchman* put it in 1877, 'Fully stated, it is not the "Eastern Question," but, "The Eastern Question and the Jewish People." ' However, the journal recognized that this particular phrasing of the question transcended the terms in which the general debate was conducted: 'Now we claim to approach the question neither in one interest nor the other,' it pleaded, 'neither as Sclavo-phils nor as Turco-phils, but simply *as Hebrews*.'[91] This was impossible, however, since the agitation—and, consequently, the counter-agitation—left no discursive space for an interim position. 'Hebrews' were Oriental, hence Turco-phils. As the *Nonconformist* had put it, the Eastern Question occupied the spectrum between the two questions, 'Who is to occupy Constantinople?' and 'What is to become of unarmed Christians at the mercy of Mohammedan savages?'[92] The public debate positioned Christian morality in direct opposition to imperial ambition. The question of Jewish restoration, or, broadly speaking, the future of Palestine, was not on the agenda.

This was in stark contrast to Egypt. As George Carslake Thompson testified in his pioneering study, *Public Opinion and Lord Beaconsfield, 1875–1880* (1886), following Disraeli's purchase of Suez Canal shares, the occupation of Egypt 'was present to the public mind as a possible policy, which at any moment might come to the front in some form or other'.[93] During the heyday of the crisis, even Disraeli toyed with the idea of occupying Egypt, but was deterred by the fear of offending France. Speculations and suggestions concerning Egypt continued to surface throughout the entire period.[94] For example, in his polemic with Gladstone in the *Nineteenth Century* in 1877, the journalist Edward Dicey claimed that Britain had to occupy Egypt to secure India.

---

[91] *Israel's Watchman*, Mar. 1877, 1–2.
[92] *Nonconformist*, 13 Sept. 1876, 918.
[93] George Carslake Thompson, *Public Opinion and Lord Beaconsfield, 1875–1880* (London: Macmillan, 1886), i. 184.
[94] Seton-Watson, *Disraeli*, 308–11.

Typically, however, no reference was made to Palestine:[95] whether it was the fear of frustrating French ambitions in Syria, or simply because it was deemed an improbable demand, the Holy Land did not figure in Britain's strategic plans, not at the official level,[96] and certainly not in the popular conception of the Eastern Question.

Indeed, if the Holy Land was evoked at all by the agitators or the counter-agitators—and that was seldom the case—it was only to illustrate the events in the Balkans, and never the other way round. For example, in the introduction to *Personal Recollections of Turkish Misrule and Corruption in Syria by a Syrian*, published by the Eastern Question Association (EQA), the Revd William Denton explained that the 'condition of Syria is one to which, for many reasons, our attention ought at this time to be drawn. It gives us a valuable insight into the source of Turkish misrule.... What is true of Syria is true of Bulgaria and Bosnia.'[97] Another EQA pamphlet, *Evidences of Turkish Misrule*, cited Charles Warren on 'Turkish rule in Palestine', but made no reference to Warren's own views on Jewish restoration, or, indeed, to Jewish suffering under Ottoman rule or to the future of Palestine.[98]

The absence of any reference to the future of Palestine is even more noticeable considering that Gladstone's 'Christian revolution' was immersed in biblical imagery—the same imagery so central to the premillenarians' understanding of the events. W. T. Stead, the editor of the *Northern Echo* who ascribed the agitation to the direct intervention of God, reported in January 1878: 'We have beaten the War party, hip and thigh, from Dan even to Beersheba.'[99] The counter-agitation also employed biblical imagery. As Dicey wrote, 'our Empire is the result

---

[95] Edward Dicey, 'Our Empire in the East' (Sept. 1877), repr. in *idem, England and Egypt* (London: Chapman & Hall, 1881), 267–305.

[96] There are two well-documented exceptions. When, in February 1878, government officials were searching for some territorial station conducive to British interests in the Mediterranean, Haifa and Acre were weighed alongside other ports, but considered inadequate. Cyprus was eventually chosen. See Seton-Watson, *Disraeli*, 324–6. In a dispatch to Layard of 10 May 1878, Salisbury wrote: 'we shall have to choose between allowing Russia to dominate over Syria and Mesopotamia, or taking the country for ourselves, and either alternative is formidable' (quoted in Harold Temperley, 'Disraeli and Cyprus', *English Historical Review*, 46 (1931), 277).

[97] *Personal Recollections of Turkish Misrule*...(London: EQA, 1877), 2.

[98] Henry Richard, *Evidences of Turkish Misrule* (London: EQA, 1877), 39–40. Warren was an active member of the Syrian and Palestine Colonization Society.

[99] Shannon, *Gladstone and the Bulgarian Agitation*, 14; Stead, *MP for Russia*, i. 432.

not so much of any military spirit as of a certain instinct of development inherent in our race.... "To be fruitful, and multiply, and replenish the earth," seems to be the mission entrusted to us, as it was to the survivors of the deluge. The Wandering Jew of nations, it is forbidden to us to rest.'[100] And yet, as far as the British Israelites were concerned, they were the Wandering Jew of nations, *literally*; and they were expecting to make their way to the *actual, geographical* Dan and Beer-Sheba.

Jews and jingoes

The Jewish response to the crisis is worth exploring, because the social, political, and cultural condition of British Jewry offers a more nuanced look at the relationship between centre and fringe. Following Disraeli's acquisition of Suez Canal shares, the *Jewish Chronicle* remarked that the significance of this purchase 'is self-evident. Unintentionally and incidentally—such are often the ways of Providence—England has thereby materially become more interested in the fate of neighbouring Palestine, than she was before.'[101] Henceforth, the *Jewish Chronicle* referred repeatedly to the prospect of a British protectorate over Palestine, which would allow the Jews to return to their homeland: 'Does not policy, then—if that were all—exhort England to foster the nationality of the Jews, and aid them, as opportunity may offer, to return as a leavening power to their old country?'[102]

Actually, much of the restorationist excitement expressed in the *Jewish Chronicle* was awakened by John Gawler, who bombarded the paper with appeals concerning the Palestine Colonization Society. The initiative was at first welcomed, but sympathy faded when the Society's real agenda was disclosed: premillenarian, British Israelite, and—to the Jews' dismay—conversionist.[103] Perhaps it was the threat of these premillenarian projects that spurred the Jews themselves into action:[104]

---

[100] Dicey, 'Our Empire in the East', 277.
[101] *JC*, 3 Dec. 1875, 572.
[102] *JC*, 10 Nov. 1876, 501. The ardent proto-Zionism of the journal did not necessarily reflect a wider sentiment, not least because the editor, Abraham Benisch, was hardly a typical Anglo-Jew. An immigrant from Vienna, he had advocated Zionist ideas from the 1830s. See David Cesarani, *The Jewish Chronicle and Anglo-Jewry, 1841–1991* (Cambridge: Cambridge University Press, 1994), 32–50, 60–6.
[103] Yardeny-Agmon, 'John Gawler'.
[104] Gideon Shimoni, *The Zionist Ideology* (Hanover, NH: Brandeis University Press, 1995), 61–4.

following the Ottoman default on the public debt in 1875–6, the Jewish community was awash with rumours that Ottoman financial obligations would allow Jews to obtain control over land in Palestine. Negotiations to that effect were undertaken by Haim Guedalla, Moses Montefiore's companion and nephew-in-law.[105] Articles and letters referring to the future Jewish restoration in the aftermath of the international crisis continued to appear in the Jewish press in the period leading up to the Congress of Berlin.

Frantically combing Jewish newspapers in search of appropriate signs of the times, the premillenarians were tremendously excited by these initiatives. The secular press, as we have seen, was generally amused. Ironically, the only 'mainstream' milieu which seemed to embrace these ideas in earnest was the anti-Semitic circle. In his infamous attack on Disraeli ('had England been drawn into this conflict it would have been in some measure a Jewish war'), the historian Goldwin Smith argued that it was a mistake to regard Judaism as a species of religious nonconformity. He proposed a solution to the Jewish problem: 'Judea may revert to the Jews, and that portion of the race which refuses to be Europeanized may withdraw from Europe, where it is an alien element... It would be a danger averted from Western civilization.'[106] The essay provoked a response from the Chief Rabbi, Hermann Adler, under the title 'Can Jews be Patriots?'[107] Smith, in reply, elaborated his plan:

People sneer if it is proposed in the dissolution of the Turkish Empire, now evidently impending, to give the Jews back their own land. Nobody supposes that the Rothschilds would return to Jerusalem. But some of the intensely exclusive Jews might return; and their withdrawal might facilitate the fusion of the more liberal element with European society; at all events, justice would have been done the race and its position as a separate nationality would be defined, as is that of the Greek.[108]

The idea that the establishment of a Jewish national home in Palestine could cleanse the West of its Jews demonstrates, once again, the proximity between Zionism and anti-Semitism. But Smith's 'Zionism', as he himself suggests, was still premature, an idea to 'sneer' at. European Jews

---
[105] Saab, 'Disraeli, Judaism', 573–4.
[106] *Contemporary Review*, 31 (Feb. 1878), 617–18.
[107] *Nineteenth Century*, 3 (Apr. 1878), 637–46.
[108] *Nineteenth Century*, 3 (May 1878), 885.

were not yet ready to employ these terms; they were preoccupied with emancipation, not restoration.

Consequently, although references to the restoration continued to appear in the Jewish press throughout the Eastern Question crisis, British Jewry was concerned mainly with the condition of its East European brethren, living under the savage oppression of Christian regimes. It was this oppression which prompted the cool Jewish response to the agitation:[109] the *Jewish Chronicle* pointed out that 'While all England is gnashing her teeth at the contemplation of the oppression of Christians by Turks...not a word is said about the oppression of Jews by Romanian Christians'.[110] It is hardly surprising, then, that Adler's response made no reference to Goldwin Smith's Zionist vision. Instead, Adler argued that Jews were acting as true patriots when they approached the British government to mitigate the suffering of their co-religionists in Romania.[111] If anything, Adler made the Holy Land seem even more irrelevant: 'Granted that eighteen hundred years ago our ancestors dwelt amid the vine-clad hills of Judea, is that any reason why we should be less solicitous for the glory and interest of the empire we now inhabit?'[112] The Chief Rabbi was far from oblivious to the Jewish nationalist impulse; but his response suggests that he was unwilling to divert the discussion from the more urgent question of Jewish emancipation, a question which was not only more practical, but which was already contained within the discursive boundaries introduced by the agitators themselves.

So, when the *Jewish Chronicle* was discussing 'The Eastern Question and the Jews', it was referring not to the colonization of Palestine, but to the condition of East European Jewry.[113] Similarly, Jewish lobbying in the Congress of Berlin sought ways to secure the civil and political rights of oppressed Romanian Jewry, not to secure the Holy Land for the Jewish colonization.[114] On the one hand, this merely reflected a pre-Zionist Jewish sensibility, in which the colonization of Palestine was still

---

[109] Saab, *Reluctant Icon*, 87.
[110] *JC*, 6 Oct. 1876, 425.
[111] Feldman, *Englishmen and Jews*, 123.
[112] *Nineteenth Century*, 3 (May 1878), 643.
[113] *JC*, 6 Oct. 1876, 424.
[114] David Vital, *A People Apart: The Jews in Europe, 1789–1939* (Oxford: Oxford University Press, 1999), 496–503.

not perceived as the natural solution to the 'Jewish question', an idea that would become the corner-stone of Herzl's political Zionism. On the other hand, the Jewish reaction suggests that Jews were participating in the debate by employing the rhetorical terms of the centre: the oppression of religious minorities in the Balkans as a reflection of conflicting visions of the British state. Palestine did not figure in this debate. Discursively, then, the *Jewish Chronicle* functioned as an intermediate space, in which fringe and mainstream met.[115] This position may have mirrored the limited integration of Jews in Victorian society; but it also reminds us that the division between periphery and centre is never totally fixed.

The books of Benjamin

We have already seen that the Prime Minister's Jewish origins, combined with his pro-Ottoman policy, allowed the agitators to read the crisis as a struggle between Christian virtue and Oriental despotism, both at home and abroad.[116] But Disraeli's roots also made him an extremely destabilizing figure, particularly in relation to the English self-fashioning as chosen people. Consider, for example, A. C. Shaw's satiric *The Book of Benjamin* (1879). Written in mock biblical verse, it begins with Benjamin of Israel's divine call to office: 'thou shalt no more be called De Israeli, but Beaconsfield shall thy name be called; for thou art set for a beacon unto the people of England, a stiff-necked and perverse generation, that have need of a sign.'[117] Henceforth it is never quite clear whether the work mimics the style of the King James Bible in order to represent the Hebrew or, indeed, the Hebraic. Since the Oriental is made to represent both the indigenous *and* the alien at the very same time, halfway through the plot Disraeli becomes a type of a stone-hearted (Gentile) Pharaoh, deaf to the calls of his oppressed (Israelite) people. The identification of Disraeli with Egypt, reinforced after his purchase of Suez Canal shares in 1875, was taken up by *Punch*, which repeatedly presented Disraeli as 'the Modern Sphinx'.[118] So, while one bitter pamphlet could represent Disraeli as an 'Uncircumcised

---

[115] Cesarani, *Jewish Chronicle*, 65–6.
[116] Ragussis, *Figures of Conversion*, 174–233.
[117] A. C. Shaw, *The Book of Benjamin* (1879; 8th edn. London: Charles Watts, 1880), 6.
[118] *Benjamin Disraeli, Earl of Beaconsfield, KG in a Series of 113 Cartoons from the Collection of 'Mr. Punch'* (London: Punch, 1881), nos. 87, 91.

Philistine', in another work the 'Schemers of Philistia' are actually the Russians who covet John Bull's estate at 'Goshen' (namely, India); but in a third pamphlet, 'The promised land, the Goshen of his soul' (in itself a fusion of Egypt and Canaan) actually stands for Britain.[119] The British Israelites, in particular, were perplexed by Disraeli's crypto-Judaism, which seemed to muddle their strict separation between Jews and Israelites.

All this points not only to the elasticity of biblical vocabulary, but also to Disraeli's unique position, as a puzzling figure crossing the invisible boundaries—social, religious, cultural—between fringe and centre (not unlike the enigmatic Shaftesbury, perhaps the only Englishman who could chair both the National Conference on the Eastern Question *and* the Mildmay Prophetic Conference). With Disraeli's imperial instinct, on the one hand, and his Jewish origins, on the other, little wonder that both Jews and premillenarians were intrigued by the possibility that his Eastern policy was motivated by a desire to restore the Jewish people to their homeland.[120] In the months leading up to the Congress of Berlin, these speculations reached the general press as well. The *Jewish Chronicle* cited the French correspondent of the *Pall Mall Gazette*: 'A rumour has got afloat that Lord Beaconsfield will not return empty-handed, and that he is preparing for his countrymen a sensational surprise—no less a thing, in fact, [than] a British protectorate over the Holy Land.'[121] That Disraeli returned from Berlin with Cyprus rather than Palestine did not discourage the premillenarians: after all, virtually any development in the Eastern Question could always be interpreted to mean one thing, and one thing only.

Twentieth-century historians have continued to wonder about Disraeli's Zionist aspirations. Headlem-Morley suggested in 1930 that 'in securing Cyprus for Britain, Disraeli felt the step would sooner or later bring Palestine and Turkey within the orbit of British control'.[122] As Isaiah Friedman noted, Headlam-Morley did not produce any evidence

---

[119] David Oedipus, *Benjameni de Israeli: Who is this Uncircumcised Philistine?* (London: W. Stewart, 1881); Anon., *Ben's Dream about the 'Schemers of Philistia' and 'Ishmael's Noble Sons'* (London: Smart & Allen, 1878), 6; Anon., *Beaconsfield: A Mock-Heroic Poem, and Political Satire* (London: Abel Heywood, 1878), 45.

[120] Cf. *Christian Herald*, 29 Sept. 1876, 534.

[121] *JC*, 28 June 1878, 4.

[122] James Headlam-Morley, *Studies in Diplomatic History* (London: Methuen, 1930), 206–7.

to support his assumption.[123] This did not hinder Friedman himself, however, from reaching a very similar conclusion: 'At heart, Disraeli was a Zionist. If he did not try to give his dreams a practical content, it was because during his lifetime there was no suitable opportunity for making any move without disturbing the status quo.'[124] If Disraeli was a Zionist 'at heart', he seldom wore his heart on his sleeve. There are only three evidential fragments that confirm that he was at all interested in the restoration of the Jews: Disraeli's exploration of early Jewish nationalism in his historical novel *Alroy; or, The Prince of the Captivity* (1833);[125] Lord Stanley's recollection of an odd incident in January 1851, when a frantic Disraeli pondered the possibility of buying up land in Palestine through the Rothschilds to establish Jewish colonies there;[126] and Disraeli's short-lived support of Oliphant in the late 1870s.[127]

With so little to work on, historical accounts have sometimes been informed more by wishful thinking than by fact. N. M. Gelber, a Jewish historian, has credited Disraeli with an anonymous pamphlet published in Vienna in 1877, favouring the creation of a Jewish state under British tutelage. The claim was repudiated by Cecil Roth in the early 1950s;[128] but Roth himself happily remarked that he 'has been informed that there is a marginal note in [Disraeli's] hand on one of the minutes relating to Cyprus in the Foreign Office files, to the effect that this territory might possibly serve as a place of refugee settlement for persecuted Jews'.[129] Isaiah Friedman claimed that in *Tancred*, Disraeli 'expressed his longing for a re-establishment of Jewish government in Palestine'.[130] The novel is certainly teeming with ideas which, years after its publication, became official policy: the British taking of Cyprus, the Royal Title Bill, and an increased British involvement in the Middle

---

[123] Friedman, *Question of Palestine*, p. xxxvii.
[124] Ibid. p. xxxviii. See also Robert Blake, *Disraeli's Grand Tour* (London: Weidenfeld & Nicolson, 1982), 132.
[125] Tuchman, *Bible and Sword*, 220.
[126] Blake, *Disraeli's Grand Tour*, 130–2.
[127] Friedman, *Question of Palestine*, pp. xxxviii–xli.
[128] N. M. Gelber, *Lord Beaconsfield's Plan for a Jewish State* (Tel-Aviv: Leinman, 1947) [Hebrew]; Cecil Roth, *Benjamin Disraeli* (New York: Philosophical Library, 1952), 159–62.
[129] Roth, *Benjamin Disraeli*, 155–6.
[130] Friedman, *Question of Palestine*, p. xxxvi.

East. But the novel makes no mention of Jewish restoration; if anything, Disraeli sees England's opportunity in Arab rather than Jewish nationalism.[131] Fortunately, Franz Kobler has found an interesting way out of this silence: 'That Tancred's restoration plans are only hinted at is in conformity with the subtle technique of the novel.'[132] The idea that Disraeli's imperial plan was motivated by his wish to orchestrate the restoration of the Jews is simply too elegant to be given up, even if one is forced to read absence as a subtle presence.

In fact, it could be argued that *Tancred* charts the opposite route altogether: the protagonist embarks on his Eastern adventure with Jerusalem in mind, determined to explore the Hebrew origins of English culture; but he soon finds himself immersed in the swirling politics of the Middle East and the question of British control over the passage to India. The novel, subtitled *The New Crusade*, laments the fact that Britain is busy constructing railroads instead of launching a third Crusade;[133] still, rather than refer explicitly to Palestine, the campaign envisioned by Disraeli—bringing the West closer to the great Asiatic mystery—reflects a much broader imperial project. *Tancred*, then, both narrates and performs a displacement which is analogous to our theme: it suggests that what the Hebraic is to the Hebrew, imperialism is to the 'Holy Land'. If the novel is indicative of its author's views, perhaps Disraeli's real aim in turning eastwards was to restore the imperial ethos—not the Jews—to its original birthplace.

My point is that these readings of *Tancred* reveal much more about twentieth-century Zionist historiography—or Victorian premillenarian desires—than about Disraeli himself. The great majority of Disraeli's contemporaries, who did not look for a restorationist subtext, did not find one. In his notorious biography of Disraeli, for example, T. P. O'Connor claimed that *Tancred* unfolds Disraeli's 'Arab policy'. Those who fail to perceive it, he declared, 'can only be those who have not read Lord Beaconsfield's works, or who, having read, have not intelligence to interpret them'.[134] Disraeli's novels and their interpretations swiftly

---

[131] Tuchman, *Bible and Sword*, 223.
[132] Kobler, *The Vision Was There*, 74.
[133] Benjamin Disraeli, *Tancred; or The New Crusade* (1847; London: Peter Davies, 1927), 176.
[134] T. P. O'Connor, *Lord Beaconsfield: A Biography* (London: William Mullan, 1879), 611.

became central to the Eastern Question debate. As the *Spectator* famously complained in July 1878, 'For the last eight months at least, our policy has evidently been borrowed from *Tancred*.'[135] This delicious fusion of the fictional and the political signified a disturbing breakdown of boundaries, which was analogous to Disraeli's personal position as an outsider who had penetrated and taken over the centre. The *Spectator* captured this when it wrote,

If the shrewdest political thinker in England had been told, thirty years ago, that the bizarre and flashy novelist, who had just given the world *Coningsby, Sybil* and *Tancred*, would, within a generation, be not only ruling England, but ruling England on the lines of ideas set forth in that very extraordinary series of political primers... we cannot doubt that the shrewd political thinker we have supposed would have treated such a prophecy as the raving of a lunatic. Yet that is exactly what has happened.[136]

The allusion to lunatics and prophecy is not inappropriate. The act of interpretation—which, as we have seen, separates the sane from the insane—could serve as the leading trope of this entire debate, characteristic of centre and fringe alike. While the premillenarians were scrutinizing newspapers to make sense of prophecy, the agitators were combing Disraeli's novels to make sense of the newspapers. Not only the agitators: according to the *Spectator*, 'when some one quoted *Tancred* two or three months ago in Lord Beaconsfield's presence, the Prime Minister remarked, "Ah! I perceive you have been reading *Tancred*. That is a work to which I refer more and more every year, not for amusement, but for instruction." '[137]

Disraeli, apparently, had little time for new reading material. Writing to George Eliot in September 1876 to inform her of the sales of *Daniel Deronda*, the publisher, John Blackwood, admitted, 'I could not hear whether Disraeli gave any utterances on the subject.'[138] The Prime Minister was probably busy: *Daniel Deronda* was published in eight parts (books) from February to September 1876, just as the Eastern Question was exploding; the sixth book, 'Revelation', which unfolds Mordecai's restorationist vision, was published in July, just as the

---
[135] *Spectator*, 13 July 1878, 883.
[136] *Spectator*, 20 July 1878, 915.
[137] *Spectator*, 13 July 1878, 883.
[138] *The George Eliot Letters*, ed. Gordon Haight (London: Oxford University Press, 1956–78), vi. 282.

revelations concerning the Bulgarian atrocities were shaking the public.[139] Eliot's 'Zionist' novel allows us an even more focused look at the affinity between Christian Zionism and the Eastern Question, between novels and interpretation, between centre and fringe.

Reading *Daniel Deronda*

'There is something very fascinating in the mission that Deronda takes upon himself,' remarks Constantius in Henry James's memorable review of *Daniel Deronda*: 'I don't quite know what it means, I don't understand more than half of Mordecai's rhapsodies, and I don't perceive exactly what practical steps could be taken. Deronda could go about and talk with clever Jews—not an unpleasant life.' Pulcheria, too, envisions life in the East as a most happy experience for the Derondas: 'they had tea-parties at Jerusalem,—exclusively of ladies,—and he sat in the midst and stirred his tea and made high-toned remarks. And then Mirah sang a little, just a little, on account of her voice being so weak.'[140]

The reason why Constantius and Pulcheria cannot quite visualize Deronda's mission (in terms other than the bitter comedy of manners with which the novel is almost exclusively concerned) is that Eliot herself is extremely vague about it. 'I am going to the East to become better acquainted with the condition of my race in various countries there,' Deronda informs Gwendolen: 'The idea that I am possessed with is that of restoring a political existence to my people, making them a nation again, giving them a national centre, such as the English have, though they too are scattered over the face of the globe' (p. 688). However, the novel ends before Deronda and Mirah have even left England: the one practical feature of Deronda's ambitious plan is a 'complete equipment for Eastern travel', the Mallingers' wedding-gift (p. 694).

---

[139] A cheaper reprint in four volumes without corrections was issued in December 1876. The second edition in one volume was published in October 1877, and for this Eliot made a few corrections. The third, or Cabinet, edition, which incorporates several alterations, especially in the Jewish sections of the novel, was published in December 1878. See George Eliot, *Daniel Deronda* (1876), ed. Graham Handley, World's Classics (Oxford: Oxford University Press, 1988), p. xxiii. Subsequent page numbers are cited parenthetically in the text.

[140] Henry James, 'Daniel Deronda: A Conversation', *Atlantic Monthly*, Dec. 1876; repr. in David Carroll (ed.), *George Eliot: The Critical Heritage* (London: Routledge & Kegan Paul, 1971), 423, 417.

Edward Said has claimed that Eliot's failure to address the material dimensions of the Zionist project is epitomized in her inability to acknowledge the existence of the indigenous population: 'Underlying all this', Said notes, 'is the total absence of any thought about the actual inhabitants of the East, Palestine in particular. They are irrelevant both to the Zionists in *Daniel Deronda* and to the English characters.'[141] Although Said goes out of his way to turn this silence into something altogether more eloquent, he is no doubt correct in asserting that Eliot's Zionist vision, though obscure, was embedded in an array of Orientalist/colonialist assumptions. At the same time, Said discusses 'the way Zionism is presented in the novel', as if Eliot were alluding to an already organized political movement or even a crystallized ethos: 'Eliot's account of Zionism in *Daniel Deronda* was intended as a sort of assenting Gentile response to prevalent Jewish-Zionist currents.'[142]

Of course, in 1874, when Eliot was writing her novel (set in the mid-1860s) there was no 'prevalent Jewish-Zionist current'. Far from producing an 'assenting Gentile response' to an established cause, it seems that Eliot was in fact attempting the opposite: it was precisely the lack of such a current that she was relying on. As Gillian Beer has argued, the Zionist plot enables Eliot to reinforce the parallel between Gwendolen and Deronda at the end of the novel: 'Gwendolen escapes the marriage market. Deronda escapes British culture and British manhood, though his success in his Zionist endeavour would have seemed far less certain for the first readers (and the author) than it may do now. He, like Gwendolen, is left on an uncertain edge of possibility.'[143] The Zionist mission, with its visionary, impractical, even maniacal edge, serves to reinforce the novel's open ending, so different from the closed conclusions of death and marriage in Eliot's earlier works.[144]

Daniel Deronda is so valuable for our discussion not simply for what it tells us about Eliot's own Zionism (to which I will return shortly); with its unequivocal restorationist plot, on the one hand, and its cultural

---

[141] Edward Said, *The Question of Palestine* (1979; New York: Vintage, 1992), 65.
[142] Ibid. 61, 66. For a persuasive critique of Said's thesis see Nancy Henry, *George Eliot and the British Empire* (Cambridge: Cambridge University Press, 2002), esp. 113–23.
[143] Gillian Beer, *George Eliot* (Brighton: Harvester Press, 1986), 227.
[144] Barbara Hardy, *The Novels of George Eliot: A Study in Form* (1959; London: Athlone, 1973), 153.

visibility, on the other, Eliot's novel presents an ideal surface, which the reader's own lighted candle can then arrange into a fine series of concentric circles. As Eliot herself notes in *Daniel Deronda*, 'all meanings, we know, depend on the key of interpretation' (p. 46). It is telling, then, that the public reception of the novel reproduced the same familiar pattern.[145] The Jews and premillenarians recognized the Zionist plot immediately, highlighted and embraced it, albeit in different ways not always consistent with Eliot's own vision; but as far as the 'centre' was concerned—the literary reviews, the national and provincial press—the restorationist plot was treated sceptically, sometimes even sarcastically. Some critics preferred to ignore Deronda's Zionist mission altogether, dismissing it as one of the curiosities abundant in the Jewish half of the novel. Critics who did refer to it were often left puzzled, disappointed, or simply bored. 'There is much that is simply obscure and tiresome in Mordecai's harangues,' complained the *Edinburgh Courant*.[146] 'The world in general cares no more for the Jewish part of the story about Mordecai, with his visions, and Daniel with his theories of Jewish unity, and so on, than Daniel's mother cared,' yawned the *Daily News*.[147] This indifference was shared by the religious press as well, which, with no premillenarian creed, had no particular reason to indulge in Mordecai's reveries. Discussing the Jewish philosopher's 'odd club', the *Nonconformist* asserted that 'to not a few, the report of the debates will no doubt be found somewhat tedious'.[148] The High Church *Guardian* thought the Jewish part of the story 'simply odd and inexplicable', regretting that Eliot's 'powers should be so often expended on offensive subjects and wasted in elaborating effects which are uselessly disagreeable'.[149]

---

[145] My analysis is based on an extensive reading of the Evangelical and Jewish press, as well as on five sources which reproduce or annotate reviews from the national press: John Holmstrom and Laurence Lerner (eds.), *George Eliot and her Readers: A Selection of Contemporary Reviews* (London: Bodley Head, 1966); Carroll (ed.), *George Eliot*; Constance Marie Fulmer, *George Eliot: A Reference Guide* (Boston: G. K. Hall, 1977); Carol A. Martin, 'Contemporary Critics and Judaism in *Daniel Deronda*', *Victorian Periodicals Review*, 21/3 (1988), 90–107; J. Russel Perkin, *A Reception-History of George Eliot's Fiction* (Rochester: University of Rochester Press, 1990), 59–84.
[146] *Edinburgh Courant*, 4 Sept. 1876, quoted in Martin, 'Contemporary Critics', 101.
[147] *Daily News*, 31 Aug. 1876, quoted in Martin, 'Contemporary Critics', 97.
[148] *Nonconformist*, 16 Aug. 1876, 823.
[149] *Guardian*, 4 Oct. 1876, 1312.

More sympathetic critics, like the *Spectator*'s, felt that the problem was rooted in Eliot's failure to establish the exact nature of the plan: 'We cannot dismiss Deronda on his journey to the East without feeling uncomfortably that he is gone on a wild-goose chase,—to preach ideas which have only been hinted, and which must rest on a creed that has hardly been hinted at all.'[150] The *Manchester Guardian*, on the other hand, claimed that while a belief in the genius and destinies of his people 'may be a noble and fruitful inspiration to one of the chosen nation', Deronda in his role as a second Moses 'hardly presents himself to our eyes as a serious figure'.[151]

The conviction that a character like Deronda would not have kept the company of a raving recluse like Mordecai echoed the uncomfortable feeling that Eliot should not have associated herself with a Jewish plot. Critics may have felt that in sending Deronda to the East with Mirah, Eliot was not only frustrating the traditional generic expectations, but also transgressing, in her choice of topic and theme, the boundary between centre and fringe. The respect for Eliot was immense; but it was precisely with her reputation in mind that critics pondered over her eccentric decision to retreat to a subculture which seemed so distant from the central, 'middle', English world of her previous novel, *Middlemarch*. As the *Saturday Review* stated, 'the fact is that the reader never—or so rarely as not to affect his general posture of mind—feels at home. The author is ever driving at something foreign to his habits of thought.'[152] And the *World*'s critic wrote, 'The aspirations of Judaism, the consciousness of the great mission which is said to haunt, even in these latter days, the remnant of the Jewish race, have been exhaustively described in *Tancred*; and Daniel Deronda himself is nothing more than a hero after Mr. Disraeli's own heart, somewhat more solemn and scientific, as suits the attendant circumstances of George Eliot's novel.'[153] The idea that Jewish aspirations were a suitable topic for a Disraeli, but not an Eliot, reflected not only the authors' different backgrounds and reputations, but also the different ways in which their novels were read and understood and their position in the literary

---

[150] *Spectator*, 9 Sept. 1876, repr. in Carroll (ed.), *George Eliot*, 370.
[151] *Manchester Guardian*, 4 Sept. 1876, quoted in Martin, 'Contemporary Critics', 102.
[152] *Saturday Review*, 16 Sept. 1876, repr. in Carroll (ed.), *George Eliot*, 377.
[153] *World*, 6 Sept. 1876, quoted in Martin, 'Contemporary Critics', 103.

hierarchy. So, while *Tancred* was no longer judged aesthetically but merely as an extension of Disraeli's foreign policy (playfully presented, in itself, as a work of fiction), no one—not even Eliot herself, it seems—made the connection between Deronda's Zionist quest and the Eastern Question that was unnerving the country at the very same moment.

By 'no one', I mean only the mainstream critics. As early as July 1876, Haim Guedalla, writing in the *Jewish Chronicle*, yoked Eliot's vision to his detailed plans for the colonization of Palestine: 'The matter is not as visionary as many seem to imagine. Public attention has been much directed to it lately, and as the talented authoress of "Daniel Deronda" in book 6th, published in July, has eloquently sketched out a new Judea, poised between East and West, a covenant of reconciliation, the subject is now sure to be well ventilated.' He concluded with the warning that a 'momentous crisis is near at hand in Turkey'.[154] In the following months, the *Jewish Chronicle* dedicated many columns to the book, including several editorials, notices, and reports, which considered the practicality of these plans and explored the enthusiastic Jewish reception. With the novel's theme limited to the 'Restoration and re-constitution of the Jewish polity, as of old', the *Jewish Chronicle* apparently cared little for Gwendolen.[155] The newspaper admitted, however, that its reading was not a literary one: 'With "Daniel Deronda" as a work of fiction we have, journalistically, no concern in these columns. It is not our province to discuss its merits or demerits as a work of art. These have been fully dealt with elsewhere. Our interest in the story is, we apprehend, confined to such portions of it as deal with Jews, their observances, and their ideas.'[156] The *Jewish Chronicle*, in its familiar capacity as a mediating arena, conforms here to the mainstream reading: it suggests that since Jews *did* 'feel at home' in the narrative, they were not genuine readers in the conventional, literary sense.

It is indicative, moreover, of Jewish aspirations in the 1870s that the novel was often seen as a significant contribution not necessarily to the dreamy Zionist cause, but to the more urgent question of Jewish emancipation. In his well-known defence in the *Gentleman's Magazine*, James Picciotto admits that Deronda's quest 'can scarcely enlist the

[154] *JC*, 21 July 1876, 251. See also George Eliot to Haim Guedalla, 26 Sept. 1876, in *George Eliot Letters*, ed. Haight, vi. 288.
[155] *JC*, 15 Dec. 1876, 586.
[156] *JC*, 22 Sept. 1876, 394.

warm sympathy of the general reader. Few of the novel-reading public are likely to have thought much about the restoration of Israel or to be aroused to any special enthusiasm in its favour.' But Picciotto, too, swiftly deserts the Zionist cause and concentrates thereafter on Eliot's faithful depiction 'of modern Anglo-Jewish domestic life', which 'has accomplished more for the cause of toleration and enlightenment than could have been achieved by any amount of legislation'.[157]

The premillenarians, on the other hand, were precisely the sort of people whose warmest sympathy would be enlisted to Deronda's quest. Their journals and newspapers recognized immediately that the publication of the novel—and its Jewish reception—was another divine message. 'To students of prophecy who in the present crisis of the world's history are watching the modern phases of Jewish thought with eager interest', wrote Evelin Smith in *Israel's Watchman*, 'the enthusiastic reception which has been lately accorded by the Jews to "Daniel Deronda" can hardly fail to be of deep significance.' It is 'a sign of the times worthy of very special notice', explained Smith, who went on to attack Eliot's attempt 'to present in popular form the principles of Positivism'.[158] The 'popular' nature of the work was also commented on by the *Jewish Intelligence*, the organ of the London Jews Society, which published the familiar extracts from Mordecai's speech as evidence 'that this subject has passed from the restricted area of students and thinkers to the wide circles of readers of popular fiction'.[159] This view was shared by Ellen Whiting, a correspondent to the British Israelite *Nation's Glory Leader* who addressed the editor in a somewhat meek tone:

I do not suppose that one like yourself, occupied with a most important mission, would be likely to read the so-called light literature of the day; but my tastes, being somewhat gregarious, lead me occasionally into that field of reading. George Eliot's last book—a remarkable one—has largely taken up the Jews and their aspirations, and, as the return of the Jews (the Tribes) to Palestine is bound up with the fulfilment of such wonderful prophetic events, I have

---

[157] *Gentleman's Magazine*, Nov. 1876, repr. in Carroll (ed.), *George Eliot*, 409, 408, 416.

[158] *Israel's Watchman*, Oct. 1877, 202–3. This was a revised version of an article which had appeared in the Presbyterian (hence non-millenarian) *British and Foreign Evangelical Review*, 26 (July 1877). Significantly, the original article made no appeal to students of prophecy.

[159] *Jewish Intelligence*, Dec. 1876, 296.

thought it worth while, to send you the following extract, for it proves that the world bears witness to God's Word that is true.[160]

While the Jewish response preserved the canonical status of the work by evading the question of its literary merit, the British Israelite reaction reversed the centre–fringe relationship. Comments like this position the 'students and thinkers', with their 'important mission', at the centre of cultural production, while Eliot's novel gains an almost ephemeral, light-headed quality.

Still, the premillenarian excitement was somewhat reserved. The *Jewish Intelligence* wrote that *Daniel Deronda* showed 'how wide-spread and popular such an expectation of a restored land and polity has become. But the Christian, zealous for the honour of his Lord, will observe with some misgiving that Christian truth forms no element in these glowing anticipations.'[161] These misgivings were well justified, for the novel's plot is nothing less than a grand subversion of the premillenarian model of restoration and conversion. Eliot preserves the colonial and Orientalist aspects that were typical of some threads of Christian Zionism, but her vision—centring on a protagonist who 'converts' from Christianity to Judaism—is concerned first and foremost with Jewish, not Christian, interpretation of prophecy. Thus, while the novel 'occupies a pivotal historical position in the transition from realism to modernism',[162] it also occupies a pivotal position in the shift from Christian Zionism to Jewish Zionism. 'Daniel's view of the restoration is not conceived as the sign of Christian power—the conversion of the Jews—as it is in traditional millenarian discourse,' Michael Ragussis noted: at the end of the novel, 'Daniel and Mirah step outside the predominant configuration of Jewish identity in English discourse.'[163]

It is tempting to read the plot back into Eliot's own bitter aversion of millenarianism, bitter as only a devout Evangelical upbringing could make it. In a letter to a friend, in May 1853, she claimed that 'For good [news], I have nothing better than that the "Society for the Conversion of the Jews" has converted *one* Jew during the last year and has spent

---

[160] *Nation's Glory Leader*, 1 Nov. 1876, 153.
[161] *Jewish Intelligence*, Dec. 1876, 297.
[162] Tony E. Jackson, 'George Eliot's "New Evangel": *Daniel Deronda* and the Ends of Realism', *Genre*, 25 (1992), 247.
[163] Ragussis, *Figures of Conversion*, 290.

£4400'.[164] Two years later, in her damning portrait of Dr Cumming, Eliot presented the successful premillenarian preacher as rivalling 'Moore's Almanac in the prediction of political events'.[165] These views are reproduced in the novel (as is the deliberate slip in the Society's title): Lady Mallinger, much interested in Mirah, observes 'that there was a Society for the Conversion of the Jews, and that it was to be hoped Mirah would embrace Christianity; but perceiving that Sir Hugo looked at her with amusement, she concluded that she had said something foolish' (p. 192). Later in the story, having expressed a similar hope, a mortified Mrs Meyrick admits that she was 'wagging [her] tongue foolishly—making an almanac for the Millennium, as [her] husband used to say' (p. 318). This odd pattern of foolish women and correcting men is perhaps not so odd, considering that it seems to sum up the relationship between Gwendolen and Deronda.

By elaborating a vague nationalistic restoration plan, *Daniel Deronda* presents a bold critique of the conventional premillenarian plot. Eliot's final attempt to exorcise the Evangelical spirit was recognized by her premillenarian—and certainly appreciated by her Jewish—readers; but it was simply lost on her mainstream critics. For them, *Daniel Deronda* presented not a subversion of the premillenarian design, but a frustrating subversion, both generic and thematic, of the leading artistic form of the period: the realistic novel. Eliot's escape from the generic 'bounds of realism'[166] is reproduced in her deviation from the cultural preoccupations of the centre. But in 1876, both Modernism and Zionism still seemed very distant indeed.

Edwardian Culture and Jewish Zionism

In 1917, as chief intelligence officer to the Egyptian Expeditionary Force (EEF), Richard Meinertzhagen played a vital role in the British conquest of Jerusalem. Later, as chief political officer in Palestine and military adviser to the Colonial Office, he helped nurture the Jewish colonies in the Holy Land. In the 1930s, his uncle, Lord Passfield (Sidney Webb), served as Colonies Secretary in the Labour government

---

[164] George Eliot to Sara Sophia Hennel, 28 May 1853, in *George Eliot Letters*, ed. Haight, ii. 102.
[165] George Eliot, 'Evangelical Teaching: Dr Cumming', *Westminster Review*, 8 (Oct. 1855), 437.
[166] Terry Eagleton, *Criticism and Ideology* (1975; London: Verson, 1995), 123.

that struggled to redefine Britain's policy towards what was undoubtedly a Jewish state in the making. A devoted Zionist, Meinertzhagen tells us that he often thought of his great-grandmother, Mary Seddon; of her mission to restore the Jews, single-handedly, to the Holy Land; and of her long years in the lunatic asylum.[167]

Seddon died in 1874, and we can only speculate what her reaction to the Eastern Question crisis or to *Daniel Deronda* would have been—not to mention her view of the Balfour Declaration. After all, the premillenarians were right: the dissolution of the Ottoman Empire during the War did lead, eventually, to the colonization of Palestine by the Jews, under a British protectorate. What, then, can we make of the fact that in just two generations the idea of restoring the Jews to the Holy Land shifted from the sphere of prophecy to the sphere of practical politics? What does this transition, from confinement in Bedlam to geographical Bethlehem, actually signify? And if the Christian Zionist tradition in the nineteenth century was indeed as peripheral and eccentric as this chapter has claimed, what does this tell us about the wider cultural resonances of the Balfour Declaration?

On one level, this shift illustrates how social and political changes can redefine the cultural demarcations on which categories of difference rely. The 1880s and 1890s saw the establishment of several Jewish agricultural colonies in Palestine; under the charismatic leadership of Theodore Herzl, these sporadic Zionist efforts gained an unprecedented sense of urgency and coherence. Writing in 1900, three years after the first Zionist Congress convened in Basle, the *Leeds News* noted the dramatic change in the public perception of the Zionist cause:

For years, the late Laurence Oliphant and others spent time and money, presumably to little purpose, in the furtherance of the restoration of Israelites to 'the land of their fathers.' Their efforts were looked upon as idealistic and nothing was considered so unlikely as the actual realisation of their dreams. Within the past four years, matters have assumed an altogether different aspect. Instead of the work being left to Gentiles, it has been taken up by the Jews themselves.[168]

---

[167] Richard Meinertzhagen, *Middle East Diary, 1917–1956* (London: Cresset, 1959), 1.
[168] Weizmann Archive (WA), Rehovot (Israel), Fourth Zionist Congress press clippings notebook, *Leeds News*, 14 Aug. 1900.

Naturally, the emergence of Jewish political Zionism redrew the eccentric–mainstream division: the Christian Zionist hope no longer seemed so ridiculous. With an increasingly visible body of Jews now committed to the colonization of Palestine, the vision of a Jewish restoration suddenly became feasible: far-fetched, perhaps; dreamy, certainly; but not impossible. As the *Sheffield Telegraph* noted when the Zionist Congress opened in London in August 1900, 'the scheme for the reoccupation of Palestine which was laughed at at one time is assuming a shape that has some resemblance to practicability.'[169] Comments like these were precisely what Herzl had hoped for when he decided to transfer the Congress from Basle to Britain's imperial capital. More than forty newspapers, national and provincial, covered the Congress, usually in a very favourable tone, stressing not only the romantic appeal of the movement, but also its considerable achievements in mobilizing public support.[170] But the response, as a whole, was somewhat sceptical. 'The restoration of Palestine as a home of the Jews seems a highly poetic conception,' mused the *Express*, but went on to note that 'The Palestine idea is, we believe, more poetic than practical... We respect the idea of Zionism, though we cannot believe in its realization.'[171] 'The Zionist movement', wrote the *Morning Post*, 'is one of those manifestations of the romantic and the ideal which are foredoomed to failure'.[172]

Several newspapers linked the Zionist quest to the problem of alien immigration to Britain, which had intensified in the late 1890s, as tens of thousands of persecuted Jewish immigrants from Eastern Europe settled in London's East End. The *Nottingham Express* noted that the English should wish success to the Zionist scheme 'if only from a selfish motive', because it would divert the Jews from Whitechapel to Jerusalem: 'If the Zionist movement will lessen the tide of this foreign immigration, the sooner it takes definite shape the better.' This, however, was quite unlikely:

No doubt millions of the poorer Jews in Eastern Europe would be glad to flock back to the old land, but the wealthier members of the community, the men with the brains, would remain in the countries of their adoption, for where the

---

[169] WA, *Sheffield Telegraph*, 14 Aug. 1900.
[170] Benjamin Jaffe, 'The Fourth Zionist Congress in London and its Reflections in the British Press', *Ha-Uma*, 51–2 (Sept. 1977), 394–405 [Hebrew].
[171] WA, *Express*, 13 Aug. 1900.
[172] WA, *Morning Post*, 14 Aug. 1900.

treasure is there will the heart be... Mr. Zangwill has a simple solution for the problem of repopulating Palestine. Let gold be discovered in six months, he says, and they will get a large population in Palestine, sufficient, at least, to force a franchise from the Turks. No one can deny the force of this analogy from South Africa. But unfortunately—or shall we say fortunately?—there is no gold in Palestine, and therefore no attraction, save that of sentiment, for the modern Jew. There is something touching in the yearning with which thousands of Jews look back to their ancient land: but while we may sympathise with their aspirations, it would be folly to ignore the difficulties that stand in the way of their fulfilment.[173]

Zangwill's wry comment about the unfortunate deficiency of Palestine gold was gleefully quoted by virtually all the newspapers reporting from the 1900 Congress: after all, here was a prominent member of the Jewish community who was corroborating the old–new myth of the greedy Jew. But Zangwill's observation was also taken up because it shifted attention from the dreamy Zionist aspiration to a much more topical question—namely, the role played by the Jews in the current crisis in South Africa. According to claims made in both Liberal and Labour circles, the Boer War was initiated by international Jewish financiers, and fought for Jewish interests:[174] as long as these Jews were more interested in their gold mines than in their old homeland, the Zionist project would never succeed.

By the early 1900s, then, the 'Jewish Question' was seen to occupy a range of geographical sites, which the Jews were either fleeing, invading, or—it was believed—seeking to control: the Russian pale and Romania, the East End, New York, South Africa. Regardless of the growing visibility of the Zionist movement, Palestine was still not perceived as a vital part of this global map. But if the Holy Land was not crucial to the representation and understanding of the alien problem in the 1900s, the 'Holy Land' certainly was: yet again, the metaphor seemed more useful, more relevant, than the actual place itself.

In some instances, Zion was in Africa. Having examined 'the structure of industry and society upon the Rand', the journalist J. A. Hobson declared in his influential book, *The War in South Africa* (1900), that 'not Hamburg, not Vienna, not Frankfort, but Johannesburg is the New

---

[173] WA, *Nottingham Express*, 14 Aug. 1900.
[174] Colin Holmes, *Anti-Semitism in British Society, 1876–1939* (London: Edward Arnold, 1979), 68.

Jerusalem'. Touring the city, Hobson was disgusted by the sight of these immigrants, 'a rude and ignorant people, mostly fled from despotic European rule'.[175] Ironically, just three years later, the vision of an African New Jerusalem—a colony which would receive these 'rude and ignorant' Jews—became an official British policy. In August 1903, Colonial Secretary Joseph Chamberlain offered to establish a Jewish homeland in the Uasin Gishu plateau, part of the East Africa Protectorate. The 'Uganda plan', as it came to be known (or 'Jewganda', in Arnold White's notorious phrase[176]) proposed the establishment of 'a Jewish colony of settlement, on conditions which will enable the members to observe their National customs'.[177] According to the draft of the Charter, prepared by the solicitor David Lloyd George, MP, the perspective settlement was to be called 'New Palestine'.[178] Israel Zangwill, an ardent supporter of a Jewish colony in Africa, came up with some other options: 'British Judea', 'British Palestine', or 'New Judea'.[179]

Chamberlain's plan was devised essentially as a practical measure: there is no reason to suppose that Africa eclipsed Palestine as a possible outlet for Jews, either on the official level or in the popular imagination. The territory was offered to the Zionists simply because it was under British control; Palestine was not—at least not yet. And in addition to the various objections made in the British press—like the danger of assigning British territory to an alien community, or the conviction that Jews were incapable of engaging in agricultural work—there was also a moral, or aesthetic, objection: the African plan lacked that sense of poetic closure which was embodied in the re-establishment of a Jewish centre in Palestine. Even those who knew very little about Zionism— but knew their Bible—could easily sympathize with the *Jewish Chronicle*'s indignation at the idea that, rather than return to the 'ancestral home of the race', the Jews were now expected to establish a 'a settlement among half savage tribes, remote from the haunts of civilisation.

---

[175] J. A. Hobson, *The War in South Africa, its Causes and Effects* (1900; New York: Howard Fertig, 1969), 189–90.
[176] *Daily Mail*, 4 Sept. 1904, 4.
[177] Quoted in Robert G. Weisbord, *African Zion: The Attempt to Establish a Jewish Colony in the East Africa Protectorate 1903–1905* (Philadelphia: Jewish Publication Society of America, 1968), 79.
[178] Ibid. 74.
[179] Central Zionist Archive (CZA), Jerusalem, Zangwill Papers, A36/91, Zangwill to Lyttleton, 30 Nov. 1905.

Is Zion to be exchanged for Kikuyu and the cedars of the Lebanon for the Taru jungle?'[180]

Yet, the Uganda plan followed its own poetic logic. If, as Zangwill had suggested three years earlier, the Jews would flock to Zion only when it became Africa, it was only appropriate for the British government to offer them an African Zion. Thus, while opposition to the scheme was often based on this comic gap between Zion and Kikuyu, Lebanon and Taru, the almost universal anxiety with which the scheme was received, in both Zionist and white East African circles, merely illustrates the swiftness and immediacy with which biblical vocabulary could be applied to other geographical spheres, even to the Uasin Gishu plateau—the New Palestine. Frustrated with the Zionist rejection of the plan, Zangwill now observed that 'if gold were found in East Africa the Jews would go there soon enough':[181] paraphrasing his earlier statement by transforming 'Palestine' back into Africa, Zangwill's new comment simply forced the analogy between the two territories.

More often than not, however, it was England, not Africa, that was imagined as Zion. 'The Zionist longs for the re-establishment of the Jews in Palestine,' observed the *Cardiff Echo* in 1900; 'but the real Zion of the Jew is England, where with wealth scarcely any social ostracism is felt and position and power are open.'[182] Numerous references to the 'Exodus' of East European Jews constructed Russia as Egypt, and England as Canaan: when the Royal Commission on Alien Immigration, set up in 1902, submitted its conclusions in August 1903, its Report referred openly to the 'main causes of this exodus'.[183] Giving evidence to the Commission, one witness complained that Whitechapel and the Mile End had become a 'Jerusalem'; another that it was 'a second Palestine'.[184]

By this stage of our narrative, the idea that England is imagined as a second, or even first, Palestine, should hardly come as a surprise. But the new Jewish Exodus destabilized this unequivocal Hebraic self-fashioning (just as Disraeli had done, several decades earlier). On the one hand,

---

[180] *JC*, 28 Aug. 1904, 15.   [181] *JC*, 24 Mar. 1905, 12.
[182] WA, *Cardiff Echo*, 14 Aug. 1900.
[183] *Royal Commission on Alien Immigration*, British Parliamentary Papers, IX (1903), 11.
[184] Ibid. 298, 178. See also Juliet Stein, *The Jew: Assumptions of Identity* (London: Cassell, 1999), 59–78.

it was certainly possible to yoke the new presence of these poor Jews to the old Bunyanesque image of the English as the chosen people. For example, one of the witnesses to the Commission, a school superintendent, observed that the Jewish child 'will not, if he can help it, be, if I may say so, a hewer of wood or a drawer of water. He will not be at the bottom if he can help it, and he generally will help it.'[185] In this version of the Old Testament story (Joshua 9), the Jews are cast as Gibeonites, Gentiles, refusing to serve the Israelites—that is, the English. On the other hand, this Jewish Exodus was so unsettling precisely because it constructed the English not as Israelites, but as the indigenous nations of Palestine, the Hittites, Amorites, and Canaanites, soon to be dispossessed by the invading tribes of Israel. Major William Evans-Gordon, MP for Stepney, leader of the British Brothers League and member of the Royal Commission, stated this explicitly in *The Alien Immigrant* (1903), which describes the Jewish invasion of the East End: 'The Christian fares as the Canaanite fared. He is expropriated. Chapel after Chapel has been closed, many mission halls have been abandoned, and the congregation of the few that remain are dwindling every day.'[186] At the same time, it was in the East End that these Israelites became once again slaves. As Evans-Gordon himself noted, 'these descendants of Pharaoh's brickmakers, at two or three in the morning, after fifteen or eighteen hours of work, drop in their tracks in the workrooms from sheer exhaustion, and snatch a few hour's sleep'.[187] Perhaps England was not Canaan, but actually Egypt, home of the slave.[188]

All this suggests that while the biblical vocabulary continued to dominate the discourse surrounding Jewish immigration to Britain, the metaphorical 'Canaan' and 'Egypt' seemed much more relevant than the actual locales themselves. The premillenarian press, as expected,

---

[185] *Royal Commission*, 407.

[186] Major W. Evans-Gordon, *The Alien Immigrant* (London: William Heinemann, 1903), 12.

[187] Ibid. 11.

[188] The Victorian fascination with all things Egyptian meant that the analogy between ancient Egypt and Britain could be viewed quite favourably. A popular novel like H. B. Proctor's *The Mummy's Dream* (London: Simpkin & Marshall, 1898) retells the scriptural story of the Exodus, but this time from an Egyptian perspective, which suggests that the Jews were to blame. The analogy is obvious: 'During the time of the XIXth Dynasty, Egypt was as England is to-day—the center of light, learning, wealth, and liberty' (p. 69); but both nations suffer from the unfortunate presence of unclean, ungrateful Jews.

followed the fortunes of the Zionist movement closely and enthusiastically; for those immersed in prophecy, even the Uganda plan was a divine sign. But the excitement did not become universal. While many in England felt that there was a Jewish problem, only a few were aware of the practical solution offered by the Zionist programme, or took it seriously. In a letter to Herzl, in which he discussed the work of the Royal Commission and considered the possibility that the Zionist leader might be called to give evidence, the journalist and Zionist activist Leopold Greenberg noted that the idea of a Jewish homeland in Palestine simply did not occur to the Commissioners:

> We shall have to get the Zionist view in, in a diplomatic manner. Curious as it doubtless will seem to you, and absurd as it is in reality, the very last thing any of the Commission think of as a remedy for the evils complained of in regard to Immigration is the possibility of the Jew creating for himself a Centre where the Jew will not be de trop. It is a remedy altogether out of their purview, and of the Commission I suppose Rothschild is the only one who knows more than the name of the Zionist movement.

And he continues:

> I had a chat the other day with one of the members of the Commission, and just hinted that Zionism could not be well left out of the Commission's consideration. I don't think he saw the full force of what I said, and seemed to infer that I was anxious to represent merely the movement's influence on the lives of Jews in the East End. I mention this to show that there is not in contemplation much more than the Local aspect.[189]

Little wonder, then, that Benjamin Jaffe, who explored the reception of Zionism in the British press from 1895 to 1904, has been reluctantly forced to admit that 'Zionism was at the period in question a marginal topic from the point of view of the public, and the Near East issue was not in the forefront of such interest'.[190]

The Zionist plot in fiction

The growing visibility of the Zionist cause—but, at the same time, its enduring liminality—was reflected in the popular literature of the early

---

[189] CZA, Herzl Papers, H 1287, Greenberg to Herzl, 3 Apr. 1902.
[190] Benjamin Jaffe, 'The British Press and Zionism in Herzl's Time (1895–1904)', *Jewish Historical Society of England: Transactions*, 24 (1974), 89–100. His survey is based on 110 publications, dailies, and weeklies, both national and provincial.

1900s. It has become 'a continually increasing fashion for the Jewish question to be taken up by the novelist,' noted the *Jewish Chronicle* in 1904.[191] And although the 'Jewish question' often featured in Edwardian fiction in the form of greedy villains who answered to names like Woolf Finkelstein or Israel Herstein, it was a sign of the times that the Zionist project, too, was now taken up. Several of the newspapers covering the 1900 Zionist Congress noted, for example, that the events they were now witnessing resembled something out of Sydney Grier's *The Kings of the East: A Romance of the Near Future*, published earlier that year. 'If any one is concerned to realise the diplomatic labour of founding a new State,' noted the *Yorkshire Post*, 'a really clever picture of it may be found in Sydney Grier's latest novel, which is precisely the story of an attempt to repatriate the Jewish race.'[192]

The Kings of the East is the third in a series of four books in which Grier (pen-name of Hilda Caroline Gregg) unfolds the high politics and social intrigue in an imaginary Balkan state, Thracia.[193] The plot centres on Cyril Mortimer, a cunning British aristocrat who served as the Thracian Prime Minister, but was overthrown as a result of foreign intervention and domestic conspiracies. Mortimer is now hired by the great financier Israel Goldberg and his 'Children of Zion' guild, in the hope that his unique diplomatic skills will assist them in realizing their object—'to colonise Palestine with Jews from Europe, buying out the present inhabitants where necessary'.[194] A United Nation Syndicate is established to finance the colonization; but only Cyril Mortimer, a 'Moses and David rolled into one' (p. 4), can trick the international powers into accepting the scheme.

What follows is a series of diplomatic crises and manœuvres in the capitals of Europe: Mortimer's many foes try to jeopardize the plan, but the great man's brilliant mind always prevails. The story then shifts to the Holy Land, which the Jews are already busy colonizing. Having persuaded the Arab natives of Palestine to accept the Jewish scheme, Mortimer has yet to convince the stubborn Ishmaelite tribesmen who

---

[191] *JC*, 4 Nov. 1904, 23.
[192] WA, *Yorkshire Post*, 14 Aug. 1900.
[193] Vesna Goldsworthy, *Inventing Ruritania: The Imperialism of the Imagination* (New Haven: Yale University Press, 1998), 51–60.
[194] Sydney C. Grier, *The Kings of the East: A Romance of the Near Future* (London: Blackwood, 1900), 7. Subsequent page numbers are cited parenthetically in the text.

control the wilderness between Damascus and Baghdad. But the perilous adventures in the desert prove too much even for Mortimer: a long illness weakens his mind considerably, leaving it incapable of further international intrigue. His enemies act quickly. After an anonymous pamphlet reveals that the Jewish Syndicate is actually a plot 'for rendering the Jews absolutely masters of the world' (p. 303), the kingdom of Scythia (a thinly disguised Russia) captures Jerusalem, and the United Nation Syndicate collapses: the Jewish financiers, 'who had no sentimental care for Palestine' and merely yielded to Goldberg's pressure, welcome the opportunity of throwing off the yoke (p. 305). Mortimer has just enough common sense left to advise the Jews to establish a Jewish Legislature sitting at Nablûs and wait for a chance to bring down the Scythians.

The *Jewish Chronicle* called the novel 'a clever newspaper romance founded on the Zionist's hope... The court scandals of Vienna, Servia and Bulgaria have been suggestive to the author as have been the schemes of Zionism, and the result is a strange mixture of fact and fancy quite worthy of the subject.'[195] Grier herself insisted that her work had 'no pretensions to be considered an historical novel, or even a *roman à clef*'.[196] Still, Goldberg is obviously Rothschild, Herschel Rubbenssohn ('The poet of the ghetto') is clearly Zangwill, while the Zionist leader Dr Koepfle, described by Goldberg as 'the brain' behind the movement, is of course Dr Herzl, 'intent on giving practical form to the dreams of many generations, and crystallising the vague maxims of scattered visionaries into a workable constitution' (p. 159). According to Grier, however, it is Mortimer, not Koepfle, who is celebrated as 'the Moses of this second Exodus... The genius of Dr Koepfle directed this migration with almost mathematical accuracy; but Cyril's name bulked far more largely before the world than his, and there could be little doubt that when the immigrants were invited to designate... the man who should rule them, they would vote unanimously for Count Mortimer' (p. 181).

The Zionist project allows Grier to spice up her Ruritanian romance with stirring tales of the East, reminiscent of Haggard, Henty, and of

---

[195] *JC*, 4 May 1900, 22.
[196] Sydney C. Grier, *An Uncrowned King: A Romance of High Politics* (London: Putnam, 1896), p. iii.

course Disraeli; the Zionist schemers add a mysterious, paranoid, yet extremely topical dimension to her international plottings. But all these merely offer a backdrop against which Grier can depict the plotting and counter-plotting of her princesses, counts, bishops, and ministers. The emphasis is always on Mortimer's exceptional talents: the novel suggests that although they dominate the world's markets, the Jews cannot succeed without this exceptional Englishman.

This remains true even after his mental breakdown. In the final book of the series, *The Prince of the Captivity* (1902), the revivified United Nation Syndicate promotes a scheme for making Mortimer Prince of Palestine—a sham, intended to draw attention away from their actual plan which involves co-operating with the Jesuits to free Jerusalem from the Scythians.[197] Once again at the heart of international intrigue, Mortimer is kidnapped and kept in a secluded lunatic asylum—just the place, as we have seen, for Englishmen intent on ruling Palestine. But the Zionist subplot remains marginal: Grier is chiefly concerned with Mortimer's niece and nephew, whose dazzling romantic adventures barely leave them time to rescue their kidnapped uncle. As the *Saturday Review* noted, the book 'is very nearly a description of the realisation of Zionism, but so many incidents occur that it never reaches its goal'.[198] Still, the Children of Zion do win their independence. In the final pages of the novel, Goldberg proudly presents the cargo on his ship—great blocks of marble, 'de stones off de temple which iss to be built to de Holy City'. Cyril warns him that rebuilding the Temple 'in the very midst of the holy places of Christendom, will revolt the world';[199] it is probably due to his weakened mental state that he makes no reference to Muslim sensibilities.

Like Grier's work, Winifred Graham's *The Zionists* (1902) also revolves around a man of genius—Alexander Stuart, born to a beautiful Jewess who marries a dashing Christian aristocrat. Destined, from childhood, to be as great as his namesake, Alexander is carefully raised by his parents with no religious affiliation whatsoever. But an old friend of his mother's, the ultra-Zionist Esther Cohen, takes great interest in

---

[197] As Bryan Cheyette has noted (*Constructions of 'The Jew'*, 71 n.), the title looks back to Disraeli's *Alroy; or, The Prince of the Captivity* (1833) and anticipates John Buchan's *A Prince of the Captivity* (1933).
[198] *Saturday Review*, 28 June 1902, 844–5.
[199] Sydney C. Grier, *The Prince of the Captivity* (Boston: Page, 1902), 343–4.

the splendid young man. 'You—you might have been a young Zionist,' she tells him, 'dreaming of kingship, unravelling the history of Israel in exile, ready to head a race without leaders, to become a modern Moses, and guide the wandering tribes back to a land of promise.'[200]

Since Alexander remains doubtful, Esther convinces her beautiful niece, Ruth, to lure the young man into the Zionist camp. Following her to Basle, where the Zionist Congress is convening, Alexander meets many Zionist activists, including 'the Vienna playwright and journalist, the celebrity of the hour, who had done so much for the cause in hand' (p. 171). Herzl, like virtually everyone else who comes across Alexander, is deeply impressed by the young man's extraordinary intelligence (though it is never quite clear why: we never see him say or think anything remarkable). Indeed, when Alexander kindly agrees to address the Congress—'With the vast grip of a mind as great as that of Benjamin Disraeli, the immortal Hebrew Premier, he grasped the financial possibilities of this scheme for restoring the people without a country to the country without a people'—the spectators feel that 'the great patriot of Judaism had at last appeared' (p. 179).

Having toured Palestine, examined its commercial potential, and even developed a process for extracting gold from the Dead Sea, Alexander begs Ruth to join him in his important work in the East. Ruth hesitates: 'her conscience told her only too clearly that in the feast of life's delight, Alexander's ardour for Zion might be quenched' (p. 269). So she refuses: 'Though I love you, and you only, I cannot be your wife until my people are regenerated' (p. 271). Alexander continues alone: in a series of grand, yet extremely hazy actions, he obtains a Charter from the Sultan, secures the consent of the local population, establishes the Jewish Palestine Association, and convinces Jewish millionaires to open their pockets.

All this activity does not replace the existing Zionist movement, but merely invigorates it: 'The "Man in the Street" gathered from what he read that a rather more energetic movement than heretofore was being matured in the cause, or, as many termed it, the craze of Zionism' (p. 279). Like Grier before her, Graham is suggesting that the Zionist vision cannot be carried out without the presence of an external leader

---

[200] Winifred Graham, *The Zionists* (London: Hutchinson, 1902), 111. Subsequent page numbers are cited parenthetically in the text.

whose genius and connections can realize the plan. Indeed, following many strenuous months of work—described in two to three pages—Alexander can finally note that his undertaking has been successful: even the Temple has been rebuilt (p. 286). Exhausted by this mammoth effort of reviving a nation, Alexander can now return home to Hawthorn Hall, where Ruth, his prize, is waiting. The novel ends with their embrace.

With its terribly romantic, larger-than-life gestures and aspirations, its fascination with the life-style of the rich and famous, and numerous references to the starry-skied East, *The Zionists* is clearly indebted to *Tancred*—a debt that Graham happily acknowledges by frequently referring to Disraeli's politics and fiction. There is no mention, however, of the other novel which of course looms large over the plot: *Daniel Deronda*. After all, like Daniel, Alexander was also brought up in ignorance of his Jewish heritage, but was drawn to the Zionist cause thanks to the presence of a young Jewess; and like Daniel, it is Alexander's English education—his English blood—which allows him to function as a civilizing force in the East. Moreover, by concentrating on a young man whose talents alone can restore the Jews, Graham was merely following the blueprint that Eliot herself had offered in 'The Modern Hep! Hep! Hep!' (1879):

> Why are we so eager for the dignity of certain populations of whom perhaps we have never seen a single specimen, and of whose history, legend, or literature we have been contentedly ignorant for ages, while we sneer at the notion of a renovated national dignity for the Jews, whose ways of thinking and whose very verbal forms are on our lips in every prayer which we end with an Amen? Some of us consider this question dismissed when they have said that the wealthiest Jews have no desire to forsake their European palaces, and go to live in Jerusalem. But in a return from exile, in the restoration of a people, the question is not whether certain rich men will choose to remain behind, but whether there will be found worthy men who will choose to lead the return.[201]

Alexander, of course, is precisely one of those 'worthy men' without whom there would be no return; Count Cyril Mortimer, though not a Jew, is another. Indeed, charismatic leaders like these appear in virtually every Edwardian novel that depicts the Zionist restoration—even when it is imagined as a failure. A typical example is *The Children of*

---

[201] George Eliot, 'The Modern Hep! Hep! Hep!', in *Impressions of Theophrastus Such* (1879; Edinburgh: William Blackwood, 1891), 290–1.

Endurance by Lucas Cleeve (pen-name of Adeline Georgiana Wolff). Published in 1904, the novel follows the fortunes of an affluent Sephardic Jewish dynasty, the von Ritters, who emigrate from Germany to England. When Raphael, the first-born, asks his father whether they will one day return to Palestine, the Baron answers, 'I like London better. We will stay here; there is no room in Jerusalem, it is very uncomfortable, there is no electric light; . . . where there is civilization, there is my Jerusalem.'[202] Dark, melancholic, and Semitic-looking—his nose, he says, 'could overshadow the whole of Jerusalem' (p. 65)—Raphael insists on rediscovering his Jewish roots and observing Jewish law. His father is infuriated, and so are the numerous Jewish leaders who are shocked by Raphael's attempt to present 'the image of the Jew crucified for his ideals, as the living picture which should inspire Judaism' (p. 289).

Raphael's fusion of Judaism and Christianity—'Judaism for the multitude, Judaism for the world' (p. 290)—relies heavily on Disraeli. Indeed, Cleeve, just like Winifred Graham, is always happy to allude to *Tancred*, while making no mention of *Daniel Deronda*, despite the obvious similarities between the two protagonists. Raphael, like Daniel, is torn between two women: the unmistakably Semitic Dorothea ('When I am in danger of forgetting my faith', explains her aunt, 'I have only to look at her profile' (p. 139)) and the beautiful Gentile Hermione, whose family owes money to Raphael's father. Determined to save Hermione from bankruptcy, Raphael intends to marry her, and together restore the Jews to Palestine. But when his father dies unexpectedly and leaves him nothing, Hermione—who was ready to play 'the comic opera of a modern Queen of Sheba to his kingship of Solomon' as long as 'Duchesses would have travelled to Jerusalem to stay in the palace of the Queen of Palestine' (p. 286)—now decides to decline the offer. Raphael continues to Jerusalem by himself, joined only by his friend and tutor, Fortesque, and a band of poor followers, fired with the wish 'to buy Jerusalem back from the Turk, to send out their suffering brethren from Russia' (pp. 235–6). Despite his 'impassioned cry' to the rich Jews that they 'should turn their faces towards Jerusalem, sell all that they had, and gather once more at the foot of Mount Sinai

---

[202] Lucas Cleeve, *The Children of Endurance: Being the Story of a Latter-Day Prophet* (London: T. Fisher Unwin, 1904), 36. Subsequent page numbers are cited parenthetically in the text.

and repent them of their sins' (p. 232), the Jews of the world do not hurry back. Suffering in the cursed and barren land—no mention is made of the Arab population, the Jewish colonies, or, indeed, the actual Zionist movement—Raphael eventually dies. Only his old tutor is left to tell his sad tale and spread his unique version of the Word. The novel, in short, rejects Eliot's assumption: it is on those rich men who choose to remain behind, rather than the worthy men who lead the return, that the Zionist vision relies.

A similar sense of failure permeates another novel which reworks the Derondian theme—Violet Guttenberg's *A Modern Exodus* (1904). The worthy man here is the chivalrous Lionel Montella, descended from one of the noblest Jewish families in England, and in love with a young aristocratic Anglican, Patricia. The lovers wed secretly, much to the annoyance of the new Prime Minister, an 'avowed anti-Semite and rabid Jew-hater', who introduces a Bill for the banishment of '*all* the Jews, both English and foreign, rich and poor'.[203] The Montellas move to Haifa, where the colony of British Jews resides. Lionel—who 'possessed all the characteristics which conduce to the making of a good leader...a worthy protector of his people's interests' (p. 137)—is appointed governor of the English portion of Palestine, not an easy task, considering 'the unscrupulous greed of the people' (p. 168), the contempt which some Jews profess towards others, the endless contention between secular and orthodox Jews, and the total lack of religious tolerance. When Montella's arch-enemy, the Chief Rabbi Ben-Yetzel, learns that Patricia has rediscovered her Anglican faith, she is forced to return to England without her son. There, having nursed the sick daughter of the Prime Minister back to health, she convinces him to repeal the banishment Bill: the Jews are welcome to return to Britain— with the exception of the 'pauper alien' (p. 317).

The modern Exodus proposed by the book's title, then, is not the initial emigration from England to Palestine; rather, it is Lionel's journey back to England, together with most of Haifa's Anglo-Jewish citizens. Palestine is not deserted, but simply marginalized, serving henceforth as a useful sanctuary for poor Jews or one's irritating relatives. The novel, which begins by presenting England as Egypt (the

---

[203] Violet Guttenberg, *A Modern Exodus* (London: Greening, 1904), 17, 87. Subsequent page numbers are cited parenthetically in the text.

Prime Minister is continuously compared to a stone-hearted Pharaoh), ends by suggesting that England, not Palestine, is the real Promised Land. This final movement, from the East back to the West, was not limited to Guttenburg's bleak vision: even *The Zionists*, the one novel of the 1900s which presents the Zionist colonization project in unqualified positive terms, ends not in Zion but in England: 'How soon we shall be home again!' (p. 288), remarks Alexander in Jerusalem as he yearns westwards, towards his English estate. Eliot's 'The Modern Hep! Hep! Hep!' envisions worthy men who will choose to lead the return: but none of the novels written in Deronda's shadow can allow these worthy men to remain living in the East. To be sure, whereas George Eliot was thinking about the conditions that would facilitate a national regeneration, the popular novels that followed seemed to revel in hero-worship and overlook, or play down, the national context. At the same time, it is characteristic of the period that, despite the growing visibility of the Zionist movement, these novelists found it difficult to imagine the Zionist project as a complete success. Whereas Eliot's novel leaves Daniel and Mirah just before their excursion to the East, the later novels shift to the Holy Land itself, imagining the entire restoration, Temple and all; but it is back to England that they finally direct their gaze.

The Christian Zionist novels of the 1900s thus reflect the ambiguous position of the Zionist cause. By walking where Eliot feared to tread, by making explicit what was only implicit in *Daniel Deronda*, these novels offer a somewhat vulgar version of the restoration narrative—not least because, as we have seen in the discourse surrounding the Zionist Congress and the Royal Commission, the Zionist project was still considered impractical, far-fetched, or simply liminal. This 'vulgarization' can also be understood in terms of literary hierarchies: if Eliot's 1876 canonical novel captured the transition from realism to Modernism, the Zionist novels of the 1900s are much closer to what Eliot herself called 'silly novels by lady novelists'—especially in their depiction of mesmeric, righteous, almost superhuman protagonists, who lack the disturbed psychological complexity of Deronda. Paradoxically, then, just when the Zionist cause was becoming more respectable, its literary representations were not. Situated at the margins of the canon, still haunted by Eliot's legacy, no wonder these melodramatic novels are all but silent about *Deronda*.

One could argue, of course, the opposite: there was nothing extraordinary—nothing visionary, innovative, or even provocative—about these novels precisely because the Zionist cause had become familiar, even mundane. It is telling, however, that the Zionist plot emerged not only in romantic melodramas, but also in another popular Edwardian genre which flourished in the margins of the canon: fantasy writing and early science fiction.[204] Employing the Jewish restoration to Palestine as an emblem of futurity, of the wonders to come, fantasy writers combined the millenarian vision with contemporary questions like the fear of a possible German invasion or the Jewish immigration to Britain.

The most powerful case is M. P. Shiel's fantastic *The Lord of the Sea* (1901), which tells the story of a Richard Hogarth, apparently the son of a small tenant farmer, who finds a diamond-encrusted meteorite and uses his new wealth to finance the building of giant floating fortresses that give him command of the sea lanes and allow him to blackmail the nations into peace and social progress, especially land reform. Later, crowned as the British Regent, Hogarth sets forth a series of anti-Jewish decrees: the novel, which begins with pogroms on the Continent that led to a mass migration of Jewish refugees to England, ends with the expulsion of Jews from England to Palestine, a 'great exodus'.[205] The final irony of the book is that Hogarth, too, is revealed to be a Jew—Raphael Spinoza. Overthrown by his many enemies and forced to leave Britain, Hogarth/Spinoza migrates to the Holy Land, where he becomes the messianic leader of a rejuvenated Jewish nation, a modern-day Jesus ruling Jerusalem the golden, a 'purified Babylon, a London burnt to ashes and rebuilt somewhere else' (p. 492). Considering Hogarth's lowly background, it is not surprising that many elements in the novel are reminiscent of Richard Brothers's millenarian plans: the notion that a plebian Briton can become King of the Jews; the emphasis on the material preparations needed to bring about the millennium; and, most significantly, the conviction that it is only in Palestine, 'an uninhabited land, as it were reserved, ordained, and waiting for inhabitants' (p. 242), that the common man can finally win a piece of holy land.

---

[204] The division between the two genres was not clear-cut. *A Modern Exodus*, defined by Guttenberg as 'a story of the impossible...placed in the future for the sake of convenience' (p. v), is listed in I. F. Clarke, *The Tale of the Future, from the Beginning to the Present Day* (London: Library Association, 1972), 28; Grier's work is listed in Darko Suvin, *Victorian Science Fiction in the UK* (Boston: G. K. Hall, 1983), 79.

[205] M. P. Shiel, *The Lord of the Sea* (1901; New York: Arno Press, 1975), 422. Subsequent page numbers are cited parenthetically in the text.

The millenarian theme was exploited further in other books, like Thomas Pinkerton's *No Rates and Taxes: A Romance of Five Worlds* (1902), a bizarre tale whose narrator—exiled on Mars—describes the rise and fall of Jubilee City, a utopian metropolis which was established after the rich Jews bought Palestine from the Turks. All the same, it is indicative of the limited visibility of Zionism in the 1900s that even fantasy novels obsessed with the power of international Jewry or the Jewish invasion of the East End very often ignored the Zionist solution which seemed so natural to Herzl and Greenberg. The most blatant examples are the futuristic paranoid novels of James Blyth, *The Tyranny* (1907) and *Ichabod* (1910). Offering some of the most anti-Semitic portraits in English literature, these two novels, both concerned with a mysterious hypnotizing power whose bearer can control the world, include detailed drafts for a new Aliens Act which would solve the Jewish problem once and for all. *Ichabod* goes even further, and continuously quotes from the Report submitted by the Royal Commission on Alien Immigration. Narrated in 1950, the novel looks back to those horrifying days when 'the filthy Semitic aliens were herding like vermin' in the East End. Using his hypnotic force to pass anti-alien measures in Parliament, Blyth's hero cleanses Britain of these hated Jews; one of the English patriots in the novel suggests that 'we'll boot 'em out in a jiffy, and send 'em home to Jericho!', but the Jews are actually deported to South America.[206] In *The Tyranny*, they are exiled to Mexico and the Argentine.[207] Although both plots are set around 1910, the Zionist movement is never mentioned; neither is Palestine.[208] Considering Blyth's obsession with all things Jewish, this omission is no less than striking.

In other words, while fantasies about Jews seemed to play a considerable role in Edwardian fiction, their return to Zion remained a marginal issue in a body of literature which was itself marginal, in the sense that it flourished on the outskirts of the canon. If, as the *Jewish*

---

[206] James Blyth, *Ichabod* (London: John Milne, 1910), 4, 201.
[207] James Blyth, *The Tyranny* (London: William Heinemann, 1907), 157, 176.
[208] A similar example is Henry Byatt, *Flight of Icarus* (London: Sisley's, 1907), a paranoid tale about the 'King of the Jews' who takes over Britain; there is no reference to either Palestine or Zionism. In Robert Hugh Benson's apocalyptic *Lord of the World* (1907), on the other hand, the Antichrist woos the world with socialism and humanism; although the millenarian climax takes place in Palestine, the Jewish restoration is never mentioned.

Chronicle noted in 1904, 'the novelist' had taken up 'the Jewish question', Zionism was never really seen as an answer.

From Balfour to Bedlam

Of course, sometime after 1914 there were enough people in Whitehall who believed that Zionism *was* the answer—at least as far as Britain's strategic interests were concerned. During the First World War, when the need to control Palestine directly—and the need to mobilize Jewish support—became imperative, the Zionist movement, with its colonial vision and organization, seemed a natural ally.

Britain's core interest was strategic, but it was nevertheless enmeshed with an array of widely held myths, first and foremost the image of the Jews as an all-powerful international élite. Weizmann was more than happy to encourage these ideas, allowing British officials to believe that the Jews virtually controlled both America and Russia.[209] As Mark Levene has observed, the Declaration was the product of 'a perception of the world, and of Jews within it, through the narrow, socially and culturally confined prism of Britain's traditional ruling class'. Insisting that the only real motive behind the Declaration was the need to give the Zionists in Russia a reason to fight on the side of the Allies, Levene has dismissed the idea that the Declaration had anything to do with 'an evangelical Christian Zionist ghost by the name of Lord Shaftesbury haunting the corridors of Whitehall'.[210]

This seems a bit far-fetched: the immediate British calculations may have had nothing to do with the restoration to Palestine, but there is enough evidence to suggest that for men like Balfour, Sykes, and Ormsby-Gore, the biblical and romantic resonances of the restoration added to the appeal of the Zionist cause. At the same time, one should be wary of reading the Balfour Declaration backwards, as Zionist historiography has so often done: taking the cataclysmic importance of the Declaration for granted, Sokolow and his followers sought to trace a tradition respectable enough, hegemonic, coherent, and consistent

---

[209] Tom Segev, *One Palestine, Complete: Jews and Arabs under the British Mandate* (1999), trans. Haim Watzman (New York: Henry Holt, 2000), 39–45.

[210] Mark Levene, 'The Balfour Declaration: A Case of Mistaken Identity', *English Historical Review*, 107 (1992), 76, 56. For a more complex view see James Edward Renton, 'The Historiography of the Balfour Declaration: Toward a Multi-Casual Framework', *Journal of Israeli History*, 19/2 (1998), 109–28.

enough, to correspond with what was to follow. Consequently, Sokolow over-glorified what was essentially a peripheral phenomenon in nineteenth-century Britain.

But even if we revise Levene's thesis, the problem nevertheless remains: analysing the role of the dramatis personae behind the Declaration is one thing; understanding the wider cultural climate is another story. Indeed, while the Zionist cause was gaining sympathy among decision-makers, it seems that its visibility outside Whitehall remained limited. The Balfour Declaration itself was released to the press on Friday, 9 November, to correspond with the publication day of the *Jewish Chronicle*. The national press, however, was concerned with news of Lenin's victory, and the Declaration received scant attention only. As Leonard Stein has noted, the Declaration seemed to make little or no impression even on Englishmen especially interested in Middle Eastern affairs. Ronald Storrs, future governor of Jerusalem, noted that 'with ninety-five per cent. of my friends in Egypt and Palestine (as in England) the Balfour Declaration passed without notice'.[211]

The public's indifference is best reflected in a survey of attitudes towards Zionism and the 'Palestine Question' conducted by Mass Observation in July 1946 and September 1947. A combination of street samples and a panel of voluntary observers, this was hardly a comprehensive study, but the findings are nevertheless remarkable.[212] One person in every three had either never heard the word 'Zionism' or turned out to have the wrong idea (p. 9); wrong guesses included Christian Science, the British Israelites, and Jehovah's Witnesses (p. 10). Half the sample had never heard of the Balfour Declaration; another quarter said they had, but did not know what it was. The remaining quarter was equally divided between those who knew, more or less correctly, and those who believed that the Declaration was a promise made to the Arabs (p. 24). People were asked how they felt about the idea that the Jews should have a national home; almost 60 per cent approved (even though only 24 per cent stated that they supported

---

[211] Quoted in Stein, *Balfour Declaration*, 560–1.
[212] Mass Observation Archive, file 2515, *Report on Attitude to Palestine and the Jews* (Sept. 1947), microfiche copy, Bodleian Library. Page numbers are cited parenthetically in the text. For similar polls conducted in 1948, revealing the extent of ignorance regarding the Empire as a whole, see Jonathan Rose, *The Intellectual Life of the British Working Classes* (2001; New Haven: Yale University Press, 2002), 363–4.

Zionism). Among those who approved, 66 per cent thought it was 'good, right for Jews', but only 4 per cent because of the 'Jewish (religious) attachment' (p. 15). The survey was conducted as the situation in Palestine was deteriorating; some of the interviews were held after the devastating bombing of the King David Hotel in Jerusalem and the hanging of two British sergeants by Irgun terrorists. Newsreels and newspapers showed the English public how Balfour was leading to Bedlam, but the researchers had to conclude that after thirty years of British rule in Jerusalem, 'In general, it is clear that Palestine is not a subject in which the majority of people are really interested' (p. 8).

To say that people were not interested in the Holy Land is not to say that they were not interested in the 'Holy Land' (indeed, the word 'Zionism' had 'religious associations for people, however meaningless it may be to them otherwise' (p. 10)). We have seen that during the Eastern Question crisis of 1870s, biblical vocabulary was central to the mainstream debate, although Palestine was not; and that in the discourse surrounding the Royal Commission and the Aliens Act, it was England, not Palestine, which was constructed as the Jews' ultimate Zion. The 'Promised Land' as a metaphorical entity was far more powerful, more significant, and in many ways more useful than any literal definition. As the next chapter will demonstrate, nowhere was this more visible than in the imperial encounter with the Holy Land during the First World War.

This brings us back, full circle, to Lloyd George's biblical education, which no doubt reflected a cultural climate much broader than what Levene called 'the confined prism of Britain's traditional ruling class'. In reminiscing over his Sunday-school classes, Lloyd George, too, was trying to glorify what was essentially a strategic decision. By this I do not mean to question the genuineness of his interpretation; no doubt Lloyd George's unique Nonconformist biblicalism did play a significant role in his pro-Zionist views. However, this impulse should be read in its proper context and not projected, anachronistically, to the mid-nineteenth century. It is telling that Lloyd George began his address in 1925 with a British appeal to the Jews, but quickly found himself talking about the Jewish appeal to the British,[213] a slippage which blurs the difference between active effort and 'natural sympathy'; between

---

[213] Lloyd George, 'Afterword', 47, 48.

proposing the Jewish colonization of Palestine at a time when the Jews still showed little inclination for a mass migration to the land of their fathers and supporting an appeal from the Jewish Zionist Congress. Representing the end of the Wandering Jew's saga, the prospect of Jewish restoration was inviting, both ethically and aesthetically; but it was not what Victorian Christian Zionism was about. Lloyd George's 'natural sympathy' was no more and no less than natural sympathy, not an initiative but a reaction; expecting not a literal realization of the apocalypse, but rather a final rehearsal of an old, half-forgotten Sunday-school lesson.

5

Homesick Crusaders

Propaganda and Troop Morale in the Palestine Campaign, 1917

On 9 December 1917 British and Dominion forces captured Jerusalem from the Turks; two days later, heading a solemn procession, General Edmund Allenby—chief of the Egyptian Expeditionary Force (EEF)—entered the city on foot. In London, *Punch* published a memorable illustration which epitomized the great achievement: captioned 'The Last Crusade', it showed Richard Coeur de Lion looking down towards the Holy City and nodding contentedly, 'My dream comes true!'[1] (see Fig. 12).

Punch, it seemed, spoke for many. The allusion to the campaign in Palestine as the 'new' or the 'last' Crusade was common both during and after the War, with numerous books offering their own variation on the theme: *Khaki Crusaders* (1919), *Temporary Crusaders* (1919), *The Modern Crusaders* (1920), *The Last Crusade* (1920), *With Allenby's Crusaders* (1923), and so forth. A recent title like Anthony Bruce's *The Last Crusade: The Palestine Campaign in the First World War* (2003) indicates that the analogy has yet to be exhausted.

This Crusading mania has been well documented.[2] So well, that little attention has been paid to the fact that several weeks before the British

---

[1] *Punch*, 153 (19 Dec. 1917), 415.
[2] Cf. Elizabeth Siberry, *The New Crusaders: Images of the Crusades in the Nineteenth and Early Twentieth Centuries* (Aldershot: Ashgate, 2000), 94–7; Jonathan Newell, 'Allenby and the Palestine Campaign', in Brian Bond (ed.), *The First World War and British Military History* (Oxford: Clarendon Press, 1991), 191.

Fig. 12. Bernard Partridge, 'The Last Crusade', *Punch*, 19 December 1917.

conquest, the Press Bureau—part of the government's Department of Information—issued the following D-notice to the press:

15 November 1917.   1.45 p.m.
NOTICE TO THE PRESS.
PRIVATE AND CONFIDENTIAL.
(NOT FOR PUBLICATION OR COMMUNICATION)
The attention of the Press is again drawn to the undesirability of publishing any article paragraph or picture suggesting that military operations against Turkey are in any sense a Holy War, a modern Crusade, or have anything whatever to do with religious questions. The British Empire is said to contain a hundred million Muhammodan subjects of the King and it is obviously mischievous to suggest that our quarrel with Turkey is one between Christianity and Islam.[3]

Needless to say, *Punch* was not prosecuted for this breach of the Censorship regulations. By February, newspaper articles commissioned by the Department of Information, written by British officials, and wired from Palestine via Whitehall to Fleet Street, adopted a tone which was—according to the terms laid down in the D-notice—unmistakably 'mischievous'. One such telegram opened with the words: 'As it was in [the] days [of the] Crusaders so to-day soldiers of the West are visiting the churches of Jerusalem and Bethlehem for prayer and thanksgiving.' It noted, furthermore, that 'Two of the commanders who have played a great part in the South Palestine campaign are descended from knights who fought in the wars of the Crusades'.[4] A month later, the Department of Information released a forty-minute official film entitled *The New Crusaders: With the British Forces on the Palestine Front*.[5] Yet, as late as October 1918, in response to an angry telegram from Egyptian headquarters (about a reference in *The Times* to 'this new crusade'), the Cable-Room censor dryly remarked: 'The Censors in this Room have long had instructions to be very chary about passing the word "Crusade".'[6] So which was it to be? Was this simply bureaucratic blunder, or did it hint at a more complex representational quandary?

---

[3] TNA: PRO, FO 395/152/218223, Notice D.607, 15 Nov. 1917.
[4] TNA: PRO, FO 371/3383/29296/98–9, Wingate to FO, 14 Feb. 1918.
[5] Roger Smither (ed.), *The Imperial War Museum Film Catalogue*, i: *The First World War Archive* (Trowbridge: Flicks Books, 1994), item IWM 17.
[6] TNA: PRO, HO 139/27, Censor's minute on note from MI7A to Press Bureau, 28 Oct. 1918.

What was at stake in the invocation, or suppression, of the Crusading theme?

The stakes were high indeed. Notwithstanding its strategic objectives or its historical repercussions, the Palestine campaign was consciously staged by the British government as an exercise in propaganda, shaped and filtered to enhance the nation's morale.[7] Palestine, after all, was unlike any other imperial catch: it was the Holy Land, steeped in religious and historical memories; few seemed more germane than Richard Lionheart's failure to win Jerusalem.

Nevertheless, the almost instinctive impulse to evoke the Crusade in this context exposed strains which normally remained obscured within the stiff imperial ethos—most obviously, the friction between the British Empire and its colonized subjects: there would have been no need to issue the D-notice, had it not been for the religious and political animosity between the (Christian) metropole and its (Muslim) subalterns and allies. But there was another rift within the metropolitan centre itself, between the people who were fabricating Britain's wartime propaganda and 'the people' for whom this propaganda was being fabricated. The censorial act constructed the 'Last Crusade' as a known secret: but this was a secret shared by a privileged few only. As we shall see, the Crusading imagery, far from being instinctive or ubiquitously available, as the British propagandists had assumed, was in fact socially and culturally confined.

The limited currency of the Crusading theme is exemplified most vividly in the letters, diaries, and memoirs written by the 'New Crusaders' themselves, the soldiers who fought in Palestine. For them, the Holy Land was associated not with memories of medieval European conquest, but rather with the traditions and institutions of vernacular biblical culture, from Sunday-school hymns to the family Bible. Whereas the Crusading image denoted a distinct imperial ambition concerning the earthly Jerusalem, this popular sentiment evoked a 'Jerusalem' associated, self-reflexively, with 'Home'; as such, it offered a contesting ethos which, when fused with the weariness of war,

---

[7] On the organization of British wartime propaganda see M. L. Sanders and Philip M. Taylor, *British Propaganda during the First World War, 1914–1918* (London: Macmillan, 1982), 1, 26, 64, and *passim*; on the pivotal role played by Mark Sykes in shaping propaganda concerning the Palestine campaign see Roger Adelson, *Mark Sykes: Portrait of an Amateur* (London: Jonathan Cape, 1975), esp. 241, 245–8.

presented an inward-looking vision, very different from the heroic, expansionist narrative constructed by government officials.

By juxtaposing these two representations of the Palestine campaign—the official and the unofficial—this chapter explores the relationship between public consumption and private conception, between vernacular biblical culture and the imperial ethos, and, most significantly, between those two very different visions: England in Jerusalem, on the one hand, and Jerusalem in England, on the other.

The Palestine Campaign and Wartime Propaganda

When Prime Minister Lloyd George met Allenby in June 1917 to discuss the impending advance on the Palestine Front, he informed the commander that the War Cabinet expected 'Jerusalem before Christmas'.[8] From the very outset of the War, Lloyd George's conviction that only a decisive blow in the Middle East could hasten an Allied victory was matched by his personal interest in propaganda;[9] in the Palestine campaign, the two objectives finally merged. During a discussion in the War Cabinet on 2 April 1917, 'great stress was laid on the moral and political advantages to be expected from an advance in Palestine, and particularly from the occupation of Jerusalem, which, it was pointed out, would be hailed with the utmost satisfaction in all parts of the country'. A success in Palestine, 'quite apart from its purely military aspects', would 'counteract the depressing influences of a difficult economic situation'.[10] Sensing that the public had to be prepared for the military action on the Eastern Front, the Prime Minister ordered his newly appointed director of propaganda, the author John Buchan, to initiate a campaign under the Gladstonian slogan 'The Turk Must Go'.[11]

Propaganda concerning the Ottoman Empire had long been a contentious issue. For Kitchener and his entourage, the possibility of a Muslim Holy War against Britain, and in particular a Muslim uprising

---

[8] David Lloyd George, *War Memoirs of Lloyd George* (London: Odhams Press, 1936), ii. 1090–1.

[9] Matthew Hughes, 'Lloyd George, the Generals and the Palestine Campaign', *Imperial War Museum Review*, 11 (1996), 4–17; Sanders and Taylor, *British Propaganda*, esp. 11, 38–9, 77–8.

[10] TNA: PRO, CAB 23/2, War Cabinet Minutes, 2 Apr. 1917 (1).

[11] TNA: PRO, FO 395/139/42320, Lloyd George to Buchan, 1 Feb. 1917.

in India, was a recurring nightmare.[12] A *jihad* against Britain, masterminded by the Germans and proclaimed by the Sultan in November 1914, failed to kindle a substantial Muslim response, but its explosive potential continued to haunt British officials.[13] Concurrently, of course, members of the Arab Bureau were engaged in an arduous effort to woo Arab leaders into launching a pro-Allied revolt against the Ottomans.[14] This made the religious question extremely controversial. The Muslims were enemies, but they were also subjects and allies: the best propaganda strategy, then, was to avoid religion altogether. A D-notice issued in December 1914, renewed in March 1915 and February 1916, maintained that the 'publication of any matter calculated to have a needlessly hostile effect upon the Mohammedan opinion should be avoided'.[15]

The D-notice of November 1917, with which we began, abided by the same logic. On 12 November, Major Hugh Thornton, serving at the War Cabinet offices, wrote to Buchan: 'I send you the enclosed note for what it is worth. It was sent to me the other day by a friend of Lord Milner's who has very intimate connections with the East.' Attached was a press cutting from the *Evening Standard* of 8 November, stating that 'for a thousand years [Jerusalem] has been in the hands of the "infidels." If we capture the town, it will mean that for the first time the flag of a Christian nation will float over its walls.' Lord Milner's anonymous—and annoyed—friend added: 'Could not Press Censor explain to the Editor that comments of this nature are ill advised, in view of the fact that our nearest ally to this front is the King of the Hejaz and other chiefs of Arabia, who are strict Mohammedans and greatly revere Jerusalem and all places connected with our Lord.'[16] It was probably this reprimand that prompted the Press Bureau to issue the D-notice prohibiting any suggestion 'that military operations against Turkey are in any sense a Holy War, a modern Crusade, or have anything whatever

---

[12] David Fromkin, *A Peace to End All Peace: Creating the Modern Middle East, 1914–1922* (1989; Harmondsworth: Penguin, 1991), 97; George Antonius, *The Arab Awakening: The Story of the Arab National Movement* (London: Hamish Hamilton, 1938), 126–48.

[13] Fromkin, *Peace to End All Peace*, 109; Antonius, *Arab Awakening*, 140–2.

[14] Bruce Westrate, *The Arab Bureau: British Policy in the Middle East, 1916–1920* (University Park, Pa.: Pennsylvania State University Press, 1992).

[15] TNA: PRO, HO 139/19/78, *Official Press Bureau Instructions*, D.122. 24 Dec. 1914; D.186 16 Mar. 1915; D.363, 21 Feb. 1916.

[16] TNA: PRO, FO 395/152/218223, Thornton to Buchan, 12 Nov. 1917.

to do with religious questions'.[17] Like the previous notices, and the note from Milner's friend, the new D-notice presented guidelines which were merely tactical. Anyone with 'intimate connections with the East' would instantly recognize that it was 'ill advised' to allude to the British campaign as a Crusade—even if it actually was one. It was 'undesirable' and 'mischievous' to suggest that the British quarrel with Turkey was one between Christianity and Islam—but not necessarily untrue. In its very existence as a conscious act of censorship, the D-notice was stating exactly what it was trying to suppress.

Ironically, the notice attempted to renounce the idea of a Holy War against Turkey by locating the volatile Christian–Muslim hostility within the British imperial framework, in which imperial affiliation was expected to come before, even obliterate, religious difference. This was of course a myth. That the 'Mohammedan subjects of the King' thought differently is evident from a telegram sent by Allenby to the War Office on 2 December 1917: 'Owing to reluctance of Pathans with 58th Rifles to fight against their co-religionists, the Turks, I have been compelled to withdraw the Pathan Company from front line for employment on lines of communication.'[18] As far as the Pathans were concerned, religious affiliation came *before* imperial duty, and the war had *everything* to do with religious questions.[19]

To be sure, just a few months earlier, the Department of Information itself advocated the Crusading theme in the open. Converting Buchan's broad guidelines for 'The Turk Must Go' campaign into a tangible list of publications, Stephen Gaselee—one of the Foreign Office's 'bright young men'[20]—included a section entitled 'The Holy Land: A New Crusade'.[21] In his letters to scholars, asking them to mobilize articles for the propaganda effort, Gaselee ruminated about French, Arab, and international interests in Palestine, before reaching the crux of the matter: 'However, it is particularly on the sentimental, romantic and religious side of the Palestine campaign that the Prime Minister and Buchan wish emphasis to be laid, especially in the ecclesiastical press,

---

[17] TNA: PRO, FO 395/152/218223, Notice D.607.
[18] TNA: PRO, WO 33/946/8638, GHQ Egypt to WO, 2 Dec. 1917.
[19] See also David Omissi, *Indian Voices of the Great War: Soldiers' Letters, 1914–1918* (London: Macmillan, 1999), 14–15, 25, 199.
[20] Sanders and Taylor, *British Propaganda*, 49.
[21] TNA: PRO, FO 395/139, [Gaselee], Apr. 1917.

and if you will keep the crusading idea in mind as you write the article, I feel certain that the results will be what they want.'[22] Gaselee was writing just a few days after the War Cabinet hailed the 'moral and political advantages to be expected from an advance in Palestine'. The Cabinet did not specify what these advantages were, but as far as Gaselee was concerned, they were intimately connected with 'What might be called the new Crusade for the liberation of the Holy Land'.[23] It was precisely because the Crusading image was so instinctive, so immediate, that the D-notice was issued.

But the association was not ubiquitous. To see why, we must first explore the cultural currency of the Crusading metaphor and its significations in the decades preceding the War.

The Crusade as metaphor

'Sire, only come hither and I will show you Jerusalem!' Thus spake the valiant knight, Sir Brian de Gurnay.
'Nay,' replied King Richard of England, and he buried his face in his armour, tears were in his eyes, and with hands uplift to Heaven he exclaimed: 'Lord God, I pray Thee that I may never see Thy Holy City, if so be that I may not rescue it from the hands of Thine enemies!'[24]

This paragraph, in Gothic script, opens Major Vivian Gilbert's *The Romance of the Last Crusade: With Allenby to Jerusalem* (1923), an account of his wartime service in Palestine and probably one of the most extravagant manifestations of the Crusading theme. The first chapter is a fictional prelude: it introduces a young Brian Gurnay, 'just down from his first year at Oxford, a typical product of the English public school' (p. 2), who is basking in the sun on the grounds of his estate, Ivythorne Manor, reading about King Richard's Crusade. Tremendously excited by these romantic adventures, Brian exclaims: 'To fight in thy cause, to take part in that Last Crusade I would willingly leave my bones in the Holy Land! Oh, for the chance to do as one of these knights of old, to accomplish one thing in life really worth while!'

---

[22] TNA: PRO, FO 395/139, Gaselee to Benson, Master of Magdalene College, Cambridge, 10 Apr. 1917.
[23] TNA: PRO, FO 395/139, Gaselee to Lestrange, 11 Apr. 1917.
[24] Vivian Gilbert, *The Romance of the Last Crusade* (New York: D. Appleton, 1923), 1. Subsequent page numbers are cited parenthetically in the text.

(p. 5). Just then, his old mother, Lady Mary, enters with the *Daily Telegraph* announcing the prospect of war. Brian is thrilled: 'he almost fancied the blood that had come down to him from Sir Brian de Gurnay was mounting to his head' (pp. 9–10).

Quoted at length in Peter Parker's *The Old Lie: The Great War and the Public School Ethos*, this scene is a superb illustration of the momentous role played by the gentlemanly tradition of chivalry, honour, patriotism, and sportsmanship—encapsulated here in the idea of the Crusade—in the Great War: not only in the mobilization of a whole generation of keen young men, but also in the myriad ways in which the war was anticipated, imagined, and understood.[25] Emerging in the late eighteenth century, this 'cult of chivalry' was perfected by Walter Scott in novels like *Ivanhoe* (1820) and *The Talisman* (1825), in which the Crusades—with an Anglicized Richard Lionheart storming the Holy Land—were depicted as a defining episode in the forging of English nationalism. Cheaper editions of Scott's novels sold well throughout the century, inspiring a range of late Victorian and Edwardian imitators, from G. A. Henty's *Winning his Spurs* (1882) and Haggard's *The Brethren* (1904) to the adventure book that young Brian was reading on that sweet summer day.[26]

An indefatigable network of sports clubs and boys' societies, school missions and men's colleges, popular fiction and illustrated magazines, sought to disseminate this public school chivalric ethos throughout society.[27] However, even Baden-Powell's Boy Scout movement, the most successful Edwardian organization of its kind, achieved a great and rapid success in the public school sector only, and it took decades before it reached a wider audience.[28] Vivian Gilbert believed that all British soldiers were Crusaders, whether they knew it or not: 'The spirit

---

[25] Peter Parker, *The Old Lie: The Great War and the Public School Ethos* (London: Constable, 1987), 228–9. See also Paul Fussell, *The Great War and Modern Memory* (New York: Oxford University Press, 1975); Mark Girouard, *The Return to Camelot: Chivalry and the English Gentleman* (New Haven: Yale University Press, 1981), 275–93.

[26] Siberry, *New Crusaders*, 112–30, 150–60; Joseph Shadur, *Young Travellers to Jerusalem: The Holy Land in American and English Juvenile Literature, 1785–1940* (Ramat Gan, Israel: Bar-Ilan University Press, 1999), 84–91.

[27] Cf. John M. MacKenzie (ed.), *Imperialism and Popular Culture* (Manchester: Manchester University Press, 1986); Girouard, *Return to Camelot*, 249–58; Cecil D. Eby, *The Road to Armageddon: The Martial Spirit in English Popular Literature 1870–1914* (Durham, NC: Duke University Press, 1987).

[28] Girouard, *Return to Camelot*, 255.

of the Crusaders was in all these men of mine who worked so cheerfully to prepare for the great adventure!' (p. 37). But Gilbert's patronizing tone—the lives of his men, he wrote, 'as dull and uninteresting as the ledgers they kept in their dismal London offices', were miraculously transformed when they were carried away from their 'stuffy little bedrooms' into a land steeped with 'a thousand memories of all the gallant crusaders' (pp. 110–11)—merely suggests that the Crusader image *was* closely associated with a very privileged social grouping.[29] Soldiers from the ranks, as we shall see, seldom invoked the Crusading image in their writings, but for someone like Major-General Guy Dawnay, the Palestine campaign was intimately connected with the memory of his 'old crusading ancestor who killed the Saracen and the lion on those very hills!'[30]

Similarly, for the men who were shaping the representation of the events in Palestine—John Buchan (graduate of Brasenose College, Oxford), Stephen Gaselee (Eton, King's College, Cambridge), or Mark Sykes (Jesus College, Cambridge)—the Crusading metaphor was all but innate, rooted in their education, their religious upbringing, their genealogy. Gaselee, a keen medievalist and a devout Anglo-Catholic, was described as 'a lover of the past' who 'seemed to move familiarly among princes, cardinals and patriarchs, as in some historical novel'.[31] Sykes, a Catholic, turned the sixty-foot replica of the Eleanor Cross near the gates of his estate into a war monument: friends and tenants killed in the Great War were commemorated as modern-day Crusaders. After his untimely death in 1919, his own figure as Crusader was set up in brass, with a Paynim lying under his feet and Jerusalem in the background.[32] If Mark Sykes could be said to embody Britain's complex, often incompatible British interests in the Middle East, his brass armoured figure suggests that beneath the vigilant foreign policy lay a repressed, unconditional imperial ambition.

This affinity between class, Orientalism, and the Crusades was epitomized in the enigmatic personality of T. E. Lawrence, who encouraged the legend that he was a descendant of Sir Robert Lawrence, an alleged

---

[29] Siberry, *New Crusaders*, 39–63.
[30] IWM, Department of Documents, 69/21/2, Papers of Major-General G. P. Dawnay, letter home, 13 Dec. 1917.
[31] *Cambridge Review*, 65 (23 Oct. 1943), 25.
[32] Shane Leslie, *Mark Sykes: His Life and Letters* (London: Cassell, 1923), 294.

companion of Richard Lionheart.[33] Lawrence's academic speciality was Crusading history: his BA thesis, exploring the influence of the Crusades on European military architecture, was later published as *Crusader Castles* (1936). During his service in Arabia, Lawrence's white robes and golden dagger seemed to obliterate the Crusader persona, but when put to the test, the Crusader was always outed: summoned by Allenby to take part in the entrance procession into Jerusalem, Lawrence took off his Arabian garb, and members of the personal staff lent him a uniform, red tabs, and a brass hat, 'tricked me out in their spare clothes till I looked like a major in the British Army'.[34] Lowell Thomas's lecture, the main vehicle for perpetuating the Lawrence myth, was at first promoted in London as *The Last Crusade*, despite—or, indeed, because of—the Arabian garment. At the same time as it conveys the fantasy of going native, the Lawrence legend relies on the reassurance that beneath his deceptive mantle lay as committed a Crusader as ever.

Lawrence's imperial escapades took place in Arabia, not Palestine: his 'Crusade' did not follow the original definition of the term, namely a military campaign to recover the Holy Land from the infidel; nor did it signify a religious clash, a holy war, between Christianity and Islam (his allies, after all, were Muslim). Rather, Lawrence's Crusade hinged, much more broadly, on the cultural and geographical chasm between Orient and Occident. A similar use of the 'Crusade' was made, for example, during the Eastern Question crisis of 1875–8, when both agitators and their opponents were inspired by what George Carslake Thompson called the 'Crusading Spirit': since 'to Europeans there is something shocking in the spectacle of any European people being subjected to people of a lower type of civilisation', Christians were able to transcend their differences and unite 'for common defence against the infidel'.[35] W. T. Stead himself declared in September 1876 that the Crusades were no longer an enigma: 'I felt that I was called to preach a new crusade. Not against Islam, which I reverenced, but against the Turks who disgraced humanity. I realised the feelings of Peter the Hermit. God was with me.'[36]

---

[33] Joel C. Hudson, *Lawrence of Arabia and American Culture: The Making of a Transatlantic Legend* (Westport, Conn.: Greenwood Press, 1995), 52.
[34] T. E. Lawrence, *Seven Pillars of Wisdom* (1926; London: Jonathan Cape, 1935), 453.
[35] George Carslake Thompson, *Public Opinion and Lord Beaconsfield, 1875–1880* (London: Macmillan, 1886), i. 73.
[36] Quoted in Siberry, *New Crusaders*, 84. Members of the British Israelite Syrian and Palestine Colonization Society were of course using the 'Crusade' literally. Cf. *The Rock*, 31 Mar. 1876, 227.

Figurative or domestic interpretations of the 'Crusade' were hardly novel, but they became more common, it seems, as the 'medieval revival' swept England in the late eighteenth century. The fusion of the Arthurian epic, the annals of Richard Lionheart, and the cult of St George (popularized by the Crusaders who returned from Palestine) into a seemingly unified myth of chivalry meant that the image of the Crusade was often Anglicized, internalized, or divorced from its original historical context. Protestants tended to read the Crusaders' atrocities as typical examples of Catholic wrongdoing. Although *Ivanhoe* certainly exalts King Richard and the Crusading movement, it is Rachel's Jerusalem, a purely spiritual concept, that Scott admires most. By associating the territorial dream of possessing Palestine with the brutal Templar Knight, Bois Guilbert, and his demented fantasies of world domination, Scott suggests that there is something corrupting and despotic about the desire to rule the earthly Jerusalem—a typical Protestant lesson. Even Catholics, however, could employ the temporal distance to construct the 'modern' Crusade as an enlightened, rectified version of the Holy War: contemporaries styled it a 'Peaceful Crusade'—that is, the gradual 'reconquest' of the Holy Land for Christianity through religious, cultural, and philanthropical penetration.[37] These redefinitions meant that in the decades preceding the War, the Crusading idea was often applied in a much looser way, as a metaphor for fighting a just cause, be it missionary work, suffragism, or temperance.[38] One could speak of a 'civilising Crusade' without any sense an oxymoron.

It was in this symbolic mode that 'Crusade' was initially employed in the First World War. Bishop Winnington-Ingram was being quite literal-minded when he declared, in 1915, that the Church should 'mobilize the nation for a Holy War'.[39] But the concept was usually employed figuratively, as in Lloyd George's 1916 declaration that 'Young men from every quarter of this country flocked to the standard of international right, as to a great crusade'. This latter phrase, *The Great Crusade*, was also the title of the Prime Minister's collection of wartime

---

[37] Alexander Schölch, *Palestine in Transformation, 1856–1882: Studies in Social, Economic and Political Development* (1986), trans. William C. Young and Michael C. Gerrity (Washington: Institute for Palestine Studies, 1993), 66.
[38] Siberry, *New Crusaders*, 104–11.
[39] Quoted in Alan Wilkinson, *The Church of England in the First World War* (1978; London: SCM Press, 1996), 253.

speeches.[40] The significance of the Holy War concept to British propaganda is displayed in the extraordinary variety of wartime and post-war visual images: from postcards of British soldiers in full armour and recruiting posters showing a knightly St George clashing with the Dragon, to stained-glass windows and monuments of majestic Crusaders.[41] The coffin of the Unknown Warrior, set up in Westminster Abbey in 1920, contained a real Crusader sword, donated by King George V.[42] Sykes himself acted in a propaganda film, *It is for England*, a ten-reel saga about St George reincarnated as an army chaplain.[43] All this made the Crusaders' actual historical journey to Palestine almost redundant. Britain was fighting a Holy War in Europe, with the Kaiser cast as the Dragon against Britain's St George.

Paradoxically, the nineteenth-century metaphoricalization of the Crusade was taking place at the exact same period which saw Britain expand its involvement in Palestine. Britain's 'Last Crusade' could be said to have begun in 1799, when the Royal Navy bombarded the old walls of Acre, the same walls that Richard Lionheart conquered from Saladin in 1191; exactly a hundred years later, in 1291, the last remaining Crusaders in Palestine were driven away from the very same spot. But this historical twist of fate merely exposes the incompatibility between the Crusading narrative and Britain's actual imperial interests; after all, in 1799, and throughout the entire nineteenth century, Christian British forces were fighting alongside, not against, the infidel Ottomans.

This is not to say that the Crusading spirit was absent from high Anglo-Palestine Orientalist discourse.[44] Robert Curzon, who visited Jerusalem in 1849, described his rage at 'the crimson flag of Turkey floating heavily over the conquered city of the Christians'. He longed to tear it down 'and replace it with the banner of St George'.[45] 'One may

---

[40] David Lloyd George, *The Great Crusade* (London: Hodder & Stoughton, 1918), 11.
[41] Girouard, *Return to Camelot*, 275–93; George L. Mosse, *Fallen Soldiers: Reshaping the Memory of the World Wars* (New York: Oxford University Press, 1989), 70–106, and *passim*.
[42] Michael Gavaghan, *The Story of the Unknown Warrior* (Preston: M & L Publications, 1995), 26.
[43] Adelson, *Mark Sykes*, 211–12.
[44] Siberry, *New Crusaders*, 64–72.
[45] Robert Curzon, *Visits to Monasteries in the Levant* (1849; London: Humphrey Milford, 1916), 193.

sympathize with the objects of the Crusaders,' noted H. Rider Haggard, who visited Palestine in 1900: 'Only I should prefer that it was a Protestant power, since otherwise the quarrels would be many and the oppression great.'[46] Still, this Christian zeal was very seldom channelled into a practical call for action. It was only in 1914 that the political and military conditions were once again set in a way which virtually begged for a realization of the metaphor. When Lloyd George decided to shift the military balance from the stalemated Western Front to the Middle Eastern side-show, he was also suggesting a restoration of the Crusade to its original historical, geographical, moral, and even emotional terms. Could a literal Crusade in the Palestine side-show eclipse the metaphorical Crusade—the Holy War—being waged against the Kaiser in France and Belgium?

The answer, sure enough, was no. And nowhere was this failure more visible than in the main propaganda event of the Palestine campaign: 'Jerusalem before Christmas'.

Entering Jerusalem
Two days after the conquest of Jerusalem, Allenby entered the city in 'the official manner which the catholic imagination of Mark Sykes had devised', as T. E. Lawrence had explained.[47] While the D-notice could be issued to the 'private and confidential' eye of the newspaper editors alone, the ceremony was essentially a public display, a series of visual and textual gestures. As such, it demanded an explicit expression of the signification of this pivotal event, exactly what the propagandists, with their 'secret Crusade' policy, were trying to avoid.

The War Cabinet spent much time debating the measures necessary to stage the occupation of the city and secure official control over the dissemination of reports and photographs. Britain's main concern, Lord Curzon explained, was that 'news should be made known in a way calculated favourably to impress India and the Mohammedan world'. Curzon suggested that on the occupation of Jerusalem, 'a proclamation should be issued throughout the Moslem world, announcing that we are the protectors of the Moslem religion and would pay every respect to the Moslem Holy Places'. He was requested to discuss the matter with Sykes

---

[46] H. Rider Haggard, *A Winter Pilgrimage* (London: Longman, 1901), 252.
[47] Lawrence, *Seven Pillars*, 453.

and prepare a declaration to that effect;[48] it proclaimed martial law in the city, urged people to return to business as usual, and promised to safeguard all institutions holy to Christians, Jews, and Muslims.[49] The Mosque of Omar and the Patriarchs' Tomb at Hebron were to be placed under exclusive Muslim control. Allenby, furthermore, was ordered to announce that the hereditary custodians of the Wakf at the gate of the Church of the Holy Sepulchre 'have been requested to take up their accustomed duties', in remembrance of the 'magnanimous act of the Caliph Omar who protected [the] church'.[50]

Just a few weeks earlier, on 2 November, the Cabinet issued the Balfour Declaration. The British conquest of Palestine was undoubtedly perceived as the first step towards the realization of the pledge made to the Zionists, but events in Jerusalem were handled with exclusive attention to Muslim, rather than Jewish, sensibilities.[51] This could have been a conscious effort to counterbalance the effects of the Balfour Declaration, criticized so ardently by Curzon. Britain's most immediate objective was to prevent an outbreak of Muslim hostility. The battle over Jerusalem was perceived as the mythical struggle between Christianity and Islam: Jews had little part to play in this.

This acute attentiveness to Muslim reaction is demonstrated by the idea of staging the entrance in accordance with an ancient Arab prophecy, which claimed that the prophet from the West would enter Jerusalem through the Golden Gate and bring an end to Turkish rule only when Nile water was brought into Palestine. Major-General Guy Dawnay, who discussed the prophecy in a letter to Lieut.-Colonel Alfred Parker, the Military Governor of Sinai, pointed out that Nile waters *were* carried to Palestine via the British-built pipeline. No less miraculously, 'the Chief's name when written in Arabic spells "al Nebi" ', that is, the prophet. Dawnay maintained that 'it would be a pity not to take [Allenby] in by that gate and to arrange for the fulfilment of any other details which local folk lore may expect'.[52] Since the Golden Gate had

---

[48] TNA: PRO, CAB 23/4, War Cabinet Minutes, 21 Nov. 1917 (19), 19 Nov. 1917 (6).
[49] TNA: PRO, WO 33/946/8583, WO to GHQ Egypt, 21 Nov. 1917.
[50] TNA: PRO, WO 33/946/8584, WO to GHQ Egypt, 21 Nov. 1917.
[51] On British attempts to employ the Declaration in the Zionist context see James Renton, 'British Policy towards the Zionist Movement during the First World War' (Ph.D. thesis, University College London, 2003), esp. ch. 4.
[52] IWM, Dawnay Papers, Dawnay to Parker, 16 Nov. 1917.

been walled up since Crusading times, the plan was really not feasible; but the etymological wonder which made Allenby 'al Nebi' was nevertheless employed.[53]

This unabashedly cynical attempt to woo Muslim opinion by literalizing an ancient prophecy is all the more remarkable considering the calculated suppression of any allusion that would appeal to a British, Anglican, or even Christian constituency. If the conquest of Jerusalem did hold a 'sentimental, romantic and religious side' for the British people, surely now was the time to exhibit it. This, at least, was the opinion of the Anglican Bishop of Jerusalem, who wrote to the military authorities in October to suggest that Christian buildings, which have been used for centuries as Muslim mosques, should now be restored to their original use. The proposal was considered by the Arab Bureau—and rejected:

> Bishop MacInnes appears to regard our invasion of PALESTINE somewhat in the light of a Crusade, the success of which should place Christianity in a predominant position over ISLAM and other confessions. At least, the carrying into effect of his proposals would undoubtedly have that effect upon the native mind. This is a natural enough attitude on the part of a Christian Bishop, but it does not take into account the questions of military and political expediency by which we must be guided.[54]

The Bishop, thwarted but not yet beaten, asked to join Allenby's entourage as an honorary chaplain, in uniform. This, too, was denied: '[I]t would be inadvisable for Bishop MacInnes to come in any capacity, as it would surely lead to trouble with our Allies, whose ecclesiastics (many of whom have stronger claims perhaps) would consider that a march had been stolen on them.'[55]

Subsequently, the ceremony had no Anglican, or even Christian, features. Nor did it stress, in any way, the fact that this achievement was won by the British and Dominion forces with virtually no Allied assistance. The British were highly suspicious of French efforts to capitalize on the victory; the French consul in Jerusalem was not permitted to join Allenby's procession on the grounds that these were military, not civilian, circumstances. Nevertheless, the procession was

---

[53] See *The Times*, 14 Mar. 1918, 5.
[54] TNA: PRO, FO 882/14/PA17/12, Graves to Deedes, 15 Oct. 1917.
[55] TNA: PRO, FO 882/14/PA17/13, Clayton to Wingate, 25 Oct. 1917.

carefully arranged to represent the entire constituency of the Allied force in Palestine.[56] It entered the city through the Jaffa Gate, and then made its way to the Citadel, where Allenby read the proclamation. The guards represented 'England, Scotland, Ireland, Wales, Australia, India, New Zealand, France and Italy'.[57] Symbols of British prevalence were reduced to a minimum; the War Cabinet ordered that 'no flags should be hoisted'.[58]

It would be wrong, however, to conclude that the ceremony was devoid of more complex symbolism altogether: Allenby's entrance on foot seems to be the one feature which was truly imprinted on collective memory.[59] This feature, too, was dictated by London. On 21 November, Allenby was informed that 'it would be of considerable political importance if you, on officially entering the City, dismounted at the City Gate and entered on foot. German Emperor rode in, and the saying went round "a better man than he walked." Advantage of contrast in conduct will be obvious.'[60] These stage directions constructed Allenby's entrance not so much in relation to Jesus Christ, as in relation to the Kaiser, who visited Jerusalem in 1898. It was not Christian humility which Allenby was expected to exhibit, but rather German vanity which he was expected to counteract. The press, always keen on celebrating German defeat, was quick to grasp this. The *Daily Sketch* declared that this was 'a staggering blow to the German dream of domination in the East and to the Kaiser's pretensions as "keeper" of the Holy Places'.[61] 'Allenby is rather the restorer of justice and fairness among all creeds than the arrogant conqueror that the Kaiser would have been—and tried to be before the war,' wrote the *Daily Mirror* under the subtitle, 'Un-Kaiserly'. To be people who seemed to think 'that we do not make enough of our victories', the *Mirror* explained that 'British generals and the British people hate boasting. And the fact reminds one

---

[56] It did not, however, include representatives of the Egyptian Labour Corps, despite its crucial contribution to establishing communication lines.
[57] TNA: PRO, WO 33/946/8693, Allenby to WO, 11 Dec. 1917.
[58] TNA: PRO, CAB 23/4, War Cabinet Minutes, 26 Nov. 1917 (4).
[59] Newell, 'Allenby and the Palestine Campaign', 190; Luke McKernan, ' "The Supreme Moment of the War": General Allenby's Entry into Jerusalem', *Historical Journal of Film, Radio, and Television*, 13 (1993), 169–80.
[60] TNA: PRO, WO 33/946/8582, WO to GHQ Egypt, 21 Nov. 1917. Jesus, of course, *rode* into the city, mounted on a colt (Mark 11: 1–11).
[61] *Daily Sketch*, 11 Dec. 1917, 1.

of the contrast between the German Emperor's swagger into Jerusalem (and all over the East) before the war.'[62] In other words, the symbolic act of staging the British entry to contrast with the Kaiser's visit actually drew attention away from the contentious Christian connotations by locating the Germans at the heart of the British–Ottoman (or Christian–Muslim) struggle.[63]

All in all, then, Allenby's entry into Jerusalem seemed to be underscored by an absence: the absence of any explicit reference to a British, rather than an Allied, victory; and the absence of any clear Anglican, or even Christian, gestures. This, as we have seen, was a highly calculated move, indicating British caution, perhaps even weakness. It was possible, however, to read this absence in a very different way. *The Times*, for one, understood immediately that this silence was quite eloquent: 'General Allenby and his companions were on foot, and made no effort to impress the imagination of spectators. No effort was needed. The measures taken spoke and will speak for themselves.' Nevertheless, the newspaper hastened to speak for them, too:

> To see in this attitude on the part of the British Commander a mere calculation of political expediency would be gravely to misread and seriously to underestimate its significance. In its essence it is a vindication of Christianity. At a moment when Christendom is torn by strife, let loose through the apostate ambitions of those who have returned in practice to the sanguinary worship of their "Old German god," it stands forth as a sign that the righteousness and justice that are the soul of Christian ethics guide Christian Victors even in the flush of triumph.[64]

As *The Times* explains, it was precisely the conspicuous absence of any British/Christian features that pointed so clearly to the actual presence of the British/Christian spirit. Religious toleration—a time-honoured feature of British colonial rule—becomes a quintessential Christian quality, a term that is set in opposition not so much to the Muslim Turk as the pagan German. This is not the Christianity associated with the actual holy places, the Crusaders' Christianity which stood against Islam and was renounced so ardently by the D-notice. Rather, this is the

---

[62] *Daily Mirror*, 11 Dec. 1917, 6.
[63] No reference was made to the fact that the Kaiser entered the city wearing a Crusader's outfit.
[64] *The Times*, 13 Dec. 1917, 9.

Christianity of the *metaphorical* Holy War, of the public school ethos. 'Christian' is redefined here as sportsmanlike, righteous, just, not losing one's ethics even in the flush of victory—in a word: chivalrous.[65]

But this in itself was only one possible interpretation of the ceremony. 'The ceremony was full of dignity and simplicity,' wrote W. T. Massey in his report to the London press, 'and it was full of meaning.'[66] But what *did* it mean? Sykes's 'catholic imagination' staged an event which offered multiple interpretations: with proper direction, it could be (and was) designed to appeal to the Pope, Russian peasants, Muslim Indians, the Zionists, the Arabs of Jerusalem, the Americans, and so forth.[67] Luckily, *The Times* knew what it meant specifically for the British people, and it was keen to share this knowledge with its readers. But the ceremony was not self-explanatory: it had to be explained, interpreted, represented.

Consequently, there was an acute inconsistency between the way the ceremony was arranged and the actual propaganda capital that it was assumed to have at home. Two weeks after it rejoiced in the news that 'considerable publicity' has been given to the fall of Jerusalem 'and that the event had produced a marked effect throughout the world',[68] the War Cabinet was disturbed to learn that 'scant use had been made, for propaganda purposes, of the capture of Jerusalem'. And while Sir Edward Carson (the minister responsible for propaganda) insisted that 'a vast amount of propaganda had been dispatched abroad', it was pointed out that 'comparatively little use had been made of the material by public speakers in this country. It was suggested that material of interest on this subject should be sent to the clergy and ministers of all denominations, with a view to its use in the churches.'[69] So it was back to the Crusading business, after all.

'Ring off the highbrow line'

Following the occupation of Jerusalem, Sykes made vigorous efforts to generate propaganda material. On 7 January 1918 he telegraphed

---

[65] For a discussion of the representation of pro-Allied Muslim forces as 'honorary Christians' see my 'The Last Crusade? British Propaganda and the Palestine Campaign, 1917–18', *Journal of Contemporary History*, 36/1 (Jan. 2001), 101–2.
[66] *The Times*, 17 Dec. 1917, 9.
[67] See numerous dispatches in PRO, FO 371/3061. See also Renton, 'British Policy'.
[68] TNA: PRO, CAB 23/4, War Cabinet Minutes, 17 Dec. 1917 (12).
[69] TNA: PRO, CAB 23/5, War Cabinet Minutes, 2 Jan. 1918 (12).

Gilbert Clayton, the chief political officer of the EEF in Palestine, stating that press articles were 'badly wanted'. 'We are losing precious opportunities of propaganda and enthusiasm throughout world,' he warned.[70] Dispatches from Palestine were delayed by innumerable bureaucratic difficulties, but ultimately, it was a problem of representation. 'This is vile barren stuff,' Sykes commented on one of the drafts sent to him from Palestine: 'He has no idea of propaganda and goes wrong at every turn.'[71] In a revealing telegram sent to Clayton, Sykes stormed:

> Tell Storrs ring off the highbrow line. What is wanted is popular reading for the English church and chapel folk; for New York Irish; Orthodox Balkan peasants and Mujiks; French and Italian Catholics; and Jews throughout the world; Indian and Algerian Moslems. Articles should give striking actualities, and description of scenes; picturesque details. Rivet the British onto Holy Land, Bible and New Testament.[72]

By 'ringing off the highbrow line', Sykes meant that the high, non-partisan imperial tone should be replaced by a more biased, pietistic voice. It marked an official return to Gaselee's suppressed theme. 'Holy Places of Jerusalem', a piece wired from Palestine to London, approved by Sykes and published in *The Times* of 23 March 1918 (and subsequently in other papers as well), opened with a description of the Church of the Holy Sepulchre and the tombstone 'beneath which the Anglo-Norman knight, Sir Philip Daubigny, has lain undisturbed for nearly seven centuries, waiting till the English came again'.[73] Press articles like this and a propaganda film like *The New Crusaders*, all produced and distributed by the Department of Information, now alluded explicitly to the Crusading past. The fact that the D-notice prohibiting any reference to the Crusades continued to be enforced, at least occasionally, points to a more sophisticated awareness of the separation between home and foreign propaganda.[74] It also suggests that Sykes deviated, knowingly, from the official line because he recognized that notwithstanding Muslim sensibilities, a representation of the

---

[70] PRO, FO 395/237/4282, Sykes to Clayton, 7 Jan. 1918.
[71] TNA: PRO, FO 371/3383/18, Sykes, minute on draft sent by Clayton, n.d.
[72] TNA: PRO, FO 371/3383/14, Sykes to Clayton, 15 Jan. 1918.
[73] *The Times*, 29 Mar. 1918, 3
[74] The National War Aims Committee, responsible for home propaganda, was established in August 1917. See Sanders and Taylor, *British Propaganda*, 65–70, 77.

Palestine campaign which employed only a secular (or secularized) vocabulary would simply fail to excite the British public. Another propaganda article, 'Easter Day in Jerusalem', acknowledged this openly:

During the British occupation of Palestine we have been very sedulous in considering the religious feelings of others. The shrines and festivals sacred to elder or alien creeds have been more than respected. So much so, that some have wondered whether we had any religion of our own.

This Easter in Jerusalem has been the answer. The British Army has celebrated the greatest festival of the Church in a place where the English under arms have never before prayed at Easter. King Richard never reached the Holy City; but King George's men communicated and sang the Easter hymns, in their own church of St. George outside the Damascus Gate of Jerusalem.[75]

Interestingly, although these propaganda articles began with the Crusading heritage, they gradually moved on to explore other aspects of the British presence in Palestine. 'Holy Places of Jerusalem' opens with the idea that British soldiers have at last returned to the Holy Land, but it ends with an image of the 'married soldier, with wife and children in his mind', who goes 'most often' to the Church of the Nativity at Bethlehem: 'It reminds him of Christmas, of his family, and of home.'[76] 'Easter Day in Jerusalem' concludes on a strikingly similar note:

Memories of the place, of its past of mystical tradition, of its sacred story, haunted those who worshipped within the walls of the Church of the Sepulchre; but it was of home, and of our own kin in France, and of our own customs of praise and thanksgiving at Easter that we were reminded while kneeling in St. George's—that little island of England's soil, set in Palestine to cheer us wanderers in distant lands.[77]

What begins as a quest to the East, ends with a yearning gaze towards the West; kneeling in Jerusalem, it is England's soil that comes to mind. The new Crusaders are actually wanderers in distant lands; and they are homesick.

To understand this narrational shift, we should recall that in his detailed telegram, Sykes did not highlight the Crusades. Rather, he demanded 'picturesque details' only: 'Rivet the British onto Holy

[75] *The Times*, 22 Apr. 1918, 7.
[76] *The Times*, 29 Mar. 1918, 3.
[77] *The Times*, 22 Apr. 1918, 7.

Land, Bible and New Testament.' This, it seems, was no oversight. It is here that one senses the limited cultural dissemination of the Crusading theme, its distinct social flavour and undeniable highbrow quality. The propaganda effort demanded 'popular reading for the English church and chapel folk', and Sykes was suggesting a conscious turn from the 'Last Crusade' narrative to an emphasis on the *biblical* associations of Jerusalem and Palestine, which, until that stage, were simply not alluded to.

Sykes may have taken his cue from the Prime Minister, who addressed the House of Commons on 20 December 1917: 'The name of every hamlet and hill occupied by the British Army, and over which British soldiers fought in this famed land, thrills with sacred memories. Beersheba, Hebron, Bethany, Bethlehem, the Mount of Olives are all names engraved on the heart of the world.'[78] Typically, it was the chapel-educated Lloyd George, for whom the place-names of Palestine were more familiar 'than those of the Western Front',[79] who invoked this sentimental aspect of the Palestine Campaign. Innate to Lloyd George as the Crusading image to Sykes and Gaselee, this vernacular biblical culture was the popular perspective that Sykes was so desperately seeking.

Paradoxically, Sykes's construction of the 'homesick Crusader' corresponded with the striking fact that references to the Crusading features of the Palestine campaign were seldom, if ever, anxious about the disturbing resonances of the analogy, such as the idea that the new Crusade might end like previous ones, or the question of the Crusaders' own prospects, now that they have achieved their goal. The future of Palestine was of course unclear, with incompatible British promises made to the Zionists, the Arabs, and the Allies. Some, like the Balfour Declaration, were made public; others, like the Sykes–Picot agreement, were not. Sykes told the *Observer* in December 1917 that 'we need not question who is going to be in Jerusalem. It is sufficient to know that the Turk has gone.'[80] While it seemed obvious that Britain would not give up this new threshold to India, the exact nature of the arrangement remained uncertain. The image of the homesick Crusader—duty

---

[78] *Hansard*, Fifth Series, 100 (20 Dec. 1917), col. 2211.
[79] Chaim Weizmann, *Trial and Error* (New York: Harper, 1949), 152.
[80] *Observer*, 16 Dec. 1917, 9.

distressed by longing, public commitment stained by private reluctance—captured this ambiguity.

The homesick Crusader, then, was a highly hybridized icon. Geographically, it contrasted the image of the Holy Land with the image of 'Home', as the advance eastward was balanced by a gaze westward (to England, but also to 'our own kin in France'), a double movement which is reminiscent of Dean Stanley's sermon, discussed in Chapter 2. Politically, it indulged the Crusading image, while shifting it away from the precarious Christian–Muslim context, back to domestic religious practices and the golden image of a rural English churchyard. Discursively, it combined the highbrow romance of the Crusades with lowerbrow biblical culture. In terms of the language of class, it constructed the English Tommy as a spiritual descendant of the (Norman) chivalrous knight, while ascribing to him the religious enthusiasm of Reformed culture and even (Anglo-Saxon) Dissent. Most significantly, perhaps, this image reflected a negotiated stand between official propaganda and public consumption: it perpetuated the Crusading image, but in a way that would appeal to public consent, to the weariness of war, to the tradition of vernacular Orientalism—and, last but not least, to the experiences and hopes of the New Crusaders themselves.

The Palestine Campaign and Troop Morale

There is evidence to suggest that the ambivalence concerning the nature of propaganda at home was reproduced on the Palestine Front. Edward Thompson—military chaplain, poet, future Oriel Fellow, and father of E. P. Thompson—wrote about his visits to Nebi Samwil, that hill-top from which Richard Lionheart refused to gaze at the city he was destined not to conquer: 'From this peak our own men, whom, by special and often repeated routine orders, it was forbidden to call Crusaders, saw this Holy City through terrific days when shells hurtled to and fro from Mizpeh and Olivet.' Elsewhere he states explicitly: 'We were forbidden to call ourselves Crusaders, but many of us were haunted by an older age.'[81]

[81] Edward Thompson, *Crusaders' Coast* (London: Ernest Benn, 1929), 29, 13–15. See also Armel O'Connor, *A Knight in Palestine* (London: Burns, 1923), 47: 'We were never encouraged in Palestine to speak of the war as a Crusade, probably in deference to the susceptibilities of Mohammedan soldiers.'

If such an order was indeed issued (and there is no formal documentation supporting this), it did not endure. By February 1918, an educational army newspaper, *Palestine News*, was set up in Palestine; among the officials engaged in establishing it were Clayton and Wingate in Palestine, Buchan, Sykes, and Gaselee in London.[82] The editor, General H. Pirie-Gordon, sent an urgent telegram to Sykes, asking him to arrange permission to reproduce various texts, among them Lane Poole's *Saladin*, Conder's *Latin Kingdom of Jerusalem*, Sykes's own *The Caliph's Last Heritage*, and an English edition of *Itinerarium Regis Ricardi*.[83] Indeed, the *Palestine News* included numerous references to Crusading history, constructing the affinity between early and khaki Crusaders.[84] Like the propaganda efforts aimed at the public in England at the very same period—and orchestrated by the very same men—the Crusading narrative was a way of justifying and ennobling the current campaign. Vivian Gilbert described the elevating effect that the Crusading image could have on troopers' frame of mind:

> Fortunately, just as this feeling of depression came stealing over one, and this usually occurred towards the end of a particularly trying march on an empty stomach, one remembered that the Crusaders had experienced just such privations and hardships similar to those we were going through now; and were we not descendants of those same Crusaders—just as the horses we rode were descended from the English stock that had furnished charges for King Richard and his knights and warriors?
>
> When one realised this, all the old fighting spirit came rushing back again, 'morale' was once more re-established, and one struggled on for the last few miles with renewed strength. (p. 116)

Notwithstanding Gilbert's remarkable ability to extend his genealogical observations to quadruped Crusaders, his delicate employment of the pronoun 'one' is perhaps not unjustified: a survey of soldiers' diaries, letters, and memoirs suggests that the Crusading theme played an

---

[82] The newspaper was published in five languages: English, Arabic, Hebrew, Hindi, and Punjabi. The Cambridge University Library catalogue mentions all five editions; unfortunately, none have survived there. While the Hebrew and Arabic editions are kept at the National Library in Jerusalem, I have not been able to trace the Hindi or Punjabi editions.

[83] TNA: PRO, FO 395/240, Pirie-Gordon to Sykes, 11 Feb. 1918.

[84] These references diminished with time. In April 1919 the *Palestine News* (*PN*) ceased to be an Army publication, and was henceforth published independently by the Oriental Advertising Co., Cairo.

insignificant part, if at all, in the soldiers' understanding of the Palestine campaign during their service in the Middle East.[85]

Occasional allusions to the Crusades were made, of course, but these tended to surface in hindsight only. It is telling that many published memoirs which employ the Crusading metaphor in their title—Cooper's *Khaki Crusaders* (1919), Sommers's *Temporary Crusaders* (1919), Adams's *The Modern Crusaders* (1920), and others—make surprisingly few references to it in the text itself; in some cases, especially when based on diaries written on the spot, there are none. It was easier, it seems, to employ the Crusading image from a distance, be it a temporal, geographical, or social distance. Consider Leslie G. Moore, of the London Regiment, 60th Division, employed before the War in the Midland Bank in the City, who recorded the conquest of Jerusalem in a cheerful letter home: 'looking back I must say that I am proud of our chaps. We were wet, hungry, shivering with cold and there wasn't a murmur.' This was his last letter; he was killed on 27 December 1917. His school magazine printed a short obituary:

> At school we saw mainly the quiet, thoughtful side of his nature. War, however, seems to have found him amply endowed with all the qualities we associate with the Crusader. Manly courage, enthusiasm, optimism and respect for even a Turkish foe are all reflected in the last letter home which recounted the taking of Jerusalem. Chivalrous too in the home, he advertised his school so well that his sorrowing mother requests us to continue to send her the magazine.[86]

Moore himself made no mention of the Crusading image in his letters home; his transformation to a chivalrous Crusader was carried out by the school staff, in England, posthumously. Even Vivian Gilbert's extravagant account (1923) originated as a War reminiscence addressed to his bohemian friends in New York. Gilbert was an actor, and his indefatigable Crusading enthusiasm sometimes reads like a belated thespian feat.

---

[85] My analysis is based on fifty diaries, letters, and memoirs held in the IWM, in addition to thirty printed biographical accounts, published primarily in the decade after the War, fifteen military and regimental histories, and five troop journals. I have concentrated mainly on British writers—with several Australians and South Africans—who served at the Palestine Front any time between summer 1917 and spring 1918, most of them in the ranks or as subalterns. On the methodological approach to these sources see Peter Liddle, *The Sailor's War 1914–18* (London: Blandford: 1985), 8–9.

[86] IWM, Papers of L. G. Moore, letter home, 14 Dec. 1917; press clipping from unidentified school journal.

It is always difficult, of course, to verify the absence of specific imagery. On the other hand, some themes appear in the soldiers' writings with such frequency and abundance as to make their prominence indisputable: first and foremost among these was the idea that Palestine was intimately associated with the Bible, with Christian history, and with Christian ethics. It is precisely their extensive allusions to biblical culture which makes the soldiers' silence regarding the Crusades all the more striking.

'I'm here walkin' in holy places'

The Official History of the Palestine campaign was certainly correct to abandon, for once, its sober tone and proclaim that 'Half-forgotten lessons of childhood were recalled and given new significance'.[87] As one soldier wrote, 'There was first a sense of being on familiar ground, of having witnessed the whole scene before somewhere, which was followed by the transition to the Bible stories of childhood's days.'[88] Many soldiers felt that they were witnessing a literalization of familiar biblical images and parables. At the sight of sheep and goats grazing together, Robert Clark wrote, 'those words of our Saviour came very vividly before my mind and I could imagine our Saviour looking at such a sight when he said he shall separate them one from another as a shepherd divideth his sheep from the goats'.[89] Rowlands Coldicott, a young subaltern in the London Regiment, recalled how his company ran across a sprouting field in Judea: 'The same sentences ran in the heads of all: *A sower went forth to sow*... Memory, sadly rusted, could not deliver the parable entire. How often in the churches in England had the perfect teaching fallen upon our staled ears! And now—why, the thing was true!'[90]

The corroboration of Scripture in the never-changing landscapes of the East was an Orientalist commonplace, but due to their unique living conditions—camping in bivouacs, seeking fruit to complement their

---

[87] Cyril Falls, *History of the Great War; Military Operations, Egypt & Palestine* (London: HMSO, 1930), ii. 256.
[88] Anthony Bluett, *With our Army in Palestine* (London: Andrew Melrose, 1919), 94.
[89] IWM, Papers of Robert Burnett Clark, 'My Visit to Jerusalem No. 2'.
[90] Rowlands Coldicott, *London Men in Palestine and How They Marched to Jerusalem* (London: Edward Arnold, 1919), 81. Subsequent page numbers are cited parenthetically in the text.

bully-beef-and-biscuit diet, and, most significantly, crossing Sinai by foot to enter the Promised Land—soldiers tended to identify even more with the biblical imagery. 'This day of battle seemed so unending that I no longer wonder that ancient Israelite warriors should have believed that Joshua made the sun stand still,' wrote J. Wilson of the Machine Gun Corps, 60th Division.[91] 'My camp bed is pitched underneath a figtree,' recorded Major V. H. Bailey in his diary, 'and I can lie in bed and pick ripe figs, hot in the morning sun! "Every man under his own fig tree!" '[92] Some felt that it was only by fighting in Palestine that one could truly grasp the biblical allusions. In a letter home, Lieut. C. G. Dowding commented on Psalm 18: 'Only those who have been on these rocky places as a combatant can fully understand the imagery of it all—and, Mother, I feel every word of that last bit I have quoted to you!'[93]

The EEF encouraged the study of biblical geography and history. One soldier recalled how 'the Padre gave us some interesting lectures on these parts and what we were coming to. We saw where Samson was born and where he first fell in love.'[94] The chaplain J. P. Wilson, whose 'constant aim was to reach those who were not church-goers', lectured throughout the campaign on two topics only, 'Palestine or Purity'.[95] Still, organized religious efforts were often rejected by the soldiers.[96] Private Douglas H. Calcutt, a Boy Clerk at the Home Office, referred to one compulsory church parade as 'a chronic wash out for the parson. No one sang. He preached about the good samaritan as if there were no war on at all, in the most academic fashion, and made no attempt to reconcile Church and Army. The prayers for soldiers and so on met with no responses and "God Save the King" was played by the band in stony silence.' This was still near Gaza, but even after the victorious battle of Beer-Sheba, the chaplain's efforts were not welcome: 'There is a thanksgiving service on this morning, voluntary, belt and side arms compulsory. It does not take.'[97]

---

[91] IWM 84/52/1, Papers of J. Wilson, Diary, 27 Apr. 1918.
[92] IWM 85/4/1, Papers of Major V. H. Bailey, Diary, 11 Aug. 1917.
[93] IWM, Papers of Lieut. C. G. Dowding, letter home, 9 Feb. 1918.
[94] IWM, Papers of W. N. Hendry, Memoir.
[95] J. P. Wilson, *With the Soldiers in Palestine & Syria* (London: SPCK, 1920), 21.
[96] J. G. Fuller, *Troop Morale and Popular Culture in the British and Dominion Armies, 1914–1918* (Oxford: Clarendon Press, 1990), 156–7.
[97] IWM 78/56/1, Papers of D. H. Calcutt, Diary, 2 Sept., 12 Nov. 1917.

The problem of reconciling faith and military service was a grave one. A pioneering survey entitled *The Army and Religion* (1919), based on a wide-ranging study of questionnaires, painted a grim picture of the nation's spiritual life. Despite their claim that most men 'acquired a new religious consciousness' during the War, the editors were shocked by 'the persistent evidence as to the ignorance of Christian truth' among all denominations. Soldiers, it seems, did not find Christ's teaching relevant to their lives, but 'memories of the human Jesus, of Him who walked in Galilee and blessed little children, and healed the sick, and spoke the Sermon on the Mount, have been unforgettable. They remember these things as they remember the hymns of their childhood about Him, and the pictures of Him that they have seen.' Considering 'the amount of time and labour which has been spent in the last half-century on religious education', the editors regarded this sentimental approach as a highly unsatisfactory accomplishment.[98] Yet this was precisely the stuff that vernacular biblical culture was made of.

It was this emotional, pietistic, nostalgic approach to Scripture which characterized the response of most British soldiers when they found themselves in the Holy Land. Private R. H. Sims, Royal Sussex Regiment, wrote to his mother, 'isn't it nice to know that we are treading on exactly the same ground as Our Lord trod on, the great Saviour & Son of God before he was sacrificed on the Cross to redeem the whole earth'.[99] And Albert Kingston, a young Welsh blacksmith, now a Farrier NCO, noted simply: 'We were all interested in our Christian faith, and therefore it was very interesting.'[100] These comments often reflected a genuine sense of wonder and disbelief. 'I little thought that I should ever stand in the Holy Sepulchre itself,' wrote Albert Surry to his parents.[101] Travel to the Middle East was well beyond the reach of working men like Surry; the War brought them to Palestine, unprepared. 'We were not as travellers, eager after reading and preparation to test and prove,' explained Coldicott on behalf of his London men: 'the wonderful truth of description had taken us by surprise' (p. 81).

---

[98] D. S. Cairns (ed.), *The Army and Religion: An Enquiry and its Bearing upon the Religious Life of the Nation* (London: Macmillan, 1919), 8, 108, 50, 108.
[99] IMW 77/130/1, Papers of R. H. Sims, letter home, 6 Feb. 1918.
[100] IWM 88/27/1, Papers of Albert John Kingston, Memoir.
[101] Quoted in Ilana Bet-El, 'A Soldier's Pilgrimage: Jerusalem 1918', *Mediterranean Historical Review*, 8/2 (1993), 234.

The image of the devout Tommy, thrown unsuspectingly unto the biblical landscape, was perpetuated by several writers. Vivian Gilbert—who believed that 'British Tommies are very like children anyhow, irresponsible, easily pleased, easily discouraged' (p. 33)—described 'the interest some of our men took in those far-off Bible times'. He overheard one soldier asking, 'What was that plice we marched by ter-day, Tom; wasn't that where Joshuar went after them fellers?' to which his friend, turning the pages of a Bible, replied, 'Naah; that was where Absalom caught 'is 'ead in the bloomin' trees' (pp. 180–1). John Finley, 'the first American Pilgrim after General Allenby's Recovery of the Holy Land', printed a supposedly authentic letter 'written by a British "Tommy" out in Palestine to his wife in England', in which the soldier promises that once he returns home, 'the Pastor can't say nothin' to me Dearie about the Holy Land, but I'll have sommat to say to he. He only knows it from books and such like Dearie, an' showed it on lantern slides—while all these days I'm here walkin' in holy places, an' knows 'em like Dearie, fightin' for 'em.'[102] Captain J. G. Lockhart recalled a visit to the Church of the Holy Sepulchre: 'Most curious of all was the detached attitude of the ordinary British soldier. This was Christianity as he had never known it, indeed it scarcely seemed to be Christianity at all... We were accompanied by our batmen, who withheld all comments until we were leaving, when Hubert's man shook his head doubtfully and remarked, "Take a lot of keeping clean, Sir."'[103]

These accounts all rely on a series of demarcations: between subalterns and Tommies; between official religion and popular, commonsensical convictions; between vernacular biblical culture 'there' and the actual reality 'here'. The preposterous transcription of the Cockney accent alienates Tommy from the biblical landscape, but also presents his uncorrupted faith, unimpressed by all the glories of the Holy Sepulchre. I will later return to this somewhat disturbing representation (which recalls Macleod's description of the Newcastle sea captain, described in Chapter 2); for now it is enough to note that displays of popular piety were not limited to the ranks. Captain John More took some leaves and acorns from Abraham's Oak in Hebron: 'I wonder if the

---

[102] John Finley, *A Pilgrim in Palestine after its Deliverance* (London: Chapman & Hall, 1919), pp. vii–viii.
[103] Captain J. G. Lockhart, *Palestine Days and Nights* (London: Robert Scott, 1920), 36.

acorn could be induced to germinate in English soil?'[104] Captain P. C. Duncan filled two empty soda bottles with Jordan water, which he carried safely to Yorkshire and handed to the local clergyman, 'for him to use for baptisms'.[105] Many soldiers sent home souvenirs, like olive-wood camel ink-stands or a mother-of-pearl cross.[106] Others picked flowers themselves and sent them, pressed, to their loved ones back home. 'Oh, these glorious flowers of Christ's country!' exclaimed J. Wilson: 'Why is it they sometimes bring the tears to your eyes?'[107]

No milk and no honey
By embellishing the soldiers' religious excitement, we run the risk of reproducing both the contemporary and the historiographical tendencies to regard the Palestine campaign as the Holiday—or the Pilgrimage—Front. On learning that he was to be sent to the Middle East, Siegfried Sassoon was deeply aggravated. He wrote in his diary: '*Points in favour of going*: New Country—conditions not so trying (probably Palestine)—less chance of being killed. *Points against going*: I want to go back to one of the regular battalions. The other place is only a side-show, and I'd be with an inferior battalion.' He begged a well-connected friend 'to get me back to France', but without avail: he was sent to Palestine.[108]

The soldiers in Palestine were painfully aware of their poor reputation. Ion Idriess, an Australian soldier, tells of a fellow trooper who received a parcel 'addressed to "a lonely soldier." Enclosed was a note from the lady expressing the pious wish that a brave soldier in France should get the parcel and not a cold-footed squib in Egypt.' In return, the soldier sent the lady 'some photos of our desert graves'.[109] Jack, a military clerk serving 'somewhere in Palestine', complained in a letter to Miss D. Williams:

I can tell you Dolly our life out here is far from being a picnic as some people imagine it to be, but still I suppose we are doing our bit. but it makes me wild

---

[104] John More, *With Allenby's Crusaders* (London: Heath Cranton, 1923), 129.
[105] IWM 79/51/1, Papers of Captain P. C. Duncan, Memoir.
[106] IWM 87/17/1, Papers of R. Louden, Memoir.
[107] Wilson Papers, Diary, 10 Mar. 1918.
[108] 21 Jan. 1918, in *Siegfried Sassoon Diaries 1915–1918*, ed. Rupert Hart-Davis (London: Faber & Faber, 1983), 205–6.
[109] Ion Idriess, *The Desert Column* (Sydney: Angus & Robertson, 1933), 295–6. Subsequent page numbers are cited parenthetically in the text.

when people write out + say what a lovely time you are having + lovely sights we are seeing in this "so called" Holy Land. If only they were out here + crossed the desert as we did and saw the battle field especially the last one they might think different. Perhaps they will now after they read about the last scrap, it was terrible.[110]

The notion that the Palestine campaign was an easy, almost negligible experience was no doubt related to its traditional military nature.[111] It is no coincidence that the only Middle Eastern campaign to be adequately acknowledged by First World War historiography was Gallipoli, which sustained the Western Front leitmotif of entrapped soldiers, perpetually butchered. However, the perception of a rosy, peaceful front—a 'picnic'—was essentially derived from the image of Palestine as a winter destination for Cook's pilgrims. In his diary, Idriess mentions the newspapers' 'glowing lies about the lads out here living in a "Land of Paradise," revelling in oranges, pomegranates, and all the fruits of the Orient. We wish that the idiots responsible for such lies were out here swallowing dust' (p. 293).

The gap between the strenuous reality of warfare and the biblical aura was captured by another caricature in *Punch*. It showed a humble dwelling of an old woman, visited by a portly esquire, perhaps the vicar:

The Visitor: 'I hear your boy is in Palestine. How interesting it must be for him to move among those scenes where every spot brings up some recollection of the wonderful events of Biblical history!'

The Mother: 'Ted don't say much about that in 'is letters. 'E seems to think the country is sufferin' from a fly-paper shortage.'[112]

Punch here offers a sobering view of the sentimental cliché, made all the more suggestive by the fact that it was printed just a few pages after the well-known Richard Lionheart illustration.

The harsh conditions of battle, and even the irritating shortage of fly-paper, certainly left little time for soldiers to indulge in biblical history. 'It was hard to realise at the time that many of the outlandish places we passed through or lived in were so steeped in Biblical or Historical

---

[110] IMW 85/4/1, Papers of Miss D. Williams, letter from Jack, 23 Nov. 1917.
[111] The battles of Sharon and Nablus, fought in September 1918, were in fact the last to employ a full Cavalry charge.
[112] *Punch*, 153 (19 Dec. 1917), 422.

interest,' wrote Captain John More: 'There was no time to think about such things.'[113] D. H. Calcutt explained that 'A rich American on horse back to Es Salt for instance with a comfortable bed booked at the other end would dwell on the rugged grandeur of the scenery and on the Biblical "wilderness," etc. etc. instead of abusing the place. When you have to attack it, it makes tinned stew warmed up for dinner.'[114] Later in the War it was probably much easier to reflect on religious issues. But during the months leading up to the conquest of Jerusalem, and even much later, the biblical narrative was repeatedly silenced, literally, by the firing of guns. W. N. Hendry described the thrilling first sight of Jerusalem: 'Bullets or no bullets we could not keep our eyes off this wonderful view.' But as shells began to burst overhead, they were forced to take shelter. When he looked up again, he saw 'the most ghastly sights of blood'. Jerusalem was instantly forgotten.[115]

Similarly, Coldicott recalled three events that took place in the rocky hills of Judaea, a few days before the conquest of the city: the shortage of matches, the arrival of a post-bag containing a newspaper announcing the collapse of the Italians, and the first sight of Jerusalem. 'Time has reversed the order of their importance, but if you then had asked any of the men, they would have ranked them thus—the dearth of matches, the 'mess-up' in Italy, the sight of the city' (pp. 133–4). For Coldicott, the most memorable episode of 9 December, the day Jerusalem fell, was rushing ahead of the marching ranks, and then pausing to share a tin of bully-beef with his sergeant-major: 'Of all the events of that vivid day none remains so brilliantly lighted in my mind' (p. 199). H. T. Pope, also of the London Regiment, thought Jerusalem a 'very picturesque modern place'. Nevertheless, the real 'godsend' of that day was 'to get a roof over our heads—the first time for exactly 12 months'.[116] Perhaps this explains why even Allenby's entrance into the city received relatively little attention in the soldiers' writings. All in all, Vivian Gilbert's claim that the 'first things we bought after the capture of Jerusalem were Bibles and matches' (p. 180) seems absolutely ludicrous, considering the soldiers' appalling reports of supply shortages and their own hunger.[117]

[113] More, *With Allenby's Crusaders*, 224–5.
[114] Calcutt Papers, Diary, 23 May 1918.   [115] Hendry Papers, Memoir.
[116] IWM 78/42/1, Papers of H. T. Pope, Diary, 9 Dec. 1917.
[117] On soldiers' hunger see, among many others, Robert H. Goodsall, *Palestine Memories 1917–1918–1925* (Canterbury: Cross & Jackman, 1925), 91.

A more telling indication of the soldiers' sense of priority is suggested by Donald Black:

> Coming up to Smith I asked for the tobacco I wanted, he handed me his tin and a leaf out of a Bible—it is the book of Job we are smoking. Someone had given him this Bible long ago, and he carried it about for some inexplicable reason, though he never read it. Running out of cigarette papers one day he had found the thin paper a good substitute, but care was needed not to smoke too much of it as the printing ink was liable to make one sick.[118]

What makes this anecdote so potent is that it does not hinge on the absence of a Bible; it is the *presence* of a Bible—bequeathed 'long ago' and carried ever since—which allows it to be used so subversively. Indeed, it was not that the biblical associations were lost on the soldiers. Rather, the soldiers often found that the reality of the Holy Land, and their presence in it, contrasted with the expectations they had in mind, expectations fuelled by biblical culture.

This frustrated sense of dissonance was translated into several stock insights. Some soldiers ridiculed the incompatibility between the land's historical and spiritual aura and the military bureaucracy. 'Jerusalem has been delivered from the Turk,' lamented Captain Lockhart: 'who shall deliver it from the prosaic matter-of-factness of the British Army?'[119] Sommers wrote: 'Where Samson wooed Delilah we have stood with a blanket round us, while the disinfector has attended to our clothing... In Jerusalem we have listened to "Where did that one go to, 'Erbert?" and where Joshua commanded the sun to stand still we have taught his descendants the three-legged race.'[120] Still, the juxtaposition of the prosaic and the poetic was often far from amusing. 'Jerusalem, city of peace and hope! Its byways now are roads of hell,' wrote Idriess bitterly (p. 351).

Another widespread theme was the familiar disappointment provoked by Palestine's appearance. *Chronicles of the White Horse*, a troop journal published by the 2/4th West Kents, printed a hymn, aptly entitled 'A Sand Grouse'. The second stanza read:

---

[118] Donald Black, *Red Dust: An Australian Trooper in Palestine* (London: Jonathan Cape, 1931), 122. On his solid religious faith see pp. 63, 98.
[119] Lockhart, *Palestine Days*, 27.
[120] Cecil Sommers, *Temporary Crusaders* (London: John Lane, 1919), 84.

> Jerusalem the Golden
> With milk and honey blest;
> Where is that milk and honey?
> It seemed to have 'gone West.'
> The honey that I've met here
> Is Crosse and Blackwell's brand,
> The only milk I've tasted
> Has come from Switzerland.[121]

The image of milk and honey—or, to be more precise, their irritating absence—was cited and commented upon by numerous soldiers. Captain W. Hine wrote to a friend back home about 'the Promised Land, the land reputed to be flowing with milk and honey (haven't seen much milk or honey yet) as I have heard one of our gunners remark the other day, "twelve to a tin and no b- honey" (our ration being one tin of condensed milk to 12 men)'.[122] Slightly more cheerful was Captain E. T. Townsend, who wrote to his father: 'Here we are, safely back in the "land of milk and honey"—as a matter of fact there is some honey in the mess just now, but not the product of this blessed land!'[123]

Other Sunday-school catch-phrases were scoffed in a similar manner. Private C. T. Shaw, of the London field Ambulance, wrote:

Jerusalem, as you all know, is known as 'Jerusalem the Golden'—'The Holy City'. The first glimpse does not give anyone the opinion that it is a golden city—far from it—change golden into filthy or muddy, and there you have a more correct name. The Holy City, certainly I agree with you, as it is both holy from the religious side, and it is 'hole'y' from a general standpoint.[124]

'I wonder how many times I've been told to "go to Jericho" but never expected to really do so,' wrote Richard Pedlar, a clerk in the Prudential.[125] Having fought in Jericho, the Australian Cavalry said they now understood the 'full force of the old expression'.[126] Major Lock wrote that many of the soldiers must have felt 'what a soldier was afterwards heard to express, "This may be the land of promise; it's certainly not the

---

[121] *Chronicles of the White Horse*, 3 (July 1917), 11.
[122] IWM, Papers of Miss Hilda Gosling, letter from Captain W. Hine, 3 Nov. 1917.
[123] IWM 86/66/1, Papers of Captain E. T. Townsend, letter to his father, 22 July 1917.
[124] IWM 81/23/1, Papers of C. T. Shaw, Memoir.
[125] IWM, Papers of Richard Albert Pedlar, letter home, 19 Apr. 1918.
[126] Sommers, *Temporary Crusaders*, 84.

land of fulfillment".[127] The *Palestine News* printed '*A Fragment* from the hitherto unknown *Book of Eisodus*, or the "Journey In," presumed to be some form of historical sequel to the *Book of Exodus* or the "Journey Out" ':

1. Behold, now I enter the Promised Land, whereof much hath been spoken, both by our fathers and our fathers' fathers, yea, and their fathers also, saying:
2. Verily, verily, it is a land flowing with milk and honey, a land of much beauty and of fair women; yea, even if thou seekest unto the ends of the earth there shall not be found a land like unto it.
3. And it came to pass as we journeyed that we came upon an exceeding barren land.
4. And there were many tins in the place.
5. And on the third day a messenger came unto us saying, 'Behold I have seen a tree.'
6. But we believed him not.

After a series of futile operations, the fragment abruptly ends:

37. And so we journeyed through the Promised Land, and verily we will have many things to say unto our children, and our children's children concerning it.
38. And it will come to pass that they will remain in their own homes, being wise in their generation.[128]

With a tormenting summer spent at Sinai, a muddy winter near Jerusalem ('The roads are liquid mud,' wrote Sassoon, '*c'est la guerre*— in an Old Testament environment'[129]) and a scorching springtime east of the river Jordan, it is not difficult to understand the soldiers' bitter reaction. But it is the *language* they chose to employ which is the crux of our discussion. These soft parodies of hymns, scriptural verses, and Sunday-school idioms testify to the momentous role played by vernacular biblical culture in shaping the soldiers' representation of the land. Paradoxically, it was precisely the religious vocabulary which was employed so effectively in demystifying, even debunking, the Holy Land.

---

[127] Major Henry O. Lock, *With the British Army in the Holy Land* (London: Robert Scott, 1919), 19.
[128] *PN*, 11 Apr. 1918, 3.
[129] 13 Mar. 1918, in Sassoon, *Diaries*, 223.

Peace and on earth goodwill

If it were necessary to select one specific episode which would epitomize this cultural condition, it would be Christmas 1917, celebrated just two weeks after Allenby's entrance into Jerusalem, that coveted Christmas gift for the nation. A calamitous combination of hideous weather, expectations of an imminent Ottoman offensive, and a severe food shortage made this 'easily the worst Xmas day we had spent in the army';[130] 'The worst Christmas I have ever spent, the only good point about it being that it is most improbable I shall ever be called on to spend a more unpleasant one';[131] 'As one of the officers remarked, Christmas day in the workhouse would be preferable to this';[132] 'Pouring with rain all day. Rations—3 oz. of bully and about 2 biscuits. What a Christmas dinner! Half starved and shivering with cold';[133] and so forth. There is no other topic on which soldiers' testimonies are so uniform.

William Knott, a south London Salvation Army clerk, served as a nursing orderly in the 32nd Field Ambulance. He spent Christmas in a sick-bed: the downpour was wild; gunfire was constantly heard from the distance; and their tent collapsed into the mud. 'What a contrast, then the peaceful entrance of the king of peace and righteousness into the world and today in the same vicinity is manifest all the terrors and suffering of modern warfare,' Knott recorded in his diary later that day: 'Satan trying to destroy that peace and goodwill but praise God, that day is coming when having conquered Satan—Christ with his Church shall reign for aye!'[134] Many soldiers pondered, though in a less ardent tone, the contradiction between the season of goodwill and the persistence of war. Captain John More, who, together with a few other frontline men was lucky enough to attend the service at St George's Church in Jerusalem, wrote: 'The words of the hymn, "Peace on Earth and mercy mild," seemed particularly ironical, especially as there was a regular cannonade going on at the time.'[135] Cecil Sommers, who thought Christmas Eve and Christmas Day 'the most ghastly days

---

[130] Hendry Papers, Memoir.
[131] Captain R. E. C. Adams, *The Modern Crusaders* (London: Routledge, 1920), 96.
[132] Wilson Papers, Diary, 25 Dec. 1917.
[133] Pope Papers, Diary, 25 Dec. 1917.
[134] IWM P305, Papers of William Knott, Diary, 25 Dec. 1917.
[135] More, *With Allenby's Crusaders*, 145.

I have ever spent', was compelled to devise his own hymns: 'As I stood in the mud at 4 a.m. with no one to love me, I thought out these very morbid lines—

> Roar out, roar out, proud guns,
> Screech over plain and hill,
> Glad tidings to mankind
> 'Peace and on earth goodwill.'
> Howl out your joyful news.
> No mourning requiem.
> 'The Saviour of the world
> Is born in Bethlehem.'[136]

Even when field-troopers were able to attend a church service, the effort of getting there could call in question the very need to offer thanks. The soldiers who travelled to Jerusalem to participate in the thanksgiving ceremony on 6 January, the Day of National Prayer proclaimed by the King, 'had to start at 3 am, and returned about 9 pm...quite soaked and with a conspicuous lack of the thanksgiving spirit. Anything less devout than their opinion of the day can hardly be imagined.'[137]

What is so remarkable about the soldiers' accounts of Christmas 1917 is their reluctance to rejoice in—or even attribute any significance to— the fact that they were celebrating Christmas in Palestine, not far from Jerusalem and Bethlehem, localities associated so intimately with Christ's life and teaching. Even a reverent soldier like Knott, whose diary is brimming with theological comments, makes no mention of it. Private S. F. Hatton was one of the very few to spell this out when he noted, 'It certainly was strange spending Christmas so near to Bethlehem, where had been born the Babe whose advent founded Christendom.'[138] Still, his choice of word—*strange*—hardly indicates a sense of excitement. What should have been their greatest hour in Palestine became, in fact, their greatest frustration. Once again, it was not the decline of religious fervour, but rather its persistence, which conditioned this response. The soldiers in Palestine were well aware of the emotional and formal significance of Jerusalem and Bethlehem. However, the Christmas ethos was so closely associated with the

---

[136] Sommers, *Temporary Crusaders*, 31–2.   [137] Ibid. 47.
[138] Quoted in Peter J. Scott, *Home for Christmas: Cards, Messages and Legends of the Great War* (London: Tom Donovan, 1993), 17.

memory of one's kindred, one's church and chapel, one's *Home*, that the actual sites which featured so prominently in this vernacular ambiance had long become irrelevant.

Even Private Sims, whose cheerfulness was seldom surpassed, perceived his presence in Palestine during Christmas only in terms of its signification for his loved ones back home and *their* Christmas spirit: 'won't it be fine when you all sing the Christian Hymns & Carols in the dear old Church to know that these places are once more in the hands of Christians & you may be sure Christian soldiers will ably defend it if need be.'[139] The miserable conditions of Christmas 1917 no doubt encouraged this yearning for home, but it was repeated at Easter, when their circumstances had improved considerably, and more soldiers were able to attend services in Jerusalem. Sims wrote, 'How I long to get back to do my service to God in that dear old church & among my dear ones & it is jolly nice to know that our work here is not done in vain.' And again, a few weeks later, 'I should of [*sic*] liked to have been in the dear old church on Easter Sunday dearest Mum.'[140] Knott wrote: 'Easter Sunday! What variety of thoughts flood one's mind, the recalling of the supreme events of nineteen centuries ago, counting how many Easters have been spent from home.'[141]

'It's "finish Palestine" for me'
It was not during religious festivals only that the soldiers' gaze was turned westwards, towards home. From the very outset of the campaign, the disillusionment with Palestine was practically inseparable from the idealization of green England, far away. L. G. Moore was speaking for many when he wrote to his mother in October 1917: 'I wonder if the people at home ever realize what a glorious country England is? When you've seen nothing but sand and soldiers and sun for weeks you *do* get "fed up" and long for the green field and trees and even *rain* of Blighty. There is roughly about a day's march between each tree here and *they* aren't worth looking at.'[142] Even those who identified a slight resemblance between Palestine and England did not pursue the analogy.

[139] Sims Papers, letter home, 25 Dec. 1917.
[140] Sims Papers, letters home, 1, 29 Apr. 1918.
[141] Knott Papers, Diary, 31 Mar. 1918.
[142] Moore Papers, letter home, 14 Oct. 1917.

Calcutt, for example, thought that the hills near Beer-Sheba were the 'most depressing country conceivable. In formation not unlike the downs round Winchester but *unrelieved dust colour,* not a speck of green, or a sight of habitation. Perfectly barren.'[143]

Compare this to Martineau, Stanley, and Kinglake, and the ease with which they were able to recognize a familiar Englishness in the Palestine landscape. 'The first thought or impression which I remember as occurring on my entrance into the Holy Land was one of pleasure that it was so like home,' Martineau wrote.[144] As I suggested above, the question as to whether any genuine similitude between the two countries actually existed is wholly irrelevant. What matters is that these Victorian travellers could, or wanted to, believe that Palestine resembled home, whereas the British soldiers could not, or did not want to, imagine such a likeness. If anything, Palestine was constructed as the *opposite* of home; the de-glorification of the Promised Land merely enhanced the over-glorification of Blighty.

This is demonstrated by an intense debate conducted in the *Palestine News* in June–July 1918, triggered by an article entitled 'Natural Beauty in Palestine': 'We are apt, owing to the hard realities of war, and partly through false impressions gained through other channels, to look upon the natural beauty of Palestine with a jaundiced eye. We look in vain for the familiar features of scenic beauty so common in the homeland, and consequently there passes through us a feeling of disappointment which is difficult to eradicate from our minds.' The writer went on to praise Palestine's colours, sunsets, and the 'weird desolation' of its wilderness.[145] The article provoked a wave of protests, which were printed in the newspaper in the following weeks. Texts like these, wrote W. H. Challen angrily,

> go to contribute to the false impressions current in England that Palestine is a beautiful land and that the EEF are having a glorious time out here. Palestine in books and Palestine in reality are two vastly different lands. Palestine may be unique and remarkable in many respects, but it certainly is not beautiful...I have been 1.5 years in Palestine alone and have yet to see a sunrise or sunset to equal any of those which occur in England....

---

[143] Calcutt Papers, Diary, 4 Nov. 1917.
[144] Harriet Martineau, *Eastern Life, Present and Past* (London: Moxon, 1848), iii. 53.
[145] *PN*, 20 June 1918, 6.

As far as the alleged beauty-spots of Palestine are concerned, I am at a loss to understand how anyone dares to venture to compare this land, which is so lacking in trees, foliage, flowers (except for four or five weeks of the year), rivers, etc., with England, 'this England of ours, set in a silver sea.'[146]

This was quite a common response, as another correspondent made clear: 'Judging from their freely expressed opinions, it certainly seems that a large proportion of the troops in Palestine regard the place as dull, barren, and forsaken, and can "see nothing in it." Perhaps this is not surprising when one reflects upon the conditions under which they live. They are soldiers on active service, *not* tourists—which explains a great deal.'[147] Then there were the poems. One, entitled 'Disillusion' ended with these two stanzas:

> Alas! amid these sun-kissed slopes
> Whose glorious past and brightening hopes
> Should stimulate my mind, it mopes
>   For London's clamour;
> Though tender memories hallow still
> The crooked streets of Zion's hill,
> Grey London's rainwashed pavements thrill
>   With kindlier glamour.
>
> Well, carry on! Pro tem, I must
> Enjoy this land of sun and dust;
> I'd gladly give the lot for just
>   one moment where
> The Sussex downs o'ertop the sea,
> Or Wells sleeps under Mendip lea;
> It's 'finish Palestine' for me
>   *Après la guerre.*[148]

And another poem, 'Palestine, as Tommy Sees It', ended,

> Aye! 'Palestine for Poets' is the tired Tommy's cry,
> 'Tis a lovely theme for canvas or for verse;
> We would drink in all its beauties, but they leave us just as dry,
> So you'll pardon if instead we breathe a curse.[149]

---

[146] *PN*, 4 July 1918, 11.
[147] *PN*, 18 July 1918, 11.
[148] *PN*, 18 July 1918, 6.
[149] *PN*, 11 July 1918, 5.

Similar poems, essays, and comments continued to appear regularly, at least until the end of the War and probably much later. In January 1919 the *Palestine News* still printed lines like

> We sit in the land of the Bible
> With the scorching sun above
> And dream of dear old Blighty
> The land we dearly love.[150]

All these texts share several characteristics. They favour Tommy's perspective over that of the non-combatant observer; they link the ability or the desire to appreciate Palestine's beauty with a tourist, leisured sensibility; and they offer only one parameter to assess Palestine's beauty: England. The fact that the *Palestine News*, as an educational Army paper, was willing to publish these letters and poems suggests that the paper attempted to reflect—though somewhat belatedly—the popular mood of its readers. Yet, these images also corresponded with a fundamental propaganda principle: the patriotic emphasis on 'Home'.[151]

It is useful, in this context, to return to the subaltern officer's description of the Tommy. This is how Coldicott, for example, described the London Regiment's typical soldier, the town-bred man: "Streets, shops, lamp-posts; a villa, a tram, a policeman and the cinema round the corner, these are his world, his excellent sufficiency. He does not wish to see the Seven Wonders . . . He will go to the Pyramids if he can take a tram to them. It is curious to reflect that he is now tramping in the rain towards Jerusalem because he happens to have inherited an Empire. But that is a place his mother told him about, and it has raised his curiosity' (p. 53). Elsewhere he stated: 'These men of mine always used to grin at me for talking about adventure, and were accustomed to remark that the only adventure they wanted was the return halves of their tickets—to London' (p. 206). The wonders of the world, adventure, Empire, all these were things that these London men could not comprehend. Luckily, thanks to a faint vernacular religious pulse, enough 'curiosity' is aroused to complete the task overseas. For someone

---

[150] *PN*, 16 Jan. 1919, 12.
[151] On the hegemonic colonial construction of England as 'Home' see Raymond Williams, *The Country and the City* (1973; London: Hogarth Press, 1993), 281–2. Many of the troopers in Palestine were Australians, New Zealanders, and South Africans, whose 'Home' was England only in a very figurative sense.

like Coldicott, discovering 'the man in the street' (p. 126) was no less exciting than discovering the land of the Bible. Major Gilbert, melodramatic as ever, vowed: 'Never again would I patronizingly refer to those whose opportunities for education and advancement had not been so great as my own, as "the common people"! Why, these same common people were winning the war' (p. 122).

As usual, in representing the 'common people', these writers were saying something far more expressive about themselves. With apologies to Gayatri Chakravorty Spivak, we could say that the subaltern—the junior officer—could not speak; he could not voice his disillusionment with Palestine or his longing for home without challenging the imperial, public school ethos of adventure, or, indeed, the mission of the 'Last Crusade'. Consequently, the craving for home could be voiced only through Tommy. In his 'A Song of Camberwell Green', Coldicott mimics one of his London men:

> They're for giving it back to the Jews, they say:
> Will they give me my job in the mews some day,
> In the little back street in Camberwell,
> And a bike to ride in Camberwell,
> And a girl behind the seat? (p. 74)

Similarly, when Robert Goodsall, an NCO, writes about his homesickness, he immediately lapses into 'A Cockney's Grouse':

> Then it's 'ome to good old Blighty
> And we'll all go down the Strand.
> A tidy sight more lively,
> Than this bloomin' 'oly land.[152]

Lyrics like these echo the music-hall culture that helped secure morale during the War by offering a cultural form which could transcend class differences; in concerts, even battalion commanders sang with a Cockney accent. The fine art of 'grousing', so characteristic of the stereotypical Tommy, became a legitimate, almost obligatory, pastime.[153] This was true of the *Palestine News* as well: through the familiar persona of the grousing Cockney, the newspaper could voice a sentiment which seemed to have been ubiquitous, yet depict it in such distinct social colours as to allow the grand imperial narrative to persist intact.

[152] Goodsall, *Palestine Memories*, 153. [153] Fuller, *Troop Morale*, 117, 130–1.

Hard-working, dedicated, yet not quite at ease in the foreign environment into which he was thrust, Tommy was presented as a reluctant imperialist, a homesick Crusader. However, as far as the majority of soldiers were concerned, they were no Crusaders: just homesick.

All soldiers miss home, but in Palestine, always mirroring England mirror the Holy Land, this longing attained a distinct poignancy. It was a nostalgic yearning, but it could also hint at a deeper sentiment, a weariness with imperial expansion, a wish to return to an indigenous, rather than imperial, framework. The historian David Fromkin has asserted that from a British point of view, by the time it was effected in 1922, the Middle East settlement had become largely out of date; British policy-makers imposed a settlement in which, for the most part, they themselves no longer believed.[154] Fromkin is relating to a complex web of political, military, and economic interests; but it seems to echo a very basic sentiment shared by the soldiers. In this respect, the failure of the 'Last Crusade' propaganda anticipated, and was indicative of, the failure of the 'Last Crusade' itself.

Back to the Promised Land

'Many wonders that the world held, but which had not existed for them, were now being forced upon their notice,' wrote Coldicott, describing his London men: 'The change was not apparent in their conversations, but various deep-seated revolutions had taken place within. Their experiences will find tongue in later generations; whereby our literature will be enriched' (p. 126).

Of course, as this chapter has shown, their experiences found tongue there and then. Perhaps the most significant finding that emerges from the collective body of letters, diaries, and memoirs is the persistence of vernacular biblical culture. It was this religious vocabulary, not the Crusading metaphor, which gave meaning and depth to the soldiers' operations in Palestine; and it was by employing this very same vocabulary, albeit subversively, that the soldiers were able to articulate their grievances, challenge the myth of the Holiday Front, and revel in the beauties of home. Their encounter with Palestine was experienced through the dark glass of war, but it was only the War which allowed

---

[154] Fromkin, *Peace to End All Peace*, 562–3.

the majority of these men to visit the Middle East in the first place; they could not have imagined the land any differently.

It is hardly surprising, then, to find that in March 1917, after their defeat at Gaza, the 158th Brigade was distributed over a nearby area 'rejoicing in the name of "St James's Park" ', a little garden of orange and lemon trees, surrounded by prickly pear hedges. The roads converging in the park were known as 'Kingsway', 'Dover Street', 'Oxford Street', and the 'Strand'. 'Dover Street' curled into 'Hyde Park', 'a pretty calm grove on the shore, near the mouth of Wadi Ghuzze'. 'Piccadilly Circus', a large water dump, was situated a mile from the railhead at Belah, where locomotives with the London South-Western lettering on them—sent from England for the advance—could be seen puffing through the desert, 'just as though they were in Eastleigh or Waterloo Stations'.[155] This is the negative of Blake's remarkable image, the golden pillars of Jerusalem standing between the fields from Islington to Marybone, to Primrose Hill and St John's Wood. Instead of arraying the scriptural geography in England, these soldiers were now mapping an England of their own in Canaan. On the one hand, this marks the culmination of our long narrative: with England firmly present in the actual Holy Land, Bunyan's tale could finally be restored to its pure allegorical mode. On the other hand, just like Christian, who walked to Jerusalem only to discover himself in Bedfordshire, we also find ourselves back where we began. Indeed, the familiar vocabulary—Holy Land, Promised Land, land of dreams, heaven—was now used to describe Blighty itself. Writing to his mother in September 1917, Jo Evans envisioned the coveted moment of returning home: 'Just at present the circumstances are not very entraining + we feel accordingly. but one of these days the dawn of the great day will break + then we shall be able to forget all the unpleasant things of the past + look forward to a sight of home + all the dear old faces that have for so long been only a memory.'[156] Another soldier wrote, in a piece printed in the *Palestine News*: '[I] welcomed the War as being a passport to the Land of my Dreams where Travel, Adventure, Glory and Romance awaited me. I am disillusioned...The Land of my Dreams is where I started from

---

[155] More, *With Allenby's Crusaders*, 17, 22, 42, 46; Gilbert, *Romance of the Last Crusade*, 75.

[156] IWM 96/7/1, Papers of Jo Evans, letter home, 8 Aug. 1917. Evans was killed on 31 Oct. 1917.

but I did not know it. I love the fogs and mud of London, and all the allurements of the East could not bribe me to forget a cottage in Derbyshire.'[157]

Let us end with J. Wilson's diary, one of the most eloquent wartime documents. As with many other soldiers, his first sight of Jerusalem came after a bloody day of battle. He was deeply touched by the view from the Mount of Olives, and at the sight of the Garden Tomb, he later wrote, 'I could hardly help saying over to myself, "There is a green hill far away." Somehow I was glad to find that it really was a green hill.' However, the real joy of those days came in Abraham's Vineyard, a tiny Jerusalem neighbourhood, where he found a plaque declaring that a cistern was presented by the people of Tunbridge Wells: 'It was really like a refreshing draught to me,' he wrote: 'I know now what made David wish for water from the well of Bethlehem.' This was an 'unexpected discovery of a little bit of home'.

Christmas was dreadful: 'However, we will have patience, because next Christmas Day we shall be in the Kingdom of Heaven.' With time, he felt 'the beauty of this Holy Land sinking, so it were, slowly into my soul... One must avoid trying to compare it with England's green loveliness, and try to judge it on its own merits.' But it was England that he was missing. In September, near Emmaus, he complains that the bells 'are almost the only feature of the country which reminds one of the English countryside'. A month later, after the great victory of October, he swims at Jaffa beach and is strangely reminded of Brighton. He writes candidly: 'I should like to have seen something of Galilee and Lebanon and Damascus and Beirut. But there are other places, for a sight of which once more I would cheerfully forego all the cities and rich valleys of the East, and all their mysterious spell.' In November, a rumour spreads: 'we are booked for a march in London on the anniversary of the capture of Jerusalem. Amen.' Then it is Christmas again: 'Last Christmas day in very different circumstances, I made a certain prophecy. And has it not come true?'

In France, 23 February 1919:

It seems almost impossible that we are so nearly home that we may be there tomorrow night. Not long ago, the thought of it would have seemed as far and

---

[157] *PN*, 5 Sept. 1918, 6.

faint as the Gates of Paradise; but now the gates are opened to let us in. It is wonderful and joyful beyond words; but I am thinking more of the days to come, and wondering about many things.

Two days later he reaches the Celestial City:

it was wonderful to see again the green fields of England. The rest of this great day has been like a dream. Our going ashore...; the issuing of lordly rations; the luxury of a swift English train; Wimbledon, and small boys' strange knowledge of the English tongue; the Dispersal Camp, a great dinner, a long wait, and then the bewildering speed of the routine of release, and the final exit precisely at six o-clock; the marvellous luck in the catching of trains; the stepping out into the dark and finding friendly hands there; the smiling of faces which I have loved long since.

May it be like this when I go Home at last.[158]

Facing Armageddon

'It would be rather interesting looking at the year 1917, if it were possible to project ourselves into the year 2017 and to observe the events of this particular year,' mused Lloyd George in the House of Commons just before Christmas 1917. He himself had no doubt 'that, when the history of 1917 comes to be written... these events in Mesopotamia and Palestine will hold a much more conspicuous place in the minds and in the memories of the people than many an event which looms much larger for the moment in our sight'.[159]

Lloyd George, it seems, was wrong. Notwithstanding the somewhat slim prospect of a major historiographical shift taking place in the next few years, we can safely assert that the Palestine campaign continued—and continues—to be overshadowed by the events on the Western Front. From its very outset, the Great War was presented in apocalyptic terms; as 1914 drew to a close, references to Armageddon appeared with increasing frequency in sermons, religious poetry, and pamphlets,[160] some of them even issued from the Department of Information.[161]

---

[158] Wilson Papers, Diary, 12, 22, 24, 25 Dec. 1917; 14 Jan., 14 Sept., 13 Oct., 16 Nov., 25 Dec. 1918; 23, 25 Feb. 1919.

[159] *Hansard*, Fifth Series 100 (20 Dec. 1917), cols. 2212, 2211.

[160] Albert Marrin, *Last Crusade: The Church of England in the First World War* (Durham, NC: Duke University Press, 1974), 137.

[161] Cf. *The Dawn of Armageddon, or 'The Provocation by Serbia'* (London: Simpkin, 1917), listed in *Schedule of Wellington House Literature*, PRO, T 102/20.

After the War, apocalyptic images continued to be employed by numerous artists and writers:[162] the Palestine campaign, with its linear narrative, traditional features, relatively few casualties, and unequivocal victory, simply could not be moulded into an Armageddon.

Paradoxically, an actual Battle of Armageddon *was* fought in Palestine: the battle of Megiddo—the biblical Hebrew name for Armageddon, an actual site near Nazareth—is included in the official history, part of the offensive of September–October 1918, which brought the EEF to Damascus. As Jonathan Newell has shown, military and biographical accounts of Allenby have tended to dwell extensively on this battle; he did, after all, become Marshal Viscount Allenby of Megiddo and Felixstowe.[163] However, it seems that by the time the British were fighting at Armageddon, just a few months before the end of the War, the metaphor had long been worn out, despite correspondents' feeble attempts to revive it.[164] A headline in *The Times* of 23 September read, 'Across the Field of Armageddon', but the article itself made no reference to the possible religious implications of the battle's site. Even Cyril Falls's *Armageddon 1918* (1964), a detailed study of Allenby's advance, does not elaborate on the metaphor, and it is not difficult to see why: Allenby's swift progress up to Damascus was certainly not the bloody, colossal, definitive clash envisioned in John's Revelation and anticipated so eagerly by the premillenarians and the British Israelites. That was taking place on the Western Front.

This is not to detract from the religious resonance of the Palestine campaign. In a lecture given at the Jerusalem YMCA in 1933, Allenby stated, 'Our campaign has been called "The Last Crusade". It was not a crusade. There is still a current idea that our object was to deliver Jerusalem from the Moslem. Not so. Many of my soldiers were Moslems. The importance of Jerusalem lay in its strategical position. There was no religious impulse in this campaign.'[165] Of course, the religious impulse

---

[162] Jay Winter, *Sites of Memory, Sites of Mourning: The Great War in European Cultural History* (Cambridge: Cambridge University Press, 1995); Hugh Cecil and Peter Liddle (eds.), *Facing Armageddon: The First World War Experienced* (London: Leo Cooper, 1996).

[163] Newell, 'Allenby and the Palestine Campaign', 195–203.

[164] *Armageddon*, a war film describing Allenby's campaign in Palestine, with some re-enacted scenes, was issued in November 1923. See Rachel Low, *The History of the British Film, 1918–1929* (London: Allen Unwin, 1971), 130, 293.

[165] Quoted in Newell, 'Allenby and the Palestine Campaign', 193.

was everywhere present: as we have seen, the Palestine campaign was initiated by the War Cabinet because it was believed that its religious associations would boost morale; the governmental propaganda apparatus worked to depict it as a Crusade, a Holy War, an image that was subsequently withdrawn due to religious considerations (Muslim sensitivity), but later restored, for the very same reasons (public opinion at home); British soldiers understood and expressed their presence in Palestine employing the religious vocabulary of vernacular biblical culture; and some Muslim soldiers were reluctant to fight against their co-religionists, the Turks.

Allenby's remark may be attributed to his weariness regarding the exaggerated religious subtext that had been ascribed to his victory. Still, he was right in the sense that this immense religious energy did not necessarily conform to the immediate military objective. It either contradicted it, subverted it, or simply passed by unnoticed. Yet again, the actual, geographical Palestine was eclipsed by its metaphorical resonances. At the end of the day—that long summer day which began with Brian Gurnay reading his book on the glittering lawn outside his manor—the literalization of the metaphor had never succeeded in surpassing the metaphor itself. The Holy War in Palestine was never more than a side-show to the Holy War in Europe; the Battle of Armageddon was being fought in the trenches of the Western Front, not in Megiddo; and the real Promised Land remained Blighty.

Epilogue
The Holy Places *revisited*

Evelyn Waugh visited Palestine in 1935. 'I half hate Jerusalem,' he complained in a postcard to Katharine Asquith, but a few days later he cheerfully changed his mind: 'Well that is all over and I love it dearly.' Indeed, the rejuvenated Waugh was now considering a new literary project: 'I feel obliged to write a history of Englanzd and the Holy Places. You see St Helena, Baldwin, Lord Stratford de Redcliffe, General Gordon etc. all English.'[1] Years later, Waugh tried to explain the nature of the task he had in mind:

> Jerusalem had all the air of a city of Christendom reclaimed. The prayers which, seventeen years before, had risen in thanks for General Allenby's superbly modest entrance, were still fresh in the memory. The first Christian government since the fall of the Crusaders' kingdom was the purest and the most benevolent which the land had known since the age of Constantine...Among the deeper emotions of the pilgrimage was also a deep pride in being English...So elated was I by the beauties about me that I there and then began vaguely planning a series of books—semi-historic, semi-poetic fiction, I did not quite know what—about the long, intricate, intimate relations between England and the Holy Places.[2]

In 1950 Waugh published *Helena*, a novel about the Roman empress, Constantine's mother, who marked the Holy Sepulchre when she visited Palestine in 326. By embracing the medieval myth of Helena's Colchester origins, Waugh was able to associate England with a key

---

[1] Waugh to Katharine Asquith, 23, 28 Dec. 1935, in *The Letters of Evelyn Waugh*, ed. Mark Amory (1980; London: Phoenix, 1995), 102–3.
[2] Evelyn Waugh, *The Holy Places* (London: Queen Anne Press, 1952), 1–2.

moment in the sanctification of Palestine; but his projected 'series of books' recounting the long relations between England and the Holy Land would remain unwritten. In 1952 he published *The Holy Places*, a slim volume depicting a recent visit to what was now the young state of Israel. In the introduction, entitled 'Work Abandoned', he wrote: 'The first, flushed, calf love of my theme has never completely cooled, though I now know that I shall not pursue it further. One element certainly is dead for ever—the pride of the country. We surrendered our mandate to rule the Holy Land for low motives: cowardice, sloth and parsimony.' Palestine, he wrote bitterly, was 'no longer a land where an Englishman can walk with pride'.[3]

In many ways, Waugh's abandoned theme has been the subject of this study: 'the long, intricate, intimate relations between England and the Holy Places'. It has been my contention, however, that these relations were far more intricate, and certainly more intimate, than Waugh himself seemed to recognize. The premiss behind his project was the expansionist vision which we have learnt to identify as 'England in Jerusalem': it is telling that all those 'great and strange Britons' who, for Waugh, 'embodied this association'—'Helena, Richard Lionheart, Stratford Canning, Gordon'—visited Jerusalem in an imperial framework or frame of mind, whether Roman, medieval, or modern.[4] Like Gaselee and Sykes, Waugh exemplifies the proximity between class and English Catholicism; which is why *Helena*, unfolding the fortunes of the first aristocratic, Catholic, English dynasty, reads like a *Brideshead Revisited* in Palestine. Waugh, in other words, shows little interest in the fact that, following the Reformation, the formal significance of the holy places for Protestants had increasingly declined; nor does he ponder the intimate meanings that the 'Holy Land' might have had back in England, for those men and women who could never have hoped to visit the earthly Jerusalem. As far as Waugh is concerned, the relationship between England and the holy places hinges simply on an active, physical presence in the land: no wonder that it was the British retreat from Palestine in 1948—the 'abandoned work' that was the British Mandate itself—which made Waugh realize that he would never pursue his old theme further.

[3] Waugh, *Holy Places*, 2–3.
[4] Ibid. 2.

What Waugh had contemptuously called 'cowardice, sloth and parsimony' was of course another name for decolonization, but its signs were visible long before the actual retreat in 1948. As we have seen, the disillusionment with the Holy Land began as early as the First World War, with the letters and diaries written by the 'homesick Crusaders'; and it intensified in the following decades, as the British men and women serving in the Mandate government found themselves in the midst of an unsolvable conflict between Jews and Arabs.[5] Jerusalem, far from being their 'happy home', was in fact just the opposite—the opposite, that is, of England.

A comical expression of this reversal can be found in 'Alice in Blunderland', part of *Palestine Parodies* (1938), a humorous collection written by P. E. F. Cressall, a chief magistrate in Palestine in the 1930s. Arriving in Palestine with the 'Empress of Britain', and 'beginning to get very tired of sitting in the lounge of the King Solomon Hotel with nothing to do', Alice follows the white rabbit down the narrow streets of the old city: ' "How funny it'll seem to come out among the people who think upside down, and write backwards" she thought.' On her way, she meets a strange mixture of officials and natives, Arabs and Jews, and visits a bureaucratic pool of tears, a tea-party at the Tel Aviv municipality, and a frantic courtroom scene. As one of her hosts, the poor government official, explains: 'You must realize that Palestine has undergone various changes since the times of the Crusaders. Originally, it *was* the Holy Land; then came the War when it was *wholly* occupied by Army heroes, finally becoming, owing to the League of Nations, and other what nots, as you see it now;—a most un-wholly land.'[6]

Like Alice's Wonderland, Palestine becomes a mad, topsy-turvy reflection of England, a place where people think 'upside down' and write 'backwards'. Cressall was parodying Palestine of the 1930s, but with the escalation of violence, the Holy Land became even madder. As one newsreel declared in September 1946, 'The British soldier is carrying out the dirtiest, most dangerous and most thankless job in the world today. For him Jerusalem has no glamour, no mystery and no rewards,

---

[5] Cf. A. J. Sherman, *Mandate Lives: British Lives in Palestine, 1918–1948* (London: Thames & Hudson, 1997); Naomi Shepherd, *Ploughing Sand: British Rule in Palestine, 1917–1948* (London: John Murray, 2000).

[6] [P. E. F. Cressall], *Palestine Parodies: Being the Holy Land in Verse and Worse* (Tel Aviv: Azreiel, 1938), 1, 2, 9.

only hard work and constant nerve breaking suspense.'[7] For Waugh, 'Jerusalem had all the air of a city of Christendom reclaimed,' but for most observers—and for the public back home—the reverse seemed to be true: to rule Palestine was to lose the mystery.

Palestine, to be sure, was swiftly incorporated into the popular imperial culture of the inter-war period. Visitors to the Palestine Pavilion at the British Empire Exhibition at Wembley (1924–5) could purchase olive-wood boxes which contained earth from Mount Moriah, or cards with dried flowers which had lain on the altar in Bethlehem. A committee in Jerusalem, headed by the High Commissioner, guaranteed the authenticity of the souvenirs:[8] Holy Land relics, once so despised by the Protestant Reformers, were now being merchandized in the name of the god of Capitalism. A new generation of boys' adventure books, like F. S. Brereton's *With Allenby in Palestine, a Story of the Latest Crusade* (1920), attempted to cash in on the Crusading excitement;[9] Jaffa oranges were advertised in posters distributed by the Empire Marketing Board in the 1930s;[10] relays from Bethlehem were broadcast in Christmas Day programmes on the BBC;[11] and newsreels brought images of the land to cinema-goers all over Britain.[12]

More than ever before, Sunday-school teachers had access to pedagogical tools which could draw children's attention to the reality of life in the Bible lands. It is interesting, therefore, that one of the most significant developments in popular religious culture in the 1920s and 1930s was the reintroduction of the Nativity play, with children at schools, churches, and chapels dressing up as natives of Bethlehem or as kings of the East.[13] This annual re-enactment of the birth of Christ

---

[7] Quoted in Taylor Downing, *Palestine on Film* (London: Council for the Advancement of Arab–British Understanding, 1979), 9.

[8] *British Empire Exhibition 1924—Official Guide* (London: Fleetway, 1924), 87–8.

[9] Joseph Shadur, *Young Travellers to Jerusalem: The Holy Land in American and English Juvenile Literature, 1785–1940* (Ramat Gan, Israel: Bar-Ilan University Press, 1999), 101–13.

[10] TNA: PRO, CO 956/122, 'Orange Exports from Palestine'.

[11] John M. MacKenzie, 'In Touch with the Infinite: The BBC and the Empire, 1923–53', in MacKenzie (ed.), *Imperialism and Popular Culture* (Manchester: Manchester University Press, 1986), 181.

[12] Downing, *Palestine on Film*.

[13] J. A. R. Pimlott, *The Englishman's Christmas: A Social History* (Hassocks: Harvester Press, 1978), 151. Curiously enough, the history of the popular Nativity play in the twentieth century has been overlooked by historians of modern-day Christmas (even

fused together several elements: the vernacular medieval play, maybe even the mummers' play which survived in some rural areas; the nineteenth-century Orientalist cliché of the never-changing East, where present-day Bedouin still wear the garb of biblical peasants; and the Victorian invention of a Christmas which stood at the heart of Protestant biblical culture. Even today—church or school still masquerading as Judaea, tea-towels still serving to protect the little English shepherds from the blazing Palestinian sun—the Nativity play continues to imagine the Holy Land using the familiar, the indigenous, the stuff of 'here'. Rather than gazing eastwards, to Bethlehem, this is the Blakean fantasy of discovering Jerusalem in one's own vicinity— similar to the experience offered by Schor's Palestine Exhibitions.

The Palestine Exhibition itself was hardly affected by the Mandate years. Reports and official guides from the 1920s to the 1940s suggest that speakers often turned to the memory of those 'Lads who fought bravely and brought the Holy Land back into the hands of someone who would care and look after it';[14] references were sometimes made to the Zionist colonization of the land. But the structure of the exhibition and its collection of models and costumes were not rearranged, revised, or updated: just like the Palestine it imagined, Schor's exhibition remained unchanged, as it continued to travel all over Britain, making sure that there was always some corner of a well-known field which was for ever Holy Land.

The fact that this ahistorical representation of the land could persist while the British Empire was in fact ruling Jerusalem suggests, once again, that Waugh's (abandoned) narrative is only one, very limited way of understanding the role played by the Holy Land in English culture. Schor's exhibition exposes, furthermore, the chasm between metropolitan culture and the imperial experience overseas. While recent

---

Pimlott deals mainly with adult religious drama). J. M. Golby and A. W. Purdue, *The Making of the Modern Christmas* (London: Batsford, 1986), state only that 'one of the few innovations to Christmas festivities this century has been the reintroduction of the Nativity Play' (p. 107); and Mark Connelly, *Christmas: A Social History* (London: Tauris, 1999), makes no mention of it at all. Nevertheless, a survey of the British Library catalogue (using the keywords 'Nativity'/'Christmas' and 'play') suggests that while only three titles were published between 1910 and 1920, there were nineteen titles in 1920–30; fifty-one in 1930–40; thirty-five in 1940–50 (many of them in 1949); forty-six in 1950–60; and sixteen in 1960–70.

[14] *Reading Observer*, 23 Feb. 1923, 1.

scholarship has done much to reveal the array of interrelationships—commercial, cultural, emotional, discursive—that tied the imperial metropolis to the colonial world, one must recognize that denial, suppression, or simply ignorance were equally significant in defining the affinity between 'here' and 'there'. At the same time, this discrepancy between the Palestine Exhibition's romantic day-dream of the Orient and the bloody reality in Palestine merely anticipated the end of the Mandate: since the mission of governing Jerusalem was ultimately unfeasible, all that remained was the vision of building a small-scale Jerusalem in one's own green and pleasant vicinity.

Nowhere was this disillusionment with Palestine more evident than in the British Israelite movement, whose members followed Allenby's advance in winter 1917 with a mounting sense of excitement; in a meeting of the British Israelite League at Central Hall, Westminster, Miss Augusta Cook proclaimed that the War was Armageddon, and that the British forces were Israelites.[15] Allenby's entrance into Jerusalem, in particular, was seen as a pivotal moment in British history: 'When Jerusalem welcomed the British as deliverers in December 1917, she surrendered to the wardship of her national, traditional, and spiritual inheritors,' explained G. H. Lancaster in *Jerusalem—Our National Birthright* (1919), 'for Jerusalem is part of the long-cherished Birthright of the Anglo-Saxon race, the literal and lineal Israel of God'.[16] Nevertheless, British Israelites soon lost interest in the actual, geographical Holy Land. As John Wilson has noted, the inter-war years saw a doctrinal shift: the prophesied return of the Israelites to Palestine was now taken to mean a representative one only; henceforth, it was Britain that would be regarded as the likely centre of the future Kingdom of God on earth.[17] Paradoxically, then, just when England was finally ruling Jerusalem, it was the vision of Jerusalem in England which was becoming the focus of the British Israelite hope. Even for them, the most ardent supporters of the British colonization of Palestine, the Pisgah sight was eventually preferable to Canaan itself.

---

[15] *The Times*, 13 Nov. 1917, 3.
[16] G. H. Lancaster, *Jerusalem—Our National Birthright* (Edinburgh: Northern British-Israel Council, 1919), 1.
[17] J. Wilson, 'The History and Organization of British Israelism' (D.Phil. thesis, Oxford, 1966), 430.

This, after all, has been my contention: the metaphorical appropriations of the 'Holy Land' in the English cultural imagination always surpassed any actual weight that the geographical Holy Land might have had in Britain's overall imperial design. The Mandate years, in this respect, were the culmination of a century-long process, in which the Bunyanesque image of 'Jerusalem in England' had always been a much more dominant trope in English culture than the imperial expectation of 'England in Jerusalem'. Waugh's account of England and the Holy Land is incomplete without the story of England *as* the Holy Land: to explore the long, intricate, intimate relationship between England and Palestine is also to explore England's intricate, intimate relationship with itself.

Index

Note: **bold** numbers denote references to illustrations

Abrams, M. H. 80
Acre 2, 45, 59, 120, 140, 145–6, 147, 209 n. 96, 259
Adler, Rabbi Hermann 211–12
African Association 89
Albury Park Conferences 191
Alexander, Frances:
 'There is a green hill' (hymn) 78, 129, 177, 291
Aliens Act (1905) 242, 245
Allen, William 99
Allenby, General Edmund 5, 11, 62, 92, 251, 253, 257, 275, 293–4, 295, 300
 entry into Jerusalem 3, 247, 257, 260–4, 278, 282, 300
Alps 80, 163
Altick, Richard 97, 101
Anderson, Benedict 23
Anglicanism/Anglicans 109, 145, 167, 191, 262, 264
 Articles of Faith 27
 see also Protestantism; Reformation
Anglo-Catholics 256
Anglo-Jews 2, 33, 185, 204, 210–13, 239, 241
anti-Semitism 6 n. 10, 199, 211–12, 239, 242
Arab Bureau 252, 262
Arabia 59, 87, 95, 252, 257
Arabian Nights 44, 90–1, 159
Arabic 73, 261, 270 n. 82
Arabs, *see* Palestinians
archaeology 70, 92, 166, 170, 174–6, 177, 178

 see also Warren, Charles
Armageddon 189, 292–4, 300
 see also Meggido
Arnold, Matthew 13, 29, 201
Art Journal 67, 88, 133
Ashkelon 132
Asquith, Katharine 295
Astley's Royal Amphitheatre 137
Athens 65
Auerbach, Erich 23
Augustine, St 21
Austen, Jane:
 Northanger Abbey 80
Australia/Australians 89, 263
 soldiers in Palestine 280, 287 n. 151
 see also Black, Donald; Idriess, Ion

Bailey, Major V. H. 273
Balfour, Arthur James 8
Balfour Declaration 182–4, 190, 226, 243–6, 261, 268
Bankes, William 69
Banner of Israel 207
Barker, Robert 139, 143, 144
Barrell, John 8–9, 12, 85
Bartlett, William 64, 85, 88, 139, 141, 163
Basingstoke 161–2
Bath 80, 149
bazaar 150 n. 122, 151, 154, 156
BBC 298
Beard, John 127
Bebbington, David 191
Beer, Gillian 219

Index

Beer-Sheba vii, 209–10, 268, 273, 285
Bedford, Francis 133, **134**
Bedfordshire 11, 21, 290
Bedouin 61, 66, 68, 84, 86, 91, 119, 143, 150, 159, 299
Beirut 120, 291
Ben-Arieh, Yehoshua 5
Benisch, Abraham 210 n. 102
Bentham, Jeremy 144
Bentley, Richard 96, 97, 98
  see also Colburn and Bentley
Berlin 73
Berlin, Congress of 203, 211, 212, 214
Besant, Walter 170–3
Bethany 150, 268
Bethlehem 43, 79, 110, 120, 133, 151, 159, 163, 226, 249, 267, 268, 283–4, 291, 298–9
  see also Church of the Nativity
Bevis, Richard 95
Bhabha, Homi K. 39–40
Bible:
  Daniel 22
  Deuteronomy 108
  Exodus 20, 231 n. 188, 281
  Ezekiel 53, 58
  Galatians 20–1
  Hebrews 21
  Isaiah 201
  Joshua 231
  Mark 263 n. 60
  Psalms 40, 201
  Revelation 21, 22, 35, 39, 49, 53, 164, 293
  Romans 28
  see also biblical imagery and vocabulary; Geneva Bible; higher biblical criticism; King James Bible; *and under names of specific biblical figures*
Bible lands 9, 43, 45, 70, 90–1, 298

biblical imagery and vocabulary:
  flexibility of 1–2, 4, 10–11, 13, 16, 19, 29–30, 34, 35–6, 39–41, 47–8, 53, 93–4, 106, 163, 177, 179, 180–1, 184–5, 196, 209–10, 213–14, 230–1, 245, 279–80, 293
  in imperial discourse 10, 16, 31, 40–1, 46–7, 196
  and working-class ethos 13, 37–9, 129–32
  see also England as the Holy Land; English as chosen people; vernacular Orientalism
Bicheno, James 47, 56
Binfield, Clyde 193
Bivona, Daniel 85
Black, Donald 279
Blackburn, Revd John 146
Blackwood, John 217
Blake, William 1, 2, 5, 17, 41, 57–60, 290, 299
  'Jerusalem' (stanzas from *Milton*) 1–2, 3, 13, 57, 58
  Jerusalem 1, 57–8
Blood Red Knight, The (play) 137, **138**
Bloom, Harold 58
Blunt, Lady Anne 75
Blyth, James 242
Bolton 151
Bonomi, Joseph 139, 141, 163
Bonwick, James 127–8
Booth, Michael 136
Booth, William 32 n. 44
Bowring, John 81–2
Boy Scouts 255
Bradshaw, Revd Samuel 196
Brereton, F. S. 298
Brighton 291
British and Foreign Bible Society 46, 167, 168
British Brothers League 231

Index

British Empire:
  interests in Palestine 2–3, 4, 6–7, 8, 9, 10, 15–16, 17, 30–1, 41, 45, 46–7, 59, 61–2, 92–3, 161, 177–8, 194–201, 208–9, 214, 243, 251, 256, 260–3, 268–9, 289, 292, 296–8, 300
  see also imperialism, British; Mandate
British Empire Exhibition (1924) 298
British Israelites 29, 199–202, 206, 207, 210, 244, 257 n. 36, 293, 300
  anti-Semitism of 199
  on *Daniel Deronda* 223–4
  and Disraeli 214
  and Richard Brothers 55
  see also *Nation's Glory Leader*
British Mandate (for Palestine), *see* Mandate
British Society for the Propagation of the Gospel among the Jews 191, 193, 206
Brixton 148
Bromehead, Joseph 38
Brothers, Richard 19, 45, 51–6, 59, 60, 187, 191, 196, 199, 241
Brougham, Lord Henry 112–13, 128
Brown, Wallace Cable 96
Buchan, John 235 n. 197, 251, 252, 253, 256, 270
Buckingham, James Silk 69, 70
Bulgaria 202–3, 209, 234
  Bulgarian atrocities 203, 218
Bunyan, John 11, 16, 19–23, 29, 31, 37, 41, 44, 54, 75–6, 90, 93, 104, 130, 137, 160, 164, 231, 290, 301
  and English as chosen people 19–20, 231
  and Joanna Southcott 51, 52
  and William Blake 58–9
  Pilgrim's Progress, The 11, 19–23, 31, 42, 59, 105, 107, 160; and conquest of Palestine 290; contesting interpretations of 40–1, 107; and hegemony 38–9, 40–1; and imperial ethos 40–1; Macaulay on 39; and radical culture 38–9, 130; E. P. Thompson on 40; and travellers to Palestine 75–6, 93; as vernacular Orientalist text 31–2; Weber on 22
Burford, Robert 137, 140, 141, 142, 143, 145–6, 147, 148, 163
Burrows, Revd H. W. 163
Burton, Richard 99–100
Burton, Isabel 100
Butler, George 72
Butler, Josephine 72
Byron, Lord George Gordon 18, 69, 74–5

Cairo 72, 154
Calcutt, Douglas H. 273, 278, 285
Calvary (Jerusalem) 78, 94, 110, 151
  see also Church of the Holy Sepulchre
Canterbury 24
Cardiff Echo 230
Carlyle, Thomas 191
Carmel 43, 87
Caroline, Queen 75
Carson, Edward 265
Carter, Paul 88, 89
Cassell's Family Bible 132

Catherwood, Fredrick 139
Catholicism/Catholics 256, 266, 296
  and the crusades 77, 258
  and holy places in Palestine 120, 178
  and Palestine's landscape 79
  see also Anglo-Catholics; Sykes; Waugh
Challen, W. H. 285
Chamberlain, Joseph 229
Chapman, John 100–1
Charles I, King 29
Chartism 13, 41, 45, 50, 60, 130–1, 165
Chateaubriand, François-René de 18, 77, 79, 114, 119
Chaucer, Geoffrey 24
Chew, Samuel 33
Cheyette, Bryan ix, 6 n. 10, 235 n. 197
chosen people, *see* English as chosen people; Jews, as chosen people
Christ, *see* Jesus Christ
Christian Herald and Signs of Our Times 206
Christian World 173
Christian Zionism, *see* Jews, restoration to Palestine
Christmas 251, 260, 267, 282–4, 291, 292, 298, 299
Chronicles of the White Horse 279
Church Missionary Society 46, 168
Church of England, *see* Anglicans
Church of St George (Jerusalem) 267, 282
Church of the Holy Sepulchre (Jerusalem) 24 n. 22, 78, 79, 94, 120, 122, 123, 140, 143, 151, 154, 174, 178, 261, 266, 267, 274, 275, 295
  see also Calvary

Church of the Nativity (Bethlehem) 79, 110, 139, 141, 267
Citadel (Jerusalem), *see* Tower of David
Civil War 22, 28, 47
Clark, Robert 272
Clarke, Edward 69, 78, 80, 110, 119, 121
Clayton, Gilbert 266, 270
Cleeve, Lucas 238–9
Cobbe, Frances Power 75
Cockneys 175, 275, 288
Cohn, Norman 26
Colburn and Bentley (publishers) 97, 98
  see also Bentley, Richard
Colchester 295
Coldicott, Rowlands 272, 274, 278, 287–8, 289
Cole, Henry 175
Colley, Linda 40–1
Colonial and Indian Exhibition (1886) 156
Conder, Claude 175, 270
Conder, Josiah 81
Constantine 295
Constantinople 27, 64, 163, 195, 202, 205, 206, 208
conversion, *see* Jews, conversion of
Conybeare, Revd W. J. 189
Cook, Augusta 300
Cook, Thomas 65, 69, 93
Cook's Eastern Tours 64–5, 80–1, 107, 277
Cookham 43
Cressall, P. E. F. 297
Crimean War 95, 163, 195, 204, 205, 206
Crouch, Nathaniel 30
Crusades/Crusaders 19, 24, 25–6, 33, 76, 82, 197, 216, 247–60, 262, 264, 265,

266–72, 288–9, 294, 295, 297, 298
and Catholics 77, 258
and chivalry 255–8, 265, 269, 271
'homesick Crusaders' 17, 267, 268–9, 289, 297
'Last Crusade' 247–51, 252–4, 257, 259, 260, 262, 268, 288–9, 293
as metaphor 256–60, 265, 271, 289
and *Tancred* 216
Crystal Palace:
and George Grove 168, 169, 173
and Handel Festival 169, 170
as Holy Land 163–5
in Sydenham 164–5
Cumberland 43
Cumming, Revd Dr John 207, 225
Curzon, Lord George Nathaniel 161–2, 260–1
Curzon, Robert 87, 259, 260–1
Cyprus 196, 203, 205, 209 n. 96, 214, 215

Daily Mirror 263–4
Daily News 220
Daily Sketch 263
Daily Telegraph 169, 255
Damascus 44, 65, 234, 291, 293
'Damascus Affair' 186
Damascus Gate (Jerusalem) 267
Dan (Palestine) 175, 209–10
Danby, Francis 119
David, King 20, 51, 233
Davies, Robert 95
Davis, John 107, 144
Dawnay, Major–General Guy 256, 261
Dead Sea 61, 99, 120, 129, 133, 174, 236
Denton, Revd William 209

Department of Information 249, 253, 266, 292
see also Press Bureau
De Quincey, Thomas 9
Derby, 15th earl of (Lord Stanley before 1869) 202, 205, 215
Derbyshire 87, 108, 291
Description de l'Egypt 70
Devonshire 48
Dicey, Edward 208–10
Diggers 22, 28, 29, 34, 36
dioramas 107, 139–42, 144, 147, 148
Disraeli, Benjamin 18, 66, 85, 202–5, 208, 210, 211, 213–17, 221–2, 230, 235, 236, 237, 238
Alroy 215
Tancred 18, 66, 85, 94, 101, 215–17, 221–2, 237, 238
Zionist historiography on 214–16
Dome of the Rock (Jerusalem) 41, 81, 143, 154
Donne, William Bodham 136
Doubleday, Thomas 130
Doumani, Beshara 82–3
Dowding, Lieut. C. G. 273
Drabble, Margaret 18
Duncan, Captain P. C. 276

East Africa 229–30
East End 171, 227, 228, 231, 232, 242
see also Mile End; Whitechapel
East India Company 31, 41
Easter 267, 284
Eastern Question 45
defined 61
during 1870s 185, 195, 202–18, 222, 226, 245, 257
Eastern Question Association 209
Edinburgh Courant 220
Education Acts (1870, 1880) 133

Edward VII (Prince of Wales before 1901) 77, 121, 133, 140
Edwards, Henry 197, 198
Egypt 20, 41 n. 75, 44–5, 55, 59, 64, 72–3, 77, 90–1, 92, 95, 103, 125, 128, 130, 141, 146, 154–5, 159, 196, 208, 213–14, 230, 244, 276
  Balfour on British rule in 8
  British occupation of (1882) 3, 196
  Egyptian occupation of Palestine (1832) 64
  England as 130, 231, 239
  see also Cairo; Suez Canal
Egyptian Expeditionary Force (EEF) 225, 247
  see also Allenby
Egyptian Hall (London) 141, 142, 162, 174
Egyptian Labour Corps 263 n. 56
Elijah 116, **118**
Eliot, George 184, 217–25, 237, 239, 240
  Daniel Deronda 184, 185, 217–25, 226, 237, 238, 240
  Middlemarch 221
  'The Modern Hep! Hep! Hep!' 237, 240
Emmaus 291
Empire Marketing Board 298
England as the Holy Land 1–5, 10–11, 16–17, 19, 30, 33, 35, 88, 92–3, 301
  in Blake 1, 57–60
  and British Israelites 300
  in Bunyan 21–3, 31–2, 40–1, 76
  and Chartism 130–1
  in children's imagination 43–4
  in Crystal Palace 163–5
  and Diggers 22, 28, 35
  in Edwardian representations of 'the Jew' 230–1, 239–40
  in *Jude the Obscure* 105–6
  in Owenism 130, 131
  in Palestine Exhibition 148–62
  in panoramas 137, 143–4
  in 1790s millenarianism 45, 48, 49–51
  in soldiers' writings 11, 290–2
  in Sunday-school curricula 128–9
  in Walsingham 24–5
  in working-class rhetoric 41, 130
  see also vernacular Orientalism
English as chosen people 4, 13, 28–30, 34–5, 41, 213, 231
  and British Israelites 199–201
  and Bunyan 19–20, 29
  and Crystal Palace 163
  and imperial ideology 40–1, 196
  and 1790s millenarianism 47–8, 52, 54–6
  and Palestine Exhibition 159, 161
  and working class ethos 38–40
English lakes 68, 86, 88, 90, 133
Englishness 10, 13, 31, 40, 60, 77, 88, 285
Erdman, David V. 59
Evangelicalism/Evangelicals 2, 12, 37–40, 80, 113, 141, 149, 162, 173, 183, 185–93, 195, 207, 224–5, 243
Evans-Gordon, William 231
Evening Standard 252
Exeter 48, 142
exhibitions 14, 15, 90, 105–7, 136–65, 174–6, 177, 179, 180, 298, 299–300
  see also dioramas; models; Palestine Exhibition; panoramas; *and under specific names*
Exodus 194, 234, 239–40, 241
  biblical 20, 33, 141, 281
  of Englishmen into Palestine 52

of Jews into England 230–1, 239–40
  see also Bible, Exodus
Exposition Universelle (1889) 154

Faber, George Stanley 46, 47, 54
Fairfax, Lord Thomas 28
Falls, Cyril 293
Felixstowe 149, 159, 293
Fergusson, James 99
Field, Edward 127
Fielding, Henry:
  Joseph Andrews 42–3
Fifth Monarchy Men 22, 36
films 2, 143, 151, 249, 259, 266, 293 n. 164
  see also newsreels
Finch, John 130
Finley, John 275
Finn, Constance 129
First World War, see Allenby; Lloyd George; Palestine Campaign; Western Front
Fletcher, Robert 126
Foreign Office 215, 253
Fox, Henry 186
Foxe, John:
  Book of Martyrs 29, 31, 54
France/French 4 n. 9, 77, 79, 140, 200, 208, 209, 214, 253, 260, 262, 263, 266, 267, 269, 276, 291
French Revolution 2, 36, 46
Friedman, Isaiah 194, 214–15
Frith, Francis 135
Fromkin, David 289
Fuller, Thomas 30, 34

Gallipoli 277
Garden of Eden 1, 49, 53, 62, 164
Garden Tomb (Jerusalem) 78, 291
Gaselee, Stephen 253–4, 256, 266, 268, 270, 296
Gaskell, Elizabeth:
  North and South 131
Gawler, George 200 n. 55
Gawler, John 199–200, 210
Gaza 133, 273
  as London 290
Gelber, N. M. 215
Genessaret 67
  see also Sea of Galilee
Geneva Bible 29, 33
Gentleman's Magazine 222
geographical imagination 16, 25–7, 42–5, 52, 56, 59, 128–9
George V 259
George, St 258, 259
Germany/Germans 9, 114, 198, 238, 241, 252, 263–4
  see also Prussia
Gibbon, Edward 84
Gilbert, Major Vivian 254–6, 270, 271, 275, 278, 288
Gladstone, William Ewart 136, 137, 203–4, 208, 209, 251
Glasgow 142, 150 n. 122
Glastonbury 24–5
Gloucester 150
Good Words 80, 178
Goodsall, Robert 288
Gordon, General Charles 62–3, 78, 140–1, 295, 296
Gosse, Edmund 202
Gott, Samuel 34–5
Graham, Winifred 235–7, 238
Gramsci, Antonio 38–9, 40
Grand Tour 148
Great Exhibition (1851), *see* Crystal Palace
Greenberg, Leopold 232, 242
Gregory, Derek 88, 90, 92
Grier, Sydney 233–5, 236, 241 n. 204
Grove, George 168–70, 173–4, 175, 176, 178
Guardian (High Church newspaper) 220

Guedalla, Haim 211, 222
Guttenberg, Violet 239–40, 241 n. 204
Haggard, Henry Rider 91, 234, 255, 260
Haifa 83, 209 n. 96, 239
Hakluyt, Richard 31
Halévy, Élie 38
Hall, Catherine 12–13
Hammond, J. L. and Hammond, Barbara 37–8
Hardy, Thomas:
   Jude the Obscure vii, 105–6, 107, 146, 160, 165
Harmony (England) 130
Hatton, S. F. 283
Headlem-Morley, James 214–15
heaven:
   as afterlife 19, 24 n. 19, 26–8, 36–8, 39, 42, 50, 76–7, 121–2, 125–6, 131, 141, 145
   terrestrial (heaven on earth) 1, 18, 19–23, 34–5, 40, 42; *see also* England as the Holy Land; New Jerusalem
Hebraism 2, 74, 106, 230–1
   and Disraeli 213, 216, 230
   and Matthew Arnold 29, 201
Hebrew (language) 73, 185, 270 n. 82, 291
Hebron 86, 87, 133, 261, 268, 275
Helena, Empress 24 n. 22, 295–6
Hemans, Felicia 121
Hendry, W. N. 278
Henty, G. A. 91, 234, 255
Herzl, Theodor 187, 213, 226–7, 232, 234, 236, 242
higher biblical criticism 9, 30, 82, 113, 159
Hill, Christopher 36
Hillary, William 197–8
Hine, Captain W. 280

Hobson, J. A. 228–9
Hollingsworth, A. G. H. 197, 198
Holy Land, *see* England as the Holy Land; Palestine
Holyoake, George 108
Hopkins, James 49
Horsley, Samuel 46, 47
Housman, A. E. 43
Howad, Yussif 198
Hudson, Hugh 1
Hull 48, 142, 143, 164
Hunt, William Holman 70, 84, 164–5
Hyde Park 54, 141, 290
hymns 11, 14, 18, 36–7, 38, 43, 50, 56, 78, 107, 116, 121, 122 n. 38, 126, 178, 180–1, 250, 267, 274, 279–80, 281, 282–3, 284, 291
   see also under specific titles

Idriess, Ion 276, 277, 279
Illustrated London News 133, **134**
imperialism, British:
   and biblical imagery and vocabulary 10, 16, 31, 40–1, 46–7, 196
   and millenarianism 41, 47, 55–6, 193–201, 300
   see also British Empire
India/Indians 2, 5, 12, 41, 128, 196–7, 202, 208, 214, 216, 252, 260, 263, 265, 266, 268
'invisible college' 70, 72, 73, 139, 165
Irby, Charles Leonard 69, 98
Ireland/Irish 4 n. 8, 64, 263, 266
Irving, Edward 191–2
Islam 33, 73, 249, 253, 257, 261, 262, 264
   see also Muslims
Islington 58, 59, 156, 290
Islington Agricultural Hall 149, 158
Israel, State of vii, 17, 296

Israelites 20, 28–9, 32, 35, 37–8, 40, 58, 141, 159, 160, 163, 182, 213, 231, 273
  lost tribes 29, 52, 54, 189, 199, 200, 207, 214, 223
Israel's Watchman (and Prophetic Expositor) 200, 205–6, 223
Italy/Italians 23, 84, 263, 266, 278

Jaffa 34, 85, 91, 291
Jaffa Gate (Jerusalem) 122, 263
Jaffa oranges 298
Jaffe, Benjamin 232
James, Henry 218
James, Revd John 172
Jehoshaphat, Valley of (Jerusalem) 106, 122, **124**, 176
Jericho (Palestine) 43, 133, 190, 242, 280
Jericho (Oxford) vii
Jerome, St 21
'Jerusalem' (hymn), *see* Blake
Jerusalem (Palestine), *see under specific place names*
Jerusalem Bishopric 2 n. 5
  see also MacInnes
Jerusalem in England, *see* England as the Holy Land
'Jerusalem, My Happy Home' (hymn) 38, 126, 146
'Jerusalem the Golden' (hymn) 122 n. 38, 177, 280
Jesus Christ 17, 20, 22, 24, 33, 39, 43, 44, 51, 76, 77, 80, 106, 109–10, 114, **117**, 125, 129, 164, 180, 199, 206, 241, 263, 274, 276, 282, 283, 298
Jewish Chronicle 170, 210–12, 214, 222, 229, 233, 234, 244
Jewish Herald 193, 207
Jewish Historical Society of England 182
Jewish Intelligence 223, 224

Jewish Naturalization Act (1753) 46
Jews 5 n. 10, 21 n. 6, 33–5, 37, 39, 58, 94, 130, 149–50, 151, 159, 175, 183, 261, 266, 297
  biblical, *see* Israelites
  as chosen people 28–9, 35, 39, 47, 54, 199, 224
  conversion of 34–5, 46, 47, 54, 161, 186, 188, 189, 192–3, 194, 199, 210, 224–5
  English, *see* Anglo-Jews
  restoration to Palestine 13, 17, 28, 34–5, 41, 45, 46–8, 50–1, 52–6, 150, 182–202, 205–13, 214–46, 288
  see also Aliens Act; anti-Semitism; East End; Hebraism; *Jewish Chronicle*; London Society for Promoting Christianity among the Jews; philo-Semitism; Wandering Jew; Zionism (Jewish); Zionist Congress
jihad 252
jingoism 56, 204
Johannesburg 228–9
Joppa, *see* Jaffa
Jordan, River 23, 36, 37, 64, 75, 130, 133, 174, 276, 281
Joseph of Arimathea 24
Joshua 273, 275, 279

Kaufmann, U. Milo 22
Kedron (Jerusalem) 128, 176, 181
Keith, Alexander 82, 103
Kermode, Frank 202
Kiernan, V. 36
King David Hotel (Jerusalem) 245
King James Bible 29, 213
Kingdom of God/of Heaven 35, 49, 50–1, 291, 300
Kinglake, Alexander 67, 68–9, 78, 84, 85–6, 88, 90, 100, 285
  Eothen 67, 68–9, 100, 101

Kingsley, Charles 131, 163
Kingston, Albert 274
Kipling, Rudyard 41
Kitchener, H. H. 7, 251
Kitto, John 112, 113–14, 116, 125–6, 131, 145
Knight, Charles 108, 112–14, 116
Knott, William 282, 283, 284
Kobler, Franz 216

Labourer, The 130
Labour Party 41, 60, 225, 228
Lamartine, Alphonse de 96, 114
Lancaster, G. H. 300
Land and the Book, The (Thomson) 62, 67
Lane, Edward:
  Modern Egyptians 92, 112
Laqueur, Thomas 38
Lawrence, D. H. 39, 180–1
Lawrence, T. E. 7, 256–7, 260
Layard, A. H. 98–9, 103, 172–3, 209 n. 96
Leeds News 226
Leisure Hour 143, 200
Levant Company 31, 41
Levellers 22, 36
Levene, Mark 243–4, 245
Levine, Philippa 70, 72
Lewis, C. S. 21
libraries 14, 101–3
Liverpool 149, 193
Lloyd George, David 182, 184, 201–2, 229, 245–6, 251, 258, 260, 268, 292
Lock, Major Henry O. 280–1
Lockhart, Captain J. G. 275, 279
London, *see under specific place names and institutions*
London Jews Society, *see* London Society for Promoting Christianity among the Jews
London Missionary Society 158

London Regiment 271, 272, 278, 287
London Society for Promoting Christianity among the Jews (LJS) 14, 46, 149, 161, 167, 172, 176, 186, 189, 191, 192–3, 223
  see also Palestine Exhibition
London Stereoscopic Company 135
Longman, Thomas 97, 98, 99
Low, Gail Ching-Liang 91
Lowe, Lisa 4 n. 9
Luther, Martin 26–7, 84

Macaulay, Lord Thomas Bebbington 39
MacGregor, John ('Rob Roy') 174, 176
MacInnes, Bishop Rennie 262
MacKenzie, John 15
MacLeod, Hugh 11
Macleod, Norman 30, 93–4, 275
Macleod, Walter 98
Macmillan Magazine 168
magic-lantern 11, 133, 180, 275
Malvern News 168
Manchester Guardian 169, 221
Mandate, British (for Palestine) 5, 17, 44, 244–5, 289, 296–301
Mangles, James 69, 98
Manning, Brian 36
maps 7, 31, 33, 62, 68, 72–3, 106, 127–8, 174, 177
  see also scriptural geography
Marshall, Charles 139
Martin, John 30, 143
Martineau, Harriet 86–7, 88, 100, 101, 285
  Eastern Life, Present and Past 86, 100, 101
Marx, Karl 67
Mass Observation 244–5
Massey, W. T. 265
Matar, Nabil 33

Maugham, W. Somerset 18
Mee, Jon 47–8
Meggido (Palestine) 293–4
  see also Armageddon
Meinertzhagen, Georgina 185
Meinertzhagen, Richard 225–6
Melman, Billie 9, 83
Melville, Herman 75
Mesopotamia 91, 209 n. 96, 292
Michelangelo 116, **118**
Mildmay Mission to the Jews 207
millenarianism vii, 19, 22–3, 30, 34–6, 41, 45–57, 183, 189–202, 205–11, 214, 216, 217, 220, 223–5, 226, 231–2, 241–2, 293, 300
  see also British Israelites; Jews, restoration to Palestine; postmillenarianism; premillenarianism; Second Coming
Milman, Revd Henry Hart 83
Milner, Lord Alfred 252–3
Milton, John 23, 75
Mitchell, Timothy 88, 90–1, 154–5, 161
models 107, 140–1, 146, 147, 148 n. 113, 150–1, 153–4, 155, 156, 158, 174, 178, 180, 299
  Brunetti's 107, 142
  in *Jude the Obscure* 105–7, 160
Mogridge, George 141
Mohammed Ali 120, 140, 146
Mohammedans, *see* Muslims
Mont Blanc 162–3
Montefiore, Moses 211
Moore, Leslie G. 271, 284
More, Captain John 275–6, 278, 282
Moriah, Mount (Jerusalem) 176
Morley 172
Morning Post 169, 190, 227
Morris, William 1, 165

Morrison, Walter 166
Morrissey 1
Moscrop, John 93, 167
Moses 20, 36, 100, 107–8, 111, 125, 221, 233, 234, 236
Mosque of Omar (Jerusalem) 122, 147, 189, 261
  see also Dome of the Rock
Mount of Olives (Jerusalem) 53, 79, 80–1, 92, 106, 110, 120, 122, 133, 143, 145, 146, 147, 151, 179, 268, 291
Mount Pisgah, *see* Pisgah sight
Mount Sinai, *see* Sinai
Moxon, Edward 101
Mudie, C. E. 65
Mudie's circulating libraries 102
mummers' play 22, 299
Murray, John 69, 73, 74–5, 97–8, 100
  Handbook for Travellers in Syria and Palestine 65
music hall 204, 288
Muslim/Muslims 75, 82, 126, 145, 159, 178, 205, 208, 235, 250, 251–3, 257, 260–2, 264, 265, 266, 269, 293–4
  see also Islam; Saracens

Nablûs 234, 277 n. 111
Napoleon Bonaparte 2, 45, 47, 48, 56, 59, 61, 64, 95, 140
Napoleonic Wars 2
National Conference on the Eastern Question 203, 214
National Society for Promoting the Education of the Poor 127
Nation's Glory Leader 199, 201, 206, 223
nativity play 298–9
Nazareth 25, 86, 133, 198, 293
Nebi Samwil 269
Neil, Revd James 148, 159, 198, 207

New Jerusalem:
  as afterlife 19, 37, 77, 125–6
  in Bunyan 21–3
  Oxford as vii, 105–6
  terrestrial, in England vii, 22, 34, 41, 50–1, 105–6, 164–5
  terrestrial, in Palestine 34–5, 52–3, 190
  see also Bible, Revelation; England as the Holy Land; heaven; Kingdom of God
New Moral World 130
New York 142, 143, 228, 266, 271
New Zealand/New Zealanders 263, 287 n. 151
newsreels 245, 297
Nicholson, Norman 43–4
Nightingale, Florence 186
Nile 59, 119, 130, 131, 144, 261
Nonconformist 205, 208, 220
Nonconformity 39, 181, 182, 191, 203, 245
Northern Echo 209
Northern Liberator 130
nostalgia 88, 91–2, 180, 274, 289
  'imperialist' 91
Nottingham Express 227

Observer 268
Old Masters 23, 81, 84, 114, 116, **117**, **118**, 119
Oliphant, Laurence 184, 188, 215, 226
Orientalism:
  academic, see Said, Edward, *Orientalism*
  high Anglo-Palestine 4 n. 9, 10, 62–3, 73, 92–3, 94, 104, 106, 107, 132, 179, 259; and Bible 9–10, 62; construction of 67–73; dissemination of 94–104; key images and themes 74–94; popularization of, see dioramas; exhibitions; films; Kitto, John; Knight, Charles; models; Palestine Exhibition; Palestine Exploration Fund; panoramas; *Penny Magazine*; photographs; Religious Tract Society; *Saturday Magazine*; Society for Promoting Christian Knowledge; Society for the Diffusion of Useful Knowledge; stereoscope
  vernacular, see vernacular Orientalism
Ormsby-Gore, W. G. A. 243
Ottoman Empire/Ottomans 2, 5, 24, 45, 61–2, 81, 186, 190, 194, 202–5, 209, 211, 213, 226
  conquest of Constantinople (1453) 27
  conquest of Jerusalem (1516) 27
  during First World War 251–2, 259, 264, 282
  reconquest of Palestine (1840) 64, 95
  see also Eastern Question; Turkey
Overton, Revd Charles 164
Owen, A. L. 58
Owenism 45, 60, 130, 131
Oxford vii, 107
  see also University of Oxford
Oxford Street (London) 58, 290

Paine, Thomas 48
  Rights of Man 40
Palestine:
  boundaries 17
  British interests in, see British Empire, interests in Palestine
  imagined as England 85–8
  imagined as the opposite of England 284–7

restoration of Jews to, *see* Jews, restoration to Palestine
see also under specific place names
Palestine Association 72, 89
Palestine Campaign (First World War) 3, 7, 11, 12, 17, 62, 93, 247–54, 260–94, 297
see also Allenby; Egyptian Expeditionary Force
Palestine Exhibition 148–62 (**152**, **157**, **160**), 179, 180, 299–300
Palestine Exploration Fund (PEF) 3, 7–8, 9, 14–15, 60, 72, 92–3, 94, 99, 107, 165–79, 196
Palestine News 270, 281, 285, 287, 288, 290
Palestine Park (New York) 153–4
Palestine Place (London) 149
Palestinians vii, 5, 17, 56, 66, 67, 79, 82–5, 86, 110, 111, 119, 147, 151, 154, 161, 216, 219, 233, 236, 239, 244, 265, 268, 297
Pall Mall Gazette 140, 214
palm-tree 59, 87, 100, 109–10, 111, 116, 119, 122, 151, 164
Palmerston, Lady 187
Palmerston, Lord 186, 194–5
Paris 54, 64, 73, 154, 185
Parker, Lieut.-Colonel Alfred 261
Parker, Peter 255
Parry, Hubert 3
Pathans 253
Pedlar, Richard 280
Pemble, John 95
Penny Magazine 107, 108–19
philo-Semitism 184, 199
photographs 62, 79, 84, 132–6, 147, 150, 151, 156, 158, 166, 174, 177, 260
see also films; stereoscope
Picciotto, James 222–3

pilgrimage/pilgrims 19, 24–5, 42, 65, 67, 68, 74, 103, 130, 154, 162–3, 275, 276, 277, 295
in Bunyan 19, 21
and Protestantism 19, 26–8, 30, 37, 50, 75–8, 81, 88, 92, 110, 114
Pinkerton, Thomas 242
Pirie-Gordon, General C. H. C. 270
Pisgah sight 20, 43, 80, 105, 107–8, 112, 119, 120, 133, 136, 147, 163, 179, 186, 300
Plymouth 149, 158, 159
Pococke, Richard 42
Pope, H. T. 278
Porter, Bernard 15
postcolonial criticism ix, 3, 4, 5–7, 12, 15–16, 32, 40, 137
postmillenarianism 46–7, 191
Potter, Dennis 44
Pratt, Mary Louise 63
premillenarianism 47, 191–3, 196–202, 205–8, 209–10, 211, 214, 216, 217, 220, 223–5, 226, 231–2, 293
see also British Israelites; Second Coming
Press Bureau 249, 252–3
see also Department of Information
Priestley, Joseph 46, 47, 54, 56, 191
Protestant almanacs 48, 191 n. 28
Protestantism 11, 12, 14, 26–8, 30–1, 40, 42, 63, 66, 120, 126, 178, 188, 205, 258, 260, 296, 298
and perceptions of Palestine's landscape 78–84
and pilgrimage to Palestine 19, 20–1, 26–8, 30, 75–7, 82, 84
see also Anglicans; Evangelicalism; Reformation
Prussia 2 n. 5, 140
see also Germany

public schools 254–6, 265, 288
Purchas, Samuel 30
Punch 144, 213, 247, **248**, 249, 277
Puritans 6 n. 13, 22–3, 35, 41, 189
Pyramids 90, 287

Quarterly Journal of Education 111
Quarterly Review 69, 186

Raffles, Thomas 193
Ragussis, Michael 224
Raphael 114, 116, **117**
Reformation 12, 19, 26–8, 296
 see also Protestantism
Religious Tract Society (RTS) 73, 102–3, 114, 125, 133, 145, 167, 168
Restoration (Charles II) 22, 46
restoration, *see* Jews, restoration to Palestine
Richard I (*Coeur de Lion*) 25, 247, **248**, 250, 254, 255, 257, 258, 259, 267, 269, 270, 277, 296
Richardson, Tony 1
Rippon, John 37
Roberts, David 18, 70, 78, 94–5, 143
Robinson Crusoe (Defoe) 44
Rock, The 190, 207
Rogers, Mary Eliza 83, 129
Romania 212, 228
Rome 26, 74, 128, 162
Rose, Jacqueline 5 n.
Rose, Jonathan 15–16, 44
Roth, Cecil 215
Rothschild, Lord Nathaniel 232, 234
Royal Albert Hall (London) 1, 3
Royal Commission on Alien Immigration (1902) 230, 231, 232, 240, 242, 245
 see also Aliens Act
Royal Engineers 7, 145

Royal Geographical Society 72 n. 46, 167
Royal Navy 2, 56, 259
Ruskin, John 70
Russia/Russians 53, 95, 111, 163, 183, 197, 200, 202, 205, 209 n. 96, 214, 228, 230, 234, 238, 243, 265
 pilgrims to Palestine 75

Said, Edward vii, 5–10, 12, 14–15, 32–3, 38, 62, 63, 67, 68, 75, 77, 88–9, 219
 Orientalism vii, 5–10, 12, 14–15, 32–3, 38, 63, 68, 75, 77, 88–9
 Question of Palestine, The 6
St George's Gallery (London) 141, 142, 144
St George's Hill (Surrey) 22
St Louis World's Fair (1904) 154–5
Saladin 26, 259
Salisbury 127
Salisbury, Lord 203, 204, 209 n. 96
Samson 273, 279
Sandys, George 30
Saracens 33, 137, 256
Sassoon, Siegfried 276, 281
Saturday Magazine 107, 109, 199–25
Schölch, Alexander 3 n. 5
Schor, Revd Samuel 149–50, 153, 154, 159, 160, 161, 172, 299
Scotland/Scots 4 n. 8, 87, 263
Scott, Walter 81, 255, 258
scriptural geography:
 in Sunday schools 11, 16, 43, 126–9, 132, 133, 180
Sea of Galilee 43, 79, 86, 88, 120
Second Coming 22, 34, 46, 186, 191, 205–6, 207
 see also Jesus Christ; Kingdom of God
Seddon, Mary 185, 186, 189, 226

sermons 33, 62, 72, 76–7, 92, 163–4, 189, 203, 269, 274, 292
servants 45, 48–9, 64, 66–7, 83, 84–5, 142, 143, 275
Shaftesbury, Lord 183, 185–7, 189, 190, 192, 194–5, 214, 243
Shapiro, James 34
Shaw, A. C. 213
Shaw, C. T. 280
Shiel, M. P. 241
Shropshire 43
Sidon 24 n. 22, 190
Simpson, William 176
Sims, R. H. 274, 284
Sinai 20, 87, 111–12, 261, 273, 281
  Mount 20, 111–12, 141, 238
Smith, Albert 162–3
Smith, Evelin 223
Smith, George Adam 62
Smith, Goldwin 211, 212
socialism 1, 2, 45, 60, 131
  see also Chartism; Labour Party; Owenism
Society for the Diffusion of Useful Knowledge (SDUK) 14, 98, 108, 111–13, 114, 119, 120, 129, 132
Society for the Investigation of Prophecy 191
Society for Promoting Christian Knowledge (SPCK) 14, 73, 102–3, 109, 120, 125, 129, 132
Sokolow, Nahum vii, 182, 243–4
soldiers, *see* Tommy, representation of
Somerset House (London) 146
Sommers, Cecil 271, 279, 282–3
South Africa/South Africans 228–9, 287 n. 151
South Kensington 156, 174, 175
Southcott, Joanna 19, 45, 48–51, 52, 54, 56–7, 59–60, 192
Southey, Robert 58
Southwark 128, 172

Spectator 102, 217, 221
Spencer, Stanley 43
Spivak, Gayatri 288
Stanhope, Hester 69, 187
Stanley, Dean A. P. 72, 76–7, 79, 86–7, 88, 92, 99, 121, 178, 269, 285
Stanley, Henry Morton 140, 141
Stanley, Lord (15th earl of Derby) 202, 205, 215
Stead, W. T. 209, 257
Stein, Leonard 190, 244
Stennett, Samuel 37
stereoscope 107, 135–6
Storrs, Ronald 244, 266
Stow, David 128–9
Strachey, Lytton 62
Suez Canal 3, 65, 196, 205, 208, 210, 213
Sunday school 11, 16, 37–8, 39, 43, 88, 92, 102, 108, 114, 126–9, 133, 148 n. 113, 153, 158, 178, 180–1, 182, 184, 201, 245–6, 250, 280–1, 298
Surrey 22, 29, 34
Surry, Albert 274
Swedenborg, Emanuel 121 n. 38
Sykes, Mark 243, 250 n., 256, 259, 260, 265–8, 270, 296
Syrian and Palestine Colonization Society 199, 209 n. 98, 210, 297 n. 36

Tait's Edinburgh Magazine 67
Tasso, Torquato 23, 75, 114
Teacher's Offering 126
Ten Lost Tribes, *see* Israelites, lost tribes
Thackeray, William Makepeace 67, 78, 91, 100, 101
The Times 61, 63, 66, 68, 84, 148, 156, 162, 169–70, 171, 173, 175, 176, 178, 187, 192, 249, 264–5, 266, 293

Theatrical Journal 141
Thomas, Lowell 257
Thompson, E. P. 12–13, 38, 40, 50, 173, 269
Thompson, Edward 269
Thompson, George Carslake 208, 257
Thomson, William (Archbishop of York, 1862–1890) 7–8, 10, 11, 60, 92, 95, 167, 178
Thorne, Susan 12–13
Thornton, Major Hugh 252
Timbs, John 191–2
Tommy (British soldier): representation of 269, 275, 286–9
Tonna, Charlotte Elizabeth 199
Tower of David (Jerusalem) 129, 151, 263
Townsend, E. T. 280
travel, *see* Cook, Thomas; pilgrimage; servants; working class, travel to Palestine
Trimmer, Sarah 126
Tristram, Revd Henry Baker 73, 88
Trollope, Anthony 64
Tuchman, Barbara 10
Tunbridge Wells 149, 291
Turkey/Turks 31, 34, 45, 47, 59, 77, 143, 147, 197, 200, 202–4, 206, 207, 209, 211, 212, 214, 222, 228, 238, 242, 257, 259
during First World War 247, 249, 251–3, 261, 264, 268, 271, 279, 294
see also Eastern Question; Ottoman Empire
Turner, J. M. W. 70, 71, 133
Twain, Mark 67, 75
Tyre 24 n. 22, 190
Tyron, Richard 42

Uasin Gishu (East Africa) 229–30
'Uganda Plan' 229–30, 232

United States of America 4 n. 9, 6, 64, 65, 142, 183, 188, 198, 243, 265, 275, 278
and attitudes towards Palestine 6, 88 n. 102
vernacular Orientalism in 35 n. 55
University of Cambridge 69, 256
University of Oxford vii, 72–3, 76, 128, 165, 254, 256
Urban II, Pope 25

vernacular biblical culture:
defined 11–12
see also biblical imagery and vocabulary; Bunyan, John; Hebraism; hymns; nostalgia; Protestantism; Reformation; scriptural geography; Sunday school; vernacular Orientalism
vernacular Orientalism 16, 31–3, 38, 40, 43–4, 48, 108, 116, 126, 131, 132, 137, 179, 269
and 'academic' Orientalism 12, 32–3, 38, 92, 93, 106, 132, 159–60, 179–80
in Blake 58
and British interests in Palestine 60, 92–4, 179–80, 250–1, 281
in Bunyan 31–2, 44
in children's imagination 43–5, 128–9
defined 12, 32–3
and popular millenarianism 48
and representation of Palestine as England 85–8
see also England as the Holy Land; English as chosen people
Victoria, Queen 29, 95, 163, 165, 171
Volney, Constantin François 81, 103

Wailing Wall (Jerusalem) 154
Wale, Revd Burlington B. 206
Wales/Welsh 4 n. 8, 263, 264
Walsingham 24–5, 26
Wandering Jew 48, 66, 210, 246
War Cabinet 251–2, 254, 260, 263, 265, 294
War Office 3, 93, 167, 175, 177, 196, 253
Warburton, Eliot 68–9, 79, 84, 85, 87, 88, 88, 103–4,
  Crescent and the Cross, The 69, 103–4
Warner, Charles 65, 93
Warren, Charles 166, 170–1, 173, 174, 176, 177, 178, 209
  Underground Jerusalem 178
Watts, Isaac 36, 40, 107
Waugh, Evelyn 295–7, 298, 299, 301
Webb, Beatrice 185
Webb, Sydney 225
Weber, Max 22
Weizmann, Chaim 243
Wells, Edward 73
Wesley, John 37
Western Front (First World War) 260, 268, 277, 292, 293, 294
Westminster Abbey 76, 259
Whaley, Buck 64, 66
White, Arnold 229
Whitechapel 173, 227, 230
Whymper, Josiah 132
Wilhelm II (Kaiser) 259, 260, 263–4
Wilkie, David 83–4
Wilkinson, Revd John 206–7
Williams, D. 276
Wilson, Revd J. P. 273
Wilson, John 300
Wilson, John (soldier) 273, 276, 291–2
Windsor and Eton Express 153

Windsor Castle 87
Winnington-Ingram, Arthur (Bishop of London) 258
Winstanley, Gerrard 22, 28, 34, 35, 54
Women's Institute 3
working class 2, 3, 11, 35–41, 49–50, 55, 56, 94, 107, 108, 131, 147, 172–3, 203, 274
  A. H. Layard on 172–3
  and geographical imagination 15–16, 35, 43–4
  and imperialist ideology 12–13, 15–16, 40–1
  purchase of books 101–4
  represented as heathens 13, 108
  Trafalgar Square rallies (1887) 173
  travel to Palestine 65–6, 93–4, 274
  and vernacular biblical culture 3, 11, 37–9, 40, 43–4
  see also Chartism; Diggers; Owenism; servants; Tommy
World 221
World's Fairs 154, 155, 156
Wylie, Revd J. A. 70, 82

Yorkshire 18, 23, 57, 87, 276
Young, Robert J. C. ix, 32

Zangwill, Israel 228, 229, 230, 234
Zionism (Jewish) vii, 3 n. 5, 5, 6, 17, 55, 161, 182, 184, 185, 187, 195, 210 n. 102, 211–13, 217, 219, 220, 223, 224, 225, 228–32, 243–6, 261, 265, 268, 299
  in Edwardian fiction 232–43
  see also Balfour Declaration; Jews, restoration to Palestine
Zionist Congress 236, 240, 246
  1st (1897) 226
  4th (1900) 227–8, 233